Ludlow Castle

Ludlow Castle
Its History & Buildings

Edited by
Ron Shoesmith & Andy Johnson

Logaston Press

LOGASTON PRESS
Little Logaston, Logaston,
Woonton, Almeley, Herefordshire HR3 6QH

First published by Logaston Press 2000
Copyright © Author(s) of each chapter as stated 2000

ISBN
1 873827 51 2 (Paperback)

1 873827 46 6 (Hardback)

Hardback Copy No:239 (of 300 copies)

Set in Times by Logaston Press
and printed in Great Britain by
Hillman Printers (Frome) Ltd

Contents

Acknowledgments

The warmest thanks go to all the contributors who somehow managed to find some scarce time to write their chapters, and also to Lord Powis and the Powis Estate for help and support, notably in the persons of Tom Till and Helen Duce.

Libraries and record offices have been their usual helpful selves, but special thanks must go to staff at Shropshire Records and Research Centre, Shrewsbury; Ludlow Library; the British Library and Christie's Images.

The account of extensive repairs and related developments at Ludlow Castle appearing in chapter XII owes much to collaboration with members of the project team engaged in this work which was overseen by the then Agent to the Powis Estate, Brian Evans. The principles of repair were established in the course of stimualting discussion with the conservation architect, Bob Tolley of S T Walker and Partners and the English Heritage structural engineer, Keith Weston, devised discrete technical solutions to many seemingly intractable problems. The contractors, Treasure and Sons of Ludlow, achieved exemplary standards of craftsmanship and worked constructively with the archaeological team, led by Ron Shoesmith and Richard Morriss, to record the historic fabric and conserve significant evidence for the structural history of Ludlow Castle.

Once again Logaston Press has used the services of Brian Byron for drawing maps, plans and buildings, and his skills are always appreciated. Several of the plans have been based on those accompanying the work of St. John Hope, specifically the ones in chapter XIII are based upon those of Harold Brakspear, by permission of the Society of Antiquaries of London, others on drawings provided by the contributors. Many of the current photographs used in the book are the property of Logaston Press, but specific thanks and acknowledgement for other illustrations is as follows: Roy Palmer for the photograph of Usk Castle on p.51; John Gibbs for the illustration of the misericord on p.59; Hulton Getty Images for the picture of Richard of York on p.63; David Preshous for the photograph of Hopton Castle on p.86; Shropshire Records and Research Centre for the Pritchard plans and drawings used in chapter X and elsewhere and also for the following: the watercolour on p.94, Wright's views on pp.100-2, Thomas Hearne's view on p.109, Calvert's view on p.111, the *European Magazine* illustration on p.112 and the Angus engraving on p.114; the Public Record Office for Fig. 4 on p.97; Birmingham Museum for Towne's view on p.113; Anthony Streeten for the illustrations accompanying his chapter XII; Dr John Rogers for the photograph of Richmond Castle on p.140; the Society of Antiquaries for kind permission to reproduce the plans on p.141; English Heritage for kind permission to reproduce the plan on p.142; Glyn Coppack for the photographs on pp.147, 148, Fig.5 on 149 and 150; Hereford City and Archaeolgical Trust Ltd. for the photographs on pp.162, 163, 164, 165 and 209; Michael Thompson for the photographs on pp.168, 169 and 170; Peter Curnow for the photographs on pp.195, 196 and 197; Dúchas, The Heritage Service, Dublin (who hold the copyright) for the photograph of Trim Castle on p.200; Ken Hoverd for the aerial photographs used on p.193 and rear cover. Thanks are also due to Ruth Thornhill for compiling the index.

For the illustrations in the colour section thanks are due to the British and Bodleian libraries, Christie's Images, Manchester City Art Galleries and Gareth Thomas, as recorded in the section. Gareth Thomas of The Cat's Whiskers Studio, Ludlow, also provided the front cover illustration.

Editors' Note

This is the second book published by Logaston Press where experts in a variety of fields, drawn together by a building of national importance, have been invited to contribute towards a wide ranging work. The first volume, on Dore Abbey in Herefordshire, was very well received and is now being reprinted. The editors have experienced similar challenges in this volume as in the previous one—not just questions of interpretation and terminology, but the dual problems of repetition on one side and a dearth of information on the other. There has also been the question as to which chapter should contain certain information; for example the position of the castle during the Interregnum is referred to in chapter VIII, when it could have equally been covered in chapter IX!

As the chapters have come together, the editors spent many a freezing day poring over contributions at Ludlow Castle, checking descriptions with the standing masonry and, on occasion, writing sections where parts of the buildings were not covered. Return visits were necessary to check the many plans and elevations as they were produced, and to up-date those that were based on much older drawings.

The work did not stop here, for the text had to be read and re-read before it was arranged into page format; illustrations had to be scanned and text inserted as appropriate and the whole put together, not forgetting the references and end notes. Final draft chapters had to be sent to authors and the responses awaited with anxiety as the deadline for the completed work to go to the printers rapidly drew nearer.

At the end, as with most projects that depend on historical references and analyses of buildings and previous excavations, there were many problems left unanswered. This volume has suggested some solutions, but at the same time has presented more problems. The debate about the keep will doubtless go on for many decades; will it be possible to refine building dates for many parts of the castle; will more historic documents be found? Ludlow Castle's story is far from over.

The editors would like to thank the authors of the various chapters for their kindness and understanding when they were pressurised to return their chapters almost before they had received them. Their cooperation was essential in getting the volume completed within an extremely tight time schedule, with a launch date arranged well before some of the chapters had even been completed!

Ron Shoesmith
Andy Johnson

March 2000

Foreword

Ludlow Castle was an important place of authority over the Marches of Wales for about 600 years, and it has not been that for another 300 years. It was relieved from its 'policing' duties in 1688 and by the beginning of the 19th century it had begun involuntarily to contribute materials for local housing projects. My family purchased the freehold at about this time, apparently to prevent any further depredations. Thus, it was one of the earlier attempts to preserve a ruinous castle for future generations, much as English Heritage and other similar organisations do today. At that time the Romantic movement turned people's attention from the newly perfected landscapes and buildings of the 18th century to the craggy and ruinous castles, abbeys, and natural wilds of the more ancient past.

The colourful historical associations of Ludlow Castle have made it a very desirable ruin. This was the headquarters for English control over large tracts of Welsh territory. It was for some time a part of the 'ambitious' Mortimer family's domain. The princes in the Tower began their incarceration here. Katharine of Aragon learned of Prince Arthur's death here. Milton's *Comus* was written for this setting and it was first performed here. And, rather from the sublime to the ridiculous, in my own family's time of ownership there was for a number of years a horse-race here, and presently, in echo to the performance of *Comus*, we still enjoy the Ludlow festival's offering annually of a Shakespeare play. And there remains uncertainty about its beginnings.

The popularity and enjoyment of this castle among visitors to the area and local inhabitants shows that our fascination with the ancient and broken has continued unabated to the present day, although we might now mix our interest in its past associations with a tinge of regret or shame for the behaviour of our ancestors in the name of 'law and order'. I hope that this tangible piece of British history will not only be preserved for the future but that it will also be in some respects returned to a closer resemblance to its former glory. This will require expertise and scholarship, and will-power; it will also require public support and plenty of funding from one body or another. In the meantime, this ruined castle remains a delight to both adults and children, including my own, because it is so much more accessible than the various intact castles with their precious contents and nervous public-spirited supervisors!

There is already a short guidebook available for those wishing to know something of this castle, but it is necessarily only brief in its explanations. We have prepared this book for those who want something meatier, who would like to know more of the past purposes of this place. It is the combined effort of a number of informed contributors, with chapters on both the various parts of the castle and also detailed accounts of its past. The hope is that this book will stimulate curiosity and the spirit of investigation amongst visitors and would-be visitors who want to go beyond a glimpse to uncover more of the past for themselves. It is not intended though to overawe readers, and I trust it will prove excellent reading.

Our many thanks go to all the contributors in their labours and enthusiasms, to those who have helped to put the book together, especially Andy Johnson and Ron Shoesmith, and to Helen Duce and Tom Till for their inspiration and energy put into making this project happen.

March, 2000

Part I

Introduction

CHAPTER I

Geology, Building Stone and Water Supply

by Nigel Ruckley & Andy Johnson

Today's landscape around Ludlow is often praised for its beauty and variety, a variety due to a combination of geological conditions that have left a range of hill masses, isolated peaks and river gorges.

The earliest geological 'history' for Shropshire dates to between 700 and 570 million years ago when volcanic lavas and ash formed several of the hills to the east of the Church Stretton valley. Around 590 - 575 million years ago a shallow sea lay across the county, and sandstones and shales were deposited, forming the Long Mynd. It was during this phase that the Church Stretton fault appeared in the Earth's crust, a fault that has been equated with the current San Andreas fault in terms of the intensity of its activity. Earthquakes appear to have been common and severe.[1]

Shropshire continued to lie under the sea and, during the Cambrian, Ordovician and Silurian periods, 570 to 405 million years ago, further sandstones and shales, together with limestones were laid down. Ludlow is famous for its Silurian rocks, the Silurian system being devised by Murchison in 1835 to record the group of fossil bearing rocks he found along the Welsh borders. The Silurian period is dated between 435 and 405 million years ago, a time when what is now England and Wales, together with southern Ireland, was being moved north into subtropical latitudes to eventually join with land that became

Scotland and the north of Ireland. The Silurian rocks were laid down in periods of shallow seas, which accounts for the coral-reef bearing limestones of Wenlock Edge, unlike the thicker limestones laid down in deeper waters that covered Wales. The main outcrops of Silurian rock stretch from Ironbridge in the north-east of Shropshire, to Ludlow in the south-west.

From 405 to 355 million years ago, the late Silurian and Devonian periods, Shropshire stood clear of sea water, and rocks laid down were restricted to those formed in lagoons and lakes, such as form the Old Red Sandstone rocks of the Clee Hills.

The sea then returned during the Carboniferous period, 355 to 290 million years ago, the period that saw, amongst others, the coal measures of Ironbridge and Telford being deposited. Shropshire then once more rose above the waters, and became an arid desert not dissimilar to the current day Sahara. This was a period when the New Red Sandstones were formed, rocks that have provided some of the county's best building stone, notably that of Grinshill which has been used in construction both inside and outside the county. Any even younger rocks, notably chalk, that may have been laid down around 190 to 2 million years ago have been totally eroded, if they ever existed.

About 2 million years ago our planet entered the Ice Ages, when Shropshire was subjected to at least three and possibly several more advances of the ice from north and west. The glaciers and ice sheets shaped much of the landscape that is seen today, with resultant valleys and deposited moraine. They also had a lasting effect on the area around Ludlow and the site of the castle. As the ice finally retreated around 15,000 years ago, the meltwaters were trapped by ice to the north of Aymestrey that blocked its usual outflow. Lake Wigmore formed, its waters gradually rising and eventually over-spilling the lake shores, gouging out Downton Gorge and the Teme valley to the east and through what became Ludlow.[2]

The result of all this activity, carried out over millions of years, was to leave a sandstone and silt-stone ridge perched above the Teme, with a combination of limestone, shales and old red sandstone rocks in the adjacent hills. Recent changes in geolog-ical nomenclature and some reclassification of the rock units

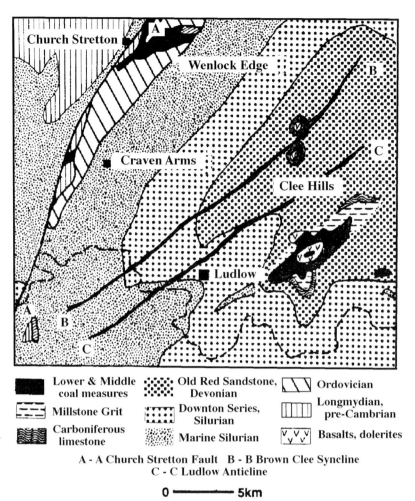

Fig. 1 The Geology of the Ludlow area

Legend:

- Lower & Middle coal measures
- Millstone Grit
- Carboniferous limestone
- Old Red Sandstone, Devonian
- Downton Series, Silurian
- Marine Silurian
- Ordovician
- Longmydian, pre-Cambrian
- Basalts, dolerites

A - A Church Stretton Fault   B - B Brown Clee Syncline
C - C Ludlow Anticline

0 ———— 5km

has brought about changes to well established geological names.[3] The oldest rocks belong to the Whitecliff Formation, formerly known as the Whitecliff Beds, or the Upper Ludlow Flags, of the Ludlow Series of Silurian rocks. They underlie the castle, the south-west part of the town where the earliest settlement took place and extend past Dinham Bridge over the river Teme. In the bank of the river Teme below the south-west side of the castle the beds dip about ten degrees to the north-west. Around Ludlow they consist of greenish grey flaggy calcareous silt-stones, with shelly limestone beds.

These rocks pass upwards into the cross-bedded sandstones of the Downton Castle Sandstone Formation, formerly the Downton Castle Sandstone Group. These lie to the east side

of a line drawn north-west/south-east approxi-mately along the line of Ludlow's Upper and Lower Raven Lane. They are represented by mainly yellow fine-grained, micaceous, well-sorted cross-bedded sandstones with siltstones and olive green mudstones. Both the Whitecliff and the Downton Castle Sandstone Formation are considered to be of Upper Silurian age.

A north-east/south-west fault (C - C on Fig.1 above), with its downthrow to the north-west brings the overlying younger units of the Raglan Mudstone Formation, formerly Red Downtonian, to lie against the Whitecliff and the Downton Castle Sandstone Formation. The line of this fault roughly coincides with the north-west edge of the high ground of Bringewood Chase and Whitecliff and eastwards across the Teme to the lower

2

ground below the north-west face of the castle. The rocks of the Raglan Mudstone Formation consists of red and silty mudstones with calcretes and red sandstones, and lie under the flat alluvial plain of the rivers Teme and Corve close to the north and north-west of the castle. Originally these rocks were classed as of Lower Devonian (Lower Old Red Sandstone), however they are now considered to be of Upper Silurian to Lower Devonian age.

The development of Ludlow Castle and its associated town demonstrates the effective use of a natural ridge of high ground defended on three sides by the Teme. A rock ridge, with steep slopes almost 100ft high on its north and west sides inhibited access to the ground within the loop of the river. The south-facing slope between the high ridge and river was an ideal location for a medieval town with adequate space for subsequent phased enlargements of both castle and town.[4] A narrowing of the Teme's floodplain on the south side of the castle allowed the construction of watermills and enhanced their efficiency due to the river's increased flow.

The castle incorporates many periods of construction and over the years a variety of stone has been used. It would appear that the greenish-grey flaggy calcerous siltstone of the Whitecliff Formation of Upper Silurian age that underlies the castle was used in its initial phase, utilising material dug out from the defensive ditch.[5] This stone was also used for some of the window surrounds in the church of St. Laurence. The stone weathered badly, being prone to chemical weathering adjacent to mortar, and also to spalling.

When better quality stone was sought, the builders turned to local sandstones which, though not of the quality of the Triassic sandstones from the quarries at Grinshill and Nesscliffe, were ideally suited for rubblestone walling. They were also used to produce ashlar blocks, but the local sandstones suffered from differential weathering and spalling, the latter often caused by lithic and mudstone clasts within the sandstone.

Two distinct local sandstones, both from the Raglan Mudstone Formation, have been used in the construction of local secular and religious buildings: the red-coloured Felton, and the purple-tinted coarse-grained pebbly Holdgate sandstone.[6] A third local sandstone was a contrasting yellow-buff sandstone of the Downton Castle Sandstone Formation, found in the Ludlow, Onibury and Stokesay area.

Felton stone was extracted from a quarry at Felton on the bank of the river Corve, about 3 km upstream of Ludlow. It is known from churchwardens' accounts of St. Laurence that this quarry was utilised between 1467 and 1471 for the reconstruction of the church,[7] and it is likely to have also supplied stone for repairs at the castle.

Holdgate stone was widely used in numerous rural buildings in Corvedale, and could well have supplied the castle with much of its red-coloured rubble walling and ashlar.

Scard considered that the yellow-buff, generally fine-grained, micaceous and cross-bedded sandstones of the Downton Castle Sandstone Formation, provided the best building stone in the area. Although in some localities it was thinly bedded and even flaggy, these characteristics were utilised for cutting stone tiles and providing the rubble core of walls. Onibury Quarry may have provided building stone for the castle from this formation as it did, for example, for the rebuilding of the tower of St. Cuthbert's, Clungunford, in 1895.[8]

With improved communications, stone could have been imported from further afield, notably that required for high quality carvings on capitals and corbels.

The Water Supply

A protected, secure and uninterrupted supply of water is of vital importance to a fortified site.[9] At Ludlow, the only secure method of supply was to construct a well through the underlying siltstones to penetrate the groundwater that was probably at a similar level to the river Teme.

The well at Ludlow lies in the inmost bailey close to the kitchen area, and by the nature of its

Fig. 2 Looking across the well in the inmost bailey. Beyond the well is the door to the Posetrn Tower, the Oven Tower is off the left of the picture

position within the early defences is probably of early construction. The well is 2.3m (7ft 6ins) in diameter and is reputed to be about 36.6m (120ft) deep, but in 1908 it was partially filled in and only about 18.3m (60ft) of shaft now remains open. The original depth of well, if correct, would have reached into the ground water and ensured a year round water supply. Such a depth of well is not unusual. The 13th-century Welsh borders castles of Beeston and Montgomery contain wells of 111.5m (366ft) and in excess of 65m (207ft) respectively. Dover Castle has wells sunk through chalk over 106m (350ft) deep.[10] Castles with wells of comparative size to that at Ludlow can be seen at Tantallon (East Lothian), Scarborough (Yorkshire) and Bamburgh (Northumberland).

Deep wells required some kind of structure or well house to cover the expensive winding machinery used in lifting the well bucket, and no doubt one formerly existed at Ludlow. But such long lifts of the well bucket inevitably meant that only a limited amount of water could be raised by hand in a given period of time. Cisterns, either for rainwater or for storage of well water, for drinking or fire fighting purposes, were present at Dover throughout most of the castle's history. More locally there was a tank in the keep at Hampton Court in Herefordshire, and it is likely that similar arrangements were also made at Ludlow.

During the presidency of Sir Henry Sidney (1560-86) a mile-long conduit was constructed to to bring water to the castle's buildings and to two fountains, one by the Round Chapel and one in Castle Street (see p.77). It may be that this followed the design at Goodrich where a lead pipe led from a spring on an adjoining hill, using a syphon mechanism to draw the water to the castle. At Ludlow such a system may have been more convenient for a busy centre of government than that offered by the well.

CHAPTER II

The Town of Ludlow

by Ron Shoesmith

'The Town lies on a hill, and in the late Middle Ages, the view of the two accents of the church
with its arrogantly high tower and the castle still standing to full height in all its parts
must have been overwhelming as travellers arrived from the south or the north.'[1]

Ludlow, well positioned close to the border between England and Wales, is perched on the edge of one of several hills that in the past have helped to create a separation between the two countries. As with most border areas, access and defence have both figured high in importance— not simply cross-border tracks for trading purposes, but, in English terms, the need for a relatively low-lying road following the whole of the border, together with the means of overall defence for the entire frontier.

Of considerable importance during many of the prehistoric periods was the Clun-Clee ridgeway, a salient of high ground that stretched from central Wales, taking a line on the elevated land to the south of the river Clun, dropping briefly through Clungunford and then up and across May Hill to descend to a crossing of the river Onny at Onibury and the river Corve just north of Ludlow. It then rises once again to the heights of Titterstone Clee and through the Wyre Forest almost to the banks of the river Severn at Bewdley. Chitty has demonstrated that the upland areas on each side of this ridgeway were probably settled during the Neolithic period and that the many find spots demonstrate the continuing importance of this trackway during the early Bronze Age.[2] A little later, in the valley between

the rivers Teme and Corve, just to the north-west of Ludlow, is an area that Stanford describes as the Bromfield necropolis.[3] Here, a relatively small area contains the remains of some 20 barrows and at least three cemeteries which were in use for a period of some 400 years around the first millennium BC.

The whole area was subject to a totally different culture during the Iron Age when the border was dominated by a great variety of hill forts. Well to the north of Ludlow, Caer Caradoc looms to the north-north-east of Church Stretton, whilst a short distance to the east a massively defended Iron Age fort sits on top of Titterstone Clee. The well known hill fort at Croft Ambrey is some distance to the south-west, but on a low hill only two miles south-east of Ludlow stands Caynham Camp. This is an unusual site for there is some evidence to indicate that the first settlement may have been as early as the end of the Bronze Age, continuing in use throughout the Iron Age. Here, the earliest timber-laced defences were apparently burnt around 400BC, to be replaced by a massive rampart, partly formed from the spoil of an internal quarry ditch. At one point the ramparts of the hill fort turned inwards to form a narrow entrance passage, doubtless flanked with guard rooms. Like others in the

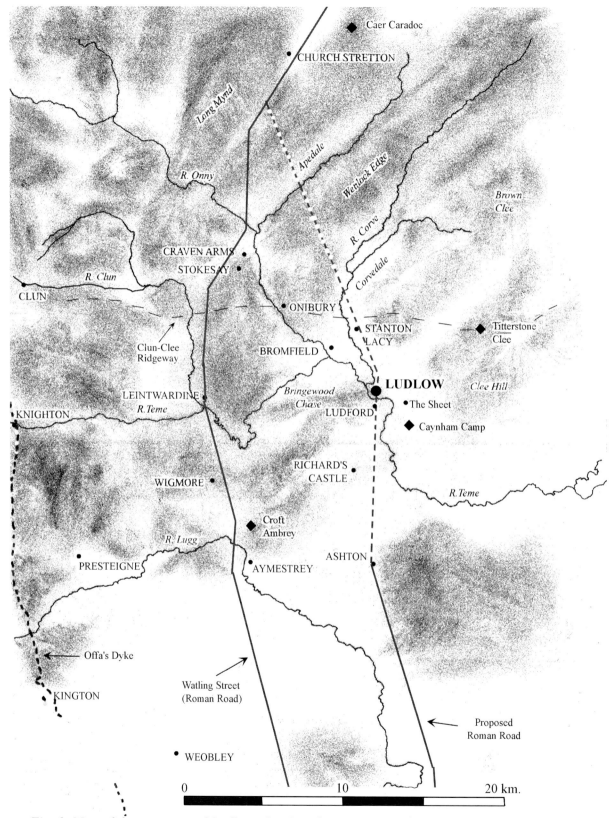

Fig. 1 Map of the area around Ludlow, showing places mentioned in this and following chapters

area, the 10 acres of Caynham were completely filled with both circular and rectangular huts, which were evidently replaced from time to time.[4] The presence of Late Iron Age pottery indicates that it continued in use for several centuries, whilst burnt timbers and charcoal, found during the excavation of many post holes, suggests a second burning, possibly as a result of the Roman invasion.[5] Other smaller sites in the area during the Iron Age give an indication of more settled occupation. One such was at Bromfield where a rectangular ditched enclosure has been shown to enclose a small Iron Age farmstead, in use for one or two hundred years.[6]

The Roman invaders created a border zone between England and Wales, associated with the strategic military road joining the legionary fortresses of Chester (*Deva*) in the north, through the centrally placed Wroxeter (*Uriconium*) to Caerleon (*Isca*) in the south. To the west was the military zone, designed to keep the native tribes in check, while to the east was the full extent of the civilised, Romanised Britain. The Roman road (which bears the traditional name of Watling Street), took a south-westerly course from Wroxeter through Craven Arms to the Roman military complex in the Leintwardine area, some seven miles west of Ludlow. Here it crossed the river Teme at its confluence with the river Clun and then took a south-south-easterly course, passing just to the east of Wigmore as it headed for the Aymestrey gap and the crossing of the river Lugg at Mortimer's Cross.

The initial impression is that the Ludlow area was apparently by-passed during the Roman occupation, but this may not be the case. A second Roman road, probably starting at Gloucester (*Glevum*), led north-north-westwards, passing through Weston-under-Penyard (*Ariconium*). It has been traced as far as Ashton, a small village on the A49 north of Leominster, but its course thereafter is unknown. It could have headed for Leintwardine, but this would have involved crossing quite difficult ground in the Gatley Park area, just to join the main road at a Roman fort. The general course of the road and the easier route stays to the east and its eventual destination is doubtless the *civitas* capital at Wroxeter.[7] Accepting this general direction, the road would have had to to cross the river Teme at some point and geographical features limit the choice. In the first instance, had the intention been to cross the Teme in the Woofferton / Brimfield area, then the road would not have taken a course as far west as Ashton. Secondly, the steep rise of Whitcliffe to the west of Ludlow would have limited a course in that direction. Following the general alignment from Weston-under-Penyard, the only reasonable crossing of the Teme is in the immediate area of Ludford, the small settlement on the southern side of the Teme, opposite Ludlow. From there, the road would have passed directly over the hill on which Ludlow is built, then, staying to the east of the river Onny, passing the Bromfield necropolis and crossing the old Clun-Clee ridgeway at Onibury on its way to join the military road at the Roman complex just to the north of Craven Arms. Here there was an important junction of Roman roads for, apart from those already mentioned, another road went north-eastwards along Corve Dale towards Bridgnorth whilst a second took a generally westerly course leading towards the important central Welsh fort at Caersws.[8] Was this road from Gloucester to Wroxeter the origin of Old Street and its continuation Corve Street, perhaps making use of a ford or possibly an earlier bridge some 200 yards downstream from the present bridge? There was a bridge at Ludford by 1221/1272, though in the second quarter of the 16th century Leland notes that the then bridge was only some 100 years old and that 'men passyd afore by a forde a lytle benethe the bridge'.[9]

Although a Roman road may well have crossed Ludlow's hill, there is no indication of any Roman settlement in the immediate vicinity. The crossing of the Teme may have led to a small *mansio* or inn, for the benefit of travellers should the river be in spate, but no trace has been found. This is not dissimilar to the situation at Hereford where, until very recently, there has been a total lack of evidence for any Roman crossing of the

Wye within the city limits, although the alignment of the Roman road points directly to the ford.

Perhaps the burning of Caynham Camp was an indication of the ferocity of the attack by the Roman troops in this area and is evidence for the consequent lack of any Roman settlement to replace the Iron Age hill fort. The opposite situation occurred in the Hereford area where the massive 50 acre hill fort at Credenhill was replaced by the Roman town at *Magnis* and, further north, the hill fort on the Wrekin was replaced by *Uriconium*. A small Roman villa at Stanton Lacy and a rectangular enclosure of uncertain date, but supposedly Roman, at The Sheet, just south-east of Ludlow, are the only definite indications of any form of settlement in the whole area during the three centuries of Roman rule.[10]

The various invasions that followed the collapse of the Roman Empire tended to force the British further and further westwards towards Wales and the Marches. Traces of large timber buildings overlying the ruins of the stone buildings at Wroxeter give some indication of post-Roman activity, but this may well be an isolated case of limited duration, for the road system would soon have fallen into disrepair, trade with the country-side would have been non-existent, and isolated villas would have been abandoned or destroyed by invaders. Such was the beginning of the Dark Ages—a 300 year period when the country degenerated into barbarism and any occupation of a permanent nature was virtually unknown.

Although Kenchester (*Magnis*) may have been abandoned shortly after the departure of the Roman army, it gave its name to the Magonsaete, a tribe that inhabited much of north Herefordshire and south Shropshire. Even so, there is little trace of activity in the Ludlow area until about 650-750AD when the Iron Age enclosure at Bromfield was reused as an Anglo-Saxon Christian burial ground. All the inhumations were orientated east-west, but the presence of grave goods in three of the 31 graves could well indicate a recent conversion to Christianity.[11]

Formal Christianity arrived in the southern Welsh Marches with the establishment of the Kingdom of Mercia followed by the foundation of the diocese of Hereford in 676AD. At that time there was no firm western border to the kingdom, and part of what is now western and southern Herefordshire continued to survive as a semi-independent kingdom called Erging. There was obviously a need to establish a positive western border to Mercia and it was during the reign of Offa (757-96) that the immense earthwork that bears his name was thrown up. Running from the river Severn near Chepstow in the south to the estuary of the Dee near Prestatyn in the north, this earthwork established a frontier that was some 120 miles long as the crow flies.[12] Offa's Dyke follows a north-westwards course through Herefordshire, from being barely five miles west of Hereford, where it leaves the river Wye, to Knighton, where it is a full 14 miles to the west of Ludlow. The Dyke not only provided a boundary for Mercia, it firmly placed the area around Ludlow together with the old Roman road passing through the Aymestrey gap well within the boundaries of Mercia.

In Herefordshire, Leland commented that 'from the decaye of Kenchestre Herford rose and florishyd.'[13] This was certainly not the case at Ludlow, where there was no Roman town for the local populace to have 'pyked owt of the best for there buildinges.'[14] However, Ludlow's hill would always have commanded the areas to the north and south and its occupants would have had a considerable influence on travellers and on the surrounding countryside. The beginnings of Ludlow town should perhaps be seen first in the Bronze Age necropolis at Bromfield and then with the Iron Age hill fort at Caynham. In the Roman period it could well have held a similar riverside position to its southern neighbour, Hereford.

The initial foundation of a settlement in the immediate area of Ludlow is somewhat controversial. Was there a late Saxon village that for one reason or another did not appear in the Domesday Survey? The available evidence, though slight, needs to be examined, but a brief description of the town and castle is essential before individual elements can be considered.

Ludlow stands on the ridge and southern slope of a broad, rocky spur that projects westwards from higher ground to the east. It is surrounded on the west and south by the river Teme and on the north by alluvial flats that include the river Corve. On the opposite side of the Teme, the ground rises steeply to the south-west to the rocky plateau of Whitcliffe. It is from there that the full defensive potential of the site can best be appreciated, with the cliff rising some 100 feet above the river.

The original road, which, it has been suggested, could be of Roman origin, rises from the Teme in the south and, as Old Street, takes a direct course up to the summit of the hill. The triangular area at the summit of the hill is called the Bull Ring and the road passes through this to drop down the northern side of the rise as Corve Street. At the bottom of the hill the road bears off to the north-west over Corve Bridge towards Bromfield.

The earliest castle occupies the north-western corner of the spur, well-defended with precipitous slopes to the north and west. As part of the original design, a broad, semi-circular dry ditch cut off the castle from the rest of the ridge—the entrance drawbridge being half way along the southern side. Some time later the castle grounds were extended to the east and south, forming a large walled outer bailey. To the south of this extension is an area of the town called Dinham which includes a 12th-century chapel, dedicated to St. Thomas, and a bridge over the river Teme.

From the main gate in the eastern arm of the extended castle defences, the Market area extends eastwards along the crest of the ridge as far as the Bull Ring. Although there has been considerable market encroachment in the eastern part of what would have been laid out as a broad open area, the part in front of the castle is once again completely open.[15] The large parish church of St Lawrence stands to the north of the eastern part of the market area, but is now hidden from view by a row of shops.

Two wide streets lead from the market area down the hill to the south. Broad Street occupies a central position, with Mill Street being closer to the castle. Between these two streets is the narrow Raven Lane; a similar narrow back lane may once have existed between Broad Street and Old Street. Broad Street continues down the hill to Ludford Bridge, the southern crossing of the river Teme. The regularity of these streets together with the cross streets, Bell Lane and Brand Lane, half way down the hill, have led several writers to suggest that Ludlow was deliberately laid out as a planned town. The town wall was probably started in 1233, but could have taken many years to complete. It enclosed the main part of the town and included six main gates.

To take up the historical outline once again, it is rather surprising to find that Ludlow is not mentioned in the Domesday Survey of 1086. Such an absence would suggest that it is reasonable to assume that it did not exist as a significant entity at that time. However, a recent reassessment of the Domesday evidence suggests that the order in which the holdings were listed—*Stantone*, *Lude*, *Ludeford*, *Castellum Aureton* (Richard's Castle)—could reflect a journey southwards from Shropshire into Herefordshire. If this is correct the identification of *Lude* north of *Ludeford* (Ludford) would be more logical as Ludlow than the alternative that *Lude* refers to Lyde in Herefordshire.[16] Whatever the case for a settlement, any castle that existed at Ludlow, as an item of expenditure rather than one of income, would in any event not be entered in the Domesday Survey for taxation purposes.

Most writers agree that Ludlow was formed out of the large parish of Stanton Lacy, now represented by a small village some two miles north-east of the town. The first Norman lord of Stanton Lacy was William de Lacy who came from Lassy in Normandy, one of the most important lords on the southern Welsh border with estates throughout Herefordshire. He was second-in-command to William fitzOsbern, earl of Hereford, and, when the latter died in 1071 and his son, Roger, was banished in 1075, de Lacy probably increased his power base. He may have initiated the stone castle at Ludlow as part of the

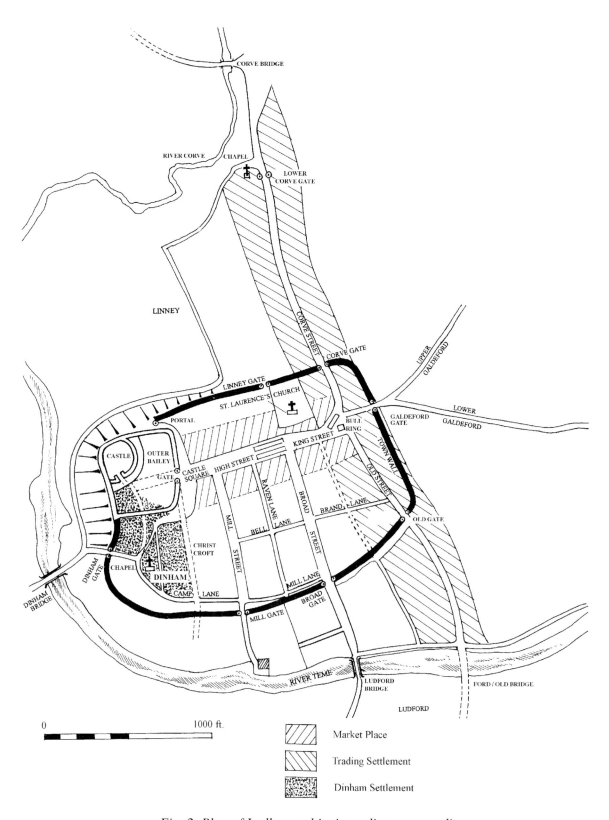

Fig. 2 Plan of Ludlow and its immediate surroundings

defensive line instigated by fitzOsbern. This started at Chepstow in the south and probably included the castles of Monmouth, Ewyas Harold, Hereford, Clifford, Richard's Castle and Wigmore. Walter de Lacy died as a result of a fall from the tower of St. Peter's Church in Hereford in 1085 and his son, Roger, took over the Stanton lordship. It is argued (see Chapter IV) that the castle at Ludlow was probably begun by Walter and that the work was continued by his son at least up to his banishment in 1095. It would seem reasonably certain that by the end of the 11th century at the latest, the strategic importance of the promontory standing starkly above the river Teme had been fully appreciated with the construction of a castle that was to become one of the finest and most important on the Welsh border.

From its inception, the castle may well have been surrounded by an embryonic borough, initially occupied by the builders of the castle and later by those who depended on the castle for a living. This could have been the beginning of Ludlow as an entity, apparently totally separate from Stanton Lacy, but not completely divorced, for apparently the keep of Ludlow Castle was still in the parish of Stanton Lacy up to the late 19th century.[17]

In any consideration of the development of Ludlow, the starting point must be the large earthen mound, containing three stone 'mausolea', which, it is recorded, was built on the highest point of the Ludlow hill. The description suggests that it was a tumulus of some type, possibly allied to those a few miles to the north-west at Bromfield.[18] It was removed in 1199 to allow for an extension to the present parish church and, indeed, its presence there may have been a factor in the choice of that particular spot for St Lawrence's church. One alternative suggestion is that it might have been re-used as the mound of an early motte and bailey castle, but a motte in this position would be unlikely for it would fail to take advantage of the defensive potential of the corner site with its steep slopes to west and north. Another alternative—that the mound was used as one of the two siege castles erected by Stephen in

1139—deserves some consideration. Similar siege castles were built (and probably still survive) at Wigmore, and the tower of Hereford Cathedral was used as a siege castle during the previous year. As there is nothing left of the Norman church and, indeed, little remaining of the comprehensive 1199 rebuild, it is not possible at this time to establish the precise position of the mound and therefore its possible use as as a siege castle.[19]

Place names often give an indication of the presence of early settlements, and it has been suggested that Galdeford—the eastern suburb of Ludlow, which gave its name to several streets and the eastern gate leading into the walled town—referred to an early settlement possibly associated with the ford across the Teme at the bottom of Old Street.[20] The same author also considers Linney—the district on the northern slope of Ludlow's hill leading down to the crossing of the river Corve—as a possible pre-Norman settlement. It is suggested that the irregular road pattern in this area could well indicate a small settlement or farmstead.

Recent writers consider that the place-name Dinham has a fine Saxon ring to it and that this part of the town still has the air of a separate village.[21] Rowley noted that in the southern part of Shropshire there are a small group of place names ending in 'ham' and suggested that when they were related to river names they were normally associated with early settlements. He quoted examples such as Corfham (river Corve), Caynham (river Key), Lydham (river Lyde) etc. On this basis he suggested that Dinham could have been derived from a Saxon village on the site of the later town.[22] However, there is a solid alternative—that it acquired its name from the mid-12th century occupant of Ludlow Castle, Joce de Dinan.

The original arrangement of streets in Dinham—the western part of the town and south of the castle—has suffered major alterations in the past, but the presence of the remains of the 12th-century chapel of St. Thomas of Canterbury opposite the top of the road that leads down to

Dinham Bridge gives some indication of the antiquity of the settlement in this area. The missing nave of this chapel would have extended well out into the present road, indicating a radical change, possibly when Dinham House was built. It is suggested that the church was originally on the edge of a small triangular area, possibly a small market, with the 'stalk' of the 'T' leading west to the bridge and the 'arms' leading north and south.[23] Such a rearrangement of the junction means that the road northwards would have led directly to the entrance drawbridge of the original small castle. At the rear of the chapel there is another narrow lane, also running north-south, and to the east again there are the curious property boundaries behind number 11 Dinham, that outline an area known as Christ Croft. This strip of ground, which is abutted on the east and west by gardens and is now cut up into individual plots, is a significant feature on the earliest Ordnance Survey maps of Ludlow. Does this represent a lost street or could it possibly indicate the position of a previous boundary ditch—the eastern boundary of the historic Dinham—cutting off the south-western end of the ridge?[24] Hints of such a ditch alignment include the foundation settlement of houses and the collapse of the corner of the castle wall immediately opposite no. 11 Dinham in 1990. There are also documentary references to a 'ditch which is called Christcrofte.'[25]

The history of Dinham is inextricably tied to the development of the castle and the construction of its outer bailey. It could well have its origins as a late Saxon village, but could equally represent the beginnings of a Norman settlement, associated with a small church and a river crossing, and growing in a slightly informal manner just outside the castle gate—a settlement that was partly lost when the castle was extended to include the large outer bailey. The extension not only cut across the main road from the castle gate to Dinham and its river crossing, but by providing a new gatehouse on the eastern side it relegated Dinham to the status of a minor suburb. This apparent reduction in status could argue for a Saxon origin for Dinham—it is unlikely that such an action would have been taken against Norman settlers—but, of course, any such settlers could well have been given alternative, high status plots in the new market place.

It has been suggested that the road over Ludlow's hill—Old Street and Corve Street—existed long before the castle was built. With the coming of the Normans and the construction of castles along the border, this road would have regained some of its earlier importance. This would have intensified once the Ludlow Castle site began to be developed, for a road along the ridge from the Castle to the present day Bull Ring and beyond would have been essential. Thus the Bull Ring would have become a significant crossroads and a straggling linear trading settlement along the line of the old road would have followed. Indeed, the development along the old road could have been reasonably extensive, for there is evidence of burgaging along much of the length and before 1186 there are references to burgages near the chapel of St. Leonard, near the bottom of the hill and close to Corve Bridge. The only logical position for the parish church of this community would be on the summit of the hill, as close to the crossroads as possible. Hindle has suggested that towards the end of the 12th century the town may have grown to have two separate parts—the Norman castle with its adjoining village of Dinham, possibly both defended, and a thriving roadside settlement stretching from the river Teme on one side over Ludlow's hill to the river Corve on the other.[26]

Accepting this scenario, the two parts of Ludlow would doubtless have been joined by a road on the crest joining the Bull Ring crossroads with the castle drawbridge and entry. It must have been about this time that the castle was enlarged and part of Dinham disappeared underneath the new outer bailey. This new work included the main castle gate on the eastern side, facing onto the ridge. It would seem likely that at this time the road along the ridge was widened to provide both a market place and grand ceremonial entry to the castle. Burgages on each side of this new market place are relatively narrow, reflecting the increasing pressure of space in the centre of the growing town.

The scene was now set for Ludlow to expand in the 13th century. Was this a carefully planned town as is suggested by most writers,[27] or should Hindle's comment that 'Ludlow's plan, so often described as a grid, is clearly nothing of the sort'[28] be accepted? The truth, as often, lies somewhere between the two extremes. Having created the market area along the ridge, there would have been a large area between Old Street on the east and Dinham on the west that was ripe for development. There would seem to be little doubt that the intention was to carve up this area into a series of burgage plots, each accessible to the main market. The two main requirements would have been good frontages and access to the rear. This is what was laid out—Broad Street and Mill Street—two magnificent wide roads leading southwards down the hill from the market all the way to the river Teme, with Raven Lane providing the necessary back lane between the two. There is sufficient topographic evidence to postulate an additional back lane between Broad Street and Old Street, whilst the burgages on the west side of Mill Street could well have had a rear access from Christ Croft—the disused defensive work around Dinham. Convenient cross lanes were provided by Bell Lane and Brand Lane to the north, Silk Mill Lane further down the hill and possibly a track close to the riverside. Broad Street and Mill Street are almost identical in design, narrowing a little towards the market where property values would have been high, widening out slightly as they go down the hill, and tending to narrow again as they approach the river where poorer people and industrial undertakings would have co-existed. Overall Ludlow was a tremendously successful development and was the 33rd largest provincial town in England in 1377 with a taxable population of 1172.[29]

The final work, which was to have a lasting effect on the town plan of Ludlow, was the construction of the town wall and gates. As has been suggested above, Dinham may have had early earthen defences, similar to other border settlements such as Longtown, Kilpeck and Richard's Castle in Herefordshire. However, the first formal murage grant was given in 1233, after a visit by Henry III, but this is of uncertain nature,[30] and was not renewed until 1260. From then grants were almost continuous until about 1470.[31] This does not mean that the walls took over two hundred years to build—the latter grants were almost certainly for repair works. A reasonable completion date would be about 1280 or 1290. In addition, the 14th-century accounts suggest that the murage grants were not always being spent on the walls, but were being diverted for other, unknown purposes.[32]

The line of the wall is reasonably certain around the whole circuit although many stretches are now missing. It left the north-eastern corner of the castle and followed the break in slope to the east, including within its line some very generous burgage plots on the north side of the market and St. Laurence's church and graveyard to the east. It cut across the upper end of Corve Street and then made an almost right-angled corner to the south to include the burgages on the east side of Old Street—burgages that are noticeably shorter towards the south. The turn to the west is more gradual and the wall has a gentle curve as it crosses Broad Street and Mill Street. From there the wall makes a long curve to take advantage of the lie of the land and to include Dinham, before joining with the castle defences again at the south-western corner. The construction of the town wall would inevitably have involved the extinction of some property rights and distorted the road pattern. The attempts to minimise this disruption show in the design of the circuit, where from time to time defensive advantages are secondary to plot design and usage. This attempt at minimal disturbance also limited access to the wall—the absence of an inter-mural road or track around much of the circuit (apart from the south-west part where Camp Lane and Silk Mill Lane probably already existed) is immediately apparent. In addition, the presence of burgages immediately outside most of the

Fig. 3 Ludlow's Broad Gate c.1900

gates would have had a substantial effect on their defensive capability.[33] Leland recorded that the town was 'well waullyd, and by estimation it is about a mile in compas.' However, he only noted five gates, Old Gate, Broad Gate and Mill Gate on the south, Galdeford Gate (Leland has it as Galfride Gate) to the east, and Corve Gate straddling the road between the Bull Ring and Corve Street. He did not note the two minor gates in the northern arm—the centrally placed Linney Gate leading to the part of the town with the same name, and the Portal, a postern gate inserted where the town wall joined the wall of the castle. More surprisingly, he did not record Dinham Gate on the western side of the town.

Broad Gate still survives and provides a pleasing break in the length of Broad Street, although partly concealed by later buildings. Preempting many writers since that time, Leland noted that Broad Street was 'the fayrest parte of the towne'.

Although the walls included the central nucleus of Ludlow, the lower parts of Mill Street, Broad Street and Old Street were all left outside the defensive circuit, as was the whole of Corve Street to the north and the eastern suburb associated with the two streets that radiated out from Galdeford Gate—Lower and Upper Galdeford Streets. From their alignment and general position, it would seem that the wall and gates had as much to do with preserving the ability to charge market tolls as it had to do with defence.

By the end of the 14th century the town plan of Ludlow had become established and, apart from the gradual loss of one or two back lanes, has remained unaltered to the present day. Ludlow's hill top position preserved the town from the damage by railway undertakings and from new relief roads that have permanently disfigured the medieval town plans of many of its neighbours.

CHAPTER III

Ludlow Castle

by Ron Shoesmith

'The Castle itself is in the very perfection of decay, all the fine courts, the royal apartments, halls and rooms of state, lye opened, abandoned and some of them falling down ...' [1]

A brief description of the castle and the changes that have taken place is included at this point for readers who are unfamiliar with what, during part of its life, acted as a royal palace.

It is most likely that the original castle made use of the strategic defensive position on the end of the ridge with the steep slopes leading down to the River Teme and the lower lying area of Linney. The Saxon settlement of Dinham, if such existed, appears to have been on the slope of the hill to the south of the ridge, and if so would not have been affected by the initial excavation of the deep ditch that was designed to cut off the corner of the ridge and thus add considerably to the defensive capability of the site. The ditch had to be cut into the bedrock and thus provided some of the building materials needed for the new castle and ensured that, in the first instance, the main parts were built of stone rather than timber.

The frontier with Wales was a turbulent area for a considerable time after 1066. Much of the area had been devastated in pre-Conquest fighting between Saxons and the Welsh, and it wasn't fully under the control of the Normans until after the uprising led by Edric the Wild in 1068-9 had been put down with great ferocity. Several border castles had been built or planned by William fitzOsbern, earl of Hereford, before his death in 1071, including Ewyas Lacy, Clifford, Wigmore and Richard's Castle, built by Richard fitzScrob, all in the area that had been laid waste by Welsh incursions in 1052.[2] Ludlow was a little way to the east of this turbulent area and, although the site guarded significant routes, the initial construction may have been a little later and was probably begun by Walter de Lacy or his son Roger as part of their holding of Stanton Lacy, sometime before Walter's death in 1085 and Roger's banishment in 1096.

The Norman castle consisted of a walled enclosure with a large gatehouse tower built towards the western end of the southern side. It was probably approached by a bridge incorporating some form of removable bridge across the dry ditch. The enclosure, which now forms the inner ward or bailey of the castle, has two gently curved sides that join in acute angles to the south-west and north-east, each angle being guarded by a rectangular projecting corner tower. The one to the north-east is called the Pendover Tower, and the one to the south-west, having undergone many changes, is now called the Oven Tower. There are two other rectangular towers, both overlooking the steep cliffs to the west and north-west. The larger one—the North-West Tower—included garderobes and was probably part of the domestic quarters of the castle; the one on the western side incorporated a dog-leg entry and is known as the Postern Tower. The walls of the towers and the intervening stretches of curtain wall are quite thick and in places incorporate internal passages

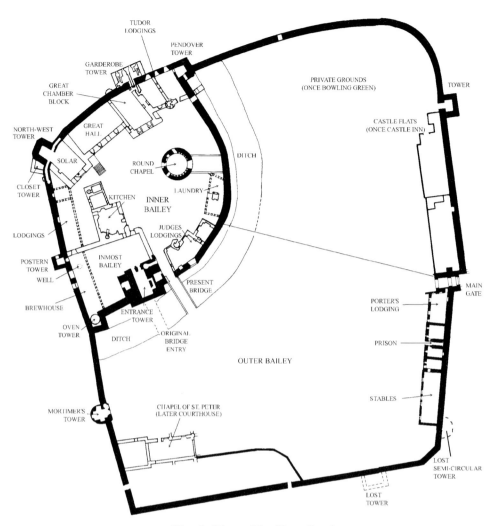

Fig. 1 Plan of Ludlow Castle

as well as wall walks. The decorative work within the gatehouse would suggest a constructional date in the 1080s if not earlier.

The only Norman building to survive within the circuit is the round chapel (probably of mid-12th century date), although the east wall of the Great Hall may incorporate some Norman work and there is some evidence to suggest that the North-West Tower and possibly others were fronted by timber buildings. Indeed, it may well be that, in the first instance, many of the internal buildings were constructed of timber—either free-standing or set against the stone curtain walls. It could well be that the stone castle was still incomplete when Roger de Lacy was banished. Shortly afterwards the castle reverted

to the Crown and, probably with little alteration, this would have been the castle that was held by troops who supported Matilda and was besieged by Stephen in person in 1139. The de Lacy family recovered the castle in the mid-12th century and retained it, apart from occasional confiscations, until the death of another Walter in 1241.

In the latter part of the 12th century a large area to the east and south of the original castle was incorporated within a new ditched defensive line forming another bailey and quadrupling the size. As part of this work the castle was re-orientated, the new entrance gateway pointing eastwards towards the new Norman market place, rather than southwards towards Dinham. The new defensive work was irregular in shape, possibly due to the incorporation of part of the earlier settlement at Dinham. It included a projecting rectangular tower north of the gatehouse and another on the south side that has since been lost. On the western side a semi-circular tower, called Mortimer's Tower, incorporated a second gatehouse. This may have been designed to replace the dog-leg entry in the Postern Tower and provide a wider and more convenient access to the Dinham river crossing. There was apparently a semi-circular tower on the curtain wall a little to the north of the south-east corner and this and the last rectangular tower would have protected the otherwise poorly-defended south-eastern corner of the outer bailey. The two semi-circular towers were probably additions to the original circuit, designed to improve the defensive capability.

The rear wall of the Entrance Tower of the original castle was eventually demolished, the building heightened and, by blocking off the original entrance, it was converted into a more conventional keep. A new entry to the old castle—now acting as an inner bailey—was then cut through the curtain wall just to the east of the keep and a new bridge was built across the ditch. An area of the inner bailey was then walled off to provide a semi-private court associated with the keep—in effect, a third or inmost bailey. It was within this court that a well was dug to provide a reliable source of water.

Apart from the Entrance Tower and the wall towers, the design and nature of the original buildings within the early castle are largely unknown, but once the outer bailey had been added, improvements could be made. The first campaign included the construction of a first floor Great Hall, built over a large undercroft, together with a two-storey Solar block that was attached to the western end of the Hall. Both were built against the safe northern curtain wall, the Solar incorporating the rectangular Norman North-West Tower. The Hall had large windows on the courtyard side and slightly smaller ones cut through the curtain wall. The main room in the Solar was on the same level as the Great Hall. Both Hall and Solar had entries from an external flight of steps as well as a connecting doorway. It

is suggested that the construction of these buildings started in the late 1280s when it was held by Geoffrey de Geneville, following his marriage into the de Lacy family.[3]

Shortly after this work had been completed, further improvements were put in hand. The Solar Block and the adjoining North-West Tower were both heightened and an approach to the upper floors was provided by a vice (spiral staircase) in the north-western corner of the Great Hall. At the same time what is called the Closet Tower was added in the angle between the Norman tower and the curtain wall. This vast improvement, again probably planned by de Geneville, was designed to provide three independent suites of rooms, together with a service basement within the Solar complex. The completion of the work may have been delayed due to de Geneville's death and may not have been finished until after the castle was taken over by Roger Mortimer in 1308. The Hall and Solar were served by a kitchen and pantry built against the wall of the inmost bailey—buildings which have long since been demolished, although their footings survive.

Although Roger Mortimer could well have completed the work to the Solar block, his principal addition to the castle was probably the construction of the Great Chamber Block which was built to the east of the Great Hall. This was effectively a second solar range which was improved by the addition of an elaborate garderobe tower that totally replaced a section of the Norman curtain wall. The new building was probably completed in the mid or late 1320s and the splendour of the work transformed what had been a relatively ordinary castle into an almost regal palace, a principal residence of the Mortimer family—the earls of March. Mortimer was also responsible for the construction of St. Peter's chapel, initially a free-standing building positioned close to the south wall of the outer bailey.

On the death of Edmund, the last Mortimer earl of March, in 1425, the Mortimer inheritance passed to Richard, duke of York, who was Edmund's sister's orphaned son. Then aged 13, he didn't receive possession of his estates until 1432. He then made Ludlow a major centre for his retinue, often basing himself in the castle whilst pondering the mismanagement of the country by Henry VI's Lancastrian advisers. When he became Lord Protector, his sons remained at Ludlow. Following his father's death, it was from here that his eldest son Edward raised a force to spearhead the Yorkist faction, first defeating a Lancastrian army at nearby Mortimer's Cross before marching on London and claiming the Crown as Edward IV. Ludlow remained a favoured possession of the new king, and in 1473 it became the home of the infant, Edward, Prince of Wales. He was crowned at the age of 12 and, together with his brother Richard, duke of York, is generally believed to have been murdered by his uncle Richard, duke of Gloucester, in the Tower of London. The presence of a royal resident and his entourage at Ludlow would have ensured that the castle was kept in first class condition, and at the beginning of the 16th century it became the home for Henry VII's son and heir, Prince Arthur and his bride, Katherine of Aragon. Arthur died at Ludlow in 1502 and his widow later married his younger brother, Henry VIII. Within a few years Ludlow had become the headquarters of the Council in the Marches and, as such, the administrative capital of Wales and the border. This new power base involved changes in use of many of the existing buildings within the castle and the construction of several new ones.

Within the inner bailey the main room in the Great Chamber Block became the Council Chamber, with further chambers above. An additional range was then added to the east, replacing buildings that had filled the gap between the Great Chamber Block and the eastern curtain wall. The new buildings, called the Tudor Lodgings, provided a necessary addition to the residential facilities of the castle. The Council Chamber was linked by a bridge to a first floor gallery in the Round Chapel and the whole of the east end of the chapel was rebuilt.

As the power of the Council grew, further accommodation was needed. This basically took the form of a Tudor house and was built within the inner bailey next to and over the entrance and against the Norman curtain wall. It consisted of a two storey suite of rooms with a kitchen to the east. This range was completed in 1581 and is known as the Judges' Lodgings. Further east was a laundry building. Even so, more accommodation was needed, and a long, probably timber-framed building was erected against the west curtain wall of the inner bailey. The main kitchens in the inner bailey were probably expanded to cater for the extra staff. The inmost court, that had once been the private preserve of the occupants of the keep, contained the Brewery, which was built over the well. This building extended to the south-west corner tower which was equipped with a large oven at ground floor level with two residential rooms above[4] and is now known as the Oven Tower.

The Council in the Marches also carried out extensive building works in the outer bailey. Adjoining the gatehouse was the Porter's Lodge and the Prison built in 1552, and further to the south a range of stables completed in 1597. The Porter's Lodge partly fulfils its original purpose—it is now the entry point for visitors. On the southern side of the ditch that ran round the inner bailey, there is an underground chamber that was used as an ice house, but may have been built as a magazine for the storage of arms and ammunition.[5]

The chapel of St. Peter in the south-western corner of the outer bailey was no longer required for its original purpose. It was extensively altered with the introduction of a first floor and and an extension to the west, was used as a courthouse and offices.

Following the abolition of the Council in the Marches in 1689, the castle was abandoned and the buildings were allowed to fall into decay. By 1771, when it was leased to the Earl of Powis, it was a romantic ruin—which was 'improved' by the addition of a series of picturesque walks around the perimeter. In 1811 the main part was bought from the Crown by the then Earl of Powis and has remained in the family ever since. The north-eastern part of the outer bailey remained in other hands and in the 18th and early 19th centuries contained the Castle Inn and a bowling green. This area, once the Tudor tennis court, now contains Castle Flats and the associated private grounds.

Part II

History

CHAPTER IV

From Foundation to the Anarchy

by Bruce Coplestone-Crow

The founder of Ludlow Castle was probably Walter I de Lacy, who died in 1085.[1] The stone castle to be seen today, however, was probably built by his son Roger, who forfeited his lands in 1096, and by Roger's brother, Hugh, who died some 20 years later. They built it at a place called Dinham within their manor of Stanton Lacy and both the castle and the town attached to it were known as Dinham 'for a very long time' before it was called Ludlow, according a late 13th century source.[2]

Walter de Lacy came to England in 1066 in the military household of William fitzOsbern, steward of Normandy and the Conqueror's closest confidant. One of King William's earliest acts was to make fitzOsbern earl over the Normans who had remained at Hereford and in Herefordshire ever since Edward the Confessor had allowed them to settle there in the 1050s. FitzOsbern was to have palatine powers within his territory, but he could not make good his earldom until after the crushing of English resistance in the western shires in the autumn of 1069.[3] Once established at Hereford Earl William sought to secure his border with an attack on the Welsh of south Wales and by building a string of castles along the border from Wigmore in the north to Chepstow in the south. He then commenced the Norman settlement of his earldom, which included the four southern-most hundreds of Shropshire[4] as well as the

counties of Hereford, Gloucester and Worcester, by the distribution of the conquered lands among his followers.

As Walter de Lacy is given the status of second-in-command to the earl in two near-contemporary sources,[5] he received the lion's share of the lands on offer. These amounted to some 163 manors across seven counties and were valued in 1086 at £423 per annum. Although the greatest concentration of Walter's power was in Herefordshire, the county central to William fitzOsbern's earldom, where he had 91 manors valued at £155 in 1086,[6] it seems from the evidence of *Domesday Book* that his lands in southern Shropshire already had a special significance for him and his family by the time of his death in 1085. The significance to Walter and his sons of these south Shropshire lands may have been related to the presence of a castle, and possibly also an embryonic borough.

The existence of a major castle at Ludlow by the time of Walter's death is perhaps indicated by a unique concentration of dominical power in the area apparent in the Domesday Survey. This was instituted only a year after his death and shows that in Shropshire as a whole his son, Roger, had 24 manors valued at £70 yearly, of which six, all of them in the vicinity of what became Ludlow—Stanton Lacy, Stokesay, Aldon, Ditton Priors, Hopton Wafers and Cleobury North—had been given to Walter by William fitzOsbern.[7] These six manors were valued at nearly £46 yearly, which represented 80% of the value of all the Lacy demesne lands in Shropshire. The Lacy demesne lands were valued at £57 per annum in 1086, and this represented 81% of the value of all Walter's lands in the county, both those he had kept in demesne and those on which had already enfeoffed some of his knights. In his barony as a whole Walter had kept lands representing only 59% of its total value in hand,[8] so the Shropshire situation was exceptional, and the situation around what became Ludlow unique.

The exceptional nature of the area around Ludlow was probably related to Walter's perception of its strategic importance. The southern portion of his manor of Stanton Lacy was located at a crossroads where an east-west route led from Knighton to Ludlow thence across the Teme at Dinham to Worcester, with a main north-south border route.[9] In his view as a Norman that crossroads would require, first, a castle to control it politically and, second, a borough to exploit it economically.

When William fitzOsbern died early in 1071 whilst campaigning in Flanders he was succeeded in his English lands and title by his second son Roger. Four years afterwards, Earl Roger joined an unsuccessful rebellion against the king and was deprived of everything he had on the English side of the Channel as a result. With the abolition of William fitzOsbern's palatine earldom in 1075, Walter de Lacy received a considerable boost to his status, since he now held all the lands he had received within that earldom as a chief tenant of the crown and not as the subtenant of an earl. It may only have been at this point, therefore, that he sought to develop the site at Ludlow into a castle that befitted his new status as one of the major tenants-in-chief of the realm and to establish beside it a borough. Both castle and borough were called Dinham initially. Neither of these are mentioned in the *Domesday Book*, but castles, being units of net expenditure, which the Conqueror could not tax, rather than of income, which he could, are only mentioned in passing and the borough may still have required capital to make it a success.

Even so, the *Domesday Book* shows a concentration of dominical power in the Ludlow area unique within the Lacy barony, and there can be little doubt that this importance was related to the presence of a castle. Walter and Roger had other castles at Weobley (Herefordshire), and at Ewyas Lacy (now Longtown, Herefordshire), but the one they had in south Shropshire was clearly the most important, requiring an unparalleled concentration of their personal resources to support it politically and to exploit it economically.

Roger de Lacy succeeded his father Walter in 1085, but less than a dozen years later he forfeited all his lands in England and Wales. Like many of his fellow chief tenants Roger regarded the succession to the English throne in 1087 of the Conqueror's second son, William Rufus, rather than his eldest son Robert, (who became duke of Normandy), as a mistake. He therefore took a leading part in the rebellion of 1088 against Rufus that was swiftly put down by the king and most of its leaders forgiven. A further rebellion in 1095, in which Roger de Lacy was also involved, proved too much for the king and in January 1096 many of its leaders, including Roger, were deprived of their lands and exiled to Normandy. William Rufus then allowed Roger's lands to pass to his brother Hugh (Hugh I de Lacy), who remained loyal to Rufus and to Henry I his successor until his death about 20 years later.

Since Hugh died childless, the Lacy barony escheated to the crown. There was a male claimant to the barony—Gilbert de Lacy, son of Hugh's exiled brother Roger—but this time the king, Henry I, chose to ignore his right to the barony (probably because he was the son of a known traitor) and arranged for it to pass instead to an heiress, whom he married off to Payn fitzJohn. This heiress was Sybil, the daughter of Roger and Hugh's sister Agnes by Geoffrey I Talbot,[10] and his intention in allowing it to pass to her seems to have been to reward Payn, a loyal household servant, since within a few years of Lacy's death he appears as both Sybil's husband and as possessor of the Lacy fief.

*Fig. 1 Map showing the Lacy manors
in Shropshire*

The barony that passed to Payn with his wife was not the same as the one that Roger de Lacy had held 30 years before. In 1096 and again when Hugh I de Lacy died in about 1115, some 20 manors in total (valued at about £35 annually in 1086) had been detached from the barony by the crown, and with the various grants to religious houses made by Hugh,[11] the barony was probably worth 20% less at his death than it had been when *Domesday Book* was written. Despite its reduction in value, the Lacy fief was still one of the largest in England and as such was a great prize for Payn fitzJohn.

Once his wife's inheritance was in his hands, Payn used his new position in Herefordshire and Shropshire, and particularly in the powerful stone castle at Ludlow, to further his interests in the Welsh border. By 1123, it seems, he was sheriff of Herefordshire; and some time between that date

and 1126, when Richard de Belmeis, bishop of London and sheriff of Shropshire, became incapacitated by ill health, he acquired that shrievality as well. He was also, it appears, justiciar in the counties under his care and this together with the offices of sheriff gave him a considerable power-base. His position was matched to the south by Miles of Gloucester, whose family had risen fast under Henry's patronage and who was likewise sheriff and justiciar in Gloucestershire. Working together in the royal service, Payn and Miles achieved a considerable degree of autonomy in the shires under their care, and the way they used this to further their own interests is referred to in the contemporary chronicle known as the *Gesta Stephani* or 'Deeds of King Stephen': 'In king Henry's time they raised their power to such a pitch that from the river Severn to the sea, all along the border between England and Wales, they involved everyone in litigation and oppressed them with forced services'.[12]

What this meant for Ludlow Castle can be seen in the marriage contract Payn drew up with Miles of Gloucester in 1137, under the terms of which Payn's eldest daughter and heiress, Cecily, would marry Miles' eldest son and heir, Roger, both of whom were minors. In the marriage contract Roger was to inherit with his wife,

> All the inheritances and acquisitions Payn held on the day he was living and dead, from whomever held; all the *maritagium* which Payn gave his daughter of the honour of Hugh de Lacy, in lands and [knights'] fees; and all the rights Payn had in the whole honour of Hugh de Lacy.[13]

As is known from other sources, this contract was not an exhaustive statement of all that Roger was to have from Payn through his wife. So, although Ludlow is nowhere mentioned within it and Payn is not associated directly with that place in this or any other surviving source, it can be inferred from the list of the 'inheritances and acquisitions' given in one section of the contract that it had been in his hands and that it was due to

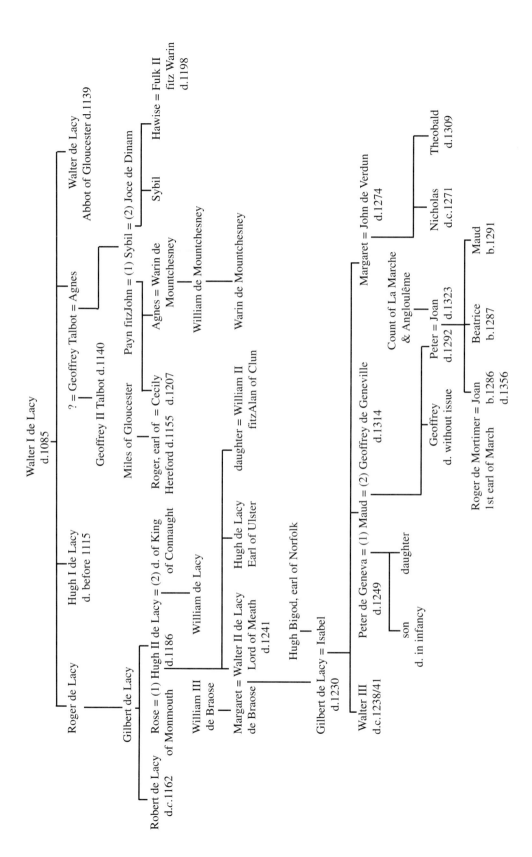

Fig. 2 The de Lacy family tree

24

pass to Roger under the heading of 'all the rights Payn had in the whole honour of Hugh de Lacy'. Some doubt has been expressed as to the extent of Payn's interest in this 'honour', whether or not it extended to the whole or just a part of it, but later in the 12th century his heirs claimed the honour or barony under the title of its three principal castles—Ludlow, Weobley and Ewyas Lacy 'with their appurtenances', so they at least believed that he had had the whole of it.[14]

It may well be that under the Lacys the castle at Ludlow had been intended to function as the caput of their whole barony in England and Wales. Indeed, it seems clear from the marriage contract that it was certainly the centre of Payn fitzJohn's interests in the Welsh border. The location of many of the lands that are mentioned within it suggests that the castle then stood at the head of a castlery, a land-unit in which most resources were directed to its support. This castlery, which Payn must have intended to support him in his role as the king's representative in Herefordshire and Shropshire, and in neighbouring parts of Wales, consisted of the Lacy demesne manors of Stanton Lacy, Onibury, Aldon and Stokesay, plus many other acquisitions Payn had made. Additionally, Payn had set about further increasing the resources available to him there by acquiring, by whatever means he could, adjacent lands and knights' fees, the greater part of which are listed in the marriage contract. (Details of them are given in Appendix I.)

Within the total number of tenements fitzJohn gained, either through his wife or by other means, there were some 17 knights' fees, all of which he made appurtenant to his castle at Ludlow. In economic terms, the *Domesday Book* value of his non-Lacy acquisitions (nearly £17) represented an increase of about one-third over the value of four Lacy demesne manors in and around Ludlow at that date. All this effectively increased and consolidated the lordship or castlery dependent on the castle there as held by Payn, and all of what he had achieved there was due to pass with his daughter Cecily to Roger fitzMiles after his death.

In fact, it was not long after the marriage contract was entered into that Payn met his sudden and unexpected death. The powerful military unit created by him at Ludlow was almost certainly his headquarters when in the March of Wales. One of his responsibilities in this area—the defence of the Welsh border—came to dominate his activities after the death of King Henry I in 1135. While Henry ruled, the Welsh border had remained relatively quiet (as a result of his campaigns of 1114 and 1121), but soon after his death there was a move by several Welsh princes to loosen the grip that many Anglo-Norman lords now had on substantial parts of their country. From the end of 1135 onwards, therefore, military activity in the March increased and it was while pursuing a party of Welsh raiders across the border on 10 July 1137, in the vicinity of a place called Cans, which may be Caus (Castle) and which lies not too far from Ludlow, that he fell dead, pierced through the head by a Welsh spear.[15]

Payn's untimely death left his plans for Ludlow and the rest of the Lacy inheritance incomplete, since his daughter was not yet married to Roger fitzMiles. Roger's father must have seen immediately that in the changed circumstances there was a danger that the new king, Stephen of Blois, who had seized the throne against the interests of the late king's daughter, Matilda, widow of the German emperor and now married to count Geoffrey of Anjou, might not allow what was in effect a private marriage agreement between two chief tenants of the crown to stand, since it was against royal policy to allow such arrangements. Not only that but since Easter 1136 Miles had had to contend with the presence at Stephen's court of a new claimant to his son's inheritance. This was Gilbert de Lacy, who had taken the opportunity of the old king's death to cross to England and present himself before the king as a 'disinherited' claimant to the fief of his father and uncle.[16] Gilbert seems almost immediately to have joined up with Geoffrey II Talbot, half-brother to Sybil, mother of the intended bride, who also had some undefined rights in the Lacy fief, and together they pressed for the return of that barony to the 'legitimate' male line.

As far as Miles of Gloucester was concerned, therefore, there was now a distinct possibility that his son's advantageous marriage might not take place, and it must have been a matter of acute frustration to him that he had to wait until Stephen's return from Normandy at the end of November 1137 before permission was granted for the arrangements to stand. The king's price for this favour was doubtless an assurance from Miles of his loyalty and a commitment not to help Matilda, daughter and heir of Henry I, against him. By charter issued in December 1137 Stephen allowed the marriage to go ahead and confirmed to Miles and his son the provisions of the original agreement between himself and Payn fitzJohn.[17]

To Gilbert de Lacy and Geoffrey Talbot of course the issuing of this charter by the king was the signal that there was now to be no peaceful, legal prospect of gaining any part of the Lacy fief. Waiting only for the return of campaigning weather in the spring, and acting on a rumour that Robert, earl of Gloucester and half-brother of the Empress Matilda, was about to make a formal break with Stephen in favour of his sister, Gilbert and Geoffrey went to the area where lay the greatest Lacy power—the Welsh Marches. There Talbot seized Hereford and Weobley Castles while Gilbert, it seems (because it appears in the hands of men opposed to Stephen in the following year), seized Ludlow Castle.[18] Gilbert was probably assisted in what must have been a

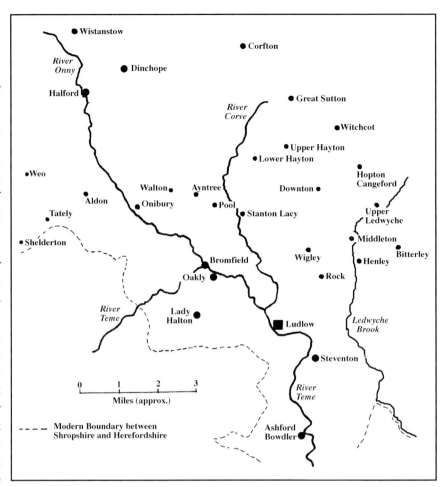

Fig. 3 Map of Ludlow and district to show places mentioned in the text

daunting task by the Lacy military tenants in Shropshire. These men, together with many of their colleagues elsewhere in the country, seem (from what evidence we have) to have acknowledged Gilbert's superior right to the fief from an early date. Also, as far as can be understood from surviving sources, neither Roger fitzMiles nor his father (acting on his behalf while he was still a minor) ever had control over Ludlow or the Lacy lands in Shropshire after the death of Payn. This means either that they were unable to make good Roger's claim to them, perhaps because of resistance from within the fief, or that if they did they were swiftly ejected from them by Gilbert and his allies within the fief. Indeed, it is difficult to see Gilbert achieving anything against such a formidable castle without help from its military subtenants.

King Stephen's reaction to the seizure of Hereford, Weobley and, probably, Ludlow by these disaffected barons was typically swift. He brought an army to Gloucester, which he reached on 10 May and where he was welcomed by Miles, the castellan and sheriff, and moved on to invest Hereford Castle a day or two later. There he remained until the castle surrendered on 13 or 14 June. Before the surrender, Geoffrey Talbot slipped away to Weobley, but that castle also fell to Stephen after a short siege, Talbot again making his exit before the final act. After this the king was away from the Welsh Marches for two months, but in August he returned to lay siege to Shrewsbury Castle, which was being held against him by William fitzAlan the sheriff. The king's army included Miles of Gloucester in its ranks. After a month's siege that sorely tried the king's patience, fitzAlan fled with his wife and children, leaving the garrison to surrender on the best terms they could.[19]

The fall of Shrewsbury left Ludlow as the only castle in the March of Wales in the hands of men opposed to Stephen. As this blocked effective communication between his forces at Hereford and Shrewsbury it was not a situation the king could tolerate for too long. Gilbert de Lacy and Geoffrey Talbot were at Bath in the late summer of 1138,[20] and it may have been this time that the king made his first move against the castle. This consisted of a marriage between Joce de Dinan, one of his knights, and Sybil, widow of Payn fitzJohn. With his new wife Dinan received from Stephen a grant of the castle of Ludlow and the lands in Shropshire associated with it, together with the dowry Payn had provided for his wife Sybil from both within and without the Lacy barony.

Although Ludlow Castle was not his to give, it was a shrewd move on Stephen's part. For not only did Sybil have Lacy blood but she had been 'lady of Ludlow' for some 20 years and could be expected to have a substantial following both among the people of the district and among the men forming the castle's garrison. After Payn's sudden death she had become a very eligible widow, her eligibility enhanced as much by the

fact that she was still of child-bearing age (she was to have two daughters by Joce) as by her Lacy lineage. It would have been unwise therefore for the king to have left her unwed for too long and her marriage to Joce de Dinan both took her off the marriage market and offered the people of Ludlow an alternative focus of loyalty that just might, in the long run, deliver the castle to a man seen as loyal to Stephen.

Joce de Dinan was perhaps not the ideal man to put against Gilbert de Lacy at Ludlow, although he was probably the best man Stephen had available to him. Like Payn fitzJohn he was of Breton extraction, being a member of a family from Dinan in Brittany who had settled at Hartland in Devon.[21] He had been drawn from Devon to the March of Wales by his affinity with the Breton lords of Monmouth and from there he entered Stephen's household. By joining Joce to Sybil the king was taking a calculated risk, since both Joce and his Monmouth friends had strong connections with Anjou, the county ruled by the Empress Matilda's husband, Geoffrey. In addition, the priory founded by the lords of Monmouth close to their castle was a daughter-house of the abbey of St. Florent of Saumur in Anjou and its foundation had been witnessed by abbot Oliver de Dinan of Saumur, who was a cousin of Joce's grandfather.[22] In the event Monmouth Priory became a powerhouse of Angevin sentiment in the southern Welsh March and Joce's connection with it doubtless influenced his eventual move into the empress's camp.

The proof of Sybil's marriage to Joce de Dinan and of his tenure at Ludlow in her right is contained in a charter recorded in the cartulary of St. Peter's Priory in Hereford. It has not been printed before and as it is important evidence for the history of Ludlow Castle it is transcribed in full in Appendix II.

Sybil's marriage to Joce means that some sort of accord regarding the division of the Lacy barony must have been reached between herself and her new husband on the one hand and Roger fitzMiles and his father on the other. In the previous December Stephen had allowed the whole of the Lacy barony which Sybil took to her first husband to pass to her daughter and to Roger fitzMiles her husband. A separate clause in the marriage contract between these two parties had stipulated that the dower Sybil had in the Lacy barony should be held from her daughter and son-in-law after Payn's death, and this arrangement had in effect been confirmed by Stephen when he allowed the marriage to go ahead. By arranging the marriage between Sybil and Joce, however, the king was now proposing that Ludlow Castle and the Shropshire lands dependent on it, as well as Sybil's dowry, should pass out of the hands of Roger fitzMiles and Cecily his wife and into those of Joce. The best that Roger and his father could have got from an accord with Joce de Dinan that allowed this new arrangement to go ahead was probably an agreement by Joce not to pursue any claim he might justly entertain by right of his wife to the parts of the Lacy barony outside Shropshire or his wife's dower. It cannot be pretended that Miles would have been happy with anything that kept his son Roger and himself apart from the lands Roger had every right to through his wife, and this may well have been a factor in his decision only a year later to desert the king in favour of the Angevin cause of the Empress Matilda. Later, after Joce too had espoused the Angevin cause, he is found witnessing Roger fitzMiles' charters, which suggests that Roger at least was comfortable with whatever arrangement there was between them at this time.

Although King Stephen made his dispositions in respect of Ludlow late in 1138 it was to be another six months before he moved to take the castle. When he did move, he clearly intended the campaign to be a 'textbook' example of the art of siege warfare—an art in which he was an acknowledged expert—since he took with him Prince Henry of Scotland, whom he was tutoring in the ways of war and kingship. That tutoring was a lively one, for Henry of Huntingdon, a contemporary chronicler, tells us that during the siege of Ludlow:

> Henry was dragged from his horse by an iron hook and nearly taken prisoner, but was gallantly rescued from the enemy by king Stephen.[23]

This machine was probably a 'crow', an engine consisting of a sort of large fishing rod on a balance, with a hook at the end,[24] and Stephen's rescue was probably made by cutting the rope or cord to which the hook was attached. John of Worcester, another contemporary chronicler, gives further details of the siege of the castle:

> The king left Worcester and camped at Ludlow. He had forts built in two places and garrisoned them with strong military forces to assault the castle which was held against him. Returning by way of Worcester, he moved an army towards London. Some of the soldiers, relentless in their cursed fighting, and driven by their boastful strength, decided to try their strength at Ludlow. A large body of soldiers gathered together for this purpose. It was dire to see one soldier raising his spear against another and running him through, and killing him, not caring what judgement his soul would have to endure. King Stephen checked these activities by his terrifying threats, and, coming again to Ludlow by way of Worcester, he settled everything peacefully. He then made his way in peace and haste to Oxford...[25]

This second account seems to suggest that Stephen found the fortifications too strong to take with the forces he had available and that he left two siege castles in front of the castle while he returned to Worcester seeking reinforcements. The locations of these siege-castles are unclear, but it would be logical for one of them to have been on Whitcliffe to dominate crossings of the River Teme and for the other to be over to the north or east to stop a relieving force reaching the castle from that direction.

What happened next according to the Worcester chronicler's account is by no means clear, but it seems that the men in the two siege castles fell out among themselves and turned on each other rather than the garrison. Then, when Stephen heard what was going on, he checked their indiscipline with threats and then returned to Ludlow with reinforcements to bring the siege to a successful conclusion.[26] Stephen probably brought Joce de Dinan and his new wife with him on his return to Ludlow and so was able to invest Joce with it as soon as it fell to him.

Joce's entry into Ludlow and the Shropshire lands at this juncture should not have affected the position of Roger fitzMiles and his father in the rest of the Lacy barony, as noted before. However, with the two Lacy 'disinherited', Gilbert de Lacy and Geoffrey Talbot, still at large, and probably with some resistance to Roger from among the Lacy feudal subtenants, what remained to them was in practice worth a good deal less than appeared on the surface. Within a few months of the taking of Ludlow Castle by the royal forces, it is apparent that Miles of Gloucester was becoming greatly dissatisfied with his position at the king's side and was ready to desert his cause for that of the empress. In the autumn of 1139 Matilda and her half-brother, the earl of Gloucester, landed in England from Normandy and made their way to Bristol. There she was met by Miles of Gloucester who expressed himself satisfied of her greater right to the English throne. Having made this decision he never afterwards faltered in his devotion to Matilda. Indeed, he eventually became regarded by friend and foe alike as the principal upholder of her cause after the earl of Gloucester.

Once he had espoused the Angevin cause Miles set about reducing Herefordshire and the neighbouring parts of England and Wales to the rule of the empress. In a vigorous six-week campaign that culminated in the sack of Worcester on 7 November he succeeded in bringing under his control virtually the whole of southern Herefordshire together with the adjacent areas of Gloucestershire and the Welsh border. However, one castle stood out against him and prevented him seizing the whole of Herefordshire and that was the castle at Hereford itself. Stephen knew well the value to him and to his enemies of a shire-castle,[27] and with a view to both to relieving it and establishing support for him in northern Herefordshire, he made two visits to Little Hereford, on the Teme below Ludlow, in the winter of 1139/40.[28] On the first visit he

achieved one aim by agreeing terms with Miles which allowed his men in Hereford Castle to go unmolested during the period of Advent, and his second by discovering that there were indeed men in the northern part of Herefordshire and at Ludlow who were prepared to remain loyal to him. These men were William de Braose, lord of Kingsland and Radnor, Osbern fitzHugh of Richard's Castle, Joce de Dinan of Ludlow and, above all, because he was by far the most powerful baron among them, Hugh de Mortimer of Wigmore.

Having met these men at Little Hereford on the first visit he returned on his second visit in February 1140 with a potential leader for them, Robert de Beaumont, earl of Leicester. Beaumont's latent capacity to lead a royalist faction in the area rested on the distant relationship between his wife and William fitzOsbern— the Conqueror's choice as earl of Hereford. Stephen must have been hoping that by making de Beaumont earl of Hereford and conferring on him all the powers of his illustrious predecessor, coupled with the relationship of his wife to the man who had effected the Norman conquest and settlement of the shire (and therefore the man to whom almost all the greater and lesser lords there owed their present fortunes) would tip the balance of power within the county in his favour.

The response from the four barons at least must have been encouraging—either that or Stephen hoped that his tactic would indeed make a difference—since only a day or two after the second meeting at Little Hereford he gave Beaumont the earldom of Hereford. Under the terms of the charter making him earl, Robert was to have the town and castle of Hereford and all the county of Herefordshire 'cum quibus Willelmus filius Osberni unquam melius vel liberius tenuit'. Excluded from the earldom, however, were the fiefs of the four barons named above, including Joce's, which is there described as being the one 'which before had been Hugh de Lacy's' ('... et feodo Gotsonis de Dinan quod fuit Hugonis de Laci'). In respect of Joce's fief, however, there was a special proviso to the effect that 'if the earl of Leicester could so deal with aforesaid Joce as that he himself would be willing to hold the aforesaid fief under the earl, that we fully allow'. ('*Et hac conditione, quod si comes Legrecestrie poterit facere versus prefatium Gotsonem quod ipse voluerit feodum illud predictum tenere de eo, bene concedo*'.)[29]

This special condition in respect of Joce's fief was probably inspired by the presence in the royalist party of his rival for Ludlow, Gilbert de Lacy. Although he had been chased from Ludlow by the king in the previous summer, the conversion of Miles of Gloucester and his son to the Angevin cause in the autumn must have been followed by Gilbert's decampment to Stephen's side. With much of Herefordshire in the hands of Miles and his allies by the end of 1139 it is likely that Gilbert now saw the better chance of gaining his Lacy inheritance as lying with the king, in spite of the fact that Stephen had recently given a substantial part of it to Joce de Dinan. There was nothing he could do to change that situation for the time being, but he could discomfort Joce somewhat by encouraging the new earl of Hereford to re-establish overlordship of all the Lacy lands within his earldom. The inclusion of the clause may indicate, moreover, that Stephen already had reason to suspect Joce's long term allegiance. His wife was, after all, the mother-in-law of Miles of Gloucester's eldest son and there must have been at least a possibility that once Gilbert had changed sides, Miles had been using his son's tie with Joce's wife to prise the lord of Ludlow away from the king. It would have been greatly to Miles' advantage and even more greatly to the king's disadvantage for this to have happened, since it would deprive the latter of one of his few friendly castles in the March of Wales and place in Miles' hands a valuable tool for use against the king's allies in northern Herefordshire. We have no knowledge of any such overtures, of course, but it is a fact that within little more than a year of the granting of the earldom to Robert de Beaumont, Joce de Dinan had gone over completely to the Angevin cause.

In the event the appointment of a new earl of Hereford by the king made little difference to his cause in Herefordshire. Hereford Castle fell to Miles of Gloucester and Geoffrey Talbot in the summer of 1140 and by the end of the year Stephen had allowed his earl of Leicester and Hereford to retire to Normandy, where his main interests had always lain.[30]

With Hereford Castle in their hands, Miles and his Angevin allies dominated all of Herefordshire except for the north, where the small royalist party held their ground under the increasingly able leadership of Hugh de Mortimer of Wigmore. In February 1141 Miles and the earl of Gloucester combined with the earl of Chester to bring Stephen to battle at Lincoln. Deserted by many of his allies the king was captured and sent first to Gloucester and then to Bristol, where he was kept in chains. The king's capture was the signal for many to desert his cause in favour of the Empress Matilda. One of these was certainly Joce de Dinan, who by April had begun to witness charters issued by members of the Angevin party,[31] and another was Gilbert de Lacy. Joce of Ludlow's defection, however, was the more serious for the king's cause since it heralded a policy of encirclement with which Miles was hoping to neutralize the royalist party in the north of Herefordshire and open up the way to the royal castle at Shrewsbury for his forces. These defections also produced the intriguing circumstance of placing all the claimants to all or part of the Lacy barony—their number reduced to three with the death of Geoffrey Talbot in August 1140—on the same side in the civil war.

For Gilbert the close ties between Miles and Joce and the arrangements they had evidently arrived at for sharing what was rightfully his was a situation he could not tolerate for too long. He remained with the empress while she made her disastrous visit to London with the intention of taking over the reigns of government and fled with her to Oxford and Gloucester and then back to Oxford when the Londoners drove her out. At Oxford on 25 July she attempted to repair some of her fallen fortunes by making Miles of Gloucester her own earl of Hereford, the position that Gilbert could well have aspired to had circumstances not been against him. Gilbert was there to witness the deed, but soon afterwards he withdrew from both parties in disgust and began working on his own account to regain Ludlow and the rest of his uncle's barony.

Within that barony it is likely, as mentioned before, that many of the military subtenants already recognized Gilbert's superior right to their feudal allegiance. Gilbert, as a male Lacy, could command the obedience of these men over either Roger fitzMiles or Joce de Dinan, whose rights in the barony were derived only through the female line or, in Joce's case, partly by grant of the crown. It was probably these circumstances that allowed Gilbert to establish himself in the lordship of Ewyas Lacy after his decision to work on his own account. This lordship had originally gone to Roger fitzMiles and his father after the death of Payn fitzJohn in 1137. A year before this event, however, in 1136, Miles had offered the Augustinian canons of Llanthony Priory in Ewyas (a house founded by Hugh I de Lacy) sanctuary at Gloucester from certain Welshmen who were making their position in Ewyas untenable. This was at the instance of Bishop Robert de Bethune of Hereford, himself a former prior of that house. At Gloucester they founded Llanthony Secunda (Llanthony-by-Gloucester) with the help and encouragement of the bishop and Miles. Later on, after Miles took possession of Ewyas on behalf of his son, but before hostilities between king and empress had broken out, he gave the land in Llanthony vacated by the canons to Oliver de Merlimond, his friend, who gave it to the house of Augustinian canons he had founded at Shobdon near Wigmore. Soon after Gilbert de Lacy established himself in Ewyas Lacy, he took Llanthony from Shobdon Priory 'by right of lordship', not so as to 'please' Hugh de Mortimer, as is claimed in the 13th-century Anglo-Norman text now known as the 'Chronicle of Wigmore Abbey', but in a bid to refound his family monastery.[32]

Shortly before Gilbert deprived Shobdon Priory of its lands at Llanthony, Hugh de Mortimer, overlord of Oliver, his steward, at Shobdon, angered by Merlimond's recent desertion of him in favour of earl Miles, had sought to disband the priory founded by his erstwhile steward by taking from them everything they had at Shobdon. The canons there were now homeless and with Lacy taking from them Llanthony, a possible refuge, they appealed to bishop Bethune (a former Augustinian canon) for assistance. His response was to gain them temporary refuge at the new house of Llanthony Secunda at Gloucester.[33]

According to the 'Wigmore Chronicle' all these events took place after Miles became earl of Hereford in July 1141 but before bishop Bethune's death in April 1148. The way Gilbert de Lacy's activities affected the history of Ludlow Castle (as well as Shobdon Priory) at this time is made clear in the late 13th century tale known as the *Romance of Fulk fitzWarin*, which now takes up the story of Ludlow Castle. In this source it is a 'Lacy of Ewyas' specifically who is the contender for the castle against Joce de Dinan in the time of King Stephen and of King Henry II.

The Romance of Fulk fitzWarin is essentially an account of the outlawry of Fulk III fitzWarin in the time of King John and of his subsequent fight to regain his patrimony. But before this account begins a lengthy prelude gives the earlier history of the family at Ludlow and elsewhere in Shropshire,[34] and it is in this prelude that the eponymous hero (actually his father, Fulk II, no distinction being made between the two) assists Joce de Dinan in his fight to retain possession of the castle and town of Ludlow against 'Sir Walter de Lacy, who at that time resided much in Ewyas'.[35]

The writer of the epic was almost certainly a Ludlow man, as his detailed knowledge of the geography of the town and its district shows. He was perhaps in the service of Geoffrey de Geneville, (lord of Ludlow from 1251/2 until his death in 1283), and his wife Maud, granddaughter of Walter II de Lacy.[36] The name 'Walter' given to Lacy in this source is generally agreed to be a mistake for Gilbert, the writer probably substituting Walter out of respect for

Maud's grandfather, the man responsible for establishing the successful castle and borough they now inhabited.

The writer seems to have been in touch with traditions regarding the history of the town and castle in the time of King Stephen and also to have had knowledge of the slightly earlier 'Chronicle of Wigmore Abbey', or of stories on which it was based, for he wove elements of both into this tale of Fulk fitzWarin. The *Romance*'s account of 'Walter' de Lacy's siege of Joce at Ludlow matches almost exactly the course of a similar siege related in the 'Wigmore Chronicle' in which Hugh de Mortimer of Wigmore is the besieger and not Lacy. According to the earlier text a 'very serious war' broke out between Hugh de Mortimer and Joce de Dinan sometime after Gilbert Foliot became bishop of Hereford in September 1148,

> in that Joce could not enter or leave his castle at Ludlow freely or without hindrance for fear of Sir Hugh, so grievously did he press him. ... And since Joce could do nothing against Sir Hugh by means of force, he positioned spies on the roads along which he learned that Sir Hugh would come unaccompanied, and he captured him, and held him in prison in his castle [of Ludlow] until he provided a ransom of three thousand silver marks, as well as his plate, his horses and his birds.

Although massive and apparently out of all proportion to Mortimer's importance, this ransom must have been paid, since when Hugh is next mentioned in the Chronicle he is a free man.[37] Mortimer's imprisonment at Ludlow may be the time in which an attempt was made on Joce's life, as bishop Gilbert Foliot reveals in a letter to him concerning his requisitioning of the church of Stanton Lacy.[38]

By contrast with the 'Wigmore Chronicle' the train of events in the *Romance* begin when Fulk fitzWarin is sent to Joce de Dinan's household at Ludlow to be raised by Sybil Talbot with Joce's own children, their daughters Sybil and Hawise.[39] According to this source Joce had completed Ludlow Castle (then called Dinham Castle, appar-

ently) which in his day consisted of three baileys surrounded by a double ditch 'the one within and the other without'.[40] While Fulk was at Ludlow 'there was a great disagreement and war between Sir Joce de Dinan and Sir Walter de Lacy ... through which strife many a good knight and many an honest man lost his life, for each one attacked his neighbours, burnt their lands and robbed their people, and did much other mischief'. 'Walter' brought an army to Ludlow and closely invested the castle, so that Joce and his knights were forced to make a sally across the bridge over the Teme below Whitcliffe to drive him off. After a lively pursuit, in which they were joined by the 'burgers' of the town, Joce and Fulk captured 'Walter' and his companion, Arnulf de Lyls, near Bromfield and imprisoned them in the castle.[41]

Thus far the two texts match each other fairly closely. Now, however, the author of the *Romance* introduces a sub-plot involving a love affair between Arnulf de Lyls and a guileless damsel of the castle called Marion de la Bruere. It is by means of this sub-plot that the prisoner gains his freedom, not by the payment of a ransom as in the 'Wigmore Chronicle', which may have been seen as too prosaic by the Ludlow author. In the course of this part of the story 'Walter' and Arnulf obtain their freedom with the aid of Marion and by shinning down a rope of towels and sheets from a window in the tower in which they are held. This tower is called Pendover Tower by the author of the *Romance*, although he also says that 'the highest tower ... within the third bailey of the castle ... is called Mortimer's Tower because one of the Mortimers was kept in it in prison for a good while'.[42] This shows that even in his day traditions concerning Ludlow Castle were circulating that may have their origins in the course of events described in the 'Wigmore Chronicle'.[43]

No further mention is made in the 'Wigmore Chronicle' of the war between Mortimer and Dinan after Hugh de Mortimer was released, but in the *Romance* the war between Lacy and Dinan continues. 'Walter' de Lacy now determines to avenge himself on Joce and, taking 'mercenaries, knights and others', he reopens hostilities.

However, at a date that seems to have been after the re-establishment of peace in England by King Henry II, (who succeeded Stephen in 1154), 'the earls and barons of England saw the great carnage and the mischief that had been committed, and which was going on from day to day. So they fixed a loveday between Sir Walter and Sir Joce, and there were all grievances redressed and the parties agreed, and they embraced each other in the presence of the great lords'.[44] That agreement, however, left Joce in possession of Ludlow and this was a situation Lacy was not prepared to tolerate. Aware of this, Joce sought to bolster his position by going to the family home at Hartland in Devon for reinforcements. While he is away, having 'engaged thirty knights and seventy serjeants and valets' to keep the castle until he returned, Lacy brought up to the castle and town by night 'knights, esquires and men-at-arms, more than a thousand'. Then, by means of the sub-plot involving Arnulf and Marion, the author has Arnulf gain access to the castle by a trick. Once inside the castle he opens its gates towards the town and then the gates of the town 'towards the river' to let in 'Walter'. In despair at being thus taken advantage of Marion stabs Arnulf to death and then leaps to her own death from a window of the Pendover Tower, which over-looked the area north of the castle known as The Linney. 'Walter' now stations men in every street of the town and as they move through it they set it alight and slaughter the burgers in revenge for the part they had played in his capture by Joce and Fulk.[45] With 'Walter' de Lacy in possession of Ludlow the end of the story is reached for despite further fighting Joce de Dinan was forced to accept that he had lost Ludlow permanently. Eventually he retired to Lambourne in Berkshire, where a manor worth £76 per annum had been provided for him by the king sometime between Michaelmas 1155 and Michaelmas 1156.[46] If the great value of this manor is in anyway compa-rable to that of Ludlow Castle and town, there is small wonder there was such stubborn fighting for it.

Although the 'Wigmore Chronicle' does not continue the story of the fight for Ludlow as does the *Romance*—doubtless because its main concern was with the founding of Wigmore Abbey—it does give details of the political situa-tion in the March of Wales in the time of King Stephen against which the Lacy recapture of Ludlow can be viewed. In this source, after Earl Miles of Hereford had died in 1143, 'the noble lord of Hereford, Roger, powerful and worthy and with a great many retainers … made so much trouble that he [Hugh] was obliged to remain behind closed doors in his castles for fear of him'.[47] Earl Roger's power, like his father's before him, lay to the south of Wigmore, but with the conversion of Joce de Dinan to the Angevin cause in 1141 the earl, the principal Angevin commander in the area, now had the castlery at Ludlow to the north-east of Wigmore at his disposal.[48] This opened up to him the prospect of an encirclement and eventual elimination of Hugh de Mortimer and the Stephanic faction in Herefordshire, although this was in the event a long time coming. It was not until after September 1148, in fact, that the prospect became a reality, when Elias de Say, whose lordship of Clun lay to the north of Wigmore, was replaced by William fitzAlan, his son-in-law and a fervent Angevin. At this point, therefore, Mortimer did indeed have 'enemies on all sides' as the 'Wigmore Chronicle' asserts and the stage was set for a final reckoning between the two factions.

Wightman notes[49] that the conflict for Ludlow between Lacy and Joce 'seems to have been private war pure and simple, and it is doubtful whether either side cared much for the fate of Stephen or empress'. However, 'Walter' de Lacy's final success at Ludlow can probably be seen as an example of Gilbert co-operating with Hugh de Mortimer though for separate ends—they were allies only in the sense that they had a common enemy. A scenario for this kind of co-operation can be provided for the year 1149, by which time William fitzAlan had probably replaced Say at Clun. In this year, while Earl Roger of Hereford was absent in the north of England with Prince Henry (the future Henry II), Mortimer, it seems, went over to the offensive and laid waste a good part of the area of

Herefordshire to the south of Wigmore in the direction of the county town.[50] A well-timed and successful operation by Lacy at Ludlow on the north-east, which saw the removal of the danger to him from that direction, would therefore have been extremely useful to Mortimer at this juncture. At the same time, Hugh's offensive in the south could be seen as an attempt to reduce the likelihood of Joce receiving reinforcements at Ludlow that might have placed Gilbert's achievements there in peril, as well as a move against the Angevin forces that dominated Herefordshire. Although the timing of these campaigns is uncertain, this kind of co-operation between the two seems to be implied in the course of events as set out in the 'Wigmore Chronicle', but whereas Mortimer's intention was to break out of the circle of enemies threatening him, Lacy's was purely to regain Ludlow and its attendant lands. To that extent Wightman is right, in that they were allies only in so far as they had common enemies, not common interests.

Ludlow and the Shropshire lands seem therefore to have been regained for his family by Gilbert de Lacy in about 1150. Thereafter Gilbert needed only to regain the lands in the hands of Earl Roger and his wife to complete his hold on the fief of his father and uncle. Opportunity to do this probably did not arise until after the death of Earl Roger at the end of 1155. Earlier in that year the earl had unwisely attempted to rebel against Henry II, so after the earl's death the king took the opportunity to reduce the power of his family by denying the earldom to his heirs and also depriving them of the lands they had acquired during Stephen's reign. Among these latter will have been Earl Roger's interest in the Lacy fief. This interest, apart from the 'maritagium' which

remained with his widow and which she took to her second and third husbands, the family were probably obliged to give up to Gilbert.

With the re-establishment of peace in the March of Wales Gilbert came increasingly under the influence of the military knights of the Order of the Temple. His desire to join them and go to the Holy Land may well have dated from the time of the Second Crusade in 1147, but this was a time when he was probably too busy fighting for possession of Ludlow to heed the call. In the 1150s, however, as peace returned to the Welsh border, he was certainly contemplating joining the Templars, as is evinced by the round-naved chapel he built in Ludlow Castle and his by grant to them of the manor of Temple Guiting in Gloucestershire.[51] Shortly after Christmas 1159 we find him setting out for Palestine as a Templar.[52] Ironically, one of his companions on the journey was Walter of Hereford, brother and heir of Earl Roger of Hereford and the man whom the king had allowed to inherit Roger's much-reduced fief (but not his earldom). Another companion was Warin de Mountchesney, husband of Agnes, the younger daughter of Payn fitzJohn and Sybil. Warin had in his possession the part of the Lacy barony assigned by Payn as Agnes' marriage portion, but which she held under her elder sister Cecily and Earl Roger.[53] Over 30 years later Warin's son William was to sue Gilbert's grandson Walter II for his rights in Ludlow, Weobley and Ewyas and their appurtenances. Gilbert is last heard of September 1163, when he was preceptor of the Templars in the county of Tripoli. There he was putting to good use his long experience of warfare in the Welsh Marches[54] by helping to defeat the Saracen leader Nur-as-Din at the Castle of Krak.

CHAPTER V

The End of the Anarchy to the de Genevilles

by Bruce Coplestone-Crow

Little is known of Robert de Lacy, the Crusading Gilbert's eldest son, but he had in any case been succeeded by his younger brother, Hugh II de Lacy, by 1162.[1] Hugh was probably present in person in King Henry II's campaign against Owain Gwynedd in north Wales in 1165, since he paid no scutage in that year,[2] but that is about all that is known of him before 1171. In that year he went with the king to Ireland, and was present when Henry took charge of affairs there from Earl Richard 'Strongbow' of Clare, who was Hugh's cousin-by-marriage.[3] Before the king returned to England in April 1172 he gave Hugh the kingdom of Meath and the city of Dublin to hold and at the same time made him his justiciar or deputy in Ireland. The Meath lands were subsequently to become the primary focus of the Lacy family's power, their value far outstripping anything they had in England, Wales or (until 1204) Normandy.

When the revolt of Prince Henry, son of Henry II, began in April 1173 the king recalled Hugh from Ireland to Normandy. There he and Hugh de Beauchamp heroically defended Verneuil against the forces of King Louis of France for a month before they were forced to surrender on 9 August. After the rebellion was put down in 1174 he remained constantly at the king's side, in Normandy until May 1175 and then in England until 1177, when he returned to Ireland once more. Sometime between May 1175 and his departure for Ireland, probably whilst at Ludlow, he arranged for one of his four daughters by his first wife, Rose of Monmouth, to marry William son of William fitzAlan of Clun, six of his Shropshire manors going with her.[4] At Oxford in May 1177 King Henry regranted to him his lordship of Meath and sent him back to Ireland as royal justiciar. In the summer the king had Ludlow Castle seized, probably as surety against Hugh's behaviour in Ireland, and placed in the keeping of one of his functionaries, Thurstan fitzSimon. Thereafter, until Michaelmas 1190, Thurstan drew a salary of £16 10s annually for his office at Ludlow Castle, the money coming from the lands of Richard Talbot (a cousin of Geoffrey II Talbot, who died in 1140) at Linton, Herefordshire, which were in the king's hands through the minority of his heir.[5]

In 1180 Hugh married a second time, this time taking as his wife a daughter of the king of Connaught. He did not have the royal licence for this, however, and as a result, in April of the following year, he was relieved of his justiciarship and recalled to England. He was sent back to Ireland in the winter of 1181/2, only to be recalled again in August 1184.[6] He returned to Ireland with Prince John the next year and built a castle within the precincts of the old Celtic monastery at Durrow. Whilst visiting it on 25 July 1186 a youth stepped out and decapitated him with one blow of an axe that he had hidden about himself, both body and head falling into the ditch of the castle.

Hugh's eldest son, Walter II, was still under age when his father died, so all his lands escheated to the crown until his coming-of-age. In 1187 Ludlow, which had already been in the king's hands for the past ten years, paid 10 marks tallage in the royal demesnes.[7] Some of Walter's lands were released to him two years later, but not Ludlow Castle, which remained in the king's hands. In 1190, when the lord Rhys ap Gruffydd of Deheubarth was showing hostility to the king and to the Anglo-Norman lords of south Wales, the castle was provisioned by the sheriff of Shropshire. These provisions included 100 loads of corn (costing £2 18s 4d) and the same of oats (costing £3 6s 8d), 2 casks of wine (£2 19s 2d) and 20 flitches of bacon (£1 5s 6d), by writ of the chancellor and at a total outlay of £10 9s 8d. At the same time he paid £5 under a similar mandate to Gilbert de Essartis for custody of the castle, Gilbert himself accounting on the roll of escheats for Northamptonshire for £3 of his expenses in maintaining himself at the castle.[8]

Walter probably entered into full possession of Ludlow Castle at Michaelmas 1190, although it seems to have been another four years before he gained the rest of the fief. In 1190 he was charged £25 12s 6d scutage on 51¼ knights' fees in the whole Lacy barony, but he did not start paying off this amount until 1194.[9] This year may therefore mark the time at which he entered into his full inheritance in England. He certainly obtained his Irish lands in that year, as he did homage to King Richard for them at Nottingham on 29 March[10] and a formal grant of his English inheritance may have followed on from this.

No sooner had Walter entered into his inheritance than it was taken from him as a result of his activities in Ireland. In 1194 he joined John de Courcy, lord of Ulster, in ravaging the lands in Ireland belonging to Prince John, who was in revolt against the king his brother.[11] The two men thought they were helping the king against his rebel brother, but were surprised by a sudden fraternal reconciliation in May. The king's reaction was to deprive Lacy of all his lands and castles. Walter's initial proffer of 1,000 marks for

their return and for the king's benevolence was rejected as inadequate,[12] and it was not until 1198, whilst he was with the king in Normandy, that he agreed to pay the huge sum of 3,100 marks for them. The agreement is recorded thus in the Herefordshire pipe roll for that year:

> Walter de Lacy renders account of 3,100 marks for having the king's good will and seisin of his land. He has paid £200 and owes £1,866 13s 4d, of which debt he pays 1100 marks [recte 1000] and will pay the residue at the Exchequer in England or at the [Norman] Exchequer, that is, £200 at either Exchequer. He owes £1200, which debt he will pay at £200 per annum.[13]

Before this, just after Christmas in 1197 the Justiciar, Hubert Walter, archbishop of Canterbury, took Ludlow, Hereford and Bridgnorth castles away from the castellans to whom they had long been entrusted and put his own men in their place *ad opus regis*.[14] This he did shortly before entering Wales with the intention of bringing peace between the two warring sons of the lord Rhys ap Gruffydd of Deheubarth (Rhys having died the previous April) and was clearly intended to provide him with a secure base from which to conduct his campaign. Hubert ceased to be justiciar in July 1198, this event probably coinciding with Walter's agreement to pay 3,100 marks for the return of his lands and for the king's good will. In the later part of 1198, therefore, Walter regained his lands and castles.

While these lands and castles were still in escheat, and while Walter was abroad with the king, the widow and nephew of Earl Roger of Hereford brought a writ of right against him for the whole of his barony. In the summer of 1198 Countess Cecily and William de Mountchesney fined 200 silver marks for having their hereditary right in 'Ludlow and its appurtenances, and Weobley and Ewyas [Lacy] with all their appurtenances'. When the plea came before the justices, however, the king intervened to forestall the case because of Walter's indebtedness to the crown.[15]

Although this plea had failed he was faced by another legal challenge in the following year, this time specifically for Ludlow. On this occasion it was Sybil de Plugenet and Hawise fitzWarin, Joce de Dinan's daughters by Sybil Talbot (de Lacy), who were the petitioners. In 1199 they fined 40 marks for having their right in the king's court in the vill of Stanton (Lacy) and its 'appurtenances' by writ of *mort d'ancestor*, that is the death of Joce de Dinan their father. Geoffrey fitz Peter, the justiciar, was told to take surety from them for the 40 marks 'and they are to have their writ',[16] but this plea also seems to have failed (or was settled out of court) as nothing more is heard of it.

Walter was certainly with King Richard in Normandy during 1198, and it seems likely that he stayed there until after the king's death in April 1199, only returning when John came to England for the second time as king in October 1200.[17] In the following month John arranged for Walter to marry Margaret daughter of William III de Braose of Bramber and Radnor, one of the king's closest confidants. Walter crossed to Ireland in 1201 and, since he is not mentioned again in the king's company until July 1207, he probably spent all of that time on his Irish estates. As surety for his good behaviour there Ludlow Castle and all his English lands were placed in the hands of his father-in-law, William de Braose, in the summer of 1202 to hold on behalf of the king. Later that year he had quittance by the king's writ of the fourth scutage of the reign owing on the 10 knights fees Walter had in Shropshire and on the 13$^{1/12}$ in Gloucestershire 'because he has custody of his lands'.[18] At the same time Walter's lands in Normandy were also committed to Braose's custody and in the following February he also also received the lands of the honour of Le Pin that had belonged to Walter's brother Hugh.[19] In 1203 the *vill* of Ludlow paid 10 marks tallage of the king's demesnes.[20] As he was fully occupied in Ireland at this time Walter was not involved in the final fall of Normandy to the French king in 1204, although he, like almost all the Anglo-Norman barons who chose to stay loyal to John, lost all his Norman lands as a result. In 1205 or early the following year Walter fined 400 marks for having the castle and land of Ludlow, his fine

being payable at a rate of 200 marks yearly,[21] and this was the point at which both were returned to him.

By 1207, however, Walter had become at variance with the king's officers in Ireland and in February Ludlow Castle was seized into the king's hands by the ubiquitous William de Braose. On 5 March Braose was told to give up the castle to Philip d'Aubigny, the king having entrusted it to him to keep during pleasure in the same way that the justiciar (Hubert Walter) had formerly held it.[22] A precept dated five days later shows that Philip had been paid 20 marks for the purpose of taking possession of it and another shows that some wine of the king's was then sent from Bristol for the stores at Ludlow Castle.[23] On 13 July Philip was ordered to return the castle and *vill* to William de Braose,[24] but by now relationships between the king and his favourite were beginning to deteriorate rapidly. On 14 April 1207 Walter had been summoned to England on pain of forfeiture and had certainly crossed to England by 16 July, when he was with John at Winchester.[25]

Over the next few months he made his peace with the king once more and on 19 March 1208 a mandate was issued to Braose saying that when he delivered up his (Braose's) son to Walter (as hostage for his good behaviour), the king from that moment acquitted him in respect of Ludlow Castle, which he had received to keep and surrender when ordered.[26] In June Walter returned to Ireland and William de Braose then used his son-in-law's castle at Weobley to attack the king's interests in Herefordshire. In the winter of 1208-9 William took refuge with Walter in Ireland and in 1210 John crossed to Ireland to root out Braose and to punish Walter de Lacy for harbouring him. Walter offered a complete submission to John on 28 June, placing all his lands and castles 'in the hand of the king, as his lord, to retain or restore as he pleases'.[27] John, however, refused to be mollified and Walter and his brother Hugh, together with William de Braose, were forced to flee to France.

Ludlow Castle and some or all of the Lacy barony in England and Wales was now placed in the keeping of Engelard de Cigogné, sheriff of Herefordshire. Early in 1213, during the period of general reconciliation that followed John's surrender of his kingdom to the Pope in return for the removal of the Interdict, Walter sent out feelers from France with a view to obtaining permission to return to England. John gave him safe conduct to come to him on 1 June and by the 24th of that month they had reached agreement on the future of Walter's lands and castles. On 29 July the king wrote to Engelard ordering him to restore to Walter all the lands under his care, except for the castle of Ludlow, once Walter had provided four hostages (one of them his son Gilbert) for his loyalty and good behaviour. A further mandate told Engelard that as soon as Walter had given security for the payment of £40 yearly towards the custody of Ludlow Castle he could give Walter seisin of Ludlow manor and its appurtenances, but not the castle. Walter seems not to have found the requisite security, however, as the borough of Ludlow was still in the king's demesnes in 1214.[28]

In February 1214 Walter went with the king to Poitou and because of his good services there John agreed that the *vill* of Ludlow should be returned to him. Engelard was instructed to let Walter have seisin of it immediately, but later the king seems to have had some regrets about it and wrote to Cigogné, rather cryptically, 'What you have done in the matter of the swine [for the garrison] is well done. And although it may be better to restore the castle of Ludlow [to Lacy] than pay 40 marks yearly for its custody, yet keep it in our hand, and let Walter de Lacy have the vill according to the agreement between him and us, because we do not wish to flinch from that agreement'.[29]

The castle of Ludlow was not included in this agreement and did not return to Walter until 12 April 1215.[30] In that year he fined 4,000 marks for the return of his Irish lands and this and the return of Ludlow Castle were probably intended by John as part of a policy designed to counter the growing power in the Welsh Marches of Giles and Reginald, sons of the late William de Braose, and their Welsh ally, Llywelyn Fawr. After the

death of Giles de Braose, bishop of Hereford, in December 1215 Walter had the guardianship of his see while it was vacant and on 8 August 1216 was made sheriff of Herefordshire.[31] Walter was by now completely reconciled with the king (either that or the king had such a stranglehold on his finances that he dared not go against him) and despite their past differences stood by him during the last months of his reign.

After the death of John in 1216 Walter became a member of the Council of Regency for his young heir, Henry III. He crossed to Ireland in August 1220 to see to his affairs there but returned to England in 1223 after war had broken out in the Welsh Marches. Early in 1223 Llywelyn Fawr raided into Shropshire and took the castles of Kinnerley and Whittington from their Anglo-Norman owners. The king and his justiciar, Hubert de Burgh, brought an army up to Shrewsbury to counter the threat and two months later William Marshal, earl of Pembroke, landed from Ireland and took back from Llywelyn the former royal castles at Cardigan and Carmarthen. In an attempt at reconciliation with the Welsh prince, a safe conduct was offered to him to come before the king, the archbishop and the council at Ludlow on 5 July. Llywelyn duly came, and so did Earl William Marshal, but the objectives of the meeting, which probably took place between 8 and 10 July, could not be met and the Welsh prince departed without anything being achieved.[32] In September Hubert assembled an army at Hereford and then moved northwards to Montgomery where he sought to improve his own and the king's position in the Welsh Marches by building a new castle. On 15 November the justiciar replaced Walter de Lacy as sheriff of Herefordshire as part of a general scheme to improve royal control over the local government of the March.

In that same year Walter de Lacy's brother Hugh returned to Ireland and tried to re-establish himself in his earldom of Ulster with the aid of his half-brother William (son of Hugh II de Lacy by his second wife) and most of Walter's knights of Meath. Despite Walter's refusal to join his brothers and his rebellious knights, his position

Fig. 1 The Norman castle walls on the south, showing, from left to right, the North-West Tower, the Postern Tower and the Oven Tower

was now regarded as suspect. So that the misdeeds of his men of Meath 'in harbouring Hugh de Lacy, pillaging and burning the king's land [and] killing and holding his men to ransom' could be dealt with, Walter was obliged to agree to a proposal by the Council of Regency that his castles at Ludlow in England and Trim in Ireland should be handed over to the crown for a period of two years from Easter 1224 and also to join in a general campaign against Hugh and William. Walter was to have free access to Trim Castle for the purposes of defeating the king's enemies and when the lands of Walter's knights were recovered the king was to hold them for a year and a day.[33] Walter was in Ireland by 30 March to carry out his part of the bargain and a patent of 15 April placed the custody of Ludlow Castle in the hands of William de Gamages, the royal agent.[34] Only a year later, in May 1225, Hugh de Lacy having surrendered to the justiciar of Ireland, Walter fined 3,000 marks to have seisin of the Irish lands forfeited by his knights and other free tenants in Ireland 'because they went against the king in Hugh de Lacy's war' and that he might have the castles at Ludlow and Trim restored to him.[35]

Walter's only son and heir, Gilbert, who had married Isabel daughter of Hugh Bigod, earl of Norfolk, died in 1230 leaving a son, Walter III, and two daughters, Maud and Margaret. On 25 December Walter II received back all the lands in Herefordshire and Shropshire that he had given to his son for his sustenance and which had been taken into the king's hand on Gilbert's death.[36]

On 1 August 1234, at Trim in Ireland, Walter made William de Lucy of Charlecote, Warwickshire, steward of his English lands and constable of Ludlow Castle. The document issued at the time gives details of the duties and allowances pertaining to the office:

Walter de Lacy certifies that he has given and conceded to William de Lucy and his heirs, for their homage and service, the stewardship of all the lands that he has or might have in England, with two carucates of land, part of the demesne belonging to his castle of Ludlow. William and his heirs are to hold the stewardship and land of Walter de Lacy and his heirs in fee. In return for the two carucates of land William and his heirs are to be constables of the castle for its safe custody; and they will maintain there forever a priest, a porter and two sentinels as formerly had been used, except at such times as Walter de Lacy himself or his heirs shall come there, and then William and his heirs shall remain in the outer ward during their stay. But in times of hostility it is agreed that Walter and his heirs shall fortify and defend it themselves at their own cost and William and his heirs will remain in the same outer ward whilst it should be so fortified. And William and his heirs may take the same taxes upon bread and beer in the town of Ludlow, in the absence of Walter and his heirs, which he [Walter] used to have or ought to receive when he was there in person. Also the repairs which William and his heirs shall make to the walls and dwellings of the castle upon occasion are to be by view of two honest men and at the charge of Walter and his heirs. And that William and his heirs shall have sufficient fuel in the woods belonging thereto [they are to have it] as other constables thereof used to have. And further that whenever William and his heirs by the command of Walter and his heirs, or his or their bailiffs, shall be called to any place where Walter or his heirs hold their courts, receive accounts, or upon other occasions, he and they shall have entertainment there for that purpose for themselves and five horses. And Walter and his heirs will provide William and his heirs with all garments and vestments as for a household knight, and if Walter son of Gilbert de Lacy, when he is of age, wishes to have the two carucates of land aforesaid in his own hand, he will provide the fair equivalent elsewhere.[37]

By the time this deed was issued Walter II was deeply in debt and its purpose may partly have been intended to relieve him of some of this burden. He owed the crown £2,700 (outstanding from his fine of 1215) and certain Jewish moneylenders a further £1,000. He therefore turned to William de Lucy, a known moneylender, for assistance. Lucy obliged him (perhaps in return for acquiring the lucrative office of constable of Ludlow) with a loan of £322 to be repaid at a rate of £80 yearly.[38] This satisfied his creditors for a while but by 1237 he was again being pursued, this time by Warin de Mountchesney, son of the William de Mountchesney who had sued for his

share of the whole Lacy barony in 1198. Warin, it seems, had bought up a number of gages Walter had given to the Jews and now sought possession of the lands they represented. Included among them were the two carucates of land William de Lucy had in the demesnes of Ludlow by virtue of his office of constable of the castle and other lands at Ludlow and Stanton Lacy. By April 1238 Walter had been forced to render Ludlow to the king as security for his debts and in that month Adam de Cusak, bailiff to Walter, came before the king at Gloucester seeking the return of the manors of Stanton Lacy and Ludlow, except for two carucates of land in Ludlow belonging to William de Lucy. This was not forthcoming, however, and the plea seems eventually to have been settled out of court, since Ludlow and its castle were in Walter's hands at the time of his death three years later.[39]

Walter de Lacy died shortly before 24 February 1241, on which day the king ordered the sheriffs of Herefordshire and Shropshire to take all his lands into custody.[40] Matthew Paris says he had lost his sight and suffered from other infirmities in his old age and, in a reference to the huge debts with which his lands were still burdened, that he left a 'wasted inheritance' to his heiresses.[41] His grandson Walter III had died some time in the previous three years, so the young man's sisters, Maud and Margaret, were his heirs. On 4 March the elder Walter's widow, Margaret, received the manor of Stanton Lacy for her sustenance until her husband's lands could be extended and her reasonable dower assigned to her. On 27 November she was given her dower in the manor of Ludlow.[42]

At the time of their grandfather's death Maud and Margaret de Lacy were unmarried and probably minors, so the Lacy barony escheated to the crown until either they came of age or suitable husbands were found for them. Early in 1244 King Henry III married the elder sister, Maud, to one of his Savoyard favourites, Peter de Geneva, and on 19 February 1244 the king commanded the sheriff of Herefordshire to extend Walter de Lacy's lands in his county and make equal partition of them between Maud and her husband and Margaret, whose portion was to remain in the king's hands.[43] As a result of this extension and partition, the king, on 15 March, commanded John Lestrange, justice of Chester, to deliver to Peter de Geneva 'the castle of Ludlow that belonged to his wife'.[44] By May of the same year the younger sister Margaret had been married to John de Verdun and in that month an equal partition of the lordship of Meath between her and her sister was ordered.[45] On 12 June the sheriffs of Herefordshire and Shropshire were to let John and Margaret have their moiety of Walter de Lacy's lands in their counties.[46] On 19 December 1245 the king told the barons of the Exchequer to acquit Maud and Peter de Geneva of their moiety of the debt of £955 13s 4d Maud's grandfather owed to certain Jews, the other moiety, owed by Margaret and John de Verdun, remaining to be accounted for.[47] Peter de Geneva died shortly before October 1249,[48] having had by Maud a son, who died in infancy, and a daughter. Maud remarried, sometime before 18 August 1252,[49] Geoffrey de Geneville, for whom, probably, the

Romance of Fulk fitzWarin was written. Geoffrey had been encouraged by the king to come to England from his home in Champagne in 1251. He soon became a friend of Prince Edward, heir to the throne, and thereafter never faltered in his loyalty to the prince, and to his father, and to the prince's son, Edward II, over nearly 65 years of service.[50]

The hundredal inquisition of 1255 in Shropshire gives an incomplete account of the various military and other tenements that owed guard and other duties at the castle in Geoffrey de Geneville's day. These are discussed further in Appendix III, but it is important to note for present purposes that in this inquisition and in the *quo warranto* proceedings of 1292 Geoffrey de Geneville and John de Verdun and their wives, 'the heirs of Walter de Lacy', were claiming a franchise at their manor of Stanton Lacy and town of Ludlow 'by conquest' (*a conquestu*). The franchise or royal prerogative they were claiming was the right to have a gallows, to hold pleas of bloodshed and hue and cry, to assize beer, and to try under their own writ of right all

Fig. 2 Looking towards the inner bailey and the Entrance Tower across the walls of St. Peter's Chapel

civil causes within their jurisdiction. All this they claimed by prescription and not by the expedient of withdrawing the lands concerned from the shire and hundred, or so they said.[51] Baugh notes[52] that Stanton Lacy begins to appear separately from the shirereeval administration of Shropshire from the 1230s onwards, so if it was Walter II de Lacy who initiated the process (perhaps to increase his revenues and so pay off some of his debts) it was the Frenchmen Geoffrey de Geneville and John de Verdun, used to such liberties in their homelands, who were now pursuing it with vigour to the detriment of the royal administration of the shire. There is now no evidence that any part of the area covered by Ludlow and Stanton Lacy was ever held separately from the kingdom of England before it came into the hands of its Norman conquerors, so the claim by these men to hold their franchise *a conquestu* cannot be substantiated as it can for other Marcher lordships.

However, it is just possible that Geneville and Verdun and their wives were harking back (not very accurately) to the days of Payn fitzJohn, when it may well have been possible for the lord of Ludlow, as both sheriff and local justiciar, to separate his lands at and around that place from the shires of Shrewsbury or Hereford.[53] After Payn's death, the civil war of Stephen's reign may have aided this process, although the return of vigorous royal rule under Henry II must have put an end to it. Henry's overwhelming response in 1155 to the challenge to his authority within the kingdom presented by the independently-minded Hugh de Mortimer of Wigmore and Earl Roger of Hereford was clearly meant to serve as an exemplary warning to other Marcher barons who might be tempted to follow their example. Thereafter, frequent royal requisitioning of the castle and town for a period of half a century from 1177 onwards may perhaps have been intended as much to ensure that a strategically important site remained within the kingdom (and so at the king's disposal) as to persuade Hugh II de Lacy and Walter his son of where their loyalties lay. The building of a new royal castle at

Montgomery in 1223 seems to have reduced the need of the crown for the use of the castle at Ludlow (it rarely appears in royal hands after that date) and it was probably at this point that Walter de Lacy began to establish the judicial and administrative independence of Ludlow and its adjacent lands. He and his heirs were undoubtedly aided in this by the geographical location of Ludlow adjacent to the Marcher lordships of Clun and Richard's Castle, where such independence already existed or was claimed to exist. As yet, however, their liberty covered only their manor of Stanton Lacy and (because they were once part of that manor) their castle and town of Ludlow. By 1274 John de Verdun had withdrawn the manor of Stokesay also from the royal administration of the shire and in the next century the lordship of Ludlow was to include Bromfield, Aldon and Onibury as well as Stanton Lacy, Ludlow and Stokesay,[54] this extensive lordship perhaps, in the long run, representing the area under Payn fitzJohn's control in the second quarter of the 12th century.

Although an interim division of the Lacy inheritance between the two sisters and their husbands had been made in 1244, it was not until 10 June 1260, as the threat of civil war loomed, that a formal partition was made by charter. Although the details of this partition are not preserved, its general outline can be reassembled from other sources. In effect it provided for an equal division of the Lacy barony in England and Wales between them, each doing service to the king for half the knight-service due from the whole barony, that is, the service of $7\frac{1}{2}$ knights' fees each.[55] At Ludlow Geoffrey de Geneville received the castle and a moiety of the demesnes and borough to go with it. John de Verdun had the other moiety of the demesnes and borough and also the castle of Weobley. There was also an equal division of the lordship of Ewyas Lacy and of the knights' fees in the whole barony, which meant, in Geoffrey de Geneville's case, that he could now command the services of 30 knights' fees.[56] The overall result of the agreement and partition as far as Geoffrey was concerned was that he was firmly established in the castle at Ludlow and had also the means with which to defend his interests there. Only a few years later the growing division between King Henry and his barons resulted in civil war, a situation in which Geoffrey could well expect the provisions for his castle to be put severely to the test, and it may have been the prospect of this that prompted a formal division of the Lacy inheritance.

The disaffection against the crown by many English barons, under the leadership of Simon de Montfort, earl of Leicester, caused a power vacuum in the March of Wales that the Welsh were not slow to fill. In November 1262 local Welsh forces took Roger de Mortimer's castle at Cefnllys in Maelienydd and when Roger and his allies moved to regain it they were forced to retreat by Llywelyn ap Gruffydd, prince of North Wales. Llywelyn went on to reduce several baronial castles in the area and then raid deep into Herefordshire. In February 1263 the king assembled two armies, one at Hereford and the other at Ludlow, to counter the threat,[57] but in April attention was diverted from the border to Sussex, where Simon de Montfort had landed in England from France. In July or August 1264, after the king and Prince Edward had been defeated and captured at the battle of Lewes, Simon took Hereford and Hay castles and in conjunction with his Welsh ally devastated the lands of Roger de Mortimer around Wigmore. The lord of Richard's Castle then quickly surrendered himself and his castle to Earl Simon, who moved on to capture Ludlow Castle.[58]

Before 28 May next, however, the castle had been recaptured for the king, presumably by Geoffrey de Geneville. On that day, Prince Edward escaped from imprisonment at Hereford and, once clear of the town, rode hard for Wigmore, where he was met by Roger de Mortimer. They then set out for Ludlow Castle, which they reached in the evening and where they were met by Gilbert of Clare, earl of Gloucester, and John de Warenne, earl of Surrey.[59] At Ludlow these four men (and, presumably, Geoffrey de Geneville) planned the campaign that would lead

in August to the battle of Evesham and the defeat and death of the earl of Leicester.

John de Verdun set out on Crusade with Prince Edward in August 1270. His wife Margaret was now dead and about a year later Nicholas, John's eldest son by Margaret, who had the management of his father's lands while he was abroad, also died. Nicholas' inquisition *post mortem* was ordered on 5 August 1271. This found that he held of the king the castle of Ewyas Lacy and a moiety of the manor there together with half the barony of Weobley and half the borough of Ludlow. In his moiety of Ludlow he had rents worth £10 4s, half a pound of pepper and two pounds of cumin annually. He also had a share of the tolls of the borough and an income of 7s yearly from certain rents. Outside the borough he had 23 acres of demesne land and a moiety of four mills valued at £13 yearly. For all this he owed the crown the service of $7\frac{1}{2}$ knights' fees for half a barony and his heir was his brother Theobald, aged 23 or more. On 18 September King Henry took the fealty of Theobald for his brother's lands.[60] John de Verdun himself died in October 1274, having returned from Crusade only the previous August, and Theobald duly inherited the Verdun share of the Lacy barony.

By contrast with the attenuated fortunes of John de Verdun, Geoffrey de Geneville's longevity ensured that he enjoyed the castle of Ludlow by right of his wife for more than 60 years until his death in 1314. At Michaelmas 1267 he granted the manor of Stanton Lacy to Catherine de Lacy, his wife's aunt, on certain conditions.[61] That same year he and Maud his wife gave a moiety of four mills at Ludlow and other revenues, worth in all 20 marks yearly, to Aconbury Priory, Herefordshire. This nunnery had been founded in 1216 by Maud's grandmother, Margaret de Braose, wife of Walter II de Lacy, on land provided by King John. John's express purpose in providing the land was for the founding a house that would pray for the soul of Margaret's brother, William III de Broase, whom he had hounded to death, and for the souls of William's wife Maud and his son William, whom he had starved to death.[62] The hundred roll for November 1274 said that Geoffrey de Geneville and John de Verdun each had half the vill of Ludlow with their wives 'and they have a franchise by conquest'.[63] It was probably about this time that a Ludlow man composed the *Romance of Fulk fitzWarin* for Geoffrey and his wife and it is possible that a rebuilding of the main domestic buildings at the castle was undertaken to provide it with a suitable setting.

Geoffrey and Maud de Geneville had several sons of whom the eldest, Geoffrey, died without issue leaving his brother Peter as the next heir. By a charter dated at Acton Burnell on 11 October 1283 Peter de Geneville received from Geoffrey and Maud the castle of Ludlow, all their part of the vill of Ludlow, all their land of Ewyas Lacy and all their knights' fees in England and Wales (30 in number), to hold to him and the heirs of his body by service of $\frac{1}{4}$ knights' fee and by performance of all capital services, with reversion to Geoffrey and to the heirs of Maud. By another charter issued on the same day Peter and his wife Joan, daughter of the count of La Marche and Angoulême, received from Geoffrey and Maud the manors of Stanton Lacy, Mansell Gamage and Wolferlow, except the knights' fees pertaining to them, to hold under the grantors for their lives, to Peter and Joan for their lives, with remainder to the heirs of Peter's body and with reversion to Geoffrey and the heirs of Maud. Peter and Joan were to do service of one-tenth knight's fee to the grantors for the lands and to perform all capital services. After the death of Geoffrey and Maud, Peter and Joan were to hold the lands under the chief lord of the fee (i.e. the king).[64]

Peter de Geneville died in 1292, within his father's lifetime, leaving three daughters by Joan. His inquisition post mortem shows that he had the castle of Ludlow, 5 marks rent of assize from his share of the vill of Ludlow, two-thirds of 2 carucates of land yielding 10 marks yearly, and tolls of the vill, together with fairs and pleas and perquisites of court, yielded £4 per annum. He also had all the knights' fees his mother and father had in England and Wales and the whole of their share of the inheritance of the heirs of Walter de Lacy, plus the manors of Walterstone in Ewyas Lacy, Stanton Lacy, Mansell Gamage and Wolferlow jointly with his wife. His heirs were his daughters Joan 6, Beatrice 5 and Maud 1, and all that he had was held of Geoffrey de Geneville and Maud his wife, his parents, who held them of the king in chief by service of $2\frac{1}{2}$ knights' fees.[65]

Geoffrey de Geneville died in 1314, aged about 85.[66] Joan, his eldest granddaughter, took his share of Ludlow to her husband, Roger de Mortimer, who later became the first earl of March. Her two younger sisters became nuns at Aconbury and so do not figure in the later history of the Lacy barony. In 1316 Roger de Mortimer and Theobald de Verdun were joint lords of Ludlow.[67] Peter de Geneville's widow Joan died in 1323 when she held at Ludlow 20 acres of arable land, a meadow and 60 burgages as dower of the castle of Ludlow.[68] Joan de Mortimer, her daughter, died 19 October 1356 holding the manor of Stanton Lacy and a moiety of the town of Ludlow with the castle and the advowson of the church, which she held in fee tail of the king by service of $\frac{1}{2}$ knight's fee of the gift of Geoffrey de Geneville and Maud by a fine levied in the king's court to Peter de Geneville, father of Joan, whose heir she was, and the heirs of his body. She also had 10 knights' fees at Bitterley, Henley, Hopton Cangeford, Wilderhope, Aldon, Wigley, Cressage (in Cound), Pool and Stanton Lacy, and at Downton, Over & Nether Hayton, Wootton and Ayntree, all in Stanton Lacy, of the king in chief by service of $\frac{1}{4}$ knight's fee, and the manors of Mansell Gamage and Wolferlow.[69]

CHAPTER VI

The Mortimer Lordship

by Reverend David Harding

Although the Mortimers had been established at Wigmore on the Welsh March since the Norman Conquest, their rise in landed wealth and political influence largely took place in the course of the 13th century.[1] Judicious marriages enhanced their fortune throughout the 14th century until the family was seen by many as possible heirs to the English Crown. According to the family chronicler the first of these marriages, the one which ultimately brought Ludlow under Mortimer control, took place at Pembridge on 20 September 1301 when Roger Mortimer the 14 year old son and heir of Edmund Mortimer of Wigmore married Joan de Geneville.[2]

When his father died in 1304, Roger Mortimer inherited lands in 21 counties which included the manors of Kingsland, Eardisland and Pembridge and the castle and town of Wigmore in Herefordshire, and in Shropshire the manor of Cleobury Mortimer, Earnwood an outlying part of Cleobury manor and the hamlet of Leintwardine as well as property in the Welsh inhabited towns of Knighton, Norton by Knighton and Pilleth.[3] Some of his father's lands and rents to the value of £120 had been assigned to Geoffrey de Geneville and his wife for a term of years which had not expired, in acquittance of a debt. More of the inheritance was absorbed by the dower of his mother, Margaret Mortimer. Being under age, the wardship of the rest of Roger's lands was granted to Piers Gaveston, but they were eventually rendered to him before he came of age, even though it was noted in July 1307 that he had not done homage for them.[4]

Much of Mortimer's attention before 1321 was directed towards consolidating his lands in Ireland. Joan Mortimer as heir of her grandmother, Maud de Lacy, wife of Geoffrey de Geneville, inherited the lordship of Trim which included a moiety of the Lacy palatinate of Meath where Mortimer interests were soon bedevilled by the hostility of other members of the Lacy family. Mortimer was in Ireland in 1308 and 1309 and again in 1315-16 following the invasion of Ireland by Edward Bruce and the Scots. Defending his lordship of Trim, Mortimer was defeated at Kells by the Scots who were guided by the Lacys who, when later accused of treason, argued that they had parleyed with Bruce at Mortimer's instigation.[5] Mortimer himself escaped capture, but was obliged to return to England in January 1316 to defend his Marcher lands in the face of the Welsh rebellion of Llewellyn Bren.[6] Appointed King's Lieutenant in November 1316 he was back in Ireland the following spring. He exacted revenge on the Lacys and forced Bruce and the Scots to retreat northwards. Superceded in May 1318 he returned as Justiciar ten months later and was able to consolidate his personal position before a final recall early in 1321.[7] This close involvement in Irish affairs meant that Roger set a precedent, followed by his descendants, of spending comparatively less time in Wigmore—and now Ludlow—and the March in general than their predecessors.

However, when Mortimer did involve himself with other Marcher lords in taking a stand against the pretensions of Edward II's minister, Hugh Despenser, the outcome was disastrous. The enemies of the Despensers spent the summer of 1321 plundering their lands, and when the king eventually took action Mortimer and his uncle, Mortimer of Chirk, fell back to the March aiming to keep the river Severn between themselves and Edward. In January 1322 a royal advance guard seized the river crossing at Bridgnorth but were routed in a night attack by the Mortimers and the earl of Hereford who then burned the town. The king had no alternative but to secure the bridge at Shrewsbury which he did, effectively cutting the Mortimers off from their most powerful ally the earl of Lancaster who was in Yorkshire. For this reason and persuaded by false promises Roger and his uncle submitted to the king. They were arrested and sent to the Tower of London while orders were sent out for an immediate assessment of Mortimer property.[8]

Hugh de Burgh was sent to Ludlow with instructions to make an indenture with Ralph le Butler, keeper of the castle and town, and keeper of the manors of Stanton Lacy and Cleobury, concerning Mortimer's goods. De Burgh was to be paid wages of 4s a day from the issues of Butler's bailiwick. Joan Mortimer was arrested at Ludlow and imprisoned in London and later Southampton. When in the summer of 1323 her husband escaped from the Tower after drugging his gaolers, Joan was sent to Skipton in Yorkshire accompanied by a damsel, a squire, a laundress, a groom and a page. The Exchequer was to pay 13s 4d a week for their maintenance, and 10 marks a year for clothes.[9]

Roger Mortimer's exile was spent in Picardy and Paris at a time when King Charles IV of France, the brother of Edward's queen Isabella, was at war with the English in Gascony. Early in 1325 the queen was sent to France to explore the

Fig. 1 Fulk fitzWarin, Peter de Geneville and Roger Mortimer, from 1859 glass in the west window of St. Laurence's church, Ludlow

possibilities of peace. It was agreed that Edward should grant Gascony to his eldest son, the future Edward III, who would do homage for the lands while King Charles would return to him those parts of Gascony which the French were occupying. The prince journeyed to Paris where he did homage as had been arranged, but then both mother and son refused to obey King Edward's orders to return to England. Increasingly strident letters passed between London and Paris as it became clear that Isabella and her son were adhering to the king's exiled enemies. 'Openly and notoriously she has drawn to her and keeps in her council Mortimer and others of his conspiracy. She keeps his company in and out of house while she obliges the prince to go with Mortimer'. Soon the chroniclers were remarking on Isabella's over-familiarity with Mortimer, referring to an illicit union.[10] When it was reported in the spring of 1326 that they were in

Hainault recruiting an army it was clear that Isabella and Mortimer posed a real threat to the regime of Edward II and the Despensers. On 22 July 1326 the sheriff of York was ordered to go to Skipton and take Joan Mortimer to be confined in greater security at Pontefract. On 24 September 1326 Isabella, Prince Edward, Mortimer and their supporters landed at the mouth of the river Orwell in Suffolk.[11]

The king and Hugh Despenser vainly sought refuge in South Wales. They were taken prisoner and Despenser was brutally hanged at Hereford and the king deposed in favour of his son by a parliament of doubtful validity.[12] There is little doubt that responsibility for Edward II's subsequent murder at Berkeley Castle in September 1327 lies with Roger Mortimer. Ruling in the name of the 14 year old Edward III the regime of Isabella and Mortimer lasted almost four years, from January 1327 until October 1330. Like the rule of the Despensers before them, it was autocratic and greedy and rapidly alienated its supporters. A broadly based council which parliament demanded should advise the king never functioned properly. An abortive military campaign against the Scots in Weardale in the summer of 1327 reduced the young king to tears of frustration and was followed by a humiliating peace signed at Northampton the following year. The extravagance of the regime's financial expenditure may be gauged by the fact that although the Exchequer received its normal income and loans were made by the Italian bankers, the Bardi, reserves at the Exchequer which in November 1326 amounted to £62,000 had dwindled to £41 2s 11d by December 1330.[13]

Both Isabella and Mortimer personally enriched themselves and in particular Mortimer revived his fortunes on the March. Old lands were regained and new ones acquired when parliament revoked the judgement which had been passed on him in 1322.[14] He was granted Denbigh, all the earl of Arundel's castles and lands in Shropshire, the manor of Stretton, the castles of Builth and Montgomery with the hundred of Chirbury and, on the Herefordshire

March, the reversion of the castle of Clifford and the manor of Glasbury.[15] He was appointed Justice of Wales and the addition of other offices gave him viceregal powers. When, in 1328, he was created earl of March it was no empty title.[16] His son however had a different title for him—'King of Folly'.[17] But such mockery could not hide the fact that with Isabella, Roger Mortimer dominated not only the borders, but the whole of England.

Ludlow benefited from his success. In November 1328 he, his wife and their heirs were granted the right to hold an annual fair at their manor of Ludlow on the Vigil and Feast of Saint Katherine, 25 November, and the three following days, perhaps the oldest fair that Ludlow holds by charter.[18] Mortimer's escape from the Tower in 1323 was commemorated by the building of a chapel in the castle's outer bailey. This was dedicated to St. Peter to recall that it was on the Feast of St. Peter's Chains—1 August—that he gained his freedom. In the chapel one priest was to celebrate divine service in perpetuity, while Mortimer received licence to alienate in mortmain land and rents to the value of 10 marks for two chaplains to say Mass there for the souls of the king, Queen Philippa, wife of Edward III, Queen Isabella, the bishop of Lincoln, Mortimer himself, Joan his wife, their ancestors and children.[19] In 1354, Mortimer's widow Joan and their grandson Roger were granted another licence in mortmain to alienate to the prior of St. John's Hospital, Ludlow, four acres of land and 34s of rent in Ludlow and Hawkebatch to enable him to find a chaplain for the Chapel of St. Peter.[20] At Mortimer's request the men of Ludlow were granted murage for six years from February 1327 while the town's Palmers' Guild had its fraternity confirmed by royal letters patent.[21]

Several writers have referred to the *Wigmore Chronicle*'s account of Edward III's journey into Wales when he was lavishly entertained at Ludlow and Wigmore.[22] Unfortunately royal accounts have a gap between 3 September 1329, when the king was at Leominster, and 13 September when he was at Hereford. The

Wardrobe accounts show that the king gave Mortimer several rings on 5 September while the next day the king was presented with a gold cup valued by weight at 51s 2d and a silver gilt ewer valued at 58s 7d. But this was at Wigmore. His presence at Ludlow cannot be confirmed.[23]

But all this came to an end with Mortimer's fall and execution for treason in the autumn of 1330 when Edward III took personal control of his kingdom. Mortimer's castles and lands were seized and the sheriffs of Hereford and Shropshire were ordered to pay 2s a day to John de Piercebridge who was sent to survey his goods. The order to take his treasure and property into the king's hands did not extend to Joan Mortimer. There was to be no interference with her wardrobe, jewels or other belongings nor with those of the ladies and children with her at Ludlow. Their expenses were to be surveyed and met out of her late husband's goods.[24] The lands of her inheritance at Mansell Lacy and Wolferlow were restored and in January 1331 the sheriff of Shropshire was ordered to deliver to her Ludlow Castle, one-third of a moiety of the town of Ludlow, a carucate of land, six acres of meadow and two watermills there and the manor of Stanton Lacy which she held of her own inheritance of the king in chief by barony, the king having postponed taking her homage until Michaelmas.[25]

Joan's eldest son, Edmund, and his wife Elizabeth Badlesmere had the castle and manor of Wigmore restored to them.[26] But Edmund did not enjoy their possession long. On 16 December 1331, at Stanton Lacy he was 'seized by a sudden infirmity and went the way of all flesh'.[27] At the time of his death his son and heir, Roger, was only three years old. An inquest to take proof of his coming of age was held at Ludlow in November 1349 when it was agreed on the testimony of William Orleton, aged 52, who was in the church at Roger's baptism that

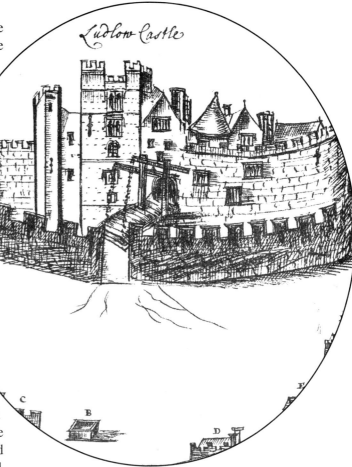

Fig. 2 Thomas Dinely's drawing of the inner bailey of the castle in 1684

the boy had been born at Ludlow on 11 November 1328.[28] Because of the heir's minority the Escheator was ordered to take Edmund's lands into the king's hands, but their keeping was committed to others. For a time Joan Mortimer held the castle of Wigmore and the manor of Cleobury rendering £90 yearly for the manor, but she eventually relinquished them to her daughter-in-law Elizabeth.[29]

Joan was more interested in making provision for her own children. In May 1336 she was given licence to grant the manors of Stanton Lacy and Ludlow, and in Herefordshire the manors of Mansell Lacy, Ewyas Lacy and Wolferlow to her son Geoffrey in tail male with reversion to her in fee. This ensured that if Geoffrey had no male heirs, the manors would revert to Joan. Three months later she was given permission to grant John de la Forde, parson of the church of Croft, the manors of Ludlow, Stanton Lacy and Walterstone, a moiety of the towns of Ludlow and Ewyas Lacy and the advowson of the church of Ludlow, and for him to regrant them to her for life with remainder to Geoffrey in tail male and to her right heirs.[30] With his mother holding lands in dower and his grandmother manipulating her own holdings, the young Roger Mortimer's inheritance was considerably divided. It took him almost the whole of his life to reassemble them.

His success was partially due to the fact that by his military prowess he gained the respect of both Edward III and his son the Black Prince. At the age of 18 he served in the prince's retinue on the Crécy campaign of 1346, being knighted on the sea shore when the expedition landed in France at La Hogue.[31] (For an illustration of English troops embarking for service in France, see colour section). He was present at the siege of Calais for which he and his grandmother Joan had been ordered to provide Welshmen from their lands in the March.[32] A founder member of the Order of the Garter (see colour section), he took part in a daring operation when the security of Calais was threatened.

Aimeric of Pavia, a Genoese member of the garrison, having agreed a price for handing the town to a French force led by Geoffrey de Charny, then revealed the plot to Edward III. The king, accompanied only by the Black Prince, Roger Mortimer and a few knights, arrived secretly in Calais where they planned to trap the French. A false wall was built inside the castle entrance for the knights to hide behind, while the timbers of the drawbridge were weakened. On the appointed night part of the French force entered the castle as arranged. Stones were then thrown down to smash the drawbridge as the king, Mortimer and their companions emerged from their hiding place to attack the trapped men. The French soldiers who had not entered the castle fled. They were pursued by the king and some of his knights who found themselves

outnumbered when the retreating French were reinforced. The king was only rescued when the Black Prince brought his men to his father's aid. The French were driven off and Charny was captured. Six months later in the summer of 1350 Mortimer took part in a battle at sea against the Spaniards when the English were victorious, and he served again in France with the king in 1355 and 1359. By that time he had rebuilt his family's landed fortunes.[33]

Following the battle of Crécy, Roger was granted seisin of all the lands which his father had held in demesne as of fee in Herefordshire, Shropshire, the Welsh March and elsewhere, his mother's dower lands excepted. Although he was not of age the king had taken his homage.[34] Described as a man of robust spirit, vigorous in war, prudent in counsel, and praiseworthy in the probity of his conduct,[35] in 1354 Roger obtained the reversal of the sentence which had been passed on his grandfather in 1330. Not only did he now inherit the title of earl of March, but he also obtained restitution of the earl's forfeited lands which included Denbigh and Montgomery and the hundred of Chirbury and the lordships of Blaenllyfni and Bwlchyddinas. The existing holders did not surrender them without protest.[36]

The death of the two Mortimer dowagers within four months of each other in 1356 meant that at long last their holdings could be incorporated in earl Roger's estate.[37] On 6 January 1357 he received delivery of all his grandmother's lands in Shropshire, Herefordshire and the adjacent Welsh March. By the king's special grace he received the issues, the estate's profits, since her death.[38] He was later granted exemption of all reliefs due at the Exchequer for the lands in England, Ireland and the March of Wales which he had inherited from his grandfather, his father, his great-grandmother and Joan, his grandmother.[39]

Roger now took steps to consolidate his holdings. On 15 May 1358, by indenture, he granted William de Ferrers the manor of Long Crendon in Buckinghamshire in exchange for a moiety of the manor and town of Ludlow. Ferrers had inherited this moiety from his mother Isabel who had died in 1349, a moiety in which there was no messuage or demesne land, only £6 rent of burgesses and it was held of the king by service of ¹/₂ a knight's fee. The unity of Ludlow was thus restored in Mortimer's favour.[40]

In a further effort to protect his lands Roger took advantage of a legal fiction known as 'the use'.[41] A landowner's right to give away his lands and their revenues by will after his death was restricted, and his lord's rights of marriage and wardship imposed further restraints. 'The use' enabled land to be granted to a person or group of persons for the use of another, often the grantor, who could also require the grantees to dispose of the lands according to his directions after his death. There were also financial advantages since customary feudal reliefs could be avoided. Utilising this method, earl Roger granted the Bishop of Winchester, Sir Ralph Spigurnel, John de Bishopston clerk, John Laundels and John Gour lands which included the manor and town of Ludlow and the manors of Cleobury, Highley and Earnwood in Shropshire. In effect they were to hold them as trustees for life rendering jointly to the earl and his heirs a rose for the first eight years and then £1,000 yearly.[42]

Six months later, aged 32, Roger died in Burgundy while accompanying the king on another expedition against France.[43] Significantly he died before his feofees had made for him and his wife Philippa Montagu the agreed estate.[44] Since the heir was his son Edmund, born at Llangoed in 1352, yet another minority ensued.[45] The bishop of Winchester and his associates surrendered to the king in right of Edmund the lands including Ludlow which the late earl had granted them. These the king re-granted to them for eight years from the date of the earl's death to hold without render to him.[46] As part of her dower Edmund's mother, Philippa, was assigned the manor of Stanton Lacy valued at £30, the manors of Cleobury and Bewdley in Shropshire and other lands in Herefordshire and Wales.[47]

Amongst Earl Roger's executors was his steward, John Gour. He assumed responsibility for Ludlow when he was appointed keeper and steward of the castles, manors, lands and fees of the late earl in Shropshire, Herefordshire, Worcestershire, Wales and the March. He was given power to hold the king's courts, receive fines, remove bailiffs and ministers and to appoint others, receivers of issues only excepted. His fee was £60 a year,[48] This lasted only three months. The Prince of Wales successfully claimed from his father custody of the Mortimer lands in his principality while the Countess Philippa secured her dower. This greatly reduced the area of Gour's responsibility and his appointment was revoked. He was then appointed keeper of the residue, which seems to have included Ludlow, at the reduced fee of £45.[49] When, in 1361, the king granted wardship of two parts of the lands to his daughter Isabella provided she paid 100 marks a year for Edmund's sustenance and the fees of the steward, Gour was ordered to be intendant to her respecting the farms, rents and issues.[50] Isabella subsequently leased part of what she had been granted to Edmund's mother who had the keeping of the boy. The lease included the manor and lordship of Wigmore and the manor of Mansell Lacy.[51]

The eight years stipulated in the king's grant of 1360 expired in February 1368. In consideration of the king's 'affection' the lands held by the trustees, including the castle and town of Ludlow, were now granted to the 16 year old Edmund.[52] A further mark of royal approval was Edmund's marriage to Philippa, the king's grand-daughter and heiress of Lionel, Duke of Clarence and his wife Elizabeth de Burgh. In turn, Elizabeth was the heiress of William de Burgh, earl of Ulster. She had died in 1363 and, as a result, Edmund in right of his wife inherited lands in East Anglia, Gloucestershire, Dorset, Wales, and Ulster and Connaught in Ireland,[53] thereby amassing one of the largest landholdings in the kingdom. Even more significantly, by right of their mother, Edmund's children were brought into the line of succession to the throne. On her father's death in 1368 Philippa and Edmund were granted seisin of his lands. However, it was not until January 1373,

Fig. 3 Usk Castle, another Mortimer holding

when the king took his homage, that Edmund gained seisin of his own father's lands.[54]

Edmund's involvement in national affairs came at a time when English success in the Hundred Years War had come to an end. In 1372 he took part in a naval expedition to relieve La Rochelle which was a disaster, and again in a failed expedition to Brittany in 1375.[55] Two years earlier he had been ready to cross to Ireland as the king's lieutenant, but he was superceded before he could take up the appointment.[56] Described as being sustained in his conduct of affairs by a superlative statesmanship,[57] it is not surprising to find Edmund in opposition to the way the country was being run for the aged Edward III by his fourth son, John of Gaunt, duke of Lancaster. When Lancaster ordered him to cross to Calais to inspect the defences there, Edmund, who was Marshal of England, was suspicious of the motives behind the order and declined to go, resigning his office.[58] At last appointed lieutenant of Ireland in 1379,[59] during the next two years he brought the island to unity, peace and submission to England.[60] But before he could consolidate those achievements he caught a chill when crossing a river and died, apparently of pneumonia, at Cork on 27 December 1381. He was not yet 30 years old.[61]

Like his father Edmund had looked to protect his estates. In 1374 he granted the castle, manor and town of Ludlow, the castle, land and lordship of Radnor and other holdings to Sir William Latimer of Danby, Sir Richard le Scrope, Nicholas de Carrew, Sir Peter de la Mare, John Bishopston and Walter de Colmpton clerks and Hugh de Boraston for life with remainder to the bishops of London, Winchester and Hereford, Sir Roger Beauchamp and John de Bridewode clerk, for life, with remainder over to himself and his heirs.[62] Five years later the donees alleged that Edmund had not carried out the terms of the gift and still held the lands. He agreed this was so and that he would execute the grant.[63] They then made a regrant to him for 20 years at what must have been a nominal rent of £100 a year. At Edmund's death the lands passed to his executors.[64]

Two of the trustees, de La Mare and Walter de Colmpton, were also amongst the earl's executors who included John Piers, a clerk holding the living of Ludlow. In his will Edmund left 40 marks to the Master and Community of the Hospital of St. John, Ludlow and to the Austin Friars at Ludlow and at Woodhouse near Cleobury Mortimer. Although bequests were made to many religious houses including Wigmore Abbey, where Edmund was buried beside his wife who had predeceased him, the chapels in Ludlow Castle did not benefit.[65]

Edmund's eldest son Roger had been born at Usk on 11 April 1374.[66] Another minority gave King Richard II the chance to exploit the widespread Mortimer estates. Escheators were ordered to take into the king's hands and make inquisitions touching the lands of Philippa late countess of March, and her son Earl Edmund.[67] An inquest held at Shrewsbury in March 1382 reported the earl's holding in Shropshire was small because with the king's licence he had demised the castle, town and manor of Ludlow and other lands.[68] As the earl had intended, they were protected when

Fig. 4 Wigmore Castle, the centre of Mortimer power until the end of the 14th century

the king ordered that all moneys from the Mortimer estates in England and Wales should, from Michaelmas 1382, be applied to the expenses of the royal household.[69] While a number of Mortimer servants were retained by the king he also appointed a number of royal squires, yeomen, and serjeants to be constables of castles, stewards, bailiffs and keepers of parks and chases. Philip Holygot, a Mortimer servant, appointed steward of the manors of Stanton Lacy, Cleobury, Earnwood and Highley was soon replaced at Stanton Lacy by David Hanmer.[70]

To protect the estates from being exploited by the king, the royal Council advised that until Roger Mortimer came of age the inheritance should be committed to the earls of Arundel, Warwick and Northumberland and Lord Neville of Raby, receiving all rents, services, profits and court perquisites from all the honours. They were to pay £4,000 a year to the Exchequer and ensure that buildings were maintained and annuities and the wages of officers paid.[71] The widespread Mortimer estates were run by a central council to which the local receivers, auditors and stewards

were answerable. This council was headed by the chief steward who during Earl Roger's minority was Sir Thomas Mortimer, an illegitimate brother of his father, the late earl Edmund.[72] The steward's most important colleague was the chief financial officer, the Receiver General. This post was held by the clerk, Walter Brugge, who served the Mortimers in various capacities from the 1370s until his death in 1396.[73] In the autumn of 1387, accompanied by the earl's auditor, Brugge made a tour through the March which lasted two months during which time officials and their accounts were examined. Much of the month of October was spent at Wigmore. The expenses for the day spent at Ludlow totalled 4s 10¼d.[74] Two years later in 1389 Brugge set out from Ludlow in April on a similar journey through Wales and the March.[75]

Responsibility for the day to day running of the estates, for the productivity of the land and for the maintenance of castles and manors rested with the local ministers and servants who ensured that the profits of the estates in their charge were available to Brugge as needed. In December 1387 carts under armed guard carried £1,400 from Wigmore to London for the earl's use,[76] while in 1394 the receivers of the earl's lands handed over their profits at Wigmore during one week in May to Roger Patrick, the local receiver, who was responsible for passing them on to Walter Brugge.[77] Some of these profits would have come from the sale of wool. Sheep were reared both at Ludlow and Stanton Lacy where some 260 fleeces were sold in 1388-89.[78] In addition to the income from land there were the fines levied in the lord's court. Justice was often swift. In 1357, for example, William Dodemour and John de Morton who had fought and drawn each other's blood, appeared before the earl of March's steward, Hugh Boraston, in his court at Ludlow and were fined 'then and there'.[79] Supplies could often be transferred from one manor for use on another. In his account for 1328-29 the receiver of Cleobury Mortimer reports the transport of items to Ludlow which included wine, salt from Bewdley, iron from Doddington and hemp ropes for the castle well.[80] In 1391-92 the bailiff of Kingsland paid a servant there for his great labour in cutting down and transporting timber to Ludlow for the repair of the castle.[81]

When the 19 year old Roger Mortimer was granted possession of his lands in England, Wales, the Welsh March and Calais in February 1393,[82] he immediately undertook a tour to inspect his estates (see colour section for an illustration of how such an inspection may have been undertaken). During the months of March and April he journeyed through Wales and the March at the cost of £162, which included payments for cloth of gold, silks and woollen cloth for his own apparel costing £13 (see colour section for a costume which this sum may have acquired). This should be compared with the wages of all the grooms and squires who accompanied Roger on his 40 day journey which totalled £23.[83]

Most of Roger Mortimer's short career was spent in Ireland where he was appointed the king's lieutenant in Ulster, Connaught and Meath.[84] This removed him from the English political scene at a time when Richard II's abso-lutist tendencies were arousing opposition. Some regarded Mortimer as the childless king's rightful heir[85] and a suspicious Richard summoned Roger from Ireland to be present at the parliament which met at Shrewsbury in January 1398.[86] His appearance can hardly have reassured the king since 20,000 people wearing hoods in Roger's livery colours of red and white went out to meet him in the hope that they might be freed from Richard's tyranny. In an atmosphere of tension the young earl acted cautiously and returned safely to Ireland.[87] His appointment was initially renewed for two years but the king then changed his mind and three months later Roger was dismissed.[88]

It came too late. At Kells, on 20 July 1398, riding ahead of his army dressed as an Irishman, Roger rashly attacked the hostile O'Briens and was cut down unrecognised.[89] The king seized his opportunity, for once again the Mortimer heir was a minor. Roger's son, Edmund, was not seven years old. Wardship of Roger's English lands was granted to the queen and then transferred to the king's cousin, the duke of Aumerle.[90] As was customary, one-third of the estate was assigned in dower to Roger's widow, Eleanor, the daughter of the king's half-brother Thomas Holland. This included Cleobury valued at £20 and Stanton Lacy worth 100s, above the £20 due from it to Roger Patrick by her late husband's grant.[91] Within a year she had married Sir Edward Charlton who became lord of Powys on his brother's death in 1401.[92] When Eleanor died in 1405 the manor at Winforton was valued at 20 marks and Mansell Lacy at 30 marks; Eardisland, however, was worth £23. All her dower lands were committed to Edward Charlton's keeping during the minority of her son at a render of 600 marks a year.[93] £100 of the issues of her estates were later granted to her daughters Anne and Eleanor who are described as being destitute.[94]

With Richard II's deposition the status of Ludlow changed. Some 19th century historians have argued that when the Mortimers acquired Ludlow it soon eclipsed Wigmore in importance[95] and recent writers have tended to agree.[96] In terms of money values this could be true although direct comparisons are difficult since records are not complete. It is difficult to know how to assess information that in 1324 Wigmore rents amounted to £8 4s, while half of Ludlow was farmed for £20; or that Wigmore was valued at £120 in 1398 though rents produced only £9 13s in 1425.[97] It is likely that Wigmore remained the financial and administrative centre of the estates until the Welsh rebellions in the early part of the 15th century made border lands vulnerable and gave Ludlow a greater strategic importance. Ludlow was certainly important enough in 1400 for the bailiffs to be ordered to display part of the quartered body of the rebel Gronw ap Tudor on the town gate facing Wales as a salutary warning to others.[98]

As early as November 1399 Henry IV had committed two thirds of the Mortimer lands to the earl of Northumberland, his son Henry Percy (Hotspur) who had married Elizabeth Mortimer the sister of the late earl, Sir Thomas Erpingham, Sir Thomas Grey and Sir Hugh Waterton.[99] Custody was removed when the Welsh rebellion under Owain Glyndŵr broke out although Waterton remained the king's receiver.[100]

Glyndŵr's rebellion brought into prominence the younger brother of Earl Roger, another Edmund Mortimer. This Edmund had been born at Ludlow on 9 November 1376, strange portents accompanying his birth—his father's stables ran with blood so deep that it reached the horses' shins; the scabbards of swords and daggers filled with blood and axes turned red; the boy in his cradle would only stop crying when shown a sword and he could only be quietened at his foster-mother's breast when some war-like weapon was given to him. Thus a bloody future was foretold.[101] When Glyndŵr threatened the March, Edmund, who was at Ludlow, opposed him. In the battle of Pilleth near Knighton in June 1402 Edmund was defeated and captured.[102]

With Ludlow under threat John Lovel was appointed to hold the castle, town and lordship against the rebels.[103] The sheriff of Shropshire was ordered to send victuals to Ludlow and also to Hereford and Shrewsbury for the king's forces moving into Wales. The bailiffs of Ludlow were instructed to see that the town's victuallers, inn-keepers, vintners and bakers also produced supplies.[104] But Lovel was superseded within a month by the more authoritative figure of the king's half-brother Sir Thomas Beaufort,[105] who in December 1402 was paid £88 18s 9d for wages for himself and the garrison of Ludlow Castle.[106] When the king refused to ransom Edmund Mortimer who was not powerful enough to ransom himself, Mortimer married Glyndŵr's daughter as a way of easing his captivity. He was to die during the siege of Harlech Castle in 1409 by forces led by the future Henry V.[107]

The lack of ransom was one factor which brought the Percies to rebellion and created further chaos on the March. However, the immediate crisis at Ludlow was ended by Henry Percy's death in the battle of Shrewsbury, Sir Hugh Cheyne then being given custody of the town and castle with an annual fee of 40 marks, paid from the issues of Ludlow.[108] Cheyne had previously been retained to serve the earl of March as far back as 1376, when his fee had also been 40 marks. Earl Roger had increased this by another 20 marks in 1397, and it is not clear if Cheyne's latest fee for the custody of the castle was over and above this.[109] By August 1404 Cheyne was dead and the king's esquire Roger Acton was installed in his place at the larger fee of 110 marks.[110] Because of their good service in resisting the Welsh rebels the burgesses of Ludlow had been granted quittance of tolls, lastage—a tax on those trading at fairs, pontage—a levy for bridge repairs, danegeld—a land tax, and all other customs so long as the town remained in the king's hands.[111] They served with parochial interest, being un-cooperative in fighting Glyndŵr elsewhere. In May 1405 the town bailiffs were ordered to arrest any who had been summoned to serve in South Wales and who were now either refusing to go or had deserted despite having been paid.[112]

The Constable, Roger Acton, also found himself in trouble. Following orders issued in May 1407 for the bailiffs to arrest anyone found preaching doctrines contrary to the Catholic faith, Acton had been outlawed and gone abroad, refusing to perform his duties until he had received the king's pardon. John Brigge was appointed captain of Ludlow in his place.[113] It seems likely that religious differences also lay behind the appointment of a commission in September 1408 to enquire into reports that John Bradeston, late lieutenant of Ludlow town, who had been arrested for trespass and misprision, had resisted arrest by causing men of the town to be arrayed for war and had then assaulted the sheriff. Acton's Lollard sympathies ultimately brought him to the gallows in 1414.[114]

Ludlow remained firmly in the king's hands throughout the reign of Henry IV. He also kept firm control of the young earl of March whom some regarded as having a better claim to the Crown than he did. Following Richard II's deposition, Edmund, who had been born on 6 November 1391,[115] was held with his brother Roger at Windsor.[116] For a time they were brought up with two of the king's own children, John and Philippa, at Berkhampsted.[117] Abducted from Windsor in 1405, they were retaken near Cheltenham almost certainly on the way to being re-united with their uncle, Glyndŵr's son-in-law.[118] The boys were held in tighter custody, the prince of Wales taking over responsibility for them in the last years of the reign.[119] When the prince ascended the throne as Henry V in 1413, by which time the younger boy had died, Edmund was granted his inheritance.[120] The idea that he was released from custody because he was too mediocre in his abilities to threaten the Lancastrian dynasty[121] has to be set against the judgement of the family historian that he was 'prudent in worldly affairs, a youth of sober character, studied in his behaviour, cautious in speech, wise and wary and one who followed his interests in redeeming the time when days were evil'.[122]

Two concerns affected Edmund's career. The first related to his finances. In November 1413 he entered into a recognisance with the king for 10,000 marks to be of good behaviour to the king and people.[123] Two years later, without royal permission, Edmund married Anne Stafford, a grand-daughter of Edward III's youngest son, Thomas of Woodstock. A £2,000 fine was levied at the Exchequer which Edmund was to pay to the keeper of the Great Wardrobe.[124] But it looks as if the king also called in the recognisance. To pay his debts Edmund quit-claimed his rights in his Welsh estates, the lordship of Ludlow and other lands to a group which included the earls of Arundel and Warwick, Edward Charlton, lord of Powys and two of his own dependents, Walter Lucy of Richard's Castle and Richard Wigmore. The amount involved is said to have been £100,000 an impossibly large sum which has not gone unquestioned.[125] What is certain is that Edmund was in debt to the Crown at the time of his death.

The other concern was Edmund's association with the Southampton Plot of 1415, when his brother-in-law Richard, earl of Cambridge, Sir Thomas Grey and Henry, lord Scrope of Masham, taking advantage of Edmund's rights to the Crown, challenged Henry V.[126] The plot failed, the conspirators were executed and Edmund survived to become the king's lieutenant in Normandy, a member of the royal council during the minority of Henry VI[127] and Lord Lieutenant of Ireland.[128] But, once again, and this time fatally and finally, Ireland ended Mortimer ambitions. On 18 January 1425 Edmund died of the plague at Trim.[129] He was 33 years old and since he was childless the 200 year Mortimer domination of the March came to an end.

The heir to the Mortimer inheritance was the orphan son of Edmund's sister Anne and Richard, earl of Cambridge. Richard, duke of York was 13 years old, and faced with another minority the Crown appointed auditors to examine the accounts of Edmund's ministers with special reference to his castles in Wales and on the March which ought to be taken into the king's hands by reason of non-payment of a fine for his marriage or for any other reason.[130] On 28 November 1427 Sir Richard Neville, James Strangeways, Thomas Banaster and John Symonde were appointed to keep the castle and town of Ludlow, the manors of Stanton Lacy and Cleeton in Shropshire and holdings elsewhere.[131] Subsequently, and for a brief period, with the exception of the widow's dower and some lands in eastern England and west Wales, the estates to the value of about £2,100 were in the hands of Henry VI's uncle, the duke of Gloucester. In February 1429 his holding was passed to the keeping of Richard, duke of York, the bishop of Norwich and the earl of Northumberland.[132]

Richard of York received full possession of his estates in May 1432. When the dowager countess of March died in September of that year her dower lands reverted to him. These transfers were not without their problems, but with the extinction of the Mortimers, Ludlow and all their inheritance passed into the hands of the future Yorkist royal dynasty.[133]

CHAPTER VII

Ludlow During the Wars of the Roses

by Ralph A. Griffiths

The 15th century was one of the most prosperous in Ludlow's history. Its baronial castle was often the residence of a high-ranking lord and his household, the commercial life of the town flourished during the Lancastrian and Yorkist periods, and contemporary investment in its buildings left an indelible mark on Ludlow's townscape. In the first three decades of the century, the Mortimer lords of Ludlow rarely visited the town, but thereafter their descendant Richard Plantagenet, duke of York, his son King Edward IV, and his grand-daughter's husband, King Henry VII, lavished personal attention on Ludlow and gave it a unique political profile among England's provincial centres.

A stone's throw from the castle stood St. Laurence's parish church, whose relationship with the castle was a close one. Its fortunes during the 15th century reflect Ludlow's prosperity. One year after Richard (1411-60), duke of York, secured possession in 1432 of most, if not all, of the inheritance of his maternal uncle, the last Mortimer earl of March, an extensive rebuilding of the church began and lasted, with some interruption, until about 1471, by which time it had become one of the largest parish churches in England and Wales.[1] This rebuilding included the great bell tower, the chapel of St. John the Evangelist, and as many as 20 chapels donated by townsmen and others; the nave was reconstructed and extended in the fashionable

Perpendicular style. In the chancel, new stalls with finely carved misericords reflected the loyalties of the townsfolk and the daily round of their lives: the misericords carry commemorative badges of the Lancastrian monarchy and the house of York, as well as illustrations of social and commercial activities. Most of these misericords were carved in Richard, duke of York's time, although a minority of them are thought to be earlier in date. Contemporary stained glass in a fine chancel window illustrates the life, miracles and martyrdom of St. Laurence, and is a tribute to the wealth and civic pride of Ludlow's inhabitants.[2]

The town's population seems to have recovered well from the plague attacks of the 14th century. In 1377, a year for which poll tax records enable a calculation to be made, the population stood at about 1,725; by 1545, when the number of communicants over the age of 12 was assessed, another calculation suggests that the town's population had risen to about 2,500. It may well be that during the first half of the 15th century, the pre-plague complement of about 2,000 souls had already been reached.[3] This would have made Ludlow, if not one of the larger provincial towns of England, certainly the second town in Shropshire, after Shrewsbury.

Such growth may be attributed in part to relatively peaceful conditions following the Welsh rebellion of Owain Glyndŵr (1400-10),

Fig. 1 St. Laurence's Church, Ludlow c.1930

and especially to Ludlow's role in the wool and cloth trades of the West Midlands and Welsh Marches. Many of the town's bailiffs were drawn from the ranks of the wealthier clothiers and merchants, leading townsfolk who produced long-cloths and broad-cloths of exceptionally high quality for sale not only in Ludlow itself but as far afield as London, Southampton and Bristol, and even to merchants from Genoa, Venice and Portugal.[4] Weavers and dyers, clothiers and drapers, hosiers and the rest provided the town with its ruling class. These officials were drawn from the families and trades that were largely responsible for much of the building in 15th-century Ludlow, and whose handiwork can still be detected in Ludlow's streets. Broad Street, according to Sir Nikolaus Pevsner 'one of the most memorable streets in England', has been surveyed in detail, and a number of its buildings with timber-framed lower storeys can be dated to the first half of the century—as well as others in Mill Street and (significantly) Drapers Row.[5] The Talbot earls of Shrewsbury had their own Talbot Inn in the town, whilst crafts and trades occupied, to some extent, their own quarters, the meat traders in Butchers' Row, the drapers in Drapers' Row.[6]

The town's government, placed on a chartered footing most recently by King Henry IV during the Welsh rebellion, was in the hands of 12 aldermen and 25 councillors, with one—and, after 1461, two—bailiffs elected annually from among the burgesses who also, again after 1461, elected two MPs to represent the town's interests in Parliament.[7] The urban establishment, along with Ludlow's powerful Palmers' (or Pilgrims') Guild, dominated the social, religious, political, and economic life of Ludlow, providing an élite among the townsfolk who moved readily from one post of responsibility to another, in town, guild and Parliament. The wardenship of the guild was perhaps the post of highest standing in 15th-century Ludlow.[8] The burgesses elected the 12 and the 25 and the MPs according to an oligarchic order that allowed fair opportunity for personal advancement within the town. The connection between the Palmers' Guild and the urban administration was close, and civic improvement—including the rebuilding of the parish church—depended heavily on support from the guildsmen, who were patronised in turn by the lords of Ludlow. The guild's reputation enabled it to attract recruits and subscriptions well beyond the town itself in southern and western counties of England as well as in central Wales, and prominent figures were eager to join it.[9] The duke of York's uncle, Edmund Mortimer, the last earl of March, attended the guild's feast in 1424, along with John, Lord Talbot, and the Shropshire landowner, William Burley. The duke of York himself and his wife, Cicely Neville, became guild members in 1437-8.[10] St. Laurence's church was served by a group of priests provided by the guild, along with four 'singing men', two deacons, six choristers and a porter for the church.[11]

Plantagenet lordship contributed to the town's good fortune, especially after Richard, duke of York's son became King Edward IV in March 1461. Such connections were not without their dangers, and in the 1450s Ludlow, like its lord, fell victim to the violence associated with the Wars of the Roses and the struggle between Lancaster and York for possession of the crown.

The last earl of March, Edmund Mortimer, had died of plague at Trim Castle in January 1425, still only 33 years old. His heir was his sister's son, Richard Plantagenet, duke of York, a young man of 13. It was several years before Richard was old enough to take possession of his estates, in 1432. In the meantime, the castle and town of Ludlow lay in the crown's hands. In November 1428 three commissioners—Sir Richard Neville, whose sister Cecily was betrothed to Richard of York; James Strangeways, a loyal Lancastrian knight; Thomas Bannaster, a Shropshire gentleman—and several others, received custody of Ludlow's castle and town while Richard was a minor; they were answerable to the treasurer of England for Ludlow's income so as to defray the Mortimer debt to the crown.[12]

Richard entered his inheritance as duke of York, earl of Cambridge and earl of March in 1432, though not all of his property was restored to him at this juncture. In February 1436 the duke, along with Sir Walter Lucy and Richard Wigmore, were licensed to enfeoff several loyal Lancastrian figures, headed by William Alnwick, bishop of Norwich, Richard Beauchamp, earl of Warwick, Sir Walter Hungerford, and Sir John Beaumont, with Ludlow and other extensive properties in order to reach a settlement with the crown for the outstanding debts.[13]

Although Duke Richard spent much of the following decade as the leading Lancastrian commander in France, it is easy to demonstrate the interest which he and his wife came to show in Ludlow. Ludlow Castle continued to house the administrative headquarters of his Mortimer estates in the borderland and the adjacent Welsh March; in 1436-7 Richard and Cecily joined the Palmers' Guild; and Richard's links with the town were

expressed in about 1447, not long after his return from France, in the carving of his personal emblems of the fetterlock and the falcon on the new misericords in St. Laurence's church—York may even have contributed to their cost.[14] Then in 1449 Richard, who may have taken to residing frequently in Ludlow in the late 1440s, granted a new charter to the town.

The reason why this charter was granted a full decade and a half after the duke came of age is not immediately apparent. However, in July 1449 Richard went to Ireland, where he had been appointed the king's lieutenant two years before. The townsmen of Ludlow may have decided to seek a new charter in order to protect their liberties during his absence; the charter itself, which may have been drafted by clerks at Ludlow for the duke's approval, drew attention to uncertainties that faced a prospering urban community whose lord was about to depart—the presence of outsiders in the town and of gentry retinues in the countryside around. As for the duke, he was amenable to the suggestion of a new charter perhaps because of his regard for the town and its administrative importance to him during his absence, and even, as events were later to prove, as a potential source of assistance when he returned.[15]

This charter of 1449 did not alter the detailed structure of Ludlow's government or its relation-

Fig. 2 Richard of York's personal emblem of the falcon and fetterlock on a misericord in St. Laurence's Church

ship with the duke. Rather did it confirm existing arrangements, including the roles of the 12 aldermen and the 25 councillors elected by the burgesses. It reiterated the townsmen's liberties, and the role of the bailiff, at the same time acknowledging oversight by the duke's officers in the castle and the king's officials in the shire: 'the correction and governance that longeth and concerneth to oure Stuard there in holding our courtes [declared the duke] and except also that that appertaineth to the constables for the king'.

Such a close connection between a great English magnate and a prosperous provincial town was not unusual in late-medieval England and Wales, and York valued his links with Shrewsbury, Denbigh and Usk in a similar fashion. But the frequency with which Ludlow Castle was his and his family's home and sanctuary in the 1450s, and its importance to him as the administrative heart of his Welsh and border estates, cemented the relationship and doubtless sustained the wealth of Ludlow as a market and business centre for a ducal household and a castle garrison.

When Duke Richard returned from Ireland early in September 1450, his bond with Ludlow became yet tighter: he resided there; he sought refuge in the castle when his political fortunes fluctuated, and it was from Ludlow that several of his challenges to the Lancastrian king, Henry VI, were issued in the years that followed. To begin with, in an exchange of letters with Henry VI in September-October 1450, as Richard made his way from the Welsh March to Westminster, he appealed to the king directly against those of the royal advisers who were defaming Richard and were regarded as responsible for the misgovernment of the realm that had attracted a welter of popular and parliamentary protest in recent months.[16] York may not have been without his sympathisers, and two members of the king's household who had been associated with recent disasters in France as well as misgovernment at home were sufficiently alarmed to wait on the duke: John, Lord Dudley and Reginald Boulers, abbot of Gloucester (and about to be elected

bishop of Hereford), rode to Ludlow out of concern for their safety, according to one chronicler; they were lodged in the castle while the tide of protest continued to flow.[17]

York's efforts were, however, far from successful, and in the ensuing months he withdrew to Ludlow, emerging occasionally to demonstrate his concern for public order and his own position—as he did in September 1451 when, supported by Sir William Herbert, one of his retainers, and Robert Hungerford, Lord Moleyns, he travelled from Ludlow to Somerset to settle a dispute between the earl of Devon, one of the duke's allies, and Sir William Bonville.[18] He was certainly in Ludlow for the Christmas festivities three months later. His time appears to have been partly spent in gathering support for a more concerted confrontation with his opponents. The result was a series of risings in the early months of 1452, both at Ludlow and further afield. This violence was sparked off by York's public appeal for assistance which he launched from Ludlow Castle on two occasions in the first weeks of 1452. On 9 January, he released a statement which rehearsed his complaints, though he now focussed them more specifically on the king's kinsman, Edmund Beaufort, duke of Somerset, whom York may have come to regard as his rival for recognition as the childless king's heir. York's statement declared unequivocally his allegiance to Henry VI.[19] It was a great regret to him that the king was 'my heavy lord, greatly displeased with me and hath in me a distrust by sinister information of mine enemies, adversaries, and evil-willers'. Anxious to persuade Henry otherwise and to give the lie to counteraccusations against him, York invited to Ludlow the highly respected John Talbot, earl of Shrewsbury, who had a house in the town, and Bishop Boulers of Hereford, to whom he had given sanctuary the previous year; they heard York's profession of loyalty and, with authority, could report the duke's willingness to swear on the sacraments that he was indeed the king's true and faithful subject.

Doubtless warned by Shrewsbury and Bishop Boulers, Henry VI moved to pre-empt more drastic action on York's part. On 27 January it was resolved to send Thomas Kent, a clerk of the king's Council and a senior official in the king's privy seal office, to Ludlow. He returned a fortnight later with the news that York was in no mood to be conciliatory or to be deflected from his purpose of removing the duke of Somerset from the king's side and restoring York himself to favour.[20]

On 3 February, a couple of days after Kent departed on his mission, York had been emboldened to issue a second public statement—this time it was addressed specifically to the townspeople of Shrewsbury. He repeated elements of his earlier appeal, but on this occasion set great store by Englishmen's pride and patriotism which Somerset had betrayed by his disastrous military record in attempting to defend the English position in Normandy and in protecting Calais. The prospect of commercial loss and the spectre of an enemy invasion would have struck chords in an urban community in Yorkist country.[21] Duke Richard also skilfully introduced his own grievances, implying that his proposals of 1450 would have remedied the realm's condition and that it was Somerset who had engineered their rejection. This enabled him to conclude with a personal indictment of Somerset for plotting 'my undoing and to corrupt my blood, and to disinherit me and my heirs'. This publicly-declared intention of proceeding against the wicked duke, with the help of York's kinsmen, friends and supporters, seemed eminently reasonable; what he required of Shrewsbury was a force that would be placed under his command—as presumably Ludlow was already providing.

At about this time some of York's retainers were indeed assembling at Ludlow, led by Sir Edmund Mulso, a notable soldier, Roger Eyton, a Shropshire man, and John Milewater, who was receiver-general of York's Marcher estates. They were later apprehended at Bridgnorth and were then transferred to Westminster, where, despite their conviction as rioters, Henry VI felt it prudent to order their release.[22] These events were preparatory to the raising of a major force

with which York marched across country to Kent later in February 1452 and eventually confronted the king and the duke of Somerset at Dartford, only to find himself disarmed and forced to come to terms. He spent the next two weeks confined to his own residence at Baynard's Castle, in London, and was required to swear an oath in St. Paul's Cathedral on 10 March that he would never rebel against King Henry again. Three days later, York and Somerset undertook to observe an arbitration award made between them. York may have been able to extricate himself from this situation when a rumour spread that his ten-year-old son, Edward, was bringing another force from the Ludlow area to rescue his father. York was then allowed to retire to the borderland, first to Wigmore Castle and then to Ludlow to join his wife.[23]

Some weeks later, in April 1452, further disturbances occurred, this time involving several Ludlow tradesmen—John Mason, John Mattys and John Preene—under the leadership of John Sharpe, an esquire from London. They were accused of murdering a valet of the king's Chamber, Richard Fazakerley, who had been sent to Ludlow with instructions for York to take action against Sharpe; instead, Fazakerley was said to have seduced Sharpe's wife. One of the town's bakers then helped to raise the angry townsfolk; he was later arrested and taken to Kenilworth Castle, but Sharpe himself was acquitted.[24] Later still, on 6 August, more trouble took place at Ludlow. John ap Richard, the rector of St. Laurence's Church, together with one of York's leading retainers, Sir Walter Devereux of Weobley in Herefordshire, with whom the duke shared the patronage of the rectory, led a band of 40 men to expel Humphrey Blount from his manor of Ashton in Shropshire for reasons that may reflect local gentry rivalries. Within a week the king himself was in Ludlow, on 12 and 13 August, as part of a lengthy tour of pacification of the western shires. Henry VI stayed at the Carmelite Friary, not in York's castle. The duke was not there to greet him. Somerset, who accompanied the king, was reported to have treated

York's tenants harshly, including (one might suppose) the inhabitants of Ludlow.[25]

Richard, duke of York had forged an intimate relationship with Ludlow: the town and its castle had been a refuge for him in difficult times, a centre for the recruitment of supporters, and a place in which to formulate and publicise political objectives of the most ambitious sort. If Charles de Gaulle had his Colombey-les-deux-églises in the 1950s, Richard of York had his Ludlow in the 1450s.

A new and unexpected opportunity presented itself for the duke of York to press his personal and political demands when Henry VI's health collapsed in August 1453; the king remained incapacitated for almost 18 months. In March 1454 York was eventually appointed protector of the king and defender of the realm, but not without serious misgivings in some quarters and in the face of hostility from the queen, Margaret of Anjou, and the duke of Somerset. York's commission as protector and defender was a difficult one. It may have kept him away from Ludlow more than in the past, but his growing family maintained its links with the town. York's two eldest sons, Edward (born in April 1442) and Edmund (born in May 1443) at least were brought up there. Copies survive of two of their letters, written apparently in 1454 from Ludlow Castle to their father.[26] In one, dated on a Saturday in Easter week (which would be 27 April in 1454), the boys referred to the protector's daunting responsibilities. They wished him well in his 'prevaile ayenst thentent and malice of your evilwillers' and were grateful for the news of him which had been brought by his dependable retainers, Sir Walter Devereux, John Milewater and John at Nokes, a yeoman of the duke's chamber. They also thanked him for his fatherly gift of 'our grene gownes' and requested (as young boys might) 'summe fyne bonetts' to go with them. Life was not without its trials for the youngsters, however, and they took the opportunity to instruct William Smyth, the duke's servant and messenger, to report the 'odieux reule and demenyng' of Richard Croft

and his brother, of Croft in Herefordshire, who may have shared their upbringing at Ludlow. Edward signed himself as earl of March and Edmund as earl of Rutland, courtesy titles which their father had evidently given them.

The second letter written jointly by Edward and Edmund is more securely dated, on 3 June 1454. In this, they sought to reassure their father that they were properly attentive to their studies in Ludlow Castle:

> And where ye commaunde us by your said lettres to attende specially to our lernyng in our yong age that shulde cause us to growe to honour and worschip in our olde age, plaese hit your Hieghnesse to witte that we have attended our lernyng sith we come heder. And schall hereaftur, by the whiche we trust to God your graciouse Lordeschip and good fadurhode schall be plaesid.

The king's recovery at the end of 1454 did not signal a reconciliation between the duke of York and the royalists, though disturbances at Ludlow seem to have abated. One chronicler, it is true, noted that York's eldest son, Edward of March, led a force, presumably from Ludlow, to join his father and the Neville earls of Salisbury and Warwick as they prepared to confront the king under arms at St. Albans in May 1455; but this is not confirmed by any other source.[27] Later in the 1450s, some of York's younger kinsmen may have gravitated to Ludlow or were brought up there in the ducal household. In August 1458, Henry Bourgchier, the son of his brother-in-law, Viscount Bourgchier, died suddenly at Ludlow.[28] Nor was the bond with the town weakened in these years: in 1458 the chapel of St. Mary Magdalen in the castle was made over to the Hospital of St. John of Jerusalem, situated near the Ludford Bridge, on condition that the hospital arranged regular masses to be said for the duke and his family.[29]

It was in 1459 that the relationship between Duke Richard and his family, on the one hand, and their town of Ludlow, on the other, was put to its greatest test by the complete breakdown of the relationship between the duke and Henry VI's court. More so than the skirmish between a Lancastrian force, under James, Lord Audley, and the Neville retinues at Blore Heath in Staffordshire on 23 September 1459, the confrontation at Ludford Bridge was a decisive moment in the Wars of the Roses, even though little actual fighting occurred.[30] The duke of York and his allies, the earls of Salisbury and Warwick, planned a union of their forces in the last week of September. Warwick arrived from Calais and managed to avoid being intercepted as he and his men made their way across England, intent on joining Salisbury and his younger sons on their way south from Yorkshire. Their objective was Ludlow, where they would rendezvous with York. In the cathedral at Worcester, they concluded a solemn, yet defiant, indenture that declared 'oure sayde trouthe and dewtee' to the king and at the same time expressed their determination to destroy their enemies. Despite the indecisive encounter at Blore Heath and the failure to apprehend Warwick, the king and the queen, supported by the bulk of the English nobility, pursued the Yorkist lords as they retreated from Worcester in the face of the approaching king. They made their way southwards towards Warwick's town of Tewkesbury and then across the River Severn and north-westwards towards York's refuge of Ludlow. By 9 October the king's army in pursuit had reached Leominster. On that day, in a letter signed by each of them, the three leading Yorkist lords sought a final interview with King Henry, provided he would guarantee their safety, in order to express their 'exclamacione and compleynt' against the enemies who were plotting their disinheritance and downfall.[31] The meeting never took place. The king offered a general pardon and, by means of heralds, gave those who were opposing him six days in which to avail themselves of it. By the time the king approached Ludford, the small village just to the south of Ludlow across the stone bridge over the River Teme, loyal contingents were arriving from Exeter (and

Fig. 3 Richard, Duke of York after the south window of Penrith church, Cumbria

presumably elsewhere) to swell the royal army.[32]

With York and his eldest sons, Edward and Edmund, and the earls of Salisbury and Warwick, were only two other noblemen, John, Lord Clinton and Richard Grey, Lord Powis. York's two nephews, John and Edward, the sons of his sister and Viscount Bourgchier, were also at Ludlow, where they may have been brought up. A number of the duke's retainers and councillors were naturally with him: Sir John Wenlock, who had once been a servant of the queen; Robert Bold, Roger Eyton and Sir Walter Devereux, from the borderland, and his councillors John Clay and Thomas Colt. With Warwick was Walter Blount, from Elvaston in Derbyshire, who had served York before joining Warwick at Calais; he and Andrew Trollope commanded the force of Calais men present in the Yorkist camp.[33]

Fig. 4 Buck's engraving of Ludlow Castle

The lines of battle faced each other south of Ludford Bridge on 12 October. The Yorkists' defensive position was fortified with carts, guns and other obstacles, and they began to fire on the king's position a little further to the south. To attack a royal army in the presence of the king himself, with his banner unfurled, was a most serious step. The Calais men, under Andrew Trollope, were especially reluctant to commit themselves to such an action. York sought to counter the king's strategy by spreading a rumour that Henry was in fact dead; mass was even said in the Yorkist camp for the salvation of his soul. But the Calais contingent nevertheless began to withdraw. In these circumstances, and under cover of darkness, York, his sons and the Neville earls decided to abandon their men rather than risk submitting to their enemies.[34] They retired into Ludlow during the night and then made off, leaving their followers to cope as best they could.

With the immediate crisis over, Henry VI was willing, out of reverence (so it was later said) for God and St. Edward the Confessor, the feast of whose translation fell on the next day, 13 October, to receive the surrender of all those who were prepared to submit.[35] Lord Grey of Powis, Sir Walter Devereux's son, Walter, and Sir Henry Radford gave themselves up. Ludlow was given over to pillaging by the royal forces, as was the Carmelite Friary; but there seems to have been little structural damage to buildings.[36] According to one contemporary, the king's men, 'whenn they hadde drokyn i-nowe of wyne that was in tavernys and in othyr placys they ulle ungoodely smote owte the heddys of the pypys and hoggys hedys of wyne, that men wente wete-schede in wyne, and thenn they robbyd the towne, and bare a-waye beddynge and clothe and othyr stuffe and defoulyd many wymmen'.[37] The duke's tenants were harried and their property despoiled, while the duchess of York and her younger children, who were presumably discovered in the castle, were taken into custody.

While the king was still in Ludlow, commissions were appointed to seize the properties of the leading traitors. Two weeks later, on 30 October, widespread commissions were issued throughout the West Midlands and the Welsh borderland for the arrest of all who had been implicated in the recent treason.[38] Parliament, which had been summoned on 9 October while the pursuit was in progress, met at Coventry on 20 November to complete the Yorkists' humiliation and punishment. Ludlow was left sacked and apprehensive. On 21 October, the castle and town were placed in the charge of Edmund de la Mare, an esquire who had distinguished himself in the recent action, though his position was not formally regularised until 21 May 1460, when he was made constable of the castle for life. On 20 June 1460, the earl of Shrewsbury was appointed steward of York's town and lordship of Ludlow, again for life.[39] The intention appears to have been to make the subjugation of Ludlow and the destruction of York's power permanent.

York and his second son, Edmund of Rutland, eventually reached Ireland; his eldest son, Edward of March, and the earl of Warwick made for Calais. They planned their return and yet another challenge to Henry VI's regime—and eventually, in 1460, his throne.

When the duke of York returned from exile in October 1460, he landed in north Wales, as he had done on his earlier return from Ireland in 1450. He then made his way southwards through the borderland, attracting support at Shrewsbury, Ludlow and Hereford.[40] Although the duke was killed on the last day of the year, at a skirmish with a royalist army near Wakefield in Yorkshire, his cause soon triumphed. Edward, earl of March, who had returned from Calais to meet his father, was crowned king as Edward IV after mustering an army in the vicinity of Wigmore and Ludlow and defeating a Lancastrian force at Mortimer's Cross early in February 1461.[41] He became king on 4 March. Ludlow's loyalty was handsomely rewarded by the new monarch. In several respects, the years after 1460 proved a golden age for Ludlow and its inhabitants, a prospect hardly to be contemplated at the time of Ludford Bridge.

Following a week spent in Ludlow in mid-September 1461, in December King Edward granted the town a new charter which placed its government on a new and even more independent footing; it also consolidated the influence of the town's élite. Most of the remaining Mortimer rights of lordship in the town, previously enjoyed by the lord's representative in the castle, were now transferred to the 12 aldermen and the 25 councillors as the town's corporation. Only the right to nominate the rector of the church in alternate years—which rested with the loyal Devereux family—and possession of the castle and Castle Meadow, and certain life interests in

town property enjoyed by individuals, were exempt from this grant. In return, the burgesses were required to pay an annual fee farm or rent of £24 13s. 4d. to the king. As the charter put it, Edward was moved by 'the laudable and gratuitous services which our beloved and faithful subjects the burgesses of the town of Ludlow had rendered unto us in the obtaining of our right to the crown of England ... in great peril of their lives. And also the rapines, depredations, oppressions, losses of goods and other grievances for us and our sake' in the dark days of 1459.[42]

Henceforth, the burgesses were to elect two bailiffs, rather than one, from among the 'foremost and fittest' of their number, and also to elect two members of Parliament; accordingly, they were exempted from contributing to the expenses of Shropshire's MPs. The burgesses of the town and suburbs were exempt from local and national taxes themselves, as the burgesses of other comparable towns were. Furthermore, they were authorised to have their own guild merchant which enjoyed a monopoly of trading in the town. They could elect their own recorder or steward, and the recorder and bailiffs together should act as Ludlow's justices of the peace. A coroner, also elected by the burgesses, would discharge the other duties that elsewhere were undertaken by the county's sheriff. As great producers of fine-quality cloth, the burgesses were allowed to dye cloth for sale just as Bristol merchants were permitted to do in their city. In all, these privileges and liberties amounted to a notable degree of independence of both lord and shire, and a confirmation of the administrative and commercial grip of the town's oligarchy. Even the collection of the annual fee farm was a reminder of the continuing intimacy between Ludlow and the Yorkist dynasty, for on 28 November 1461 £20 of it was assigned per annum to the king's personal physician, Master James Fryse, for his lifetime.[43]

This charter of 1461 was the foundation of Ludlow's urban liberties. In 1478 it was extended by a further grant from Edward IV which conceded that the annual fee farm should now be paid to the king's receiver of the lordship locally rather than to the more distant Exchequer. At the same time, the bailiffs were given control over the aulnage or tax imposed on cloth manufacture in the town; henceforward, the corporation appointed their own aulnager to assess the levy. Further confirmations of these privileges were granted by Richard III in February 1485 and by Henry VIII in the first year of his reign, presumably at the request of an ever vigilant corporation.[44]

The procedures of urban government were well established by the end of the century. The high bailiff, the senior of the two bailiffs, was chosen by the 25 from among the more select group of 12 aldermen, whilst the lower bailiff was chosen by the 12 from among the 25. Such a procedure of simple symmetry bound the élite of Ludlow together; it ensured a breadth of representation and experience in the town's government; and it confirmed the place of the aldermen as the most influential group of townsmen. For example, in the year 1469, eight of the aldermen had been, or would soon be, high bailiff, and five of them warden of the Palmers' Guild. The low bailiff was the more junior of the elected officials and very few burgesses took the post more than once. On the other hand, about a third of these low bailiffs are known to have graduated to become high bailiff, a minority of them more than once; Walter Hubbold, indeed, was high bailiff on five separate occasions in the 1470s and 1480s. Those who presided over the Palmers' Guild were the more respected townsmen. John Dodmore, warden from 1468 to 1471, had been high bailiff in 1464 and was MP for Ludlow in 1467-8; whilst Richard Sherman, the warden in 1472-94, though apparently never a bailiff, was highly thought of by his fellow burgesses, who elected him their MP on two occasions (in 1467-8 and 1478).[45]

As for Ludlow's other MPs, Piers Beaupie was a lawyer and recorder of the town from 1466, and a member of Edward IV's household; he regarded Ludlow as his home, and when he died in 1480 Piers' wife and two sons established a chantry there in his memory. Both John Sparchford, MP in 1472-3, and Thomas Stephens, MP in 1478, had sound records as high bailiffs to commend them. By 1475-6 the town had its own chamberlain, previously known as the catchpole, who exercised regulatory and disciplinary powers in the town, and had charge of the town gaol and the gates, and the conduct of the town's court.[46]

Circumstances after 1461 facilitated the resumption of the urban building programme, with the king himself contributing to the rebuilding of the parish church and the restoration of the Carmelite Friary when it sought help in 1465.[47] In 1469 a mason from Gloucester was brought to Ludlow to advise on completion of the parish church's tall tower. The Plantagenet connection with the Palmers' Guild was also sustained in the early part of Edward's reign: its register reports over 50 royal servants and office-holders, along with the duke of Suffolk and other noblemen, as members, and the king donated £5 to the guild in 1472-3.[48]

The wealth of individual townsmen and merchants was consolidated in the second half of the 15th century. John Hosyer, high bailiff in 1465 and a clothier who was connected with the important Bristol merchant, Robert Sturmy, at his death in 1485 endowed almshouses in College Street; Richard Sherman was one of the executors of his will.[49] About the same time, the influential Bradford family was installed in what later became known as 'the great house' in Corve Street, outside the town walls.[50] By 1482, Broad Street was a major thoroughfare and a much-sought after residential district. Its 64½ burgages were in the hands of only 28 proprietors. Apart from the Hospital of St. John of Jerusalem and the Palmers' Guild, which owned one-third of the properties in Broad Street, three substantial burgesses were each holding as many as four or more burgages, especially in the upper part of the street closest to the centre of the town. Among these three were the heirs of William Griffith, whose family was well established in Ludlow though doubtless of Welsh origin: William had been high bailiff in 1467 and 1472, and his father John was warden of the Palmers' Guild in 1451-

62. The Griffith, Sherman, Hoke and Moreton families provided between them bailiffs of Ludlow on as many as 11 occasions between 1461 and 1512. It is possible that No. 1, at the foot of Broad Street, close to Ludford Bridge, was rebuilt in 1462 because it had been pillaged and damaged in the fracas of 1459.[51]

Edward IV's designation of a substantial Council to govern his Welsh and other estates, and its despatch to Ludlow as its semi-permanent residence from the end of 1473, created an additional factor to cement relations between the town and the Yorkist royal family. This Council had the effect of deepening the integration of castle, guild, church and commercial interests, and it ensured that Ludlow was thriving when a number of other provincial towns in England were languishing. The presence of this Council and, indeed, of the king's first-born son, Prince Edward, at Ludlow up to the king's death in April 1483 meant that a number of royal servants resided there, and, like Piers Beaupie, became benefactors of the town.[52] Castle Meadow, which had been excluded from the properties conceded to the burgesses in 1461, was often leased to these servants, including to John Broke before 1475 and to Thomas Neville in 1476, as well as to Ludlow merchants like John Tewe and Richard Sherman.[53] The king's uncle, Richard duke of Gloucester, may have remembered Ludlow with affection, even though he spent most of King Edward's later years in the north of England. In about 1478 Richard promoted one of his chaplains to be prior of the Hospital of St. John of Jerusalem and required the prior or one of the Hospital's brethren to celebrate mass for Prince Edward's household in St. Peter's Chapel in the castle.[54]

The prince's presence at Ludlow is well attested on a number of occasions in the 1470s and early 1480s, whether authorising letters to bailiffs of Shrewsbury to end disorder in their town, or travelling to Shrewsbury in 1478 and again in 1480. And in March 1476 the king arranged a conference there with his son's Council to which the Marcher lords were invited in order to discuss levels of crime in Wales and the March. When Edward IV died somewhat unexpectedly on 9 April 1483, the prince was still at Ludlow, with his maternal uncle, Anthony, Earl Rivers, and he celebrated St. George's feast-day (23 April) there before leaving for London next day to be acclaimed king.[55] The unique role which Ludlow had played under Richard, duke of York was sustained for a full generation under his son and grandson.

On the other hand, precious little documentary evidence survives to indicate that either Duke Richard or King Edward or the prince of Wales authorised significant building works at Ludlow Castle. The classic account of the castle's architecture, by W.H. St. John Hope, notes that the north face of the Norman Keep-tower was rebuilt in the third quarter of the 15th century.[56] It is tempting to attribute this work—which may have been in the nature of repair—to Richard of York, if only because the castle was a family residence for a decade and more before 1459, when he also patronised building and other works at St. Laurence's Church. After 1461, when several financial accounts of the earldom of March survive, only modest sums are known to have been spent by Edward IV on repairs to the castle (a total of £32 1s 8d in 1464-6 and nothing in 1467-8), whilst for the prince's lordship and occupation after 1473 no records relating to Ludlow Castle are known to exist.

Henry Tudor, who married Edward IV's daughter and regarded himself, in part, as King Edward's true heir, extended his patronage to Ludlow and came to appreciate its strategic and governmental value in establishing secure rule in the western shires of England and in Wales. Thus, the violent overthrow of the usurper Richard III in 1485, and the change of dynasty that resulted, had no perceptible effect on Ludlow's fortunes or on the town's élite.[57] Some years after his accession, in November 1493, Henry VII granted to his son, Prince Arthur (1486-1502), the castle, town and lordship of Ludlow, along with other former Yorkist estates, and he realised the value of sending his young son to Ludlow with a Council after the pattern established by Edward IV. Indeed, when Prince Arthur died in 1502, the king allowed the Council to remain at Ludlow in the interim before Prince Henry was created prince of Wales. Like Edward IV, Henry Tudor visited Ludlow on occasion; and the fee farm of the town was assigned to meet the pensions of royal servants, including Edward Haseley, who had tutored the king presumably during his exile.[58] In November 1490 the king granted the keepership of the new park at Oakley, along with 51s. from Ludlow's fee farm, to Richard Sherman, doyen among the burgesses.[59]

The Palmers' Guild continued to attract high-ranking members, including Earl Rivers (in 1489) and the duchess of Buckingham towards the end of the king's reign.[60] And when Prince Arthur died in the castle on 2 April 1502, it was symbolic that his heart was interred in the parish church while his body, after a requiem mass in Ludlow, was solemnly conveyed to Worcester for burial in the cathedral; that day was 'the foulist, caulde, wyndy and rayny day, and the werst wey that I have seen—ye, and in some place fayne to take men to drawe the chare, so ill was the wey'.[61] When Prince Henry (later Henry VIII) arrived to take up the reins of conciliar government, at least ten members of his household joined the Palmers' Guild in 1502-3 as a sign of continuity and continued royal favour.[62]

John Leland's visit to Ludlow in about 1540 produced some significant comment. He noted that Broad Street was 'the fayrest part of the town', and few burgesses would have disagreed with him. In the parish church he noticed the graves of Piers Beaupie, servant to Edward IV, of a gentlemen-servant of Prince Arthur, and that of John Hosyer, merchant of Ludlow, as well as memorials to members of the princes' councils.[63] It was a roll-call that testified to Ludlow's unique history during the Wars of the Roses.

CHAPTER VIII

The Council in the Marches of Wales

by Michael Faraday

For two centuries, apart from short intervals, Ludlow Castle was the home of the Council in the Marches of Wales, which gave Ludlow an importance which, otherwise, it would not have had. Ludlow became 'the capital of Wales' as the result of an historical accident—that since the early 14th century it had been the *caput* of the earldom of March, which in 1461 became merged with the Crown upon the accession of the House of York.

A great nobleman with extensive estates normally maintained a household to match his status. Organising and financing this required servants and officials, who were directed by a council of trusted and, usually, professional administrators, whose task was to run the estates and raise revenue, but who also had to look after the political interests of the lord in those parts of the country where his estates were. Raising troops when the lord was called to war, running the manorial courts on his estates, advising on appointments where their lord had influence: all these were normal duties of a magnate's council.

Wales had long been a source of political trouble for the kings of England and having a 'presence' there became important to them in the 15th century. In July, 1471, Edward IV established his son, Edward, prince of Wales, with his own household and council and responsibility for Wales and Chester. At first this council had no judicial responsibilities, but the very fact that it was there as a grander version of a magnate council gave it a *de facto* political presence. In 1473 it was enlarged and the prince was sent to live in Ludlow Castle. A prince would need his own establishment somewhere; in Ludlow his servants could also keep watch on a fractious part of the country, cultivate the classes who had most influence there, and generally be the eyes and ears of the king. In 1473 the beginnings of political and judicial functions can be seen when the Council was required to suppress crime in the border counties. The Council achieved some success in overcoming the widespead intimidation of juries and increased the number of cases indicted in the King's Bench at Westminster. In November, 1473, John Alcock, bishop of Rochester, was appointed president of the prince's Council, for the prince himself was an infant and was no more than a figurehead signifying the authority of the Council. Although the Council was still primarily part of a royal magnate's household, it began to acquire *ad hoc* political and legal powers, chiefly in investigation and in judicial appointments, both essential to enforcing governmental authority. Settling disputes within towns soon became an important activity, as in 1478 when the Council laid down ordinances regulating the trades of Shrewsbury.[1]

This Council probably came to an end when, on his accession in 1483, Edward V left Ludlow, going to his death at the hands of his uncle.

There is no evidence of the existence of any council in Ludlow without a prince, which demonstrates the fact that hitherto its function did not involve any established machinery of either government or justice. It had been an *ad hoc* body, acting as the occasion seemed to demand or as opportunity arose.

There was to be no subsequent Council in the Marches until 1493 when Prince Arthur, eldest son of Henry VII, was given powers very similar to those of Edward, and again exercised by others on his behalf. This coincided with the grant to Arthur of the earldom (although not the title) of March, including Ludlow Castle, and other Marcher lordships, which from this time onwards were falling into Crown hands. Arthur's Council was still essentially a medieval magnate's council, exercising justice and control as a function of his lordship but with the specific addition of over-riding public supervisory responsibilities.[2] Among the measures to be enforced was a requirement that lords marchers and the officials of royal marcher lordships were to be bound by indenture for good rule and order with a system of redress of grievances from the lords' courts to the prince's Council. In practice these powers were exercised by Jasper, duke of Bedford, and others until Arthur himself went to Ludlow in 1501.[3] Whether the prince's Council as such played any governmental role in the Marches is disputed. William Smyth, bishop of Coventry and Lichfield, and later bishop of Lincoln, seems to have been president of this Council in the 1490s and, after Arthur's death in 1502, continued to exercise the functions of the office. How effective the Council may have been is open to doubt; it was one thing to have the legal powers, quite another to exercise them effectively.

It was 23 years before another royal household was established at Ludlow, but the Council was there throughout the period. In 1512 William Smyth was succeeded as president by Geoffrey Blythe, bishop of Coventry and Lichfield, and the supervisory powers continued to be exercised in much the same way as before. In 1525 Princess Mary was sent to Ludlow and the Council, under a new president, John Veysey, bishop of Exeter,[4] ran her household there as well as performing its continuing public duties. Councils were instruments of Wolsey's policy for asserting royal authority in the further-flung parts of the kingdom, so the Council in the Marches of Wales was given powers similar to those of the Council in the North. The establishment of this Council comprised both a household and a hierarchy of public officials.

The Council could now be seen to be acting as a court of law, exercising both criminal and civil jurisdiction, as a court of first instance and as an appellate body hearing appeals from manorial courts. Settled procedures were being developed. Nevertheless the distinction between having powers and being effective became obvious under Veysey. The departure from Ludlow of Mary's household did not end the activities of the Council there but the determination with which it conducted its responsibilities diminished. In 1532 Thomas Philips asked Cromwell to ensure that a Council was in place which would make the officers in Wales 'quake' if found in default of their duties; he also accused the retinue of the household of using their position to obstruct rather than to expedite justice in Wales.[5] In 1533 Sir Edward Croft and his son, Thomas, claimed that Veysey was not up to the task of imposing peace and justice and that no one had been punished for a hundred murders committed during his period of office. It is evident that habituated bad behaviour required determination and energy to overcome it. It was in 1534 with the appointment as president of one of Thomas Cromwell's associates, Rowland Lee, bishop of Coventry and Lichfield, that a kind of revolution began.

Lee was a vigorous, even ruthless, man, constantly on the move, who went out looking for trouble, in 1536 proudly declaring to Cromwell, his political master in Westminster, that 'all thieves in Wales quake with fear'. A public hanging on market day after a humiliating journey to the scaffold trussed in a sack was Lee's preferred remedy for a thief. He took care to keep Cromwell on his side at all times and with that assurance was not afraid to arrest and hang male-factors of any rank. Lee was lord president at the time of Cromwell's reform of the political structure of Wales through the Act of Union of 1536 and, after Cromwell's fall, almost until the passing of the great consolidating Act of 1543. These Acts reformed the old courts of great sessions in Wales and introduced the system of justices of the peace, so that in most essentials Wales was for the first time governed in the same way as England. These reforms greatly augmented the formal powers of the Council in the Marches. Lee, however, thought that the reforms would put the people who caused most of the trouble in charge of the day-to-day working of the system. On this matter he did not have Cromwell's backing, but, until 1540, Cromwell had the king's and the policy went through. Although Lee's activities were dramatic, it is not to be supposed that he could solve the lawlessness of Wales and the Marches merely by a personal reign of terror, however many thieves he hanged. Social changes were required to amend modes of behaviour and to remove opportunities for misconduct and these took time. Cromwell's policy of assimilating Wales into the English system had more effect in the long term.

Until 1534 the court of the Council had been in strictness a 'prerogative court', existing by royal will alone, but in that year it received statutory powers both to hear suits and to supervise and intervene in judicial proceedings in Wales and the Marches. The Act of Union of 1543[6] included a provision that 'there shall be and remain' a president and Council 'with all officers, clerks and incidents to the same, in manner and form as hath heretofore been used and accustomed' with the power to 'hear and determine ... such causes and matters as be ... assigned to them by the King's Majesty, as heretofore hath been accustomed and used.' This was a curious provision since it both established the court and at the same time acknowledged that it had already been in existence for some time.[7]

From Lee's death in 1543 to the appointment as lord president of Sir Henry Sidney in 1560 the

Fig. 1 Sir Henry Sidney, president of the Council in the Marches from 1560 to 1586

presidency of the Council in the March was subject to the fortunes of factions at Court. Richard Sampson, 1543-1549, was a supporter of Gardiner, not a reformer; he was replaced in 1549 by John Dudley, earl of Warwick, who a year later put in William Herbert, earl of Pembroke, to be his successor after Somerset's fall. When Dudley too fell from power, Herbert was replaced by a cleric of the orthodox faction, Nicholas Heath, bishop of Worcester, who stayed three years. When Heath was promoted to lord chancellor, Pembroke had found favour with Mary and recovered the lord presidency, which he kept for three years, until he lost favour again. Gilbert Bourne kept the post for a year, and his successor, Lord Williams of Thame, died in Ludlow Castle after only eight months.

The judicial function of the Council derived from its political function of keeping the region loyal. Seeking out and punishing crime, since crime was a source of disorder, was one aspect; providing justice to the king's subjects was in recognition that its lack also led to vendetta and disorder. The courts in Westminster were thought to be too far away and to discourage poor men from seeking their protection; this was a particular disadvantage to a poor region. Criminal jurisdiction was acquired through statutory powers to oversee the courts of great session in Wales, after their reform in 1534-1543, and through a grant of commissions of oyer and terminer and of the peace, although the Council was able to act on powers similar to those of Star Chamber and was one of the few courts empowered to use torture. Civil jurisdiction was derived from the Council's prerogative power and took on aspects of both the court of Chancery and of the Court of Requests (the poor men's court).[8] It was claimed that the court's fees were lower than those at Westminster; this was a source of annoyance to those who practised in the latter as they lost business to Ludlow.

The court was, however, beset by problems of conflicting jurisdiction which remained unresolved. This was a general problem of the age which had not wholly defined each court's jurisdiction, but allowed a kind of free-for-all in which courts protected their own by trying to ignore or override the decisions of competing courts. From the outset the Council in the Marches intervened as it could in the legal proceedings of the courts of the marcher lords; this became a statutory power in 1534. In 1543 the lordship courts lost most of their powers and the courts of great session, reformed and with wider common law powers, became the courts of first instance throughout Wales. Although the Council's court had appellate powers in relation to these and the Council itself had considerable influence through interlocking memberships of commissions of the peace, this was untidy. In the English shires subject to the Council, the system of quarter sessions continued to exist and here too the Council had an influence on appointments. But a similar untidiness of overlapping jurisdiction prevailed. In the boroughs the same occurred with the town courts. Ecclesiastical courts had jurisdiction over morals and matters of conscience, this latter extending to anything involving oaths and even 'good faith'. Wills, breaches of contract, even debt, could be sued in a bishop's court. Apart from the probate of wills, all these were matters in which the Council's court also got involved. Sexual morals were in the 16th century left to the church courts, but by the early 17th century the Council's court prosecuted them too. This was to some extent a reflection of the increased interest both the ecclesiastical and secular authorities were taking at this time in the reform of private conduct; the church courts' records also show a greatly increased volume of 'moral' cases. In the period 1618-25, for which comparative figures can be compiled, five times as many Ludlow people were prosecuted in the bishop's court for sexual offences as were prosecuted for such offences in the Council's court; so the entry of the latter into this area must therefore not be exaggerated. Nevertheless, the Church, far from welcoming the assistance of the secular courts in suppressing vice, resented the competition. Between 1617 and 1636 about a quarter of the criminal cases heard by the Council's court involved adultery and other consensual sexual misconduct. (As a comparison, over a third of criminal cases involved violence, often affray, which might be thought to have been closer to the original proper interests of the court. A significant proportion of prosecutions in this period were of the Council's own officials for neglect or breach of duty! Even more were of persons who had ignored earlier orders of the same court.) The court at this time also concerned itself with scandal, slander and misconduct, like that of William Sherwood of Ludlow, fined £3 6s 8d in 1620 for 'singing rybaldry songs in an alehouse and using undecent speeches to Richard Bulkeley clerk'.[9]

The Council was in origin a prerogative court and exercised powers akin to those of the London prerogative courts—the Privy Council, Star Chamber and Requests—but, unlike these three, it also had common law and equity jurisdiction. Nevertheless, its procedures were essentially modelled on those of Star Chamber.[10] It was therefore competition with the courts of

Westminster, King's Bench, Common Pleas, Chancery and Exchequer, which led to the worst overlapping and which ultimately led to the abolition of the Council's court. The latter had intentionally been given both common law and equity functions in order to make access to the law easier for local people. There is evidence that the common law courts in Westminster lost income to the Councils in the March and the North after 1537, but by the 1550s they were resorting to prohibitions to stem the loss.[11] In the time of lord president Sampson the Council protested against a *certiorari* issued to it in connexion with a matter before its court.[12] In 1574 the court of Exchequer issued an inhibition against the Council proceeding with Agnes Bulkeley's case against her stepson, Richard, who had found friends in London. The Exchequer court claimed jurisdiction where Crown revenues or staff were even indirectly involved, as where the subject-matter was a Crown lease, so this was potentially a very serious threat to the Council, which protested, but probably lost, as it may have done again two years later in the case of an Exchequer official, Arthur Salwey, suing for a Droitwich property. In another case Burghley stated that the principle to be adopted in these cases was to allow the Council to proceed where the rights of the Crown, even though involved, were not at risk. This was a pragmatic counsel of perfection which did not allow for the ability of persons with influence at Court to manipulate the Exchequer into asserting its legal rights. The question remained unsettled, for neither side was prepared to accept its defeats as binding precedents.[13]

The administration of justice was not improved by undefined jurisdictions. In 1580 John Hughes ignored the Council's court order and sued 17 Montgomery residents in the Westminster courts; the Council was incensed and asked the lord chancellor to deal with Hughes 'as may breed in him a more quiet disposition henceforth'.[14] This was a not uncommon occurrence; circumstances virtually invited litigants to claim and counter-claim in different courts where they thought a better outcome might be forth-

coming. There were many 16th and 17th century examples of litigants suing each other in different courts and claiming oppressive and malicious litigation on their opponents' parts and of being thereby put to unnecessary expense. Agnes Clayton sued Edward and John Trevor in Star Chamber, *tempore* Henry VIII, having, they alleged, already worn them down by suing them in the Council in the March.[15] In 1587 Philip Bradford of Ludlow sued John Passey in the Council's court as well as several times in Star Chamber; this case took eight years.[16] In 1592 Richard Season sued two other Ludlow residents in Chancery for a property there which they had wrongfully obtained; they asked for the case to be referred to the Council in the Marches.[17] Unsurprisingly, Anne Devaux, widow of the sergeant at arms of the Council, asked in 1599 that the case she was defending in Chancery against John Passey of Wigley be referred to the Council's court at Ludlow.[18] Even the poor men's court, the Court of Requests, was not immune. In 1580 William Bevan, defendant in a suit begun in that court by John Croft, asked for the case to be taken to the Council in the Marches, as he was a Radnorshire man.[19] The 1603 case of William Sherwood and the alleged abduction of Susan Blashfield came before both Star Chamber and the Council's court, with Sherwood being prosecuted in the former for riot and suing in the latter for theft; later Sherwood himself prosecuted his Broughton opponents in Star Chamber, winning in both courts. Broughton's sister, Frances Blashfield, alleged that Sherwood had illegally 'maintained' another's suit against her before the Council's court. This case was in some respects a reflection of faction in the Council in the Marches; Broughton had been a senior follower of Essex, while Sherwood had been a minor member of the Pembroke household.[20] Some litigants used the multiplicity of courts to pursue cases already lost elsewhere. Catherine Whitton of Ludlow lost her case against John Posterne before the Council's court in 1609, so in 1612 she began again in Chancery.[21] The bailiffs of Ludlow sued Richard Edwards, their rent-collector, in the Council's court for arrears of rents and in 1620 had obtained the decision that Edwards should pay the bond he had given and pursue defaulting tenants himself. Instead, Edwards sued the bailiffs in Chancery.[22] The most famous case in which various courts were involved was the 1590s struggle between political factions in Ludlow over the borough's charters and property. This began in the Council's court, which referred it to the Privy Council because of its essential political content, only to have it promptly referred back to settle with the benefit of local knowledge. In the end it became an Exchequer case on a *Quo warranto*.[23] The opportunities for vexatious litigants and for those who had the resources to support endless litigation were greatly increased by the ill-defined jurisdiction of the Council in the Marches.

The Council's court began with a very wide jurisdiction which was gradually limited. Bristol obtained exemption in the mid-16th century and Chester not long after. As the great sessions of the Welsh counties and the quarter sessions in the English counties became better organised there was less apparent need for the Council's intervention, but its jurisdiction remained. It is probable that only a minority of criminal cases came to the Council rather than to these lower level courts.

The court was levying fines as early as 1517.[24] The gradual formalisation of the Council in the Marches as a court of law gave it and its officers sources of income. Some formed part of the perquisites of the various officers additional to any formal salaries they were paid by the Council. Others, however, were expected to help finance the Council's own costs. The more cases the court handled the greater its income. Curiously, for a court designed primarily to ensure that law and order prevailed in Wales, most of the income from fines derived from its English jurisdiction, which became a source of grievance. In the late 1570s fines levied averaged £1,060 a year, but only 80% of this was collected. In the 1580s fines levied rose to £1,336 a year, of which 84% was collected. By 1601-1602 fines levied had risen to £2,417 a year of which 82%

was collected. So great were the arrears carried forward from year to year, indeed from one receiver of fines to another, that some of the sums collected in a year may have related to fines levied in earlier years. It may be assumed, however, that most arrears rapidly became uncollectable bad debts.[25] From time to time there would be both informal and formal cancellations, waivers and writings off. Although the instructions given to the Council included a requirement for proper and frequent accounting for revenues and expenditure, this seems never to have been enforced. On occasion the clerk of the fines took it upon himself to remit fines, possibly because he lacked the energy or the incentive to pursue defaulters or was able to exercise undue favour.

The problem of arrears became a besetting one. There were attempts at reform; Bishop Whitgift tried, but was opposed by Sidney, whose motive is unclear. The expenses of the court itself, salaries, fees and allowances, were the first charge on the fines, which gave an incentive to the judges to fine heavily to ensure that their own salaries were paid. Arrears, however, meant that salaries, properly charged to the clerk of the fines, were themselves in arrear, perhaps never paid in full.

In 1600 a panel of four professional lawyers was appointed to assist the lord president in hearing cases—and also to hear cases during the frequent absences of lord presidents. This improved the efficiency of the court but may not have permanently improved the level of fining. In 1603/4 the fines levied came to only £1,189, while arrears of the current and the two previous receivers came to £4,418. Twelve and 13 years later fines levied amounted to £1,987 for the two years, of which only £938 was received and £412 was formally discharged.[26]

Few of the accounts kept by the receivers of fines have survived and where they have they are rarely in a form which enables clear comparisons to be made. They are clearer on expenditure than they are on income. The fining activity of the court was open to criticism—if the fines collected were too low to pay for the expected

Lord Presidents of the Council in the Marches of Wales	
1473 - *c*.1483	John Alcock, bishop of Rochester
1490s - 1512	William Smyth, bishop of Coventry and Lichfield
1512 - 1524	Geoffrey Blythe, bishop of Coventry and Lichfield
1525 - 1534	John Veysey, bishop of Exeter
1534 - 1543	Rowland Lee, bishop of Coventry and Lichfield
1543 - 1549	Richard Sampson, bishop of Coventry and Lichfield
1549 - 1550	John Dudley, earl of Warwick
1550 - 1553	William Herbert, earl of Pembroke
1553 - 1555	Nicholas Heath, bishop of Worcester
1555 - 1558	William Herbert, earl of Pembroke
1558 - 1559	Gilbert Bourne, bishop of Bath and Wells
1559	John, Lord Williams of Thame
1560 - 1586	Sir Henry Sidney
1586 - 1601	Henry Herbert, earl of Pembroke
1602 - 1607	Edward, Lord Zouch
1607 - 1617	Ralph, Lord Eure
1617	Thomas Gerard, Baron Gerard of Gerard's Bromley
1617 - 1630	William Compton, earl of Northampton
1631 - 1641	John Egerton, earl of Bridgwater
1661 - 1672	Richard Vaughan, earl of Carbery
1672 - 1688	Henry Somerset, marquis of Worcester
1689	Charles Gerard, earl of Macclesfield

(Sources: Penry Williams; DNB; Complete Peerage; National Library of Wales, Great Sessions, Writs)

disbursements and if they were so high that those who paid them felt that they were being unjustly oppressed.

Fines, which in theory were intended to punish and deter offenders, were in reality needed to support the running of the court. The expenses of a royal household, such as that of Princess Mary, would more easily be accepted as charges on central finances. In 1528-1530 *ad hoc* payments were made by Sir Brian Tuke, treasurer of the Chamber, to Mary and her officials.[27] As late as 1534 Council salaries and expenses were generally met by grants from the King's Chamber but later it seems that the Council was expected to live of its own as far as possible.[28] In 1579/80 the fees of the vice-president, the chief justice, the chaplain and messengers, as well as the steward of the household and the armourer were paid from the fines, as were payments to the bailiffs of Ludlow for the hire of beds,[29] (presumably for visiting officials, couriers and others on transient

Council business in Ludlow). In 1581 Charles Booth, receiver of fines and amercements, paid out of the fines fees to two former vice-presidents, three councillors, the current and previous justices of Chester, the Queen's attorney, the current and previous solicitor, himself and the auditor of fines, the secretary to the Council, the chaplain, the keeper of the castle, the keeper of armour and two messengers. Several of these officials would have had little or nothing to do with the court as such. Payments to former officials demonstrate that payments in arrear were commonplace.

In 1587 Oliver St. John, then receiver, reimbursed the expenses of Sir Henry Sidney incurred in attending the Privy Council four years earlier, those of Sidney's chaplain and even the six-year old expenses of two attorneys, Roger Morgan and Thomas Evans. He also paid out fees to the councillors, the secretary, the castle keeper, the chaplain, himself, the auditor, messengers, Richard

Clenche, the keeper of the castle's clocks, and a plumber. This pattern of expenditure continued in 1600-1602 but also included a laundress, underporters and suppliers of goods and services to the Council (chiefly coopers) and repairs to the castle. In 1607 substantial household expenses were disbursed. By 1614 payments out of the fines, in addition to the usual fees, included £83 on castle-repairs, the clerk of the kitchen, rewards for musicians, £195 on fuel, coopers, a seamstress, candles in the chapel and brewing costs. In short, the area of expenditure for which the receiver of the fines was expected to disburse funds was not confined to the running of the court, nor was there any clear definition of what he was responsible for. One or more of the senior officials of the Council seems to have decided who was to be paid what and from where as opportunity and occasion arose. From time to time the Council would be instructed from Westminster to pay certain salaries from its own fines. None of this was conducive to prudent accounting.[30]

The lord president had an allowance from the King's Chamber for the costs of his establishment, although Sidney found it inadequate and made ineffective appeals for more money. He was aware of the inflation which afflicted the age, but his superiors were unmoved. He was reduced often to laying out his own money. It is not surprising that the Council would live hand-to-mouth and 'raid' any funds nearer to home, such as the fines, nor that there should have been contemporary accusations of bribery and extortion. People forced to spend their own money might well have thought it legitimate to take such advantage of their offices.

The Council was a household as well as a court; it was also an administrative centre. From Sidney's time onwards a grand household was maintained at Ludlow Castle. Large sums were spent on its furnishing, its staffing and its 'diet' and entertainment. We know that in 1615 13s 4d was spent on musicians and 40s on a company called 'the Queen's players'. The latter were called upon again in 1616.[31] In 1634 Ludlow castle also saw the first performance of Milton's

Comus, written for Bridgewater's household entertainment. The cost of this threefold establishment would have been considerable at all times. In 1615-1616 various officials petitioned to have their expenses met; they included servants of the vice-president, odd-job men (including Thomas Gruffith who wanted a wage of 15s 'for killing noysome vermin as ratts and mices in Ludlow castle'), a joiner for repairs to furniture and to the fabric of the officials' private chambers, a goldsmith, a cooper, and the receiver of fines himself, Alexander Roberts, who wanted reimbursement for books and fuel purchased.[32]

Repairs to Ludlow Castle itself formed the biggest continual financial worry for the Council. Before the establishment of the Council custody of and repairs to the castle had been a charge on the estates of the earldom of March.[33] From about the time of the establishment of Prince Edward's council these expenses appear to have fallen, not to the earldom of March, but to the Council, emphasising how much the Council was seen as a natural successor to and development of the earldom. There was a succession of supervisors of building works at the castle, from John Broke in 1463, through Walter Rogers in 1525 to Thomas Blashfield in 1583. It is unclear whether the office was a permanent one or whether it was an appointment made only when work was contemplated. In 1534 Lee was forced to borrow money for this purpose, but it is unclear where he raised the money and how he repaid it.[34] He claimed that his major programme of repairs would have cost the king £500. In 1602 the then president, Lord Zouch, was permitted to charge castle repairs to the fines and forfeitures. Complaints about the state of the castle were continual, but it is not known whether previous repairs had been ineffectual, whether there was always something needing repair, or whether rising expectations of living and working standards led to continual expense. Certainly most surviving accounts contain references to work on the fabric of the castle. Rowland Lee ordered the removal of a great quantity of lead—over five fothers—from the former Carmelite friary in

Ludlow to use on the castle. Whether this was part of the eight fothers of lead he claimed in 1534 to have bought for the same purpose is not known as there is no evidence that he paid for the Carmelite lead.[35] Thomas Eyton, clerk of the kitchen, had wider responsibilities than his title implied, for he claimed from the lord president in 1615 for the two casements in Mr. Alured's chamber and for the mending of the lower gate 'being ready to fall' in 1616.[36]

During Sidney's presidency (1560-86) a great deal of work was done on the fabric of Ludlow Castle including the construction of the Porter's Lodge and associated buildings. In addition repairs were effected at Wigmore Castle, still in official use as a prison, and as a residence, Bewdley and Tickenhill. At Ludlow Castle these works included making a walled walk for prisoners to use, constructing a courthouse with two offices beneath it in which to keep its records, kitchen buildings and chambers for the Council's officers. This programme included 'making a fayre stone bridge into the castle with a great Arch in the myddest and two at both ends conteining in leingth about 30 or 40 yards and in height upon both sides with free stone a yard and a half.' The castle chapel was also substantially repaired, glazed and tiled, furnished with seats and the arms of the Queen and the Council. Sidney's programme included a tennis court in the castle, roofing the castle with lead, the building and glazing of a number of large windows, made possible by the fact that the castle was no longer perceived as a defensive stronghold. It also included a mile-long conduit to bring water to the castle and to distribute it within the buildings, with two fountains, one in the garden of the castle and the other in Castle Street.[37] Only the presence of the Council and a nobleman's stylish household with the need both for a good many official and domestic buildings would have justified such a programme. It is also unlikely that it would have been carried out unless a man like Sidney had been president there for a long time. Without the Council, Ludlow Castle would have decayed long before the 18th century.

Fig. 2 The arms of Sir Henry Sidney, as drawn by Thomas Dinely in 1684 and of which the weather-worn remains are above the entrance to the inner bailey

Fig. 3 The chapel as drawn by Dinely in 1684, also showing one of the fountains installed by Sidney

Sidney was succeeded in 1586 by his son-in-law, Henry Herbert, earl of Pembroke, son of William, earl of Pembroke, an earlier lord president. He remained in office for 15 years, when the Council was at the height of its powers and influence. Herbert, like most of the presidents, did not spend a great deal of his time in Ludlow, but for the most part worked through his vice-president and the councillors. The vice-presidency, usually vested in the Chief Justice of Chester, was for long periods the effective headship of the Council.

There were complaints of malicious prosecutions and of corruption made against the court of the Council which may well have been true, since these were not abuses confined to that court at the time. The court was an aspect of a political institution which was manned in the same way as other political institutions—by patronage in return for loyalty. It could not help getting caught up in the family and factional rivalries of noble families, Where there were scores to settle, advantages to be won and debts to be paid, corruption was likely. The court was often riven by political faction. The court was also alleged to make too much use of informers (relators), a practice which disrupted local communities. The region had long been used to, and equally disliked, the apparitors of the ecclesiastical courts, a version of such informers.[38]

There was, however, opposition to the very existence of the court from two sources. The first was the gentry of the area for which the Council was responsible. These resented the loss of potential influence in their 'countries', where the Council, rather than they, exercised the last word in causes. Even this source of opposition was not evenly distributed; the gentry of Shropshire were generally much less antipathetic—for Shropshire gentlemen occupied a disproportionate number of posts in the Council's hierarchy. The second source of opposition came from the lawyers who practised in the Westminster courts, who were very well placed to make their enmity felt. Even these were not an homogeneous class, since London lawyers were often appointed to posts in

the Council. Although the opposition was able to present itself in terms of principle, it was in fact based on a shifting bloc of individual and personal grievance and envy, powerful on occasion, especially during a crisis, but for the most part ephemeral.

A substantial move against the judicial powers of the Council began early in James I's reign. The Council's court imprisoned a defendant to a civil suit for disobeying its order, whereupon he obtained a writ of *habeas corpus* from the King's Bench. A dispute developed in which Lord Zouch, the new lord president, (and who was married to Sir Henry Sidney's niece) appealed to the king 'as a point of government, not of law', a compelling argument at the time, but one which perhaps rashly potentially tied the fate of the Council's court too closely to that of the main prerogative court, Star Chamber. Sir Edward Coke, the attorney general, denied the court any jurisdiction in England, a severe line since most of the court's income arose in England. In 1606 Sir Herbert Croft and John Hoskyns, M.P. for Hereford, brought in a bill to restrict the Council's activities to Wales; this failed in the Lords. Fresh royal 'instructions' were, however, issued to the Council removing its power to use torture, its jurisdiction over sexual offences and its criminal and civil jurisdiction (except for small cases of debt and trespass) in England.[39]

Lord Zouch resigned, largely over this, and was replaced by Ralph, Lord Eure, who was given fresh instructions which restored all the Council's powers except that of torture. A renewed attack in the parliament of 1614 went the way of the parliament itself, falling when the Commons were dismissed. Eure died in 1617 and was very briefly replaced by Thomas Gerard (whose relative, Sir William Gerard had been a vice-president under Sidney), who gave way to William Compton, earl of Northampton, the grandson of the second wife of William Herbert, earl of Pembroke.[40] This began the 'golden age' of the court when it had an unprecedented volume of business, high income and little opposition. Nevertheless, arguments were in the making. The provision in the Act of Union relating to the court referred to the 'Marches' but did not define them. The defence was that the court originated in the prerogative, which was plainly true, but did not resolve the question of whether prerogative acts still applied where relevant subsequent statutes were silent. At this time they almost certainly did, but there would come a time when such an argument would not be accepted. In any event, arguments were mere decorations to the issue. What mattered was who had friends in the government since the existence of the court was, in the last analysis, political. Zouch's troubles had been made worse because of the opposition of Lord Ellesmere, the lord chancellor, but Compton gained by the support of Francis Bacon, a later lord chancellor.

Compton's successor as lord president in 1631 was John Egerton, earl of Bridgewater, who—ironically—was the son of Lord Chancellor Ellesmere. Political opposition was renewed under Sir Robert Harley and his wife, Brilliana, who were prosecuted before the Council by their enemies, the Crofts.[41] In another curious reversal, whereas Croft had been a catholic, Harley was a puritan. In the 1630s the Council was under attack from several directions; William Somerset, earl of Worcester, whose family had in the past been members of the Council, was now intent on building up his personal political interests in the area. In 1640 he obtained the king's support for his own independent control of the militias of South Wales and Herefordshire, which was an unprecedented derogation from the authority of the Council. In 1636 Archbishop Laud ordered the Council to suspend its jurisdiction over sexual cases.[42] There were always lawyers with influence in high places who opposed the Council. Popular antagonism developed when the Privy Council used the Council in its unremitting campaign to enforce the collection of ship money and 'coat and conduct money' for the raising of troops for Scotland. In both these matters the Privy Council became closely involved in the day-to-day administration and saw to it that the Council in the Marches took on some of this burden and, with it,

some of the odium. Although the Council was involved more in the routine casework and not in the 'high-profile' cases which Star Chamber initiated and which created the latter court's later reputation for arbitrariness and tyranny, particularly during the period of 'personal rule', it was inevitable that the Council would suffer by association in any political attack on Star Chamber. So it proved in the Long Parliament.

Ludlow was the only defender of the Council and sent a petition to the king and to Parliament pointing out how much the town depended upon the 'great conflux of people [who] did resort to the said Town to have justice administered unto them ... But now since the jurisdiction of the said court in the Council ... hath been questioned in this present Parliament there hath been little resort to the said Town'. It achieved nothing.[43]

The court's end came in the Act for the Abolition of the Court of Star Chamber, 1641,[44] which declared 'that the like jurisdiction now used and exercised in the Court before the President and Council in the Marches of Wales ... shall from the first day of August 1641 be also repealed and absolutely revoked and made void'. It may be significant that the presidency and Council were not abolished, only their judicial powers, although what was left was executive power dependent upon instigation and guidance from Westminster, which in the climate of the times was no longer forthcoming. Nevertheless the fact that the Council was technically still in existence may have assisted its re-emergence after the Restoration. Certainly the various seekers after office and favour took for granted the continuance of family rights to themselves.

The theoretical existence of the Council, shorn of its judicial powers, does not imply an actual existence, for which there is neither evidence nor acknowledgement. Ludlow Castle, the former seat of the Council, fell within the command of a series of military governors, first Royalist, until the fall of the castle in late May, 1646, and then Parliamentarian until the Restoration. Ludlow Castle was surrendered by its Royalist governor and commander, Sir

Michael Woodhouse, and within days, Samuel More, commander of the Shropshire Parliamentarian forces, was appointed in his place. Only Shrewsbury and Ludlow were allowed garrisons thereafter and even Ludlow's was disbanded in 1655, only to be revived in 1659-60 during the uncertainty caused by Richard Cromwell's resignation. Under the Royalist governor Ludlow had suffered from the billeting of soldiers of the garrison; this problem continued, if on a lesser scale, under the Parliamentary governors. In 1648 there was a brief flurry when a Royalist plot to seize the castle was uncovered, but this was the only event to be noted during the Interregnum.[45]

The government of the Marches fell to the county committees and later to the major-generals. There was no place for the Council. Its personnel scattered. Several of its officials, including six under-secretaries of the Signet, became Royalist army officers and eventually suffered the penalties accorded to 'delinquents'. Lord President Bridgewater had already joined the king at Newcastle in 1639 and never returned, dying at his Herefordshire home in 1649. Secretary Goring had probably exercised his several appointments by deputy in any event; there is no evidence that he came anywhere near Ludlow before or after the abolition. Bridgewater continued to be appointed by the commissions of the peace in the counties of Wales while those areas were still under Royalist control, although there is no reason to suppose that he ever exercised any functions or even attended any sessions.[46] The reality was that, although the Council had political and administrative functions outside its (now lost) judicial functions, these were exercisable only in a settled and unified region, since much of what it used to do had been by way of influence, advice, mediation and intervention. Without a base, officials, income and general subordination to its wishes, it could not act as an effective body. As the counties formally under its control fell to Parliamentary forces or factions, even this ghost of its former activity was exorcised.

Less than three months after Charles II was restored to the throne, Richard Daulbin had been granted the office of clerk of the fines at a fee of £50 a year, despite the fact that the Council had not yet been formally re-established. A month later John Butts obtained the examinership there. It was not until January 1661, that the lord presidency was granted to Richard Vaughan, earl of Carbery, who was a son-in-law of the previous holder of that office, John Egerton, earl of Bridgewater. There was then a flurry of petitions asking for various offices in the Council—remembrancer, examiner, sergeant at arms, protonotary, yeoman of the wardrobe, clerk of the billets.[47] The Council was not re-established until a royal proclamation on 28 September 1661, although appointments to it were being made long before this. An orchestrated campaign of petitions, often in identical terms, from Gloucestershire and other places began in the summer of 1661 asking for the re-establishment of the court. Even Worcester, which in the 16th century had tried and failed to remove itself from the Council's jurisdiction, petitioned for its restoration to cut the cost of litigation. The circumstances of the petitions do not, however, suggest a wave of popularity; they resulted from a small number of persons hoping to gain from it.[48] Carbery was given an allowance of £1,106 13s 4d a year back-dated to 2 January that year; this was to be paid by the receivers of north and south Wales, but from what revenues is unclear. The proclamation declared the Council in the Marches of Wales to be established *and continued* by the king and to have full power to determine causes and complaints. It enjoined obedience and submission to its orders; possibly the draftsman had in mind the general disobedience to the court's orders which developed in 1640-1 when its status had been in doubt.[49] The wording of the proclamation implied perhaps deliberate ambiguity; did it establish the Council or merely declare its technical survival? Where there were 20-year old claims to offices this may have been important to some people.

Most of what is known about the working of the Council or of its court over the next 28 years concerns the continual jockeying for jobs, or, more precisely, for offices, since many of the successful applicants appointed deputies to carry out the duties. Applicants were happy to ask for very different offices, such as sergeant at arms or clerk of the billets, as alternatives, so demonstrating that it was the income therefrom which interested them, fitness for the particular duties being irrelevant. Offices were often granted with survivorship to other persons.[50] New councillors were appointed during 1662 to replace those long dead. The Crown, and everyone else, treated the Council as never having been abolished, which technically may have been the case. Its jurisdiction had been abolished in 1641, but no mention was made of its offices. After the Restoration applicants were anxious to show some family or other connexion with the previous holders, many of whom were now dead.[51] In 1667 Richard Daulbin was able to surrender the clerkship of the fines to his son, John.[52]

As they had been since the late 16th century, the offices of the Council were treated as a form of private property,[53] but it was increasingly so after the Restoration. In 1661 George Goring, earl of Norwich, who had been secretary, clerk of the Council (so keeping the records and taking fees for references to them) and clerk of the Signet (so taking fees for sealing almost all court paperwork) as long ago as 1630, was re-appointed secretary, and his son, Charles, clerk of the Council. The latter obtained both offices on the father's death in 1663. Henry Wynne, a lawyer, was made secretary, clerk of the Council and clerk of the Signet in trust for him with the liberty to appoint a deputy to perform the duties. The duties were apparently not performed well by John Lynne and after eight years he was replaced by Luke Clapham. A dispute arose which was settled, not on the quality of the services provided by the contenders, but upon the footing that Lynne's deputyship should not have survived the death of the first earl.[54] The reversion of these offices was granted in 1673 to Henry Bennet, earl

of Arlington, also in trust, since he came nowhere near Ludlow to carry out any duties.[55]

In 1672 Henry Somerset, marquess of Worcester, later duke of Somerset, became lord president, to remain in that office until the Revolution, when he was briefly replaced by Charles Gerard, earl of Macclesfield, the last lord president (and great-nephew of Thomas Gerard, equally briefly lord president in 1617).

The Restoration government, being very anxious about republican plots and risings, may have been prepared to countenance the Council's revival on security grounds. One of Carbery's first duties was to spend £2,000 on the repair and furnishing of Ludlow Castle, £100 of which was donated by the borough, wishing to ingratiate itself.[56] In March 1663, a small garrison was stationed at the castle, whose chief duties were to guard funds and ammunition for the Welsh militia.[57] Nevertheless Thomas Hunton, keeper of the wardrobe, complained in 1669 that Carbery had kept most of the funds he had been given, had neglected repairs and kept only half the soldiers paid for. Hunton however had personal axes to grind.[58] The Council, either as a body, or through its members individually, was expected to oversee the politics of the region, as it had a century earlier. Beaufort kept a close watch on the 'insolent' Whigs of Leominster in 1683, and in 1688 was asked to propose the names of men to be chosen for parliament.[59]

The judicial records of the Council have not survived in the State archives (apart from those for 1616-37 which are in the British Library) so not much is known about the working of the court. That so many offices were filled by deputies who would have drawn smaller salaries than the offices carried, suggests that either second-rate people were employed or fees charged were excessive. The court was an equity court, for a page of the royal bedchamber complained in 1674 that he had been granted £120 from the duty of 2d levied at Ludlow on every defendant in equity proceedings.[60] The public were unlikely to have enjoyed a good service.

As Wales and the Marches attained social standards enjoyed elsewhere, the argument for a separate judicial structure became weaker. Hostility from Westminster lawyers was unlikely to have been less than it had been 50 years earlier and the Revolution provided an opportunity to bring about the end of the Council.

The fate of the Council was not immediately sealed in April 1689 for the new king ordered Macclesfield to instal John Trenchard as chief justice at Ludlow; but by May the House of Lords was considering its fate.[61] The 'Act for taking away the Court holden before the President and Council of the March of Wales'[62] was a short one, consisting mostly of preamble, reciting the establishment of the court by the Act of 1543, and stating that the 'proceedings and decrees of that court have by experience been found to be an intolerable burthen to the subject'. It declared that this provision of the 1543 Act was repealed, effectively from 1 June 1689. That the court had already been abolished by Statute in 1640 and re-established by proclamation in 1661 was not mentioned, nor was the technical position that the Council might have had an existence separate from that of the court. The Council ceased with this Act.

CHAPTER IX

The Civil War

by Jeremy Knight

When the newly raised army of Charles I left Shrewsbury for the Edgehill campaign in October 1642, 'The town of Shrewsbury, and all that good county … he intrusted only to that good spirit that then possessed it, and to the legal authority of the shirers and justices of the peace. And it fared … as in all other parts of the kingdom, that the number of those who desired to sit still was greater than of those who desired to engage of either party; so that they were generally inclined to articles of neutrality.'[1] If Shropshire, like other Marcher counties, was Royalist country, Ronald Hutton has made clear in his *The Royalist War Effort* that at the outset only a militant few sought to bring its community to war.[2] The county justices were specifically 'Of the Peace', and their primary duty was to maintain that peace. Once the die had been cast, however, there were reasons (quite apart from his armed presence) why the area favoured the king. There was a strong Catholic recusant community, and, more significantly, a conservative regard for traditional forms of religion and popular culture.[3] Attempts by Westminster to impose radical change (of whatever political hue) affecting the customary ways of people in such areas will inevitably meet with a degree of resistance. In June 1642 'At Loudlow [local Royalists] set up a May Pole and a thinge like a head on it … and gathered a great many about it, and shot at it in deristion of roundheads.'[4] Such 'popular' demonstrations may not have been wholly sponta-

neous, but May games, church ales and Sunday sports had attracted particular hostility from Puritans. The conflicting cultures were seen again when a London Roundhead regiment attended morning service in Hereford Cathedral that October. 'The pipes played and the puppets sang so sweetly, that some of our soldiers could not forbear dauncing in the holy quire; whereat the Baalists were sore displeased.'[5]

The local Puritan community seems to have been small and compact. Sir Robert Harley used the newly established Ludlow post to send 'advertisements of the proceedings of the Parliament' to the bailiff of Ludlow, for 'the puritan party' of the neighbourhood.[6] Nehemiah Wharton, the London Puritan officer quoted above, claimed that there were only three supporters of Parliament in the whole city of Hereford, though one man who stared rudely at a local Puritan outside Ludlow church and cried 'Roundhead' found himself knocked down and beaten with a cudgel snatched from a bystander.[7] At a more popular level, pre-war resistance to de-afforestation and interference with traditional rights of common under royal grant had brought many forest edge communities into sharp conflict with local grandees and with the Crown, as in Wentwood Forest in Monmouthshire, and in the Forest of Dean.[8] The wooded and upland areas of Shropshire and Hereford were to be Clubmen territory late in the war.

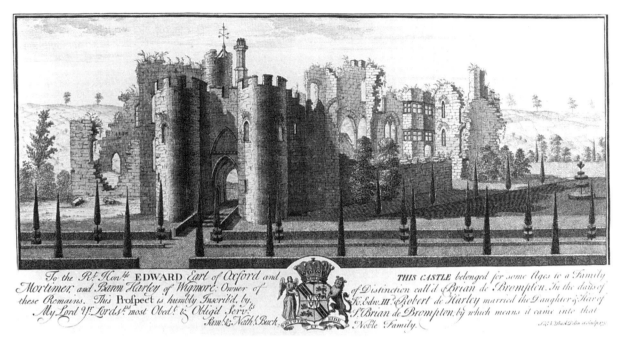

Fig. 1 Buck's engraving of Brampton Bryan Castle

In a sense, the story of Ludlow Castle in the Civil War is a short one. Garrisoned for the King at the outset, its governor surrendered on terms when it was obvious that, nationally, further resistance was hopeless.

After the stalemate of Edgehill in October 1642 (as in a much later war, many thought that it would all be over by Christmas), both sides prepared for new efforts in the spring.[9] When Lord Capel was made lieutenant general of the Royalist forces in north Wales and Shropshire in March 1643, he brought with him a professional soldier, Michael Woodhouse, who had served in Ireland, as sergeant-major general, with a commission to raise a regiment of foot for the King's field army among the gentry of north Wales and their tenants. The regiment raised, Woodhouse's Bluecoats, fought at the siege of Gloucester and at the first battle of Newbury, where it took heavy casualties and where Woodhouse was knighted in the field for bravery.

Orders were given for the defences of Ludlow to be strengthened,[10] and whilst Woodhouse was away the town was left in charge of Lt. Colonel John Marrow, a professional soldier newly arrived from Ireland. In late September, Woodhouse's

Bluecoats returned to Shropshire with Sir Richard Herbert's regiment and was put into garrison at Ludlow, where Herbert became governor. The following month, however, Capel's little field army was defeated at Wem by Sir William Brereton. Marrow now took command of a cavalry regiment formerly commanded by Lord Cholmondeley, which he led like 'a second Nimrod' until he and his regiment were ambushed and destroyed near Northwich in the following August.[11] When Prince Rupert, the new regional commander, re-organized Royalist garrisons in April 1644, Richard Herbert became governor of Aberystwyth and was replaced at Ludlow by Woodhouse. Montgomery Castle was, unusually, left in the charge of its civilian owner, Lord Herbert of Chirbury, Richard Herbert's father.

We know the names of 16 officers of Woodhouse's Bluecoats known to have been in Ludlow garrison, and can probably add a few more, but sources do not specifically indicate whether they are members of the regiment; other regiments were also present at times, such as Richard Herbert's.[12] About half were from north and central Wales, the remainder were locally recruited Shropshire men. There is also a list of

25 'Ludlow delinquents'—townsmen who served as royalist officers and who had to compound after the end of the Civil War to retain their property. Four 'took arms for the defence of Ludlow', one of whom, Captain Richard Phillips, certainly served in Woodhouse's Regiment, as did Major John Williams, a Brecon man, who exacerbated his offence by cursing Parliament as 'rebels and rogues'. Thomas Fisher not only raised an infantry company in Ludlow, but brought ordnance from Bringwood Forge to defend the castle. William Colbatch and Charles Hawkins were in the garrison of Stoke(say) Castle and Thomas and Roger Powis were at the siege of Brampton Bryan, the home of Sir Robert Harley, but others in the list may have served in other regiments.[13] Three other local men, accused of training royalist troops, denied this, and pleaded that, living as they did in Ludlow, they had been forced by the governor to collect tax contributions.[14]

The Welsh saying that anything irrevocably lost had 'gone to Caerphilly' illustrates an aspect of castles often ignored by military historians. The impact of garrisons, even on individuals uninvolved in military affairs, can often be glimpsed in diaries or petitions—hay crops burnt (sometimes by both sides), cattle and horses carried off or 'half diminished ... by soldiery or murrain', houses looted, neighbours murdered by soldiers, gentry imprisoned for failure to collect tax arrears or their estates confiscated on malicious claims that they had been 'Papists in Arms'. This catalogue, taken from the recorded experiences of just two Monmouthshire men[15] can be matched in the Ludlow area. Humphrey Walcot of Walcot near Clun was imprisoned by the Royalists in Ludlow Castle until he ransomed himself with a large sum of money. He later pleaded that he had only done this in self defence 'to save his estate from utter ruin', but still faced a further heavy fine from Parliament as an alleged 'delinquent'. Edward Vernon similarly had to pay £500 to the Royalists to free himself from imprisonment at Ludlow.[16]

At the beginning of 1644, Prince Rupert was created regional commander for north Wales and the northern Marches, with the rank of captain-general. From the outset, his firm but diplomatic handling of local affairs contrasted with the harsh approach of the two professional soldiers, Michael Woodhouse and John Mennes, that he had sent ahead of him to Shrewsbury.[17] Clarendon claimed that the King had entrusted the county to its legally appointed civil magistrates, but these got short shrift if they challenged any of the diktats of Rupert's two Cavalier officers.

In the spring, Rupert's subordinates cleared most of the Marches of Parliamentary garrisons. In Shropshire, only Wem held out. Brampton Bryan, west of Ludlow, had successfully withstood a siege from July to September 1643 under Lady Brilliana Harvey. On a rumour that the Royalists now intended to blockade it closely by a garrison at Hopton Castle, the governor of Brampton Bryan (where Lady Harley had now died) put a garrison of about 20 men into Hopton on 18 February under a local man, Captain Samuel More of Linley. In early March,

Fig. 2 Lady Brilliana Harley

Woodhouse attacked Hopton, but was repulsed with heavy losses following a rash frontal attack on the castle, losing two officers of his regiment—Major Henry Vaughan and Captain Thomas Vaughan of Burlton. Woodhouse then brought up two heavy cannon and mined below the small keep, forcing the garrison to surrender. Their subsequent murder in circumstances of cold blooded brutality was long remembered, 'Hopton Quarter' (there was none) became proverbial. Woodhouse could have argued that technically, under the laws of war, his action was justified, for the garrison had refused an offer of quarter, whilst the Royalist Lord Byron had set a bloody precedent when he massacred the garrison at Barthomley in Cheshire a few months before. Only Samuel More was spared, which led to peculiar consequences. He was freed in exchange for Edward Cressett of Upton Cressett,[18] and rejoined the Parliamentary forces. When Woodhouse subsequently had to yield up Ludlow, one condition on which he insisted was that he should not have to surrender to More, by then governor of Montgomery Castle. He was later to become governor of Ludlow.

Meanwhile, Woodhouse went on to besiege Brampton Bryan. He may have learnt caution from Hopton, for though he undermined the walls, he did not attempt to storm them. His men may also have had their morale damaged by their losses at Hopton, for during one sally by the garrison, officers and men alike fled from the siege-works. 'All deserve to be hanged' growled Woodhouse to Rupert. Only after More, then a prisoner at Ludlow, had been persuaded to write to Lt. Col. Wright at Brampton Bryan advising surrender did they yield. On 17 April, Woodhouse reported to Rupert 'The place delivered up, giving the rebels their lives'. The castle was burnt down and the prisoners taken to Ludlow, where 'The inhabitants of Ludlow baited us like bears' reported one of them 'and demanded where our God was'.[19] The Harley children stayed at Ludlow until May, when they then went to London.

This was Woodhouse's last field campaign. As governor of Ludlow, he set about improving the defences with characteristic disregard for the unfortunate townspeople. Though locals who later claimed that their aid to the Royalist war effort had been under compulsion were trying to avoid ruinous fines for 'delinquency', their claims that living as they did in Ludlow, they had little choice in the matter, rings true. It was common enough for commanders to burn standing hay and corn to deny them to the enemy, or to pasture horses on growing grass, but Woodhouse went one better. A Ludlow widow had the turf stripped from her meadow for use in the fortifications, leaving only bare earth. Someone else, having already lost his three horses, had his spade taken for use in digging new fortifications, leaving him with no means of tilling the ground, and a wife, family and billeted soldier to support.[20] Woodhouse's exactions on the north Welsh cattle drovers who passed through Ludlow even drew protests from the

Fig. 3 Hopton Castle

86

archbishop of York.[21] Such actions were counter-productive, for destitute civilians could not provide the taxes necessary to pay the garrisons. As the war proceeded, there was increasing desperation on all sides—from military commanders, from taxpayers, and from unpaid soldiers. When disaster struck in September, however, it was from an unexpected quarter.

Montgomery Castle had been left in charge of Sir Richard Herbert's father, Lord Herbert of Chirbury. He was a retired diplomat, elderly and in poor health, and had a garrison of some 30 men with few provisions. On 5 September Sir Thomas Myddleton appeared before the castle with 200 horse and 500 foot, demanding its surrender.[22] Richard Herbert wrote to Prince Rupert that his father hoped to hold out until help came, but he actually surrendered the same day.[23] Samuel More, the survivor of the Hopton Castle massacre, became governor. In view of his own experiences, it is interesting that he signed and witnessed a document setting out the reasons why Lord Herbert had surrendered the castle, for by that stage in the war, it was not unknown for Royalist commanders who surrendered without good cause to be shot.[24]

The Royalists immediately responded. Lord Byron drew troops from neighbouring garrisons, including Ludlow, in an attempt to recover the castle, adding to them five of Ormonde's Irish regiments, as well as Rupert's and Byron's own regiments. This provided a force of a total of around 2,000 foot and 1,500 horse with which he then laid siege to the castle. On 18 September, facing an equally matched Parliamentary force under Myddleton, the Royalist field army was lost when the Lancashire horse broke at the Battle of Montgomery, leaving the infantry to their fate. 'Not 100 foot came off' admitted the Royalist Colonel Trefor.[25] Well over a thousand were captured, and the large quantities of somewhat obsolete armour recovered from the inner ditch of the castle during excavation had probably belonged to the Irish foot.[26] The last Royalist army in the west was destroyed.

The Tudor president of the Council in the Marches, Bishop Rowland Lee, had described Montgomery Castle as the 'second key of Wales', Ludlow being the first.[27] With Montgomery lost, and the Royalist field army destroyed, Ludlow was vulnerable. The defeat had also removed Woodhouse's ability to supply his garrison from the surrounding countryside, as he himself admitted.[28] One Ludlow officer complained that after Montgomery 'the malignancy which has lain in many men's hearts has now burst forward to a manifest expression'.[29] Nevertheless, there was no immediate threat. Indeed the following February Prince Maurice drew a Royalist force from various garrisons, including Ludlow, to raise the siege of Chester, but in the same month, whilst Maurice was still in Cheshire, Shrewsbury fell to a surprise attack from Wem.[30]

In June 1645 Woodhouse's outpost at Stokesay Castle fell, blocking in Ludlow from the north-west. Woodhouse drew in reinforcements from the Royalist garrisons from Monmouth up to Worcester, and tried to re-take Stokesay, but was defeated by the Shropshire Parliamentary forces on 9 June, a week before the king's final disaster at Naseby. Caus and Shrawardine were abandoned, their garrisons presumably being drawn in to strengthen Woodhouse's depleted forces at Ludlow.[31] By this stage in the war, both Woodhouse at Ludlow and Lord Charles Somerset at Raglan were resorting to large scale cavalry raids on newly won Parliamentary territory, in an attempt to regain the initiative. In September 1645, a raiding party of 140 of the Ludlow garrison under Colonel Davelier, a Florentine professional soldier who, like Woodhouse, had served in the Irish wars, were routed outside Bishop's Castle, but despite this setback, in the following January the 'Ragland and Ludlow Horse' were still proving 'very active'.[32]

It was not until 24 April 1646 that Sir William Brereton and Colonel John Birch's army, made up of soldiers based at Hereford where Birch was governor, strengthened by local forces, approached Ludlow. Woodhouse began destroying the suburbs in preparation for a siege, but before he could finish his work, Brereton was upon him.[33] Birch invested Ludlow in his normal businesslike way, requesting 'three whole culverins with their equipages' from Gloucester, and defeating a Royalist relieving force drawn from the garrisons of Worcester, Madresfield and Goodrich.[34] By 20 May, Woodhouse was ready to treat for terms. He was unwilling to surrender to the local men, led by Samuel More, presumably because of the episode at Hopton Castle, and this led to much rancour between Birch and the 'Shropshire men'.[35] According to Birch's secretary, Woodhouse, 'expecting fair terms ... out of knowledge of the said Colonell [Birch] and others there [presumably Brereton] yielded sooner than otherwise he needed.'[36] It appears that Woodhouse, a professional soldier, took a realistic view of the situation and sought the best terms available. On about 26 May the garrison marched out.[37] Birch had apparently already left for the siege of Goodrich, and had to return for the surrender. A number of Royalists were later to claim to the sequestration committee that they were protected by these 'Ludlow articles'.[38] Woodhouse left to join the exiled court in the Hague. One of Cromwell's agents reported him visiting Queen Henrietta Maria in Paris in March 1647, but thereafter there is no trace. He may have died in exile.[39]

Governors of Ludlow Castle continued to be appointed under the Commonwealth, though in 1653 most of the arms and ammunition were removed and sent to Hereford for safekeeping.[40] In July 1659, in the political crisis after the abdication of Oliver Cromwell's son, Richard, William Botterell was ordered to garrison Ludlow with 100 men, but the following year found himself petitioning parliament for the 'considerable arrears' of pay that resulted.[41] Even after the Restoration, there was much unfinished political business, as the various plots and alleged plots of Charles II's reign showed. Castles like Chepstow and Ludlow still had a part to play in local security. In 1663-5 a small garrison was put into Ludlow under the Earl of Carbery, as lord lieutenant of Wales, with Henry Herbert commanding a company of foot. This was ostensibly 'for securing of the militia money, and the plate and jewels kept there' or for 'the safety of plate, furniture etc there', but only when this little garrison was stood down did the story of Ludlow and the Civil War really end.[42]

CHAPTER X

The Castle in Decline

by Pat Hughes

The ruinous shell that is Ludlow Castle to-day provides little understanding of the activity, the colour and the importance of the 17th century site. Some idea of the luxury and importance of the castle in its heyday can be gained from the inventory made of the goods 'belonging to the late King' which, after the surrender of the castle in June 1646, were sold at Ludlow in 1650 by the Commonwealth.[1] A careful study of the inventory shows that, while many of the more valuable and portable items had already been removed, the beds with their hangings and particularly the wall coverings indicate the standard of living in the castle, as does the great number of chambers dedicated to officials and servants of all sorts.

The clerk who took the inventory seems to have started in the Solar block, at the west end of the Hall and worked his way round the building in an anti-clockwise direction. He came first to the Prince's chambers, the suite of rooms on the top floor, where Prince Arthur and his ill-fated wife, Katherine of Aragon once lived. These contained the grandest furniture, a bed covered with watered damask, valued, with its bedding, at £36 10s. The walls were hung with tapestries worth £15 and the andirons had brass knobs. In the same part, the shovelboard room had walls covered with 'green carsey [a woollen cloth] hangings paned with gilt leather', valued at £25. Below these were the lodgings of the gentlemen ushers, and, between the Solar block and the kitchen, was a range which seems to have accom-modated the secretary and the steward. The clerk to the kitchen had a room over the kitchen.

The clerk then skipped the service rooms to deal with what he termed the governor's quarters—the lodging of the judges of the Council in the Marches—which adjoined the gate to the inner bailey. The governor's quarters boasted tapestry hangings, darnix or dornix (a woven patterned woollen material) hangings, three beds with green curtains, Turkey work chair coverings and window curtains.

The clerk then went back to the Great Kitchen, Brewhouse, 'Wetthouse', Bakehouse and Coalhouse. The wethouse was probably near or over the well, while the great oven in the bakehouse can still be seen in the south-west corner of the courtyard. In the same area there was a laundry and dairy and sundry rooms above. There was also a chamber above the porch to the chapel.

The Hall, council chamber, withdrawing room and the private chambers of the lord president of the Marches were all in the range on the north side of the inner bailey. The Hall had, in addition to the necessary tables, chairs and forms, 'two wooden figures of beasts', while the withdrawing room walls were covered with watered cloth paned with gilt leather. There were two pictures of the late king and his queen. The constable's rooms and the marshal's lodgings were probably in the keep.

It has been said that Ludlow Castle never recovered from the Civil War, and this appears to be the case. The short-lived reinstatement of the Council in the Marches after the Restoration failed to restore it to its former glory, and, after the Council had been abolished in 1689 the castle began to fall into disrepair. Still in the possession of the Crown, the castle was left in the hands of 'governors', half-pay officers, who lived in a few of the rooms and who seem to have been able to do what they liked with the fabric.[2] An inventory taken in 1708 shows how far the castle had already slipped into decay.[3] The impression gained is that only three main rooms were in use in the Hall range—the president's with-drawing room, the president's bed-chamber with the adjoining servant's room, and the ladies with-drawing room. The with-drawing room was still quite grand and the 'watered cloth' on the walls had been replaced by gilt leather panels of which one piece was missing. There were 11 gilt chairs, an elbow chair and four tables, but two of the four sconces were 'broke'. Of seven chairs in the council chamber, three were broken, the looking glass in 'my Lord's closet' was cracked and the bedstead in the servant's room next to the closet, rotten. Prince Arthur's room held, instead of the grand bedstead, a grey stuff bed, the featherbeds were 'gutted' and, in place of the tapestries, the room was 'hanged with green'. The cellar held 18 stinking hogsheads, and six butts, six hogsheads with their heads out, one leather chair, one large broken tundish, one table, and one broken bedstead.

In the Judges' Lodgings only one room, the second judge's chamber, was adequately furnished for use, while the marshal's lodgings in the keep, parlour, kitchen and rooms over, contained basic furniture, but no bedding other than torn sheets. Some of the rooms, furnishings and all, had apparently just been abandoned and their contents left to rot and to the mice.

There is some indication that, even at this date, part of the range between the Solar block and the great kitchen had ceased to be used and may even have been partly demolished. Only two rooms are listed in this area, the chief justice's room and that of his servant, both obviously unoccupied and filled with old, broken or rotten furniture.

The decay of the castle was accelerated, according to the antiquarian Thomas Wright, by an order for unroofing the buildings and stripping them of their lead, made soon after the accession of George I in 1715. Wright claimed that this move 'was quickly followed by the decay of the floors and other parts constructed of wood, and by the plunder of the furniture'.[4] This may have been the sight that greeted Daniel Defoe when he visited Ludlow in the early 1720s. He described how 'the Castle itself is the very perfection of decay, all the fine courts, the royal apartments, halls and rooms of state, lye open, abandoned and some of them falling down; for since the Courts of the President and Marches are taken away, here is nothing to do that requires the attendance of any publick people; so that time, the great devourer of the works of men, begins to eat into the very stone walls, and spread the face of royal ruins over the whole fabrick'.[5]

The destruction, however shocking to Defoe, was still not in any way complete. Even in the 1760s a later travel writer, Francis Grose, claimed that Hall and chapel still contained panelling and that the Hall was decorated with 'lances, spears, fire-locks and old armour'. Another visitor, in 1768, stated that 'the floor of the great council chamber was then pretty entire, as was the stair-case. The covered steps leading to the chapel were remaining, but the covering of the chapel was fallen; yet the arms of some of the lords president were visible'.[6]

The last of the 'governors' was a man called Alexander Stuart, who was credited with pulling down and selling large portions of the fabric. One later report (1829) claimed that 'Old Mr. Andrew Stuart, a half-pay Army Captain was Governor … He shockingly delapidated the Castle and sold the materials he purloined, as I believe, living Persons remember'.[7] The name is wrongly given but the feeling of outrage is clear. Certainly, by the 1760s most of the buildings in the service court had disappeared. The outer bailey had been partitioned and half made into a bowling green, 'originally for the recreation of the inhabitants of Ludlow, but for many years the Bowling Green has been converted to another use'. Some of the stone went to the building of the Bowling Green Inn, a small public house, erected 'many years ago'.[8]

In the early 1760s the earl of Powis, who had been Member of Parliament for Ludlow, cast his eye on the castle and, in 1765, required the architect, Thomas Farnolls Pritchard of Shrewsbury, to make a series of drawings and plans showing the walls and the adjacent buildings in some detail. Six years later the earl applied to the Crown for a lease of the castle for 50 years and caused something of a stir. There has been considerable speculation about the his plans for the premises, some holding that he intended to dismantle the building and sell off the materials. However, a bundle of papers in the Public Record Office sheds a rather different light upon the matter. A government report made in 1811, and quoting earlier papers stated that: 'The motive which the late Lord Powis assigned for applying for that lease was his desire to erect a House on the said Ground for his own Residence, at a considerable expense, which would be an improvement to the Land Revenue'.[9] Another report, also of 1811, states that: 'His Lordship proposed to build himself a residence within the Scite with the aid of the Materials of the Ruins of the Castle'. Yet another memo made in 1829 adds to this: 'I suspect that he had an intention to make it his occasional residence on having parted with Oakley Park, but he died in 1772'.[10]

In the event, when Lord Powis applied for a lease, the surveyor general looked through his files and could find no information about Ludlow Castle, 'finding no Account of the Premises in his Office, he caused a Survey to be made thereof'.[11] The name of the surveyor chosen by the government is not recorded on the plan or survey of the castle, now in the Public Record Office, but Wright states that 'a surveyor from Shrewsbury , named Pritchard was employed to value it' and there seems no reason to doubt his information.[12] Certainly a plan and survey of the castle was commissioned and was duly delivered in 1771.[13]

The plan is of interest, but the detailed survey of the state of the castle, taken with the plans and the 1765 drawings, is most enlightening. The main gate from the town was then described as 'the Entrance of the Castle at a Tower', and must

have been a much more impressive introduction to the castle than the present shell of a building. Even in 1771 it was 'extremely ruinous … the upper parts daily trickling down and scarce can the Old Gates be made fast to enclose the Castle'.

What is now part of the reception area was once the prison. Only the outer walls remained. 'The Cross walls are almost down without Roof or Walls'. The stables, next door, fared slightly better. They retained a first floor and a roof 'in bad condition half Thatched half slated'. Some maintenance had obviously been done by the tenant, Mr. Hill, of the Bowling Green House, who used it as a stable. Beyond these buildings, in the angle of the wall, was once a tower and a sally port. In 1771 this was 'Reduced to Low Burr Walls in Bad Condition'. Now no trace exists above ground.

The 'Offices for the Inferior Courts of Law', re-modelled in the 16th century from St. Peter's Chapel, had lost all roofing and had 'only a few Rubble Walls standing'. They were being used as part garden, part wood store or 'Faggot Yard'. The Dinan Gate, one of the town entrances was in a 'very indifferent State'. The survey of the outer bailey finished with a look at Mortimer's Tower. At a slightly later date this tower was rebuilt and became a dwelling, but at this stage it was without floors or roof, although the rear part had been reinforced with a cross-wall.

The main castle buildings were in no better shape. The bridge across the ditch had no parapet walls and the state of the Judges' Lodging was a cause for horror. The roofing and floors of these buildings had almost all fallen in and rotted away and what remained hung 'impending in a frightful and dangerous manner'.

The keep, 'the Old Tower on the left hand side the Gateway', had no roof and the internal walls were disintegrating, but one floor was more or less intact and some of the timberwork below this was still preserved. Beyond the keep, the service area had virtually disappeared. The tower containing the oven still stood—the measurement was noted as 16ft x 14ft—but the well was blocked up with rubbish and the kitchen walls were down to 'a low Height'. Only the arch of the

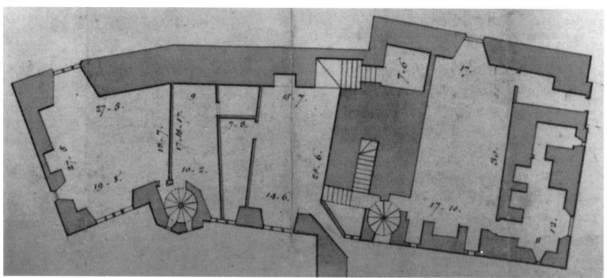

Pritchard's plans of 1765 showing Fig. 2 the 'Plan of the Chamber Story of the Gatehouse, together with Fig. 1 the south elevation (top) and Fig. 3 north elevation with the great oven to the right (bottom)

kitchen chimney, and the oven and chimney in the pastry remained to mark the place where there was once such bustle and activity.

The description of the hall range is evocative. 'The principal part of the Body of the Castle formerly containing the Hall, Council Chamber and other apartments—Now in so ruinated condition that it is dangerous to go under the Walls, and the small part of the Roof that remains is hanging and just supported by a few Braces. There are some large Timbers and pieces of Lead fallen from the Roof in this place with a few Iron Barrs in the Windows. The Walls are mostly Rubble and the Battlements greatly decayed'.

The chapel, which remains such a feature of the castle, was already a total ruin. The chancel had disappeared and the round entrance porch was roofless. 'The Walls at top are craggy and in places fallen. The Doorway and a few small Pillars with Arches over them being rather perfect are the only Ornament about the Castle'.

A graphic, if fragmentary, picture of the castle in the 1760s and 70s can be ascertained by comparing the 1771 description with the drawings that Pritchard had made seven years before. The outer bailey was of no apparent interest to the earl of Powis; his concern started with the inner gate, the outer walls of the keep and the judges' apartments. These buildings retained most of their window mullions and possibly some glass, but although the roof of the judges' apartments looked more or less intact from the outer bailey, the views from the other side show that little of the roof was left and the timbers were indeed rotted and dangerous as described in the survey.

The inner views of these apartments, looking south are not completely consistent; one, (opposite) shows the façade with rafters and purlins, in the other (below) no timbers are visible. In the illustrations opposite the little stair turret, crowned with a pepper-pot roof is complete; that below shows the same turret with cracked masonry and little of the roof surviving. Even the foliage hiding much of the keep is different and suggests that the drawings were produced on two occasions, separated by a period of time. A later watercolour (see overleaf) shows further decay.

Pritchard's drawing of the hall and Council chamber range differs little superficially from what can be seen to-day, although, once again, some of the windows appear to be glazed, the battlements and chimneys are more or less complete—the extent of the 'decay' mentioned in the survey is not visible—and all the tracery survives in the windows. 'The small part of the roof that remains' cannot be seen, being hidden behind the battlements.

The state of the service area can only be deduced from the plan accompanying the drawings. This shows the outline of the kitchen, more than exists today, and also includes the pastry chimney and oven. The great oven, now hardly more than a hole in the wall, is shown opposite. The chapel likewise only appears on the plan.

The government, alerted by the earl's interest in this forgotten asset on the Welsh

Fig. 4 Pritchard's alternative drawing of the Judges' Lodgings showing the north elevation in greater disrepair

Fig. 5 A watercolour of 1789 shows the deterioration of the Judge's Lodgings to be continuing. The roofs have gone and presumably it is their timbers that litter the bailey

borders, were obviously considering its economic potential. Would the sale of the stone off-set the cost of demolishing the castle and developing or selling the site? It has been suggested that Pritchard minimised the value of the castle in order to preserve it, but it is also likely that he wanted to further the schemes of his noble patron, the earl of Powis. Pritchard's emphasis on the dreadful state of the fabric and the cost that would be incurred if demolition took place was certainly intended to deter the government from pulling the place down. The letter from the Ludlow lawyer, Somerset Davies, which was attached to the survey, emphasised this view, indicating that there would be 'some advantage to the crown to be relieved of such an unprofitable charge'. Both men most likely stood to gain if the earl succeeded in renting the castle and built a house at Ludlow.[14]

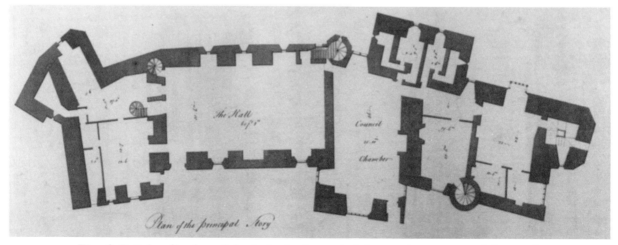

Fig. 6 Pritchard's plan of the 'principal story' of the northern range of the castle

Fig. 7 Pritchard's drawing of the south elevation of the northern end of the castle

The Crown authorities were not convinced. They claimed that 'the land was of greater value than the building' and offered a lease for 31 years only at a rate of £20 12s with 'convertible old materials' at £7 10s, making a total of £28 2s. The lease was made out to the earl of Powis, with an expiry date of 30 June 1803, but although the lease was duly executed, the earl died in 1772 and the projected house was never built. The governor apparently continued in place and the rent was paid to him until 1785. After this date it was collected by the 'Receiver for Salop' on behalf of the Inland Revenue.[15]

In contrast to the attitude of the government, anxious to obtain as much money as possible from the site, the Powis family seem to have cared for the place. The trustees and the countess took responsibility for its upkeep and set out to improve the site. The accounts for 1784 - 1811 survive in various versions and indicate the involvement of the family with the castle.[16] Their first action was to lay out paths on the castle mound above the river, and open the site to the townspeople, as a place to indulge the fashionable pastime of strolling with their friends. Trees were planted to soften the bleak profile of the castle and, by 1798, when the castle was painted by Turner, had grown to some height. The accounts show yearly payments for cleaning the walks and maintaining them with gravel, for providing and repairing gates and seats and, eventually, in 1799, for fencing the walks with wooden railings. At the same time the more obvious faults in the castle were remedied, starting in 1785 with the repair of the gateway tower. Walls which fell down were rebuilt on various occasions and the inside of the castle tidied up and levelled.

After so much investment in the castle, and particularly after their efforts in laying out the grounds and walks, the Powis trustees expected

Fig. 8 Pritchard's 'North West View of Ludlow Castle'

to be able to renew the lease without difficulty, and when the fifth earl died unmarried in January 1801, they applied for a new lease in the name of Lord Clive, who had married the earl's sister and heir. There appears to have been no formal reply to this application, although, it seems, preparations for a survey were put in hand. In September 1803, however, there was a new development; Mr. Probert (executor and trustee for the late earl) sent a letter, via his solicitor Mr. Ryder, to the Office of the Commissioners of Woods, the government body then responsible for the castle, telling them how Lady Clive was shocked to discover that:

> some person had lately been making a survey of Ludlow Castle, and that she was told they were from the Barrack Office that survey in order to convert the Castle to a Depot for French Prisoners of War and Mr. Probert in his letter desired Mr. Ryder to enquire of Mr. Harrison [the deputy surveyor general] whether the persons who had surveyed the Castle were sent for the Inland Revenue Office to make that survey preparatory to the renewal of the Lease of the Castle for which he had applied or whether he knew any thing of an intention on the part of Government to employ it as a depot for prisoners.[17]

The concern of the countess that the castle should remain with the family was clearly stated.

In the same letter Mr. Probert expressed an anxious desire to retain the castle as an appendage to the Powis property 'now possessed by my Lord Clive', and mentioned that Lord Powis 'had been at some expense in planting and decorating the Ground belonging to the castle as a Public Walk for the accomodation (sic) of the inhabitants of Ludlow'.

It appears that the action of the Barrack Office was as much a surprise to Mr. Harrison as it was to Lady Clive. He claimed that he had 'not till that moment' heard of the scheme and 'had no reason to suppose that Mr. Telford, who had been engaged to survey it [the castle] for the Land Revenue Office would have made the survey without apprising him of his going thither'.

Accordingly Harrison set off with Ryder for the Barrack Office to ascertain the truth of the matter. Once there he was informed that the castle had

> indeed been surveyed by their Officers, on an order from the Commander-in-Chief, and was shown a very minute plan which had been taken of it and the reports of the Assistant Barrack Master General who had viewed it and who stated it to be one of the fittest and most commodious places for the purpose of a Depot for prisoners of war that he had ever seen - and - from the reports & the information of the gentlemen of the Barrack Office there appeared to be every reason to believe that it would be employed for that purpose.[18]

A copy of the letter from the assistant barrack master general survives among the correspondence regarding Ludlow Castle. Written on 29 August 1803, it describes how Mr. Boyd, the surveyor has been 'employed since Day-light' and how he 'thinks that the present buildings, if roofed in, might be made to contain about Three Thousand Prisoners and, by the addition of other buildings, to be erected against the Walls, One thousand more'. Mr. Boyd had more plans for the rest of the castle.

> There is a circular Building in the Centre, Twenty Eight feet diameter, formerly a Chapel the lower part of which may be Converted into a cooking house, and the upper into a Guard room, in the same manner as the Block house at Norman Cross.
> On the outside of the Ditch (which is dry) is a space with a range of outhouses and Stables chiefly uncovered which might readily be converted into a barracks for a Regiment at least (with some additions) and Water is conveyed into the interior by pipes from an adjacent Hill, sufficient, as I am told, for every purpose; there is also a river at a very short distance. The Wells are all choaked up, but probably there would not be occasion for them.

The report ends: 'The property of the Castle, from what I hear, but cannot rely on, is in

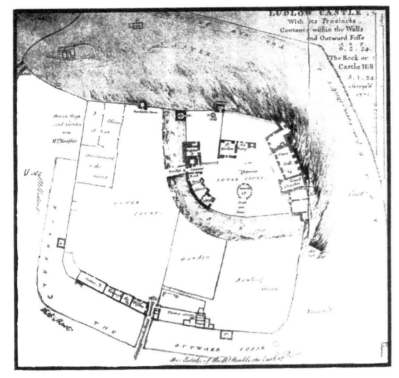

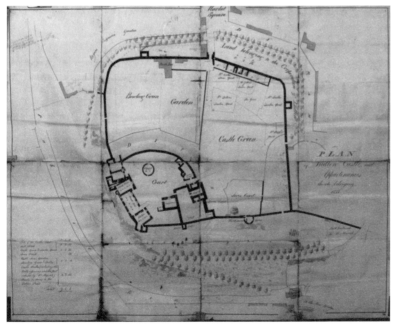

Fig. 9 The plan of 1771, now in the Public Record Office (top), and Fig. 10 that of 1811 (below)

This was the report shown to Messrs. Harrison and Ryder and they concluded that the staff of the Barrack Office had been very badly briefed and 'prior to the survey knew very little about the property or tenure of the Castle'. Not until they were 'on the spot' had they discovered the government involvement or the nature of the agreement with the Powis family.

It is something of an anti-climax to find that no further action was taken on the matter. The Barrack Office did not proceed with their truly horrendous plans for housing upwards of 4,000 men within the castle's draughty and crumbling fabric, but neither was the necessary lease granted to Lord Clive. It may be that inter-departmental strife delayed any resolution of the problem. The Commissioners for Woods would hardly be pleased to have their property commandeered and a rash of temporary buildings run up on the premises.

The situation remained static until December 1810, when Lord Clive, by this time created earl of Powis, applied either for a continuation of the lease or for permission to purchase the property. The Commissioners for Woods conceded that no new lease had been made and wrote to the Barrack Office asking for a copy of the plans made in 1803. In a manner that seems typical of the organisation, they received no answer for some time, but in January, after some pressure, the Barrack Office replied they 'they are sorry the plans are no longer in the office' and suggested the commissioners apply elsewhere. The Inland Revenue, when asked, claimed that 'the plan before alluded to has been given to some other office'. In the end a

Government. Lord Powis had lately the custody, on his demise it reverted to Lord Clive, but by what means or on what terms, or by what right I am unable to account'.

third plan, and accompanying report, had to be prepared, but still delays occurred. Mr. Haycock, the Shrewsbury surveyor commissioned by the Office of Works to draw up the plan, wrote to Mr, Probert that these were due to the 'inclemency of the weather' and his own 'slight indisposition'.[19] This third plan is now in the Shropshire Record Office.[20]

After reiterating the history of the leases made to the earls of Powis, the 1811 report relates some of the developments that had taken place in the castle over the previous 40 years and it is apparent that any repair work must have been superficial. The walls were still regarded as being 'in a very delapidated state'.

> Those of the eastern tower so dangerously so as to render it necessary to take part of them down; some of the Walls stand firm, would admit of Roofing and may be fitted up as Dwelling Houses or for other purposes but the Rents which could be obtained would not be sufficient remuneration for the Expences incurred.
> The Circular Building in the centre, from the inconvenience of its form, and its defective state, is not capable of being applied to any advantageous purpose.
> The South Side of the Castle is in so bad a state as to entirely prevent any attempt to alter or repair the part of the building to advantage.

The Mortimer Tower, however, ruinous in 1771, had been repaired.

> That part of the Castle called Mortimers Tower is occupied as a Dwelling House and may with some attention still be applied to the same purpose; the Occupier lives Rent free, his Father having, by permission of the Lessee, expended nearly £300 in making and keeping it habitable.

A dwelling house and offices 'within the walls', was let as an inn, and was also habitable.

It was suggested that 'it may with some repairs be still continued for the same purpose'. There are records of building work relating to these premises in the 1820s.[21] The range of buildings on the opposite side of the outer gate, 'part used as Stables, may be repaired and occupied as at present, or converted into workshops for artificers'. One of these buildings was later rebuilt as a museum by the Powis family and set out with showcases for fossils and rocks.[22]

> A Dwelling House on the land belonging to the Crown (at the South-West extremity) in a good and tenantable State of Repair; the Occupier is rent free, he having built the House, nearly 12 years since with consent of the late lesee & and expended on it about £300.

This dwelling house, now no. 47 Linney Road, is still in existence.

The recommendation of the Crown surveyor was that the castle should be let for 61 years at £50 per annum. This seems to have been his preferred option, but it was also agreed that the premises might be sold, and, in this case, their value 'in perpetuity, free from the payment of any rent to the Crown, including 316 Timber Trees of Elm, Lime, Fir, Sycamore, Beech & Chestnut, is in his opinion £1,560'.[23] However, the earl continued to press for an outright sale and in May 1811 he was informed that 'The Treasury had been induced to rescind its former position and has directed a warrant for the absolute sale to his Lordship'. In July a draft lease was made out, and finally, in September the Bank of England were authorised to pay to the Office of Woods the sum of £1,560, plus £11 6d. for the fees payable to the Treasury, the auditor and for the proceedings for the conveyance.[24] Lord Powis had at last achieved his goal, the ownership of the castle.

CHAPTER XI

Symbolism and Assimilation

by David Whitehead

Notwithstanding the advances in archaeological techniques, late 20th century antiquaries should not forget that their pursuits are part of a great tradition of interest in ancient buildings which stretches back into the Middle Ages. In our rational age the study of historic buildings calls upon a wide range of techniques, which provide the tools of analysis, that unlock the creative processes that produced the monuments. What is often forgotten in the course of this study is the emotional appeal—both in the past and the present—which an ancient structure held for both its owner and the casual observer. Victorian antiquaries rooted in the romantic *milieu* were only too eager to register their feelings about buildings such as Ludlow Castle, albeit at the same time they were beginning to deploy those new techniques of study, which were later refined by 20th-century archaeologists. Indeed, picturesque perceptions, which dominated the 19th century assessment of the castle, and still flourish in the popular mind today, have been defined by modern cultural historians as an aesthetic position straddling the cultural tropes of reason and romanticism. Even well-qualified antiquarians like Thomas Wright, who skilfully utilised the new archeo-architectural language in his many descriptions of Ludlow Castle, was just as keen to promote the castle in the light of contemporary aesthetics (see illustrations overleaf). He felt that the meaning of the building was enhanced by repeating many of the popular stories with which

the fabric had become associated by the late 18th century. Thus he was promoting the monument as an object of scientific discourse as well as a catalyst for emotion.

It is the object of this chapter to consider Ludlow Castle as a cultural artefact of symbolic significance, satisfying in many different ways and in many different periods, the emotional as well as the intellectual sensibilities of its owners, and, more recently, the visitors who come to admire it. Gradually, as the story unfolds, the interests of the latter subsume or eclipse the interests of the former. The functional considerations of those who possessed the castle have gradually been eroded by the fantasies of those who come to visit it.

Chivalric Symbolism

Charles Coulson and others have taught us to fundamentally review our perceptions of the pragmatic purpose of castles like Ludlow.[1] Ludlow Castle is patently a fortress protected by its elevated position and chosen, we might logically assume, for its defensive potential. However, this high terrace vibrates with ancient importance. Throughout Wales and the borderland the Norman conquerors sought out the sites of Dark Age *dins* to tap into the ancient order of things and annex princely prestige.[2] Dinham is such a place and the name was employed with pride by one of the earliest possessors of Ludlow, Joce. We may also speculate that Roger de Lacy's

Fig. 1 Thomas Wright's castle view, 1852

impressive keep at Dinham proclaimed his political aspirations on the border just as surely as the
great keep at Thornbury signalled to Henry VIII
Edward Stafford's ambitions in the early 16th
century.[3] Dinham, it may have been assumed, had
once been occupied by a princely palace and in de
Lacy's name a new one was rising. The
symbolism which Roger restored to Ludlow, was
garnered more subtlety by subsequent owners.
Moreover, during the Early Middle Ages, the
castle obtained a heroic history which considerably enhanced its emblematical importance and
elevated its attraction for all subsequent owners.
It made it a place to possess less because of its
defensive qualities—which were in any case
severely compromised by the development of the
town in the 12th century—but more because of
the quality of its cultural associations.

Roger Mortimer (1287-1330) was perhaps the
first owner of Ludlow to view the castle with a
yearning for the past. He held court here in the
early 14th century and added the Great Chamber
block and garderobe tower for the convenience of
his guests. This functional building also adds

considerably to the north-west prospect of the
castle, sprouting organically from the rock-face
with its cavernous shutes and complementing the
existing Norman towers. It has deliberately
revivalist qualities and is comparable to similar
towers, functional yet emblematic, built in this
period at Warkworth, Warwick and Windsor—the
last within an Arthurian context.[4] Mortimer was
part of the courtly *milieu*, which produced the
chivalric longings of Edward III's reign and the
new tower no doubt enhanced the setting for the
'feasts, tiltings and other recreations' with which
Mortimer entertained the king's mother, Queen
Isabella.[5] Some indication of the esoteric atmosphere which prevailed at Ludlow in this period, is
suggested by the survival of a series of middle-
English poems which are connected with the
Mortimer household. It seems that Ludlow had
become a 'show castle'—the symbolic setting for
a chivalric lifestyle.[6]

Richard, duke of York (1411-1460) and his
son Edward IV (1442-83) both proudly maintained their titles as earls of March. The latter,
with his brother and tutors, was established by his

Fig. 2 Thomas Wright's view of the outer bailey, 1852

father at Ludlow in the early 1450s.[7] The castle became the spring-board for many of the Yorkist adventures, but never played a front-line role in the Wars of the Roses.[8] It was a bolt-hole, a breathing space and a place of assembly but never of strategic importance and, when in October 1459 Richard decided to face the king, he abandoned the castle and built earthwork ramparts for his guns at Ludford. The castle was presumably in good repair since his sons had recently been in residence there. Any Lancastrian occupation of the castle was temporary, for the possession of a castle was, it seems, no longer vital in the tit-for-tat conflict of the 15th century. Henceforward, the preservation and enhancement of Ludlow, which was frequently expensive, was primarily for residential purposes and because the ancient fortress evoked the '*moeurs* of chivalry', which Edward IV was especially determined to revive.[9]

During the 1460s considerable work seems to have taken place at Ludlow. This certainly frightened Henry VI who complained that 'certain persons', namely Yorkist sympathisers, were victualling and fortifying castles and places of strength in Wales and the Marches.[10] Between

1464-8 Edward is recorded as rebuilding the keep, inserting a new staircase and providing access via a richly decorated door. Edward's attention to the keep coincides with an era of tower building, carried out especially by the victorious Yorkists throughout England. At Ashby de la Zouche, Kirby Muxloe, Raglan, Gloucester, Warwick, Pontefract, Nottingham and elsewhere the *turris* acquired new meaning as a conspicuous symbol of lordship.[11] Ludlow was also being made ready for the reception of Prince Edward who took up residence in 1473 with a commission of oyer and terminer to rule over the Principality and the Marches. The castle provided the setting for a great assembly of marcher barons in 1476—summoned by the prince to discuss the issue of crime and disorder in his petty kingdom. The gathering presumably took place in the Great Hall, where young Edward could make a ceremonial appearance from the Great Chamber via another fine doorway, which dates from this period.[12]

During these two decades the castle blossomed again but the alterations, which can still be detected today are almost all cosmetic. Even the

Fig. 3 Thomas Wright's view of the inner bailey, 1852

great tower, it seems, was reduced in size retaining a safe, but token structure. The fabric was preserved to bolster Yorkist aspirations with the 'trappings and accoutrements of nostalgia'.[13] Prince Edward and his brother Richard were at Ludlow when their father died in April 1483, and their subsequent role as 'the little princes in the Tower' added as significantly as their father's restoration, to the rich tapestry of associations which singled out Ludlow as a national, rather than a local monument in subsequent centuries.

The Enchanted Castle

The Tudors could not escape the enticement of Ludlow and a prince with the name Arthur— conceived to celebrate the British past—was sent by his father Henry VII to enjoy his honeymoon at Ludlow in 1501. He even took possession of *Lys-twysoc* 'the prince's palace' according to the antiquary William Camden. In a sense he was at the wrong castle, for down the road at Knucklas, near Knighton, William of Worcester noticed in 1479 a castle reputedly founded by the real Arthur. Prince Arthur's death early in 1502 added a further veneer to the already thick gloss of

romantic episodes at Ludlow.[14] It presumably did not enhance the magic of the place for Princess Mary, who came in equally dismal circumstances with the divorce of her mother on the horizon in 1525. For her father, however, Ludlow was, no doubt, an outpost of his glittering court where nostalgia for the chivalric past was hardly dimmed by the first flicker of Renaissance humanism. Henry's courtyard 'castle' of Nonsuch and the great hall of Hampton Court show that the Henrican court was, in architectural terms, still firmly fixed in the Middle Ages and a many towered castle like Ludlow had enhanced appeal. Henry, however, was characteristically tight fisted with funds and although a good deal of soldering, sawing and daubing took place at the castle in October 1525 for Mary's reception, the work only came to £5 17s 9d. Clearly, Mary was expected to enjoy the symbolism whilst enduring the dilapidations, but according to the instructions provided for the 364 persons appointed to attend the princess, everything about her was to be 'pure, sweete, clean and holsome'. When the season was convenient she was to 'use moderate exercise for takeinge open ayr in gardens, sweete and holsome places and walkes', which sounds as if the immediate surroundings of the castle were beginning to be appreciated.

Rowland Lee, bishop of Coventry, Mary's successor as president of the Marches, was a bureaucrat of the Cromwellian mould. But he too realised that Ludlow and the other royal castles of the border were reflections of Tudor polity in a landscape of banditii and therefore needed to be a dignified image of that august court. Notwithstanding Henry's parsimony, he embarked upon repairs in 1534. The work was slow and another courtier, Sir Thomas Englefield, preferred to seek accommodation at the Bishop's Palace in Hereford in 1535 because 'The castle at Ludlow is in such decay that we cannot lie there until it is repaired'. The enchantment of the ancient stones was no substitute for a dry bed. The repairs continued until 1538 with Lee pursuing various strategies to raise money including the confiscation of the goods of condemned felons and materials from the 'old friar house' in Ludlow. He also made gestures towards repairing castles at Brecon, Chirk and Wigmore. Nothing dramatic appears to have been done to the castle but its antiquity was preserved. John Leland was impressed in 1539, and maybe lost for words, stating laconically that it was 'a fine castle'.[16]

The appointment of Henry Sidney as Lord President of the Council in the Marches in 1560 opened a new chapter in the appreciation of the castle as an ancient monument. Sir Henry, according to Camden, was 'the most experienced of all antiquity' and was at the centre of the chivalric revival, which swept through the Elizabethan court, a movement brought to a climax by Sir Henry's son Philip.[17] His interest in the castle was almost compulsive and St. John Hope in 1908 found traces of his restoration—always in a sympathetic late perpendicular style—in every corner of the building. Sidney had already 're-edified' Dublin Castle whilst he was lord deputy in Ireland, but his work at Ludlow took place during the last few years of his life when he retreated from court, disappointed by Elizabeth's apparent ingratitude for his services in Ireland.[18]

In 1560 Sidney had been given a commission to remedy the 'great ruin and decay' of the queen's 'castles, houses and edifices' at Ludlow, employing 'fines, amercements and forfeitures taken in our court there'. Apart from repairing the 'ancient edifices' he could also erect 'new buildings' and during the 1580s these activities were taking a major part of the income collected in fines. He was determined, it seems, to create an 'old soldier's' dream castle, a suitable setting for the Arcadian knights who accompanied his son Philip. He provided the castle with a new show entrance a 'fayre lardge stone bridge'—30 to 40 yards long, in fine stone of three arches. The Norman round chapel was carefully repaired and given a new nave, enriched with 'divers noblemen's armes'. According to Churchyard:

> most trim and costly sure
> So bravely wrought, so fayre and firmly fram'd
> That to world's end ye beautie may endure.[19]

The round design of the chapel may have reminded him of the 'lays and stories of Arthur' which intoxicated his son (see illustration on p.77). He also inserted a floor into the circular nave to form a private chapel for the members of his court, separated from the household below. Such an arrangement, which existed in many palaces and country houses, may have been a product of Sidney's antiquarianism, for the most famous example was at Aachen, built for the emperor Charlemagne. Like Edward IV before him, Sidney also refurbished the great tower and integrated it into a new range of buildings known in 1650 as the 'Governor's Quarters'. The name perhaps suggests that the president may have occupied this accommodation with its easy access to the tower, the very essence of Ludlow's majesty, leaving the hall range for ceremonial occasions.[20] Sidney's delight in the gothic display of armorial bearings is celebrated on his daughter's tomb in Ludlow parish church and it became the tradition for the gentry and noblemen who were attached to the court to have their arms painted for the council chamber, adjoining the

Great Hall. This continued into the 17th century and eventually over 200 heraldic devices were displayed. They survived to be recorded in the 18th century as a comprehensive celebration of the English and Welsh aristocracy who served the Council.

The style of the new range (the Judges' Lodgings) is entirely late gothic, emphasised by the tall staircase turret and reminiscent of Sir Henry's south-west range at Penshurst, Kent, of 1574-5. An equally sensitive hand can be detected in the restoration of the north range and especially the 'fayre house' (the Tudor Lodgings) squeezed in between the Great Chamber block and the Pendover Tower. The Great Hall—the chivalric focus of the castle—was hardly touched except for the provision of a new fireplace and chimney, designed to protect the roof which had caught fire during the Christmas festivities of 1579. Like the 14th-century great hall at Penshurst, which the Sidneys preserved, this space must have been equally enthralling for them. Like the house of Kalander in *Arcadia* Ludlow had a 'refreshing of a firm stateliness ... all the more lasting than beautiful'. Ben Jonson's eulogy on the family's Kentish home makes a similar point:

> Thou art not, Penshurst, built to envious show
> Of touch or marble, nor canst boast a row
> Of polished pillars, or roof of gold;
> Thou hast no lantern whereof tales are told,
> Or stair, or courts; but stand'st an ancient pile,

and could equally be applied to Ludlow. Sadly, the manner of life at Ludlow is not recorded in Sidney's time but his successor Lord Pembroke was infected by the fantasy and at Christmas 1594 dined with his friends in the Great Hall at Ludlow in the dress of the knights of the round table.[21]

Sir Henry Sidney left his heart in Ludlow Church and he also left a castle, which was the epitome of the florescence of Elizabethan chivalry, a real gothic castle providing a backdrop for the romantic yearnings of a *parvenu* aristocracy, threatened by extinction by his Catholic majesty, Philip II of Spain. With their backs to the wall, the English élite retreated into the never-never land of the gothic past. But at Ludlow this was solid stuff, not some ephemeral sham like Lulworth, Ruperra or Bolsover, built by the next generation of chivalric dreamers. Moreover the castle was now very much a palace with a fountain enriched with coats of arms playing in the inner court. The chivalric treatment of this feature, which complemented the other gothic enrichments carried out by Sidney, deserves comment. Fountains were frequently singled out for displays of Renaissance taste—at Oxford and London—and in a similar context to Ludlow, at Kenilworth Castle, where the earl of Leicester made one a conspicuous item of display in his privy garden. The eight sides of the basin were decorated with 'storie work' i.e. Greek myths, whilst above there was a figure of Atlantis. Sydney eschewed such conceits at Ludlow and instead created an emblematic fountain, where the 'storie work' celebrated the English myths.

There was also a 'fayre tennys court' and most intriguing of all a 'ffayre and lardg seat upon the north side of the said castle, wth a howse over the same, together with a lardg walke enclosed with pall and tymber'. St. John Hope identified this to the east of the Pendover Tower where a rocky platform remains to indicate this pleasaunce. From here there are views out into an elysium landscape like that enjoyed from Basilius's lodge in *Arcadia* set up on an 'insensible rising of ground' providing 'the eye lordship over a good large circuit' and 'pleasant picture of nature ... diversified between hills and dales, wood and plains'. Not only was the castle the symbol of enchanted dreams, but it had it also become part of a picturesque landscape. Thomas Churchyard puts it well: The castle

> stands right well and pleasant to the vewe
> With sweet prospect, yea all the field about,
> An auncient seate, yet many buildings newe
> Here are great works that now doth beare no
>   name,
> Which were of old. And yet may pleasure you
> To see the same; for loe in elders daies
> Was much bestowed; that now is much to prayse.[22]

On 4 November 1616 the castle was the focus for the ceremonies surrounding the solemn declaration of James I's eldest surviving son, Charles, as prince of Wales and earl of Chester. James was seeking to stimulate 'the loyall affection of the British Nation to their Royall Prince' and Ludlow was chosen as 'his Highnesse chiefe seate and castle' for the principality of Wales. 'His maisties chappell within the castle' as well as the parish church, were used for the sacred parts of the ceremony but on the castle green there were bonfires, volleys, music and speeches, whilst within the castle itself, a great feast was provided for the principal participants and the 'best sort of gentlemen'. The scholars of the free school carried 'penons' and 'bannerolls' containing the arms and achievements of Prince Charles, which were carefully deposited within the castle chapel as 'remarkable Trophies of that Solemnitie'. James I was, perhaps, clutching at straws in trying to improve the popular perception of the regime. But the choice of Ludlow Castle as the set piece for this ceremony acknowledged that the 'prince's palace' was redolent of those qualities which the Stuarts wished to harness.[23]

Milton's *Comus* created for the household of John Egerton, earl of Bridgewater (1579-1649) and performed in the Great Hall in 1634 was a pastoral entertainment which deliberately played upon the rusticity of Ludlow and the decency of the Egerton family, contrasting their solid country virtues with those of the court, where the masque had been corrupted by lascivious plots and the 'whirling whimsies' of the set designers. Here we find the castle within a sublime setting, the tangled wood of Bringewood where the Egerton children fall into the clutches of Comus but eventually escape to the earthly paradise of their father's household at the castle. Little did Milton know that he had contributed another element to the mélange of associations that gave the solemn building so much meaning in the 18th century. It was Thomas Warton (1728-90), who wrote the *Pleasures of Melancholy* (1747) about the

Fig. 4 Dinely's drawing of the castle from Whitcliff in 1684, showing the wooden Dinham Bridge

sublime pleasures of ruins like Ludlow, who revealed the mysterious and romantic side of Milton. In 1785 he published a new edition of Milton's poems, which included *Comus* and a description of Ludlow Castle. Thus, by happy chance, Milton, whose view of the English landscape encapsulated the picturesque point of view, was associated with Ludlow. Few travellers in the late 18th century, on first seeing the castle from Whitcliff could resist quoting from *L'Allegro* where:

Towers and Battlements it sees
Bosom'd high in tufted Trees.

Apart from Churchyard's account, there are few early appreciations of the setting of the castle. Its visual amenities were extensive. To the north-west there was Oakly Park—anciently belonging to Bromfield Priory but emparked for the convenience of the occupants of the castle at least as early as Edward IV's reign. Across the Teme beyond the brow of Whitcliff was the chase of Bringwood and adjoining it the royal forests of Moctree and Deerfold, which were also part of the Mortimer inheritance. Among the facilities provided within these woods was the Haye Park, above Richard's Castle, where the Egerton children had their character-building experience. The large ditched and banked game enclosure here no doubt provided a temporary covert for the deer driven out for the convenience of the hunters from the castle. Just as the earl of Leicester built a 'fayr timberd bridge' to link the chase at Kenilworth directly with the castle, so Dinham Bridge must have served the same function at Ludlow. The origins of this second bridge at Ludlow are obscure; Dinely shows a wooden structure in 1684. The conjunction of art and nature, castle and woodland was well appreciated at Kenilworth and had been applauded by Philip Sydney on his grand tour of Italy. At Ludlow the interplay was even more dramatic and a man-made castle, linked by a bridge across a noisy torrent, with the wilderness beyond, must have appealed equally to Sir Henry Sidney and the other occupants of the castle. On a more mundane level, the castle had an immense appetite for fuel and venison, much of which would have been carried from the forests across Dinham Bridge. As the woods were gradually denuded of trees in the 16th century, aided by squatters and industrial entrepreneurs, new arrangements were made to obtain regular supplies of fuel and game from other royal forests in the region. Eventually, the Crown adopted a policy of leasing the forests and chase to the local gentry.[24]

The Moralists

Thomas Dinely attended the first duke of Beaufort, lord president of Wales, on his progress around the principality in 1684 and recorded the castle four years before the Council in the Marches was abolished in 1689. He produced the first view of the castle from Whitcliff, encapsulating with his awkward style the classical view so often repeated by later artists. His views inside the castle show many of Sidney's improvements, including the Norman chapel, which had already succumbed to mythology and become 'Prince Arthurs Chappel'. Although he feverishly records every minor inscription, there are no signs of regret or nostalgia as the castle is still a working establishment. His perspective of the inner court from a viewpoint above the outer gate shows the heart of the castle—the great tower, jostling with the high gables of Sidney's apartments—girdled with a battlemented wall, rather like the depictions of cities on medieval seals. The castle is still triumphant, not at all diminished (see illustration on p.48).[25]

By the time Stukeley and Defoe visited Ludlow in 1721/2 the castle was beginning to decay. Neither found the neglect inspirational, as it was too easy for them to picture the courts and halls thronged with litigants and clerks. Like our own appreciation of a modern building recently gutted by fire, the ruins smelt of mortality and called for a judgmental response. Stukeley cries out on viewing the great apartments: ''twas a noble structure, but now alas only groans out with its last breath the glorys of its antient state'. Defoe with one foot in the Renaissance world admires the fecundity of the surrounding countryside viewed from the castle. But this arcadia awaits its prince 'that is not now to be expected' and 'time, the great Devourer of the works of men, begins to eat into the very Stone Walls and to spread the Face of Royal Ruins upon the whole Fabrick'. Here we have the leitmotif of every ruin visitor—*sic transit gloria mundi* ('thus passes earthly glory')—but unrelieved by any pleasure or aesthetic response.[26]

The historical awareness of the enlightened mind frequently led visitors and commentators to develop a sentimental or moral response to the ruins. Geoffrey Lipscomb writing in the era of the French Revolution (1799) had no regrets about the disappearance of the Council in the Marches—'thus the iron Yoke, which had so often galled the neck of the subject in these parts, was at length broken'—and he suggested that the 'true patriot will walk around these desolated walls, and triumph in their decay. His exultation will not be interrupted by any circumstance of personal injustice having been occasioned by their fall'. Quite clearly, he is allying himself with the Freeborn Englishman/Norman Yoke ideology, which formed part of the political rhetoric of his time. The fact that Ludlow had once been a palace occupied by royal princes as well as the haunt of feudal tyrants made this reaction almost *de rigueur*. It was necessary for this imaginative leap to feed 'the imagination with ideas of the splendid scenes once enjoyed within its walls' and compare this with the present ruins, which 'affords a striking vestige of the power of the destroying hand of time over the strongest and most beautiful fabrics erected by the art of man'. Or again on contemplating the 'splendid scenes of the past' the present ruins 'will impress upon the mind a sentiment not destitute of moral use, since it will teach us the decay of magnificence however durable, and the vicissitude of every-thing that depends upon human support'. The latter has a tone of prudery born out of English nonconformity, which came to characterise the attitude of the Victorian middle class tourist.[27]

The Pleasures of Ownership

Stukeley was not the first to regret the loss of the furnishings of the castle, sold by those whom the crown entrusted to maintain it. Governorships of royal castles, however ruinous, had attracted the nobility and gentry throughout the 16th and 17th centuries, implying that the titles, albeit nominal, conveyed status. In the mid-18th century the governor of Ludlow was Alexander Stuart from Fife who, according to Hodges, was a relative of the Stuart pretenders. No doubt this dangerous connection was one reason why the government was prepared to patronise him as governor of Ludlow Castle where it could keep an eye on his activities. Nevertheless, Stuart lived at No.33 Broad Street and spent some time each year in Scotland.[28] Francis Grose noticed in 1765 that the governor kept the Great Hall 'decorated with some kind of ornaments, together with lances, spears, firelocks and old armour'. This arrange-ment can be traced back to 1708 when 'A Catalogue of goodes in Ludlow Castle, delivered

by Captain Jones to the governor' mentions in the Hall 'Fifty-eight musquettes whereof one wants a lock; 37 pikes, one olberd, four tables, 3 benches, 1 table plank, one large iron shovel, and 1 iron grate'. What appears to have been the vestige of the castle armoury in 1708 had become an antiquarian display by 1765. In the 18th century such arrangements became commonplace in medieval halls throughout England—Penshurst comes to mind—and particularly in the gothic revival castles of the following century. Martial equipment displayed in this manner stim-ulated romantic yearning for the feudal past in a place where, it was imagined, a lord and his tenants feasted in good fellowship after the fray. An anonymous *Ode to Ludlow Castle* captures the sentiment. The 'mailed host' having repulsed 'Cambria's ruthless band':

> In happier times how brightly blazed
> The hearth with ponderous billets raised,
>   How rung the vaulted halls,
> When smok'd the feast, when care was drown'd,
> When songs antisocial glee went round,
>   Where now the ivy crawls.

Governor Stuart, who perhaps, enjoyed some perquisites from the visitors to the castle, no doubt appreciated the need to evoke a chivalric atmosphere even amidst the decay.[29]

Ownership of a medieval castle conveyed even greater kudos than a mere governorship. James Brydges, first duke of Chandos, lord lieu-tenant of Herefordshire and M.P. for the city of Hereford, struggled hard, but in vain, with the Harleys of Eywood and Brampton Bryan in *c*.1725-6 to secure the site of Hereford Castle. He intended to build a house and made it clear from his correspondence that he needed a suitable base in the county to look after his 'concerns'—his social and political influence. What better spot could he hope to secure than the remains of the royal castle in the county town.[30] Henry Arthur Herbert, earl of Powis of Oakly Park, whose property adjoined Ludlow probably claimed to have more elevated concerns when he leased Ludlow Castle in 1771. He was a member of Ludlow corporation and a benefactor of the parish church but the acquisition of such a noble edifice, replete with an impeccable pedigree that included the greatest nobility of the borderland and most of the kings and queens of England since 1461, must have been an added incentive. Sadly, he died in 1772 and never enjoyed his acquisition.[31]

The Hon. John Byng informs us, incidentally, that Frederick, the prince of Wales, father of George III sent a surveyor to inspect the state of the castle with a view to making it 'habitable and princely' but decided that the £30,000 required was too much. Byng thought that the present (1784) prince of Wales, George, might 'take some pleasure in repairing (& sometimes living at) Ludlow, than in eternally ———'. *The Guide to Ludlow* (1879) states that George IV thought Ludlow 'second only to Edinburgh' and thus, it is possible, that the earl of Powis acquired in 1771 a putative royal palace on the Teme![32]

In purely financial terms the Powis family took on a burden, a factor that it was eager to point out in 1811 when the castle was sold to them for £1,560. This followed a survey carried out by Thomas Telford to ascertain if the castle could be used for French prisoners of war. In a letter of 1803 when this was first mooted, Lord and Lady Clive emphasised that 'the place, fine as the ruin is, was of no real advantage to the family, more than the pleasure it afforded in enabling it to compliment the inhabitants of that respectable place'. However, they would 'feel hurt if their son should lose even a feather (for such was the castle) that his uncle and grandfather enjoyed'. Clearly, some family pride had become invested in the ownership of this ruin and the magic, which had worked upon Henry Sidney, was apparent again.[33]

There was another ingredient in the equation. Ludlow had become the élite leisure centre of the middle Marches in the 18th century and the castle was the focus of this burgeoning tourist industry. Undeterred by Defoe's gloomy predictions that the town faced disaster with the passing away of the Council in the Marches, it continued to flourish as a social centre. A recent study of the

Easter Books, which registered the 'sojourners and lodgers' in the town shows that rich visitors outnumbered the poor, especially in the fashionable streets such as Broad Street and Castle Street. Indeed, Ludlow had a particularly high number of 'sojourners' in the 18th century, at 6-7% of the population compared with 2% in Bristol. Wealthy widows in particular seem to have been drawn to the town, often with unmarried daughters. What was the attraction? By the end of the century the town had two theatres, a library and one of the earliest racecourses in Shropshire. John Byng thought it was 'one of the best towns for a genteel family of small fortune to retire to' and on later journeys he frequently used Ludlow as a yardstick for judging the quality of other towns. Among Ludlow's additional attractions was the neatness of its streets and its cheapness, but most of all it had 'one of the most pompous antiquities of the kingdom' readily accessible, which could be explored in 'every corner'. Moreover, around it was some 'enchanting country' and 'charming walks ... overhanging the river banks'. Ludlow was thus one of the first tourist 'honey pots' in England and if the Powis-Clive family had any commercial interests in the town, the possession of the castle certainly helped secure these as it was the focus of attention for most visitors.[34]

Sublime and Picturesque

The Enlightenment legitimised rational and sober pleasures, which promoted personal gratification as well as social harmony. Indeed, they were expressions of communality—and tourism, which involved conviviality and social intercourse, fitted the bill perfectly.[35] Moreover, the intelligentsia of the era developed a series of aesthetic theories that helped to classify what they saw, thus adding to the enjoyment. Among the most influential and earliest of these theories was the concept of the sublime, given its fullest expression in Edmund Burke's *A Philosophical Inquiry into the Origin of our Ideas of the Sublime and Beautiful* (1756). This explored human behaviour in terms of two basic

Fig. 5 Ludlow Castl*e, 1797, by Thomas Hearne*

Thomas Hearne (1744-1817), whilst painting a series of views of Downton Gorge for Richard Payne Knight, produced a dramatic view of the castle. His station was further upstream than Towne, but again a low perspective exaggerates the dominating position of the castle. Notwithstanding a number of picturesque props in the foreground and the encroaching vegetation on the castle hill, this is a sublime image, replete with 'grand and awful ideas'. When it was published in the second volume of the *Antiquities*, the text stressed the completeness of the walls and the opportunity the castle afforded 'for contemplation upon the extensive and gloomy marks of our ancestors'. The sublime view provoked anxiety by displaying the massive bulk of the castle unencumbered by nature. It also complemented the antiquarian / moralist view of the ruin, anchoring it in the real past. Such images lent themselves for the engraved print, often used to illustrate antiquarian discourses—for example, the anonymous *View of Ludlow Castle* (*c.*1800 but derived from Stukeley's prospect of 1721).[38]

impulses—self-preservation and self-propagation—which were caused by sublime and beautiful experiences. The attributes of the former were horror, immensity and obscurity; the latter clarity, smoothness and delicacy. The simplest emotion of the human mind—curiosity—brought tourists into contact with the sublime, which created a tension with the other human state— indolence and inactivity. The sublime was found in rugged countryside, the beautiful in pastoral scenery. The former was particularly associated with the paintings of Salvator Rosa (1715-73), which were much admired in Britain.[36]

Among the early views of Ludlow Castle is a fine watercolour by Francis Towne (1739-1816) *A view of Ludlow Castle drawn on the spot ... July 21st 1777* which takes a low perspective from the Teme (see colour section). The gaunt grey walls of the castle are unrelieved by vegetation and it stands high on its bare knoll. The bleak treatment of the subject in an unkempt landscape is in essence a sublime image. The building oppresses its surroundings and the figures in the foreground, providing a visual trigger for the moralist's view of the castle as the abode of tyrant kings, and exhibiting a 'painful reflection of sublunary grandeur, in the awful majesty of the ruins'.[37]

The contrast with the picturesque view of a similar date (1792) by Julius Caesar Ibbetson (1759-1817) is most striking (see the colour section). Here the artist stands well back upon Whitcliff and the mood of the scene is transformed by framing the castle in an ample landscape. The result is a 'homely interpretation' mild and, perhaps, slightly melancholy. Turner produced a similar view in 1798 (published as an engraving in *Picturesque Views of England and Wales* (1825-38)). The sublime treatment of the view is again toned down by the arcadian scene in the foreground, but the brooding image of the castle, illuminated by morning sunshine, with its north front lost in blue washes, is yet another manifestation of 'agreeable horror', hardly intimidating for the female reapers.[40] Sublime

Fig. 6 The engraving of Turner's view of 1798 reproduced in
Picturesque Views of England and Wales *(1825-38)*

emotions could be stimulated in other ways. A bright autumnal view of the late 18th century by an anonymous artist, places the castle in a setting of water and trees with no other sign of human interference. The walls of the castle seen from some distance lose their medieval character and could easily belong to some pre-Columbian monument in the Americas.[41] Peter de Wint (1784-1849) produced an almost transcendental image of Ludlow in *c.*1845 (see colour section). Viewed from a distance—on Bringewood Chase—the castle and the church rise out of a bleak, undifferentiated countryside of blue and bronze washes, the work of giants erupting from an unremitting landscape.

It was the regularity of the castle walls and their lack of ruination that made Ludlow a difficult subject for picturesque composition. A late 19th-century visitor put his finger on the problem, finding that the castle viewed from Whitcliff 'looks not less massive than romantic'.

It really needed a 'picturesque genius' (Gilpin) like Cromwell to break up those great slabs of wall to create more variety and stimulation for the imagination. In a sense the interior of the castle, as John Byng found, was more satisfactory in this regard. Yet the view by Francis Towne (see p.113) of the interior shows that even here the ruin had not surrendered sufficiently to nature, the hand of man was still all too obvious and the traces of his art needed to be hidden.[42] This point is made by Richard Payne Knight in *The Landscape* (1794):

Let clustering ivy o'er its sides be spread,
And moss and weeds grow scatter'd over its head.

But harsh and cold the builders' work appears,
Till softened down by long revolving years.

By blending the castle with nature, greater variety of scenery was achieved and there were more opportunities for creating pictures.

Fig. 7 F. Calvert, Ludlow Castle, *early 19th century*

Increasingly the late 18th century tourist, educated by Gilpin and the other picturesque theorists, was concerned with matters of form and colour, so that gradually visual considerations ousted the moral reflections stimulated by the sublime. The hierarchy of pleasures associated with ruins was changing. In Wordsworth's phrase the cult of the picturesque created 'the tyranny of the eye'. The search for variety and intricacy, which became so essential to enjoy scenery, was not satisfied with natural embellishments alone and required a whole series of props such as bridges, cottages, boats, mills, waterfalls and human activity. All these were available below the castle and could be used to animate the scene.[43] In Calvert's early 19th-century view, the Teme, supporting an excessive number of boats, is turned into a rocky cove and the castle becomes a sea-side ruin.[44]

The atmosphere of William Marlowe's view of the 1770s (as reproduced in the castle guide-book) is in striking contrast to the view of Francis Towne of the same decade and from the same low perspective. The castle is much less dominating, its walls are represented by yellow hues and trees are visible over the battlements. Although the castle hill still lacks vegetation, it has been colonised by people walking the foot-paths and the foreground is busy and domesti-cated.[45] The composition leads the eye on a 'wanton chase' (Price) and so, the moral force of the sublime has been replaced by the affable delights of the picturesque. Numerous views, many reproduced as prints, exploit the same formula with little sign of originality. Most boring of all are the prospects from Whitcliff, which, because of the elevated perspective, find it difficult to import picturesque props, except for the odd figure and some vegetation. Serious painters went down to the river in this period. Nevertheless, Whitcliff, saved from enclosure in 1793 became a tourist attraction in its own right where: 'extensively rich, beautiful and grand landscape scenery enjoyed by all from elevated and elegant walks, in the vicinity of one of the neatest towns in the British dominions'.[46]

Fig. 8 The view published in the European Magazine (1788)

The picturesque canon of intricacy drew the observer closer to the castle and once there, antiquarian tendencies tended to develop. This had a long pedigree, which included Dinely and Stukeley, but the desire to classify what could be seen—both the architecture and the natural history—was encouraged by the picturesque preoccupation with detail. Price's *Ludlow Guide* (1797) urges the visitor to examine the 'prodigious thickness' of the walls and the 'fine species of architecture in which it is built' and subject all of this to 'minute attention' and 'ample delineation'. The curious antiquary, the 'tap and jot' brigade are just round the corner.[47] Geoffrey Lipscomb felt that Ludlow, 'a perfect specimen of feudal splendour', should have provided the model for Richard Payne Knight's Downton Castle and was saddened on his visit to find a building entirely 'unworthy of the dignified title of castle'. Picturesque sensibilities made tourists well informed on the particulars of gothic architecture and thus Lipscomb was not alone in completely misunderstanding Knight's precocious attempt at imitating the military architecture of the Greeks and Romans.[48]

Picturesque perceptions had a significant impact upon the manner in which the castle was preserved by the Powis estate. The first priority was the management of the castle walks, which Marlowe's view and Pritchard's survey (1765)

show were being used informally even before the countess of Powis began landscaping in 1772. The trees were planted without the benefit of picturesque presumptions in a formal manner. The view in the *European Magazine* (1788) shows them lining the lower walk as it zig-zags down to Dinham bridge.[49] There are already many self-sown trees, the result perhaps of 'artful negligence'. The views of the 1790s show the castle 'embosmed' in trees although the north slopes, where the rock outcropped, provided a different texture and was thus, kept clear. A set of accounts for the period 1785-1810 indicates, as we might suspect, that a picturesque landscape required fastidious attention and cost money. The walks needed to be kept clean and frequently regravelled. This was the work of William Matthews who was paid two guineas a year throughout the 1790s. The estate also provided seats, which required repairing and painting and were sometimes the object of vandalism. In 1799 part of the walk was fenced off with painted rails—a detail which is studiously ignored by the artists. During the proceedings leading to the purchase of the castle in 1811, Lord Powis's agent calculated that maintaining the walks between 1803-10 had cost the estate £197. It was pointed out by the government's correspondent, that this expenditure went beyond the terms of the original lease, which was simply concerned with preserving a 'monument of Antique magnificence'.[50]

The proposal to use the castle for prisoners of war—'disagreeable neighbours'—was greeted with horror because, among other considerations, it was likely to impact upon the public walks. The survey by John Haycock in 1811 clearly shows the walks. The upper walk was still tree-less whilst the middle and lower walks had matured considerably and were just like avenues. We learn

Fig. 9 Francis Towne's interior view of 1777 (Birmingham Museums & Art Gallery)

from a guidebook of *c*.1800 that they were planted with beech trees. There were also similar walks laid out either side of the lodge, on the site of the castle ditches. That to the south-east along Dinham, was known in 1811 as the 'New Walk'. As the walks matured, so the views from within it improved, providing the necessary framework for picturesque composition. John Price, who was particularly sensitive to these matters, commented that they 'surprise the traveller with their unparalleled magnificence and plenty'. Moreover, the 'various meanderings of the Teme', and the views towards Oakly Park, together with the 'charms of rock, wood and water' create scenes 'not only in themselves agreeable but true specimens of picturesque beauty'. No longer was the castle an austere monument of feudal tyranny, instead it had been softened by nature and engaged with the surrounding countryside.[51]

For much of the early 18th century the castle was a 'mouldering mansion'. Early decay in a building, as Uvedale Price observed, is simply a 'diminution of beauty, without being consoled for it by any other character'. But gradually, ruins are embellished by 'incrustations and weather stains' and various plants spring up in the crevices, the smoothness and symmetry disappears and eventually the picturesque prevails. 'The ever regular lines of doors and windows are broken, and through their ivy-fringed openings is displayed in a more broken and picturesque manner' the work of man abandoned to nature.[52]

The 'fantastic strokes of nature working upon the patterns of art' can first be detected in Pritchard's elevations of the castle in 1765 (see previous chapter). On its northern front the keep is virtually smothered in ivy. The south front is also succumbing but the Governor's House (Judges' Lodgings), with its fractured roof, still has the 'smell of fire and mortality' and has a long way to go before the picturesque prevails. Francis Towne's interior view of 1777 indicates that nature has advanced with considerable speed in a mere 12 years. The south front of the keep is now enveloped in ivy and the Judges' Lodgings is fast disappearing. Trees and shrubs are also laying siege to the round chapel. The advance of nature, with ivy in the vanguard, continued into the 19th century and a mid-Victorian watercolour

Fig. 10 'Interior of Ludlow Castle', engraved by W. Angus for the Beauties of England and Wales, *1808*

of the Judges' Lodgings shows the building almost entirely lost in vegetation, Visitors contrasted the gloomy solitude of the interior with the ever growing ivy 'alone showing signs of life' yet considerably 'festooning the ruins which it feeds upon'. In Angus's view of 1808 the vegetation is apparently so vigorous, it is providing a fall of timber and two workmen are busy with the trunk of a mature tree. The ivy darkened the interior of the keep, provided the necessary twilight to imagine the 'captives kept in the lone darkness of the donjon'. Or if you prefer Thomas Wright's flight of fancy, a place for keeping lions or wild beasts 'to be let out at pleasure to devour some ill-fated prisoner'. Midnight visits to the castle were much enriched by the ivy where '... the bat and moping owl are found, and mould'ring turrets intercept the way ...'. John Byng regretted the absence of a Welsh-harper, until recently domiciled in Ludlow, who, no doubt could be hired for these midnight

jaunts, just as he enjoyed one at Tintern in the Wye valley.[53]

Attrition and Assimilation

Not everyone found the wildlife attracted by rampant nature agreeable. Mr. Jones of Dinham House wrote to the estate office in 1836 suggesting that the birds occupying the ivy should be fumigated. By the 1870s, when photographs become available, there are signs, for example on views of the Great Hall, that the ivy was being controlled, but it was the antiquarians who eventually launched the most successful assault upon this parasite, and indirectly, upon the picturesque sensibilities. The Norman chapel, which had evinced the admiration of Pritchard in 1765, was gradually being consumed by vegetation in the 19th century until the architect Arthur Blomfield was commissioned to supervise its restoration in 1883. He appreciated 'the picturesque effect of the grass and foliage on that part of the wall' to be restored, but insisted that its removal was essential 'if the arch is to be saved from falling into ruins'. Thus, sensibility succumbed to sense and visual priorities gave way to scientific antiquarianism. During the late 19th century the ivy was gradually scraped from the walls so that in 1908 W.H. St. John Hope could applaud the 'many features (now revealed) that have long been hidden from view and others saved from imminent destruction'. Remarkably, his photographs show the struggle was far from won and ivy still dominated the upper walls of the Great Hall, the northern front of the keep and even the round chapel.[54]

In 1915 the castle was designated an ancient monument and in a letter to Lord Powis from the Office of Works its 'national importance' was stressed. The conservators moved in 1930 and this marked the death knell for the ivy. A report of the same year complained about the poor structural condition of the walls 'hastened by the presence of the roots of shrubs and ivy' and recommended that the walls should be taken down by several courses, all the vegetation eradicated, and the stones re-bedded with 'water proof mortar'.[55]

The war of attrition against the ivy and rampant picturesqueness was fought on other fronts during the 19th century as the desire to tidy-up the interior increased. The dangerous and derelict state of the castle described by Pritchard in 1765 was difficult to reconcile with public access. The accounts beginning in 1786 show considerable sums being spent on the walls, usually when there was a threat of a fall. Towne's view of the interior reveals that the ground in the inner court was rather uneven but in 1794 Samuel Hay was paid £3 16s 11d for 'levelling and improving the inside of the castle' and regular payments for similar work continue until the accounts end in 1810. In October 1806 Hay was joined by Jacob Felton who was paid £7 5s for 'levelling and carrying away soil from within the castle'. Gradually, it seems the interior of the castle was being sanitised, revealing another example of the tension between visual sensibilities and convenience—a current debate among

picturesque, and not so picturesque, landscapers. The undercrofts of the buildings—a particular area of stimulus for the popular imagination—were also being cleared. In the case of the old stables in the outer court, which in 1825 were provided with a 'good oak floor', it was to prepare the building for a new role as a museum. However, the main vaults of the residential ranges were finally cleared by the Office of Works in the 1930s and, as a result, a little more mystery evaporated from the building.[56]

The grass within the castle courts was kept under control by sheep and goats. These animals, much admired by artists and photographers composing pretty views, were also under threat in the early 20th century. When a visitor in 1924 found the 'walks and steps covered with goat and fowl manure' a letter was sent to the Health Inspector. Complaints were also made about the noxious smells, also as a result of the goats. The owner of the animals, who lived close to the castle, on being reproached by the Powis estate, pleaded poverty and the necessity of keeping the goats for their milk, needed by her invalid father. The goats survived for a few years longer, presumably because they were effective in keeping the grass down, and their owner paid a small rent. By the early 20th century the trees on the walks outside the curtain wall had reached maturity and were, for many visitors, the great ornaments of the castle but also a great liability for the estate. They began blowing down and in 1919 for the 'safety of the pedestrians' those that appeared unsafe were cut down. Nine years later the rest were viewed by Lord Powis and reluctantly clear felled. Ludlow Council protested and a visitor from Manchester wrote complaining that the 'beautiful avenue of trees had been ruthlessly cut down by some Goths and Vandals'.[57]

With the removal of the ivy, the rationalisation of the interior, the threats to the sheep and goats and the removal of the great trees, the picturesque era came firmly to a close in the early 20th century. The romantic appeal of the castle no longer moved the élite and instead rational antiquarianism held sway. The castle was to be

Fig. 11 A postcard showing the mature trees on the walks around the castle

following year the employers of Hollins Colliery, Pensax in Worcestershire. There were many more. Within Ludlow itself the castle was a natural focus for many local organisations, including the Salvation Army. Castle Green was a valuable open space. It was used for a football match in 1920 (and left full of litter) and for a gymkhana in 1928 (and left like a 'ploughed field'). The household staff of Oakly Park was brought here in 'motors' for a picnic in 1925 and the great keep was regularly used as a backdrop for pageants and theatrical events. A historical pageant was being discussed at length in 1924 and a group of old Etonians at Balliol College, Oxford, sought permission to put on Aeschylus's play *The Curse of the House of Atreus* in 1920, which included a scene with a horse-drawn chariot.[59]

In the confused world of 1918 the castle took on a new role as the *locus sanctus* for the survivors of the Great War. An oak was planted to mark the signing of the Armistice and three years later a plaque was placed on the adjoining wall. Archdeacon Maude, the tenant of Castle House had arranged a 'Patriotic Fete' in Castle Green sometime earlier and in 1924 the bishop of Hereford addressed a Diocesan Missionary Festival held here. And so the 'majestic ruins' adapted themselves to the new demands of the 20th century, providing a historic marker for the confused spirituality of the age. Something tangible, old and permanent in a landscape of shifting values; still a symbol, tinctured with nostalgia, of a golden age but seen with less clarity than by the Yorkist and Tudor princes, and the picturesque tourists—*plus ça change, plus c'est la même chose.*

preserved as a monument, to be studied by people with history degrees as an exemplar of medieval secular architecture. Its emotional and symbolic roles were of secondary importance. Remarkably, just as these new perceptions were developing, the powers of steam locomotion and the internal combustion engine were providing an opportunity for the working classes to visit the castle in large numbers. In a rather archaic way, they came to raise their spirits, feast their eyes and re-live in their imaginations the ancient lays. They came to enjoy what their social superiors had enjoyed for a couple of centuries and thus, a delight in the picturesque lived on, a little longer, among ordinary people.[58]

Several boxes of letters in the Shropshire Record Office provide the social historian with a rare insight into the role played by an ancient monument in its regional community. In August 1930, for example, 500 employees of Britannia Batteries Ltd. of Redditch visited the castle—at a reduced rate. Their spokesperson wrote to say they enjoyed themselves albeit the day was 'a wash out'. The clerical staff of the London, Midland & Scottish Railway Company at Victoria Station, Swansea came in 1924 and the

English troops embarking for France,
representing type of ships used by Roger Mortimer,
the second earl of March
(By permission of The British Library. Roy, 18, EI, f130V)

Roger Mortimer, second Earl of March,
a founding member of the Order of the Garter,
from the Bruges Garter Book
(By permission of The British Library. Stowe, 594, f15v)

Courtiers and Ladies, showing some of the
extravagant clothes which might have been bought
by the fourth earl of March with his £13
(By permission of The Bodleian Library. Bodley, 264, f181)

Lord and Lady on the Manor on their estates
from Le Livre de Rusticau *by Piero de Crescenzi.*
Though slightly later (1475–1500) this shows
an inspection of estates as might have been
undertaken by the fourth earl of March
(By permission of The British Library. Add. 19720, f305)

Clee Hill, Shropshire *(?)c.1845 Peter de Wint*

A view of Ludlow Castle drawn on the spot ... July 21st 1777 *by Francis Towne*
(reproduced courtesy Christies)

Ludlow Castle, Shropshire English School, late 18th century

Ludlow Castle, 1792, Julius Caesar Ibbetson   (© Manchester City Art Galleries)

Looking over Ludlow Castle to Whitcliff, showing the outer bailey with its wall walk to the left, and the private flats to the right of centre (© Gareth Thomas)

Looking over Ludlow Castle from Whitcliff (© Gareth Thomas)

CHAPTER XII

Monument Preservation, Management & Display *by* Anthony D.F. Streeten

Ludlow Castle is unusual among the nation's most important and well-known medieval strongholds because it has been owned privately and managed as a ruin since the freehold was acquired in 1811 by the then newly created earl of Powis. The castle was scheduled as an ancient monument in 1915, but it has never passed into State 'guardianship'. It is a cherished landmark at the heart of the town and has long been the venue for the annual Ludlow Festival, but the earl and trustees of the Powis Estate remain responsible both for upkeep of the historic fabric and for ensuring the enjoyment and appreciation of visitors. By the mid-1980s, however, the backlog of repairs exceeded the resources available to the Estate which nevertheless remained firmly committed to the long-established tradition of private ownership and management. This chapter therefore examines briefly the steps which were taken at that time jointly by the Powis Estate and English Heritage to safeguard the long term preservation and maintenance of Ludlow Castle, marking also a significant stage in the evolution of public sector policy towards the repair of privately owned monuments of national importance.

Establishing Principles and Priorities

Repairs had been carried out during the 1970s and early 1980s by the directly employed labour force of the then Department of the Environment, representing 'assistance in kind' from the public purse towards the upkeep of Ludlow Castle. This included work on the Entrance Tower/Keep, repairs to the bridge in 1981, and latterly consolidation of the Great Kitchen. Accompanying archaeological supervision also contributed information about the history of the castle. Investigations carried out during the repairs indicated, for example, that the northern span of the bridge had been dismantled and rebuilt in the 17th or 18th century, while consolidation of the inmost bailey wall revealed details of timber reinforcements probably inserted in the 16th century to stabilise the adjoining brick chimney (see Fig. 1 overleaf). By 1983, however, the need had been established for an integrated programme of recording and consolidation to tackle those parts of the castle which were most in need of repair.

Coinciding with the appointment of a new agent to the Powis Estate in 1986, agreement was reached on a new strategy which commenced with commissioning a conservation architect to carry out a full condition survey. Completed in 1987, this report was to become the first in a series of quinquennial inspections which have informed subsequent repairs and maintenance of the historic fabric and commented on public access. Under the new arrangements concluded between the Powis Estate and English Heritage—which had taken over the responsibilities of the former Directorate of Ancient Monuments and Historic Buildings within the Department of the Enviromnent in 1984—the directly employed

*Fig. 1 Evidence for intramural timbers
exposed during consolidation of the
Great Kitchen in 1981*

labour force was withdrawn in favour of a specialist contractor—Treasure and Son of Ludlow, who tendered successfully for specified tranches of work.

English Heritage offered financial assistance amounting to some £500,000 in order to help the Estate embark upon a phased programme of repairs. Negotiations a few years earlier in respect of nearby Stokesay Castle had already established the need to secure appropriate long-term benefits from substantial public investment in the repair of privately owned monuments. However, the circumstances were different at Ludlow and the arrangements which had been made for eventual acquisition of Stokesay Castle by English Heritage were inappropriate for the Powis Estate which remained committed to its responsibilities for continued repair, maintenance and public access to the castle. Instead, public investment was conditional upon the accompanying development of facilities for visitors in order both to increase income for future maintenance and to encourage public appreciation of the ruins and their history. These and similar negotiations elsewhere marked a significant development in funding policy at the time which sought to fulfil objectives for sustainable management as well as meeting the particular needs of conservation.

An assessment of around 250 castles in the English counties of the central Marches has understandably confirmed the priority for public investment in the preservation of important sites such as Clun, Ludlow, Wigmore and others. The castles at Clun and Wigmore were taken into 'guardianship' before repairs commenced, but at Ludlow the pace of work was dictated by the availability of revenue to match the offer of grants towards the substantial costs of conservation. The priorities included the comprehensive repair of the outer curtain wall and extensive work on the north range of the inner bailey. Tasks involving skilled and semi-skilled maintenance were also identified to alleviate deterioration of the buildings and enhance the appearance of the ruins. The plan of incremental action agreed between the Powis Estate and English Heritage sought to balance practical and financial considerations both in recording and conservation and for enhancing the appreciation of visitors.

It was established from the outset that archaeological recording would take place both before and during the repairs, funded jointly by the Estate and English Heritage. As a first step, English Heritage staff surveyed and plotted photogrammetric images of the principal buildings which were to be repaired. Thereafter, the City of Hereford Archaeological Unit was commissioned for successive phases of work to refine and interpret the surveys with the benefit of further examination and structural analysis of the masonry. The brief for archaeological recording acknowledged the eroded and often undiagnostic texture of the friable walling stone, noting as a specific objective the need to identify extant fabric which had not been consolidated or re-faced previously. Measured drawing was specified to show the evidence for structural changes and to record unstable areas of stonework which would need rebuilding, principally around the wall heads. Profiles were drawn as a record of the principal architectural features and the ensuing reports commissioned in conjunction with the repairs form the basis for some of the research now published elsewhere in this volume.

Consolidation and Maintenance

Repairs identified in the 1987 report as the highest priority were specified in detail using the survey drawings both for the purposes of obtaining tenders and for the necessary approval of scheduled monument consents. In the first phase of work to the outer curtain wall, repointing, rebedding and wall capping were carried out using lime mortars, while extensive voids within the core were grouted by gravity. Work progressed from west to east but before the next stage of repair had commenced there was a substantial collapse at the south-east corner of the outer bailey after prolonged rain in February 1990. The assessment of repair priorities had been correct but the devastating consequence of adverse weather conditions could not have been predicted.

The catastrophic scale of the collapse raised fundamental questions of conservation philos-

Fig. 2 The collapsed south-east corner of the curtain wall in the process of being rebuilt in 1990

ophy. Should the wall be rebuilt or should the broken masonry be consolidated as lasting evidence for this episode in the castle's history? The English Heritage structural engineer observed that the outward collapse had been 'hinged' at the higher ground level inside the castle and confirmed that rebuilding would be feasible on the existing foundations. Site security and visual integrity of the castle within the wider setting of the Ludlow conservation area were the principal factors which influenced the eventual decision to rebuild the wall in its entirety, especially since the form could be reproduced from the evidence of earlier photogrammetric surveys.

The collapsed masonry was sorted carefully under archaeological supervision in order to recover diagnostic features such as the stone quoins, which were reinstated as far as possible in their correct positions when the wall was rebuilt. The line of the fracture was expressed by a break in the coursing of the facing stone as conspicuous evidence for the occurrence and a datestone was placed to record the reconstruction.

The principles and techniques of repair established for initial conservation of the outer curtain wall were also adopted for subsequent phases of work on the north range of the inner bailey. The objective was to prevent the ingress of moisture to wall heads which had been damaged by the penetration of woody growths, yet retaining the soft appearance of the masonry with its light covering of wall flowers. The extent of repair and stone replacement was dictated partly by accessibility. Eroded stones were replaced at high levels which could only be reached from an expensive scaffold suspended against the lofty north wall of the castle, whereas stonework in comparable condition elsewhere was retained where it was less exposed and more easily accessible for future repair at lower levels on the inner elevations.

A few eroded jambs and window mullions were replaced in the Solar block where structural stability was judged to be impaired. New stone was cut and set to the recorded original profiles, while other mouldings were measured for future reference when the time comes for their eventual replacement. A weathering of lead was inserted

Fig. 3 The Solar block and North-West Tower swathed in scaffolding for the stonework repairs carried out in 1991

partly to the rather neglected appearance of the ruins and partly to the enhanced expectations and competition derived from alternative leisure opportunities. Work to improve the appearance and presentation of the castle was therefore carried out in conjunction with conservation of the historic fabric. Among the principal enhancements were the removal of a works compound from the outer bailey, the management of vegetation in the inner moat and improvements to the degraded surfaces within the inner bailey. Timber-lined steps were installed for safe access to the moat which was laid to grass, flanked by thorny undergrowth to prevent erosion of the margins. Surface profiles were reformed where necessary around buildings within the inner bailey also to allow for the controlled circulation of visitors. Floor surfaces within the ruins were dressed with quarry scalpings to reinforce the character of these internal spaces.

Oak handrails on the bridge, made of timber from the Powis Estate, established a new pattern for the safe access of visitors to elevated parts of the ruins. Oak was selected for the attractive colour and texture of its natural weathering in harmony with the surrounding stonework. The robust sectional design of the handrails anticipated the risk of vandalism and allows for the piecemeal replacement of components where necessary. Mesh infill panels on some of the the guardrails were set horizontally rather than diagonally following experiments which showed that diagonal mesh stands out more conspicuously in sunlight against the mellow stonework.

The rugged texture of the former staircase leading from the inner bailey to the doorway of the Great Hall contributes greatly to the informal character of the ruins. Consequently, it was decided to modify the surface rather than to install new stone treads when, in 1991, the new decking was installed at floor level within the Great Hall. Reinstatement of this 'floor' gives a more meaningful impression of the scale and proportions of this magnificent space than had been available previously from the basement level. Access to the spiral staircase leading to the upper floors of the

above the hoodmould of the uppermost window on the south elevation of the Solar block in preference to replacing the stone.

Since regular maintenance was regarded as an important prescription for maintaining the overall character and appearance of the ruins, stainless steel anchors were installed on the wall tops to enable safe access for inspection of the high level masonry without incurring the expense of frequent scaffolding. This enlightened approach reinforces the usefulness of quinquennial inspections which identify the need for maintenance before major repairs become necessary.

Public Access and Interpretation

The number of visitors to Ludlow Castle had fallen significantly by the mid-1980s, owing

Fig. 4 The Porter's Lodge and adjoining Prison remodelled as the new visitor reception centre in 1993

Solar block also opened up hitherto inaccessible parts of the castle with commanding views from the floors which were reinstated in the North-West Tower. Again this enables regular inspection and permits access for maintenance.

These improvements to public access were accompanied by the rationalisation of infrastructure, including seating and litter bins in the outer bailey, all to a consistent design using Powis Estate oak as the unifying theme. It was a difficult challenge to reconcile the desired atmosphere of informality with the expectations for explanatory information enabling visitors to appreciate the history and significance of Ludlow Castle. In due course, however, selected viewpoints were identified for explanatory panels—again mounted in oak frames for consistency of design and presentation. Each location was scrutinised carefully to minimise the visual intrusion of these panels, selecting for example a discrete position on the outer lip of the inner moat as the least conspicuous place for explaining the complex development of the Entrance Tower/Keep.

Maintaining the informal atmosphere of Ludlow Castle has been an important objective of the Powis Estate, yet the appreciation and enjoyment of visitors has been enhanced successfully by improved interpretation including an informative guidebook and audio tour. The quiet interior of the castle contrasts strongly with the municipal setting of the formal gardens adjoining the outer curtain wall, yet the towering defences to the north and west have benefitted greatly from enlightened management of the vegetation in a manner which has opened up the memorable vistas from hills on the opposite side of the river valley.

Tourism and the Development of New Facilities
The plan of action agreed between the Powis Estate and English Heritage in 1986 had envisaged the need to increase revenue from visitors to secure the continuing regime of repair and maintenance. These objectives were shared by the then English Toursit Board which, in 1988, took the initiative of commissioning a study to review the

scope for active marketing of Ludlow Castle as a destination for visitors to South Shropshire. The project brief was to examine ways of increasing income from visitors through improved services and management, exploring particularly the relationship between the castle and the town and the opportunities for raising public awareness of the central Marches as an attractive area to visit. The report completed in July 1989 analysed the attitude of visitors and explored far-reaching options for development. Principal among the recommendations were proposals to improve the facilities for visitors entering the castle who had hitherto purchased their tickets from the custodian at a small wooden shed near the main entrance. Possibilities for the short term included some form of reception tent in the outer bailey or a new building just inside the castle on the north side of the outer gate. Longer term options included the potential for developing visitor facilities outside the castle or incorporating them inside the shell of surviving buildings within the outer bailey.

Trustees of the Powis Estate made their own assessment of the options and concluded that operational needs and aesthetic considerations could best be satisfied by building within the walls of the former Porter's Lodge and Prison attached to the outer curtain wall. Archaeological investigations and a feasibility study indicated that a two-storey structure with a low-pitched roof could be accommodated within the available space using original structural openings and taking support from masonry without significant damage to the fabric or appearance of the buildings.

These new facilities, comprising a shop, exhibition space and toilets, which were completed in 1993, marked the culmination of an ambitious programme of repair and development at Ludlow Castle. By 1999 there were over 100,000 visitors per annum—a significant increase since the period of declining attendance in the mid-1980s. The manner and even the principle of re-roofing a ruin is invariably controversial but the solution at Ludlow Castle has safeguarded the familiar open character of the outer bailey unencumbered by substantial new buildings. The scheme has also fulfilled the original objectives to enhance the facilities for visitors and thereby to sustain public interest in the future maintenance of the castle.

Conclusion

This short account of monument preservation, management and display at Ludlow Castle encapsulates much that would now be recognised among the components of a Conservation Plan. The co-operation between English Heritage and the Powis Estate is also a familiar aspect of what has come to be known as partnership funding. Above all, however, the integrated approach to consolidation and display of the ruins serves as a benchmark for future management of the castle, highlighting the aspirations for continuing maintenance of the ruins in their informal setting. Ideas will change and the methods of presentation and interpretation will evolve but safeguarding for public enjoyment the enduring character of Ludlow Castle remains just as important as preserving the ruins themselves.

Part III

The Buildings

CHAPTER XIII

The Norman Military Works

by Derek Renn[1]

Once the rising of Edric the Wild against William the Conqueror was crushed in late 1069, a castle at Ludlow was to be expected, more particularly after Walter de Lacy's holding became directly of the Crown in 1075, and perhaps built of stone like William fitzOsbern, earl of Hereford's own castles in the Wye valley (including Chepstow and Monmouth). Walter died after a fall from scaffolding whilst supervising the building of a new church in Hereford in 1085, which suggests a close interest in stone building.[2] The earliest decorated feature in the castle—the wall arcade in the Entrance Tower—might date from the 1080s, if not before. The complete absence of arrow loops is another pointer to an early date for the masonry of Ludlow Castle's defences.

The plan and elevation of the inner bailey

Chapters I to III describe the setting of the town and castle. The natural strength of the castle site was improved by cutting off the angle by a ditch originally some 25 metres wide with vertical rock-cut sides, but now partly filled in. The resulting platform is roughly quadrant-shaped, with an internal radius of almost 70 metres. Such a layout could have been adopted at almost any time, but the relative scale of the ditch compared with the area enclosed suggest the foundation of a medieval castle rather than that of an earlier fortification. The walls and towers of the inner bailey closely follow the edge of the platform. Similar quadrant layouts on cliffs overlooking major river-crossings underlie the early stone castles of Barnard Castle (Co. Durham), Goodrich and Wigmore (both Herefordshire) and particularly Monmouth.[3]

The present inner bailey probably comprised the whole of the first castle. St. John Hope, who excavated the foundations of the demolished parts of the entrance and of the chancel of the chapel, found no trace of a bank within the ditch.[4] Although a bank might have been completely removed at an early date, perhaps leaving part of an early gate, as at Barnard Castle,[5] it is more likely that the stone quarried from the ditch (as well as from the cliffs on the other side) was used rapidly to build the curtain walls and towers. The plan of the inner bailey curtain wall is an irregular pointed oval—one side more sharply curved than the other—rather than a true quadrant. The 'quasi-radii' to north and west are each slightly bowed outward, with square open-backed towers at each end, facing open country. The 'circumference' to south and east is unbroken except by a gateway near one end. Such an angle position for the gateway is not unusual (e.g. at Barnard Castle, Carisbrooke [Isle of Wight] and Exeter [Devon]) since it frees up interior space while focussing movement. The Ludlow gateway did not face the medieval town to the east, but looked south towards Dinham and the easier river crossing from Wales (see also chapter II).

More than one wall tower (apart from the gate) is uncommon in medieval castles before the mid-12th century, but Ludlow started with four.

There were corner towers (one next to the entrance) to the square bailey at Carisbrooke, and the oval trace at Saltwood (Kent) had at least two, regularly spaced from the gate tower and each accompanied by a larger one projecting only internally. Perhaps the nearest parallel to Ludlow are the early walls and towers of Richmond (North Yorkshire) (see chapter XIV).

At first the towers would seem to have risen little above the top of the curtain wall (with the possible exception of the main entrance). Apart from a few small slits for light and air, the walls were completely plain. Seen from outside, the walls rise directly from the exposed rock outcrop, heightening it into an unscaleable cliff. This blank curved face was interrupted only by two towers, one (the North-West Tower) in the middle carrying the latrines and the other (the Postern Tower) to the west, with a small doorway partly concealed in one side. Seen from the castle's later outer bailey, the curved inner curtain wall had a tower at each end. Close to the left-hand one was the bridge leading to the first entrance (to the left of the present bridge and entrance). Of the four towers (excluding the gate) all were rectangular and all open-backed except the Postern Tower. There is evidence for an almost continuous passage around the wall tops; the towers are so sited as to command almost the entire 'envelope' of the castle but provided only passive defence— without arrowloops, active defence came from the wall top.

Generally, the early walling is of local shaly rubble, with ashlar dressings and quoins of red sandstone. Doorways are square-edged and round-headed, as are other openings. Barrel vaults are usual. Significant differences from these norms will be mentioned. The curtain wall of the inner bailey is about 1.7m thick and was built in a number of straight lengths. The entrance passage was near the south-facing angle tower. That both curtain wall and towers have been raised in height, sometimes more than once, is apparent, for example in the quoins to the west of both the east-facing tower and the entrance, as well as in the masonry between them.[6] Much of the north bailey wall has been taken down and

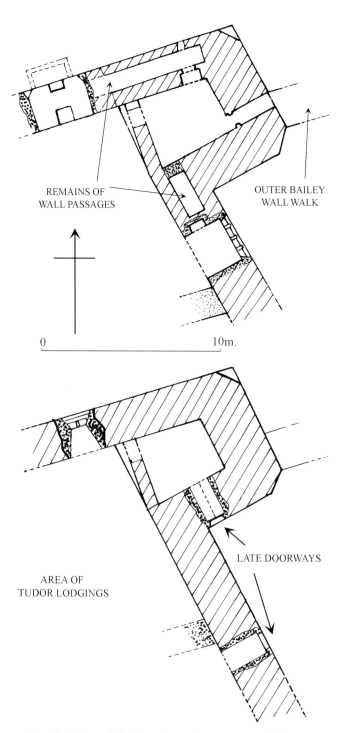

REMAINS OF WALL PASSAGES

OUTER BAILEY WALL WALK

0   10m.

LATE DOORWAYS

AREA OF TUDOR LODGINGS

Fig. 1 Plan of the Pendover Tower ground floor (lower) and first floor (upper) showing later alterations

rebuilt to accommodate the palatial domestic range, described in chapters XVI, XVII and XVIII.

Pendover (East) Tower

This tower, which lies flush with the north bailey wall but projects eastward, may be the Pendover Tower of the 13th-century *Romance of Fulk fitzWarin*.[7] The external corners are chamfered off, perhaps an alteration since the interior corners are square, making the wall there thin and weak. Chamfered angles, however, lessened the danger of quoins being levered out or knocked off by attackers. A wall built across the open back or gorge had two loops in 1903, one above the other, so there was at least one intermediate floor inside. The south wall shows evidence of two successive blocked passages, and there is another through the curtain wall to the south. These all gave access to the north end of the inner bailey ditch; latterly they gave access from the lodgings into the outer bailey, but either or both might have been a postern to the town before the outer bailey was added. That from the tower would have been a right-angled entrance, like that of the Postern Tower.

At first-floor level there are wall passages blocked by later alterations, one entered by a Norman doorway and running west and the other heading south. The passages are not continuous: the east wall of the tower has a blocked doorway which led onto the wallwalk of the outer bailey, so the doorway was presumably no older than that bailey wall. The western passage may have once continued (perhaps as an open wall-walk) as far as the eastern passage of the next (North-West) Tower, but the curtain wall has been rebuilt. The upper parts of the tower are later medieval additions.

North-West Tower [8]

This is not to be confused with the later multistorey garderobe (latrine) block further east. The tower has chamfered angles externally but not internally, similar to the Pendover Tower. On the left-hand side of the gorge of the tower, a stair with wide shallow treads rises from ground level south-westward into the curtain wall. It has three arches in the vault, and ends at the foot of a blocked spiral stair. In the north wall of the

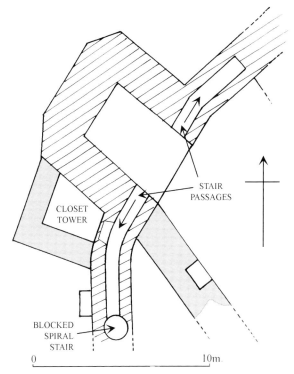

Fig. 2 Plan of the North-West Tower ground floor

passage is a blocked opening, which might either have opened into an original latrine or into a later stone-walled latrine pit added to the tower. From the top of the spiral stair, another passage ran northward, with a small loop in each side and a latrine corbelled out over a pilaster buttress.

A similar wall-stair, which starts from the opposite side of the gorge. is blocked and the walling altered a little way up. It probably formed a 'mirror image' of the other wallstair, since there is a spiral stair in a matching position and traces of an upper passage. A similar metre-wide passage runs round the tower walls at this middle level; it once linked with the others, but is now blocked at both ends (see Figs. 7 & 8, pp.162 & 163). The internal gap at this level may once have been a doorway leading from the passage into the tower space. The passage roof has small cross-vaults to carry the heads of the external pairs of loops in each wall, and there is a recess for a latrine carried on a squinch arch between tower and north curtain wall, ashlar-faced within and without.

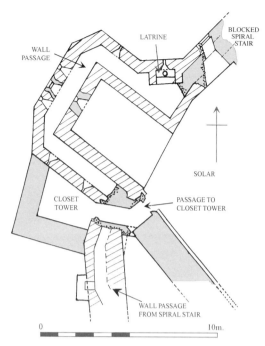

*Fig. 3 Plan of the North-West Tower
first floor*

The effect of these spiral stairs was to reverse the direction of travel and at the same time to raise the passage (to continue at a higher level) within a relatively thin wall. But why was there not simply a straight stair in the tower walls alone, rising to the middle level passage, like that in the Entrance Tower? The straight stairs might have been intended to end at a lower walltop; when the wall was heightened, the only alternative to passages going even further away from the tower (further weakening the curtain wall; compare the alterations to the Entrance Tower), was to turn them back on themselves in this way. Such an elaborate rearrangement suggests that there were Norman domestic buildings of quality against the curtain wall here. Bishop Henry de Blois' palace at Winchester (Hampshire) has a latrine block of *c.*1141 encased by 1154 with an upper passage similar to Ludlow and Bishop Alexander's gatehouse at Newark Castle (Nottinghamshire) of 1123-48 had flanking chambers and passages linked similarly by intermediate spiral stairs.[9] Since there is no evidence for a wall passage in the next (Postern) Tower, it is uncertain how far south the passage ran. Again, the top storey of this tower is a later addition.

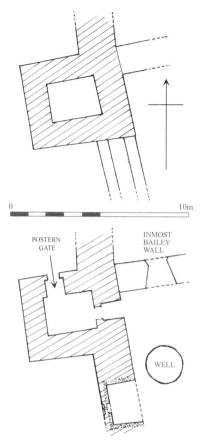

*Fig. 4 Plans of the Postern Tower ground floor
(lower) and first floor (upper)
after St. John Hope*

Postern (West) Tower

Here there is clear evidence in the masonry that the bailey wall and the tower were once only about one-third of their present height. The tower has an entrance doorway in its northern flank, some distance above the ground outside, and a similar but larger doorway in the east (back) wall into the inner bailey. There is a single loop higher up in the west wall and an added upper floor and raised parapets, so that it is impossible to establish if there were any early links along the walltop in either direction. The interior is inaccessible at present.

Oven (South) Tower

This tower is perfectly plain externally, apart from two small loops high up lighting a wall passage running north from a latrine and doorway from the interior. The passage has a second doorway facing east along the (later) wallwalk to

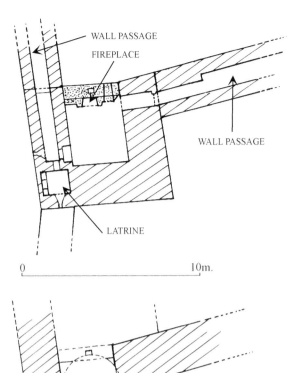

WALL PASSAGE

FIREPLACE

WALL PASSAGE

LATRINE

0   10m.

OVEN

*Fig. 5 Plans of the Oven Tower ground floor
(lower) and first floor (upper)*

the Entrance Tower. The interior is completely filled by a great oven, spanned by a back wall which, like the top floor, was a later addition. When the back wall was added the upper part of the tower was converted to residential use as indicated by the fireplaces built into the wall.

The Entrance (Great)Tower

G.T. Clark in 1877 declared this to be 'one of the most curious and perplexing Norman keeps now standing'.[10] Although he recognised that the northern wall was considerably later in date than the others, he failed to observe that the early internal arcade must have continued beyond it, or to recognize the large blocked arch in the south wall. It was left to St. John Hope to interpret this

correctly, and to excavate the foundations of at least two earlier phases of the northern part of the tower.[11] He followed Clark in believing in a T-shaped plan protruding slightly from the inner bailey wall, but originally forming an entrance passage (with an outer lobby in front of its main arch) and not an enclosed basement. (see Fig. 7). St. John Hope's description of the castle is masterly, and it is with great diffidence that I offer a new interpretation.

Ground Level

The quarrymen of the inner ditch left rock abutments for a timber bridge, levelled up with mortared shale slabs, in front of the tower. (A small brick-lined 'cave' in the outer side later formed an ice-house.) The exterior of the tower is partly of squared and coursed rubble and partly of ashlar, varying from a hard grey stone to a soft red sandstone. The ashlar is largely confined to the south exterior and to the ground-floor arcade within. Seen from the outer bailey, differences in the tower's masonry indicate the position of the ground-floor entrance arch but, apart from one or two chamfered blocks and what may be a piece of carved decoration now reset on edge, no dressings are left. Indeed, the 'cast' looks more like that of a pointed arch than of a semi-circular one: the dressings could possibly have been inserted at a later date into the inner curtain wall to the east, forming the outer arch (once of two square orders?) of the present entrance, with slight traces of a stone bridge abutment there also. The north arch of the present bridge is clearly secondary, and replaced a drawbridge (see Dinely illustration p.48).[12] But this pointed entrance arch is unlikely to have been the first. In the disturbed walling at the interior south-west angle of the tower, there is part of a chamfered impost. At ground level on the south side is a chamfered quirked offset course, partly underpinned with squared rubble, but not returned along the east and west sides. The south-east angle of the tower spreads outwards in a bold sloping batter, returned unevenly northwards to where the upper ashlar stands on shaly rubble, perhaps a plinth to the inner curtain wall at this point.

Within the basement of the tower, the pointed rubble barrel-vault, over the central section, with slots through from the floor above, replaced a timber roof or an earlier vault. The slots are too short and wide to have been for dropping missiles or water to extinguish fire set against the doors. St. John Hope suggested that the blank ashlar walling to east and west was where a pair of main doors folded back. Further north there is part of a wall arcade, of round-headed square-edged arches carried on round shafts with crude capitals (without abaci) and Attic bases on square plinths. Only part of one arch remains on the west side, the shaft supporting a plain cushion capital. On the east there are two complete arches, and the position of the major arch across the passage and of a

Fig. 6 The Entrance Tower, showing the addition on the outside of the inner bailey wall, and the blocked gateway arch at ground level

similar base excavated by St. John Hope (outside the present north wall) indicated four bays. Each of the surviving capitals on the east side has a different curling ornament: the southernmost being a slightly chamfered cube cut into two scallops (see Figs. 8 & 9). A date of around 1080 might be suggested for this arcade.[13] More assured versions of the same ornament can be seen on the capitals of the blind arcade round the nave of the nearby chapel (see chapter XV).

St. John Hope based his case for an outer lobby on what he described as 'a shaft for the main order' of an arch within the present basement. It is not clear whether this is the same as a 'respond shaft' which he also describes, extrapolating it into a two-bay arcade in front of his arch. This 'respond' is a column carrying a well-finished scalloped capital, lower (and better) than those of the arcade. It stands in a re-entrant near the south-east corner, next to one end of a narrow ashlar-lined wall passage in the east wall, partly roofed with slabs and partly with rubble, which emerges again about 3 metres further north. St. John Hope took it to be a pedestrian 'wicket' by-passing the main door.

The doorway at each end of this narrow passage has a lintel which has been re-set, perhaps because a round arch or a tympanum has been torn out. Both doors could have been barred from the inside against an attack from the main entrance passage. St. John Hope's postulated arcade arch would not have cleared the head of the south doorway.

With the position (and arrangement) of the original entrance arch unknown, it brings us back to the inner end of the original gate-passage. Here, the excavations outside the present north wall of the tower showed that the main passage arch had two square orders towards the inner bailey, probably framing doors,[14] and was flanked by a narrow doorway in the east wall leading to the foot of a straight wall-stair. Entrance passage and wall-stair alike had been blocked by masonry up to 3 metres thick at the base, with several chamfered offsets to the batter (at least on the north side). This casing returned

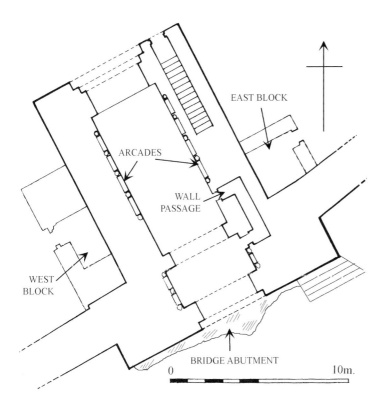

Fig. 7 Reconstruction of the ground floor plan of the Entrance Tower as arranged for a gatehouse, with added south front (see Fig. 10)

Fig. 8 (above) 1852 drawing of wall arcade in the ground floor of the Entrance Tower. Fig. 9 (right) shows a detail of a capital of the arcade

along the east and west sides to where two large blocks of masonry were built on the same alignment in the angles against the bailey wall.

The west block has very thick walls against the side of the old entrance passage, and does not quite reach the bailey wall. St. John Hope said that it was of a slightly later date and that the space within was spanned by a strong semicircular arch springing from rude imposts. He called it a garderobe pit, predating the blocking and casing of the passage. Similar additions were made to the early *donjons* at Corfe (Dorset), and Old Sarum (Wiltshire), whilst that at Newark seems to have been an original feature. The pit is badly placed for the extant latrine shafts. If the ground floor was at least partly a storage basement/ undercroft, the walls seem wastefully thick and prevent direct access from the entrance passage. The building did not extend to the original length of the main passage, possibly because an external doorway was planned, to be reached up steps from the north-west, rather like

Richmond, and as suggested by St. John Hope for the rebuilt tower. Perhaps what was begun as a forebuilding with a drawbridge pit (like Hedingham [Essex] or Rochester [Kent] for example) was converted into the basement of the private suite. St. John Hope pointed out that there is no trace of any large opening in the external walls above ground. Finding parts of two steps (on the slope of the batter to the north), lining up with the outside of the entrance passage wall, he inferred a new stair which turned east before reaching the block. That would have made an awkward entrance (into one corner of the upper chamber), but it might explain the position of the present north wall. There is no indication of the extent and date of the blocking of the wall stair and it might have remained in use (until the insertion of the spiral stair) by way of an opening through the casing.

The single-storey east block, with an altered doorway and pointed barrel vault, formed the porter's lodge to the new entrance beside the tower; a blocked opening high up in the south (bailey) wall can be seen inside.

The later rebuilding north of the porter's lodge may conceal evidence of an original eastern block matching the western one in plan, but not in height. This would explain the vaulting of the porter's lodge, which seems unnecessary for a single-storey unlit space. The blocked opening in the south wall is similar in position to the niche between the western block and the curtain wall. The latter was the shaft of the private latrine so this opening might have belonged to a public one for visitors, as well as for sentries on the wall-walk and, in particular, for the guard/porter on point duty, the space below being later converted into a porter's lodge for the present entrance.

Whether these two blocks were coeval with, or were later additions to, the main entrance passage is uncertain.

It seems more than a coincidence that the excavated foundation is exactly the same width as the T plan and that, if its thickness is deducted from the ashlar south front, we are left with an original entrance almost exactly level with the rubble faces of the bailey wall. An entire later casing might explain why the south-east corner of the tower had to be under-built where it encroaches slightly on the inner bailey ditch and for the suggested Transitional rather than Norman outer arch, as well as the entire absence of ashlar at the south end of the basement and the awkward revaulting, while still allowing for a shallower lobby and the wall passage bypassing the main door (see Fig. 10).

The Inmost (Third) Bailey

Either or both stairs would have been necessary when an 'inmost bailey' was created by building a rubble wall east from the Postern Tower as far as a porch covering a skewed doorway. From the porch, the new wall turned south (the corner being chamfered off) along the east side of the casing just inside the foundation offset line, St. John Hope's plan shows it as extending as far as the porter's lodge, which would imply that the casing was already demolished when the new wall was built. (see Fig. 10) However, the excavation photograph confirms what can still be seen, namely breaks in the rubble coursing where it formerly butted up against the sloping north face of the casing. This is confirmed by the excavation plan.

It is not obvious whether this casing was ever completed, how high it was carried up, and why or when it was demolished or collapsed, to be eventually replaced by the present north wall. It might have remained as an open platform for a military 'engine', but the heart of the castle—symbolic or defensive—still lay here. Another wall ran south on the alignment of the west side of the entrance passage and its foundations are shown on the excavation plan as butting up against the casing.[15] So there would have been a third, private, or inmost bailey enclosure, separating the Entrance, Oven and Postern Towers from the rest of the inner bailey, and containing the present well. It would have been reached either through a lobby to the north-east from the rest of the inner bailey or from the west (outside the castle) through the Postern Tower. Stairs from here to the upper floors of the Entrance Tower (perhaps one set from each 'half' of the inmost

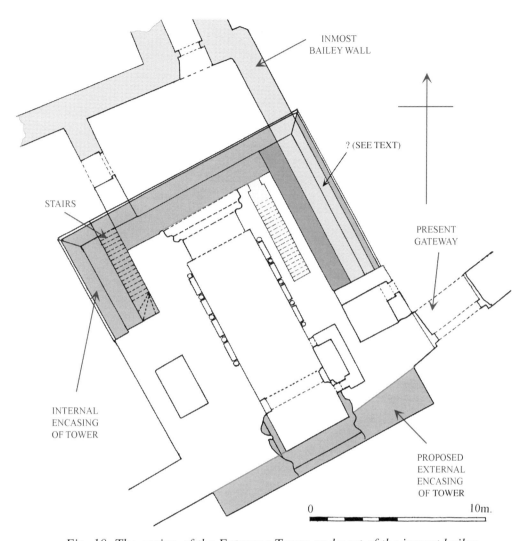

INMOST
BAILEY WALL

? (SEE TEXT)

PRESENT
GATEWAY

STAIRS

INTERNAL
ENCASING
OF TOWER

PROPOSED
EXTERNAL
ENCASING
OF TOWER

0   10m.

Fig. 10 The casing of the Entrance Tower and part of the inmost bailey

enclosure), are likely but not certain. At later stages of the castle's development, additional entrances were made in this wall.

The Building Dates of the Entrance Tower and of the Inmost Bailey

Contemporary square towers alongside the entrance doorway through the bailey wall occur from about the middle of the 12th century in Britain (e.g. Bridgend [Glamorgan], Kenilworth [Warwickshire] and Lydney [Gloucestershire]), by which time some earlier towers pierced by an entrance passage had been blocked and a new entrance made alongside. Examples other than Ludlow are Bramber (Sussex), Exeter and Richmond.[16] At Richmond a great 11th-century arch in the curtain wall had a square tower added on the outer side, which in turn seems to have been cased around on three sides.[17] I have demonstrated that both Pevensey (Sussex) and Portchester (Hampshire) towers encase an earlier building, whilst the country house at Castle Acre (Norfolk) was lined rather than cased on conversion into a great tower or *donjon* about 1140.[18] A baronial *penchant* for building similar tall towers at this time resulted in those at Bungay (Suffolk), Hedingham and Rochester, for example.

Likely historical contexts for such major works here at Ludlow are either around the time of the siege in 1139, or that of the private war between Gilbert de Lacy and Joce de Dinan, the outer date limits of which are 1148 and 1156 (see

133

chapter IV).[19] The author of the *Romance of Fulk fitzWarin* obviously knew his 'Dynan' (Ludlow). He mentions the three baileys and two ditches, and the tower within the third bailey. During the fighting, the gate towards the river was opened, a tower over a gate burnt and the high tower largely overthrown.

Repairs were completed by 1170 at the latest and no building work appears in the accounts from 1177 to 1199 while the castle was in royal hands.[20] In 1172 Hugh de Lacy II was given Meath in Ireland, and he or a later de Lacy built a great tower there at Trim. Pre-1170 is perhaps a rather early date for an inmost bailey, the royal fashion for which began at Dover (Kent) and Windsor (Berkshire) in the 1180s and continued at Corfe, Kenilworth and the Tower of London soon after 1200.[21] St. John Hope's date, (early 13th century), for the walls north and east of the Entrance Tower which form the inmost bailey, is thus likely to be correct.

The Entrance (Great) Tower:

First-Floor Level

The straight eastern wall stair rises to the level of the top of the curtain walls and originally gave access only to an (almost) continuous narrow path at this level round the perimeter of the inner bailey. But, when the western block was added, the gate-passage vaulted and the whole was cased in, the extra width provided space for two vaulted lobbies, covered by four-part plastered vaults without ribs and a large high-roofed space between them. The doorway from the stair is set in a tall recess; opposite is a tall loop, splayed widely internally and slightly externally, which has been widened and lowered to form a seat, so that it now cuts through an external half-hexagonal string-course. This string-course is on the south face only; there are offsets about a metre higher on the east and west sides of the tower. The external east face of the tower is mainly of coursed rubble, like that to the west, with ashlar on the lobby faces only. A tall doorway to the inner bailey wall walk eastward has an impost in light-coloured stone, suggesting the removal of a tympanum like that surviving on the west face.

There appears to be a vertical break in coursing further north, beyond which again is a small jambshaft with a cushion capital and re-used lintel, and a blocked rerarch jamb, both once part of a window.

Within the tower, another doorway leads up two steps onto the top of the renewed vault of the basement. It is distinctly possible that only the south part of this room was built at first (compare the west gate at Lincoln Castle), not only on account of the building break on the east wall, coupled with vertical quoins (at X on Fig. 12), but also being the reason for the change from grey to red sandstone on the opposite wall at Y and the curious three-plane west face described below. St. John Hope took the quoins to be part of a very large Norman recess (some 5 metres high), but they might mark a break or an angle, clearing the head of the staircase, to a thinner east wall comparable with that opposite which has an internal offset from the face below.

The west lobby is rather different from that to the east: it is reached through a high arch, is smaller and (almost) rectangular rather than square, and opens onto a short passage that leads to a doorway onto the wallwalk leading towards the Oven Tower. This doorway has a light-coloured stone tympanum and preserves part of the rear wall of the early wallwalk (see Fig. 11). It is in a vertical strip of wall which protrudes beyond the south-east angle of the tower but lies behind the line of the western block. To accompany the loop lighting the stairhead and east lobby, the south face of the west lobby and the central space were lit by three windows, of which the eastern $1^{1}/_{2}$ survive. Each window had a deep and wide internal recess, and the surviving windows have an outer order supported on jamb-shafts with cushion capitals.

A fourth window would have made a symmetrical façade, so why was a narrow loop made at the top of the stairs? I suggest that it denotes a difference of function within. The east lobby had door arches to the head of the stairs, to the bailey wall walk next to the present entrance, and to the main room and west lobby. The other first-floor spaces had only one doorway apiece. A single guard

Fig. 11 The doorway into the keep from the wallwalk to its west, showing the plain, light-coloured tympanum above, and the narrow window slit to the adjacent room

standing by the slit in the east lobby could control movement in several directions, with the advantage of height and the light behind him. The slit may eventually have been deliberately cut down to make a comfortable seat for a long vigil and incidentally to convert it into a proper arrowslit.

An early medieval visitor, after climbing the straight staircase or otherwise reaching the wallwalk of the inner bailey would, on passing the guard, go up more steps into an imposing high room, probably with a dais at the far (north) end, illuminated by high windows in the south wall. The room then extended further north than it does now, and this far end probably contained passages and stairs—both spiral and straight—controlling access to the smaller rooms at this and higher levels. The end wall may also have had a fireplace and chimney flue plus large windows looking into the inner bailey.

The west block, in the angle between the inside of the inner bailey wall and the tower, was

entered from the north-east corner. The main room within has a two-bay unribbed vault, with a loop in the north wall and another to the west. There are two large recesses in the east wall plus a later window. At the south end of the block is a smaller room, similarly vaulted (but east-west) with a single loop in the west wall and a latrine in the far corner which vented into the slot between the block and the bailey wall here and the shaft could be flushed (and possibly used) from the wallwalk. This was clearly a private block with *en suite* facilities. One corner of the main room has since had a corner blocked off by a latrine chute from an upper floor.

The Entrance (Great) Tower:
Upper Parts
The next level was originally part of the double-height central chamber, probably reached from below by a stair on the north side. How much of this is Norman is uncertain. Above the western chamber block is a much-altered but similar-sized room, with a lean-to roof. Only the southernmost loop is round-headed, and there is a latrine here which is immediately above the south-west corner of the ground floor space. The small size and inconvenience of this siting (particularly with respect to the floor below) must mean limited use. Was the substantial ground-floor space intended for storage (like other spaces below raised medieval halls or chambers) and perhaps adapted much later by partitioning off one end? The modern doorway here may have had an equally large predecessor; it seems unlikely that it would have been hacked through such a thickness of wall, although there may have been a rake-out arch. St. John Hope stated that there was a narrow (0.6 metre wide) dog-legged passage to a spiral stair in the south-west corner, of which the north end and two lighting loops to south and west are visible now. Two blocked square small loops on either side of the south-east angle at this level may indicate a very dark room within—perhaps a treasury for valuables—reached by a straight or spiral stair and wall passage from the north.

Above this level there is another string course and offset on the south and east faces of the tower

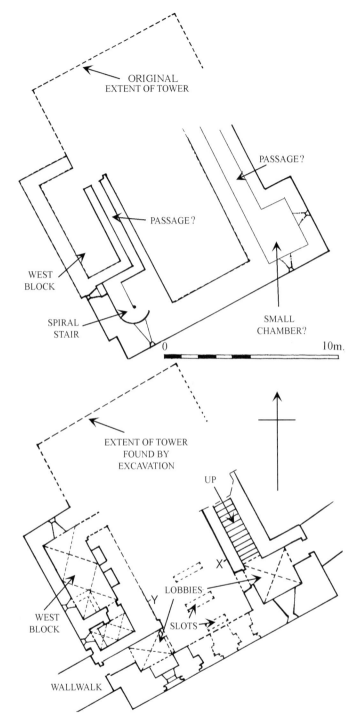

ORIGINAL
EXTENT OF TOWER

PASSAGE?

PASSAGE?

WEST
BLOCK

SPIRAL
STAIR

SMALL
CHAMBER?

0   10m.

EXTENT OF TOWER
FOUND BY
EXCAVATION

UP

LOBBIES

WEST
BLOCK

SLOTS

WALLWALK

Fig. 12 First floor plan (bottom)
and second floor plan (top) of the Entrance Tower

creasing is visible on the south wall. Generally at this level there are changes in the quoins and masonry which suggest a later date for the top floor, and there is no evidence for Norman work at the top of the tower. St. John Hope's stair implies an upper floor, but the size of the passage suggests limited use, perhaps only by sentries going to a look-out turret.

A Parade Front?

The row of windows facing south above the (now blocked) entrance passage may not have been very warlike, and showed an attacker that the wall was weak here, but they did add an impressive feature to the façade. The best example I know of such a display in a Norman castle is the gatehouse at Newark founded by Bishop Alexander 1123-48, with traces of two tiers of windows. The 'tribune' gallery approached by wallstairs at the west end of great churches exists at Jumièges, both St. Pierre by about 993 and Notre Dame begun 40 years later, or Hersfeld Abbey, a hulking *westwerk* pierced by a passage with a wall arcade of four arches on either side and stairs rising in straight flights in side blocks. These were twice the size of Ludlow, and echo both Charlemagne's chapel and the palace gatehouse at Aachen and the double chapel at Hereford.[22]

Larger openings than windows, well above ground level, for displaying either relics or people occur in a number of Anglo-Saxon church towers in England. In the Bayeux Tapestry, Harold's return from Normandy is seen by people looking through round-headed openings at two levels above a gate but below the top floor of the building.[23] Examples in 11th-century stone castles in England are the open triangular-headed arches at Exeter and the round-headed ones at the top of St. George's Tower at Oxford.[24] The same idea of public exhi-

but not on the west. There is an offset within on the east and west walls, probably for the wallplates of the high-pitched roof whose bition today is the balcony of Buckingham Palace, the theatre box, the 'platform party' at a meeting, or the appearance of an actor through the stage scenery. Symbolic features in later castles include a deliberately dramatic approach route to the most private apartments (Knaresborough [West Yorkshire], London [Wakefield and White Towers], Castle Rising [Norfolk], Warkworth [Northumberland] and prominent heraldic carvings (Bodiam [Sussex], Herstmonceux [Sussex], Hylton [Co. Durham], Warkworth again).

An equally early parallel to Ludlow is Richmond Castle. It is triangular in plan; the longest side, above a sheer cliff, is unwalled. The other sides have small square towers at the ends, one combined with an early hall and gate-tunnel. Another walltower forms a chapel with simple blind arcading on three sides. At the apex, facing the town, is the main tower (which was added in front of the original simple gate-arch) with the present entrance alongside.The basement of the tower is reached through the original gate-arch, but the upper floors can only be reached from the curtain wallwalk and thence by straight wall-stairs. The main room on each upper floor has small flanking chambers. The first floor has three large round-headed openings (the central one with a tympanum) cut straight through the outer wall. Elsewhere they would be doorways, but here they open into thin air. This is the same idea as the Ludlow gallery; the honour of Richmond adjoined that of Pontefract, the lands of the other branch of the Lacy family; Pontefract Castle is too ruined to determine whether it too had a gallery.

There is an echo of the Ludlow inner gate-house in the projecting Norman church doorways with blind arcading above, just a few kilometres down the Teme valley, at Bockleton, Eastham, Knighton and Stockton, although the closest (and probably earliest) parallel is at Stoulton, beyond Worcester, where the arcade arches (supported on nookshafts) over the doorway might once have been open.[25]

Fig. 13 The inside of the south wall of the Entrance Tower showing the creasing of an earlier roof, replaced when the top storey was added

The later alterations to the Entrance Tower

The date and reason for the disappearance of the north wall are unknown. The *Romance of Fulk fitzWarin* says that the highest tower was largely destroyed in the 12th-century fighting,[26] but deliberate damage might be expected to be mainly to the outer rather than the inner side. (This might well have been the reason for the entire casing). Ground settlement, or too many windows, chimney shafts, stairs and other passages may have led to the collapse of the north wall. The repositioning may have been due to damage affecting the east and west walls also, or to a decision to reduce the floor area, so needing shorter joists.

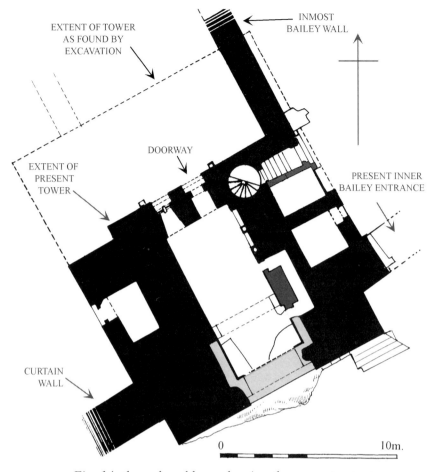

EXTENT OF TOWER
AS FOUND BY
EXCAVATION

INMOST
BAILEY WALL

EXTENT OF
PRESENT
TOWER

DOORWAY

PRESENT INNER
BAILEY ENTRANCE

CURTAIN
WALL

0   10m.

Fig. 14 the reduced keep showing the present extent

blank shields, which once carried a pediment.

Each floor is entered through a square-headed doorway at the north-east corner and with a similar one at the north-west into the rooms of the west block. Each floor has a window of two trefoil-headed lights[27] with a four-centred head to the rear-arch and side seats in the south wall, and two rectangular windows in the north wall. There are some minor varia-tions. Thus the first floor has another door in the east wall leading either to a timber balcony or the roof of the porter's lodge, the south window has been knocked out, and the north windows have four-centred heads to the reararches, and there is a fire-place between them. The second and third floors have their fireplaces in the east wall, and the north window rear arches are segmental in shape. The third floor was above the old roof, and the north windows have trefoiled heads externally. At the top of the stair, a door opens onto the wallwalk round the tower, which has low square turrets at each corner. Most of the parapet has gone, except on the south side where there are two widely-spaced crenels between the higher turrets, which themselves have traces of similar crenels on each face, placed closer together.

St. John Hope dated the tall segmental arch inside the north-east angle to the 14th century, but put the rebuilding as a whole into the third quarter of the 15th century. He gave no reason for such precision, but Sir Howard Colvin has pointed to documentary evidence for repairs to the castle immediately after 1459,[28] to which I would add the contemporary rebuilding of much of the parish church, including its tower.

The rebuilding created a domestic block consisting of a double basement and three higher floors. The lower two floors retained a second room on the west side. The basement is entered either through the holes in the vault or from the inmost ward through a square-headed doorway within a double recess and is lit by rectangular openings at two levels at each end. Rough masonry was inserted into the original entrance passage to carry a timber floor at courtyard level, below which was a low sub-basement. The upper timber floors were linked by a spiral stair (lit by small rectangular loops in the new wall) which was sited on the line of the earlier straight staircase and reached by a short passage from the east, entered through a doorway with continuous mouldings, a four-centred head below a lintel with quatrefoils, flanked by square-section shafts with cusped panelling and

CHAPTER XIV

Changes to the Castle Keep

by Peter White

The Entrance Tower, or Keep, at Ludlow presents a challenging opportunity to discuss the inter-relationship of building function and form in the context of a 12th-century castle. This chapter explores issues relating to that discussion, chapter XIII having dealt with the description and analysis of the building itself.

When G.T. Clark meticulously described Ludlow Castle, failing to recognise that the Keep had originally been constructed as a gatehouse, he remarked that the building was 'one of the most curious and perplexing Norman keeps now standing'.[1] He was left, inevitably, in some diffi-culty with his interpretation, because he simply could not establish relationships among the internal spaces. It must be assumed that dense vegetation obscured a principal diagnostic feature—the blocking to the gate arch in the elevation facing the outer bailey—although early photographs seem to indicate that it was visible. It was some 30 years before St. John Hope, following further detailed investigation including excavation, published his interpretation of the building in a detailed report for the Society of Antiquaries, and the substance of his commen-tary is still accepted .[2]

Any account of the intended function of the building must consider its location. In this regard, it is difficult today to focus attention away from the extensive, ruined evidence of Ludlow's later pre-eminence as a major Marcher castle, palace and administrative centre. However, at the core of the complex is an early masonry castle which, in its day, was strong and well located. This original castle, now the inner bailey, seems likely to have been defended by a stone curtain wall from the outset. This wall was reinforced by square towers, of which the most powerful was the one to the south, through which ran the gate passage. Clark, seeing this tower simply as a keep, nevertheless remarked that it was not constructed on the highest part of the enclosure 'nor has it any natural advantages for defence'.[3] He continued 'It was not intended to stand alone, but, as is often the case with keeps of that age, is placed upon the enceinte and forms part of the original line of defence'. Nevertheless, he remarked that it had 'communications right and left ... with the curtain wall on which it stood. This is very unusual, and quite an exception to the jealousy with which the entrances to Norman keeps are usually guarded'.

Taking this idea further, R. Allen Brown, writing over 70 years later, reflected 'There is no doubt that the enclosure type of castle, without motte or the equivalent of a great tower or keep, is a constant in medieval military architecture in England as elsewhere—witness Ludlow and Richmond at the beginning of the century ... [they] were evidently enclosed with a stone curtain wall set with mural towers and a gateway (in both case converted into a tower keep in the 12th century) from a date soon after 1066'.[4]

Fig. 1 The walls and and keep at Richmond Castle

There are few among the many examples of 12th-century castles in England where evidence survives of such well integrated stone-built defensive planning at this early period. Other locations where the substantial gatehouse survives along with the same type of square 'open gorge' mural towers, and 'communications' leading out from each side of the gatehouse to the curtain wall walk are Framlingham (Suffolk)[5] and Sherborne (Dorset).[6] Early surviving gatehouses where contemporary mural towers of a different type are evident are at Richmond (Yorkshire)[7] and Newark (Nottinghamshire)[8] and possibly at Sarum (Wiltshire)[9] and Manorbier (Glamorgan),[10] while none are evident at Exeter (Devon),[11] Tickhill (Yorkshire),[12] Bramber (West Sussex),[13] or Carew (Pembrokeshire).[14]

However, the form and size of these other examples immediately raises the question of the intended function or purpose of the Ludlow building, before it emerged as a keep rather than as a gatehouse tower. At what stage was it envisaged that it should provide for more than simply the defence of the enceinte, because in plan area it was certainly among the largest, either of the mural towers, or of the gatehouses? The comparative figures are quite striking. At Ludlow, the

overall length of the tower was some 10m and after the extension beyond the curtain wall which made the building T-shaped was about 12.5m and its width 4.5m, giving an enclosed area of 45sq m and 56sq m respectively. Richmond, from among this group, is clearly larger, with an enclosed of 69sq m. Because of extensive rebuilding, it is not possible to ascertain the detail of the Richmond building when it functioned as a gatehouse, but it too was most unusual, not least because its long axis is parallel to the curtain wall line. Like Ludlow it was converted to a keep, in its case by extensive rebuilding in the later 11th century, and it survives largely intact in this form.

Newark is of similar size to Ludlow. It was, from the outset, a very confident building, with numerous and rather generous windows. There is no doubt that it was designed for residence as much as defence, and it continued to perform this dual role throughout its useful life, the original 12th-century windows, which are still discernible, being eventually replaced.

The floor areas of the upper chambers of the gatehouses at Bramber, Exeter, Framlingham, Sherborne and Old Sarum were of 35sq m or less. Of these, the first two named, like Ludlow, did not continue in use as gatehouses, but became towers beside gateways and so could be regarded as keeps, although Exeter with an upper floor area of barely 16sq. m. hardly merits this description.[15] The others continued as gatehouses, but not enough now survives of Sarum to determine its possible domestic use, and Framlingham is windowless. Sherborne certainly housed a modest, well-lit chamber above the gate passage from the outset.

The later 11th century saw the emergence of a group of towers actually constructed beside the

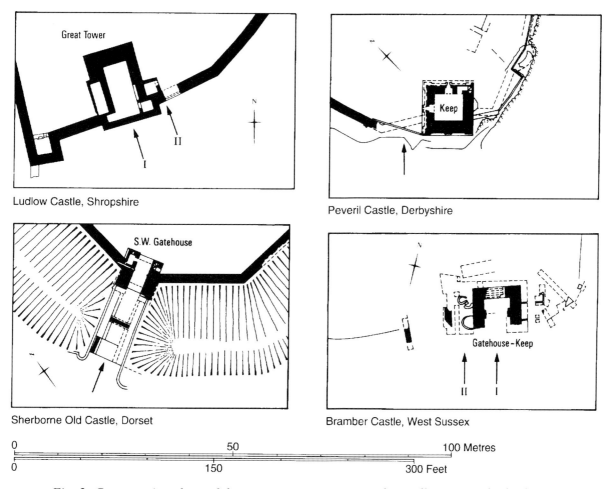

Great Tower

II

I

N

Ludlow Castle, Shropshire

Keep

Peveril Castle, Derbyshire

S.W. Gatehouse

Sherborne Old Castle, Dorset

Gatehouse – Keep

II   I

Bramber Castle, West Sussex

| 0 | 50 | 100 Metres |
| 0 | 150 | 300 Feet |

*Fig. 2 Comparative plans of the entrance arrangements for Ludlow, Peveril, Sherborne
and Bramber castles*

castle gateway. One of the earliest, and the most striking examples of this approach is to be seen at Arques-la-Bataille, Seine-Maritime, France, where Henry I considerably strengthened the castle, which had been in his family's ownership for a century or more.[16] Between 1100 and 1130 a great, multi-storey tower keep with an entrance forebuilding was constructed beside a gateway that is little more than an opening through the curtain wall. After the 1150s Kenilworth (Warwickshire) saw 'improvement' on a similar scale,[17] but the more numerous and rather more modest examples at Bridgend (Glamorgan),[18] Peveril (Derbyshire),[19] Bridgnorth (Shropshire),[20] St. Donat's (Glamorgan)[21] and possibly Goodrich (Herefordshire)[22] and White (Monmouthshire),[23]

all providing accommodation on a plan area of less than 20sq m the first, or principal floor, put the generous size of the Ludlow tower into perspective.

It seems likely, therefore, that the Ludlow gate tower was intended to provide accommodation, in a chamber above the gate passage, of more than average size for such a building. By so doing it was integrating domestic and defensive functions so as to provide both entry to and the 'strong point' of the castle. As such, its physical strength and visual power would have been considerable, even if the design concept could be considered economical. A cursory glance at contemporary castle development illustrates this. At the time when the Ludlow gate tower was built, square

141

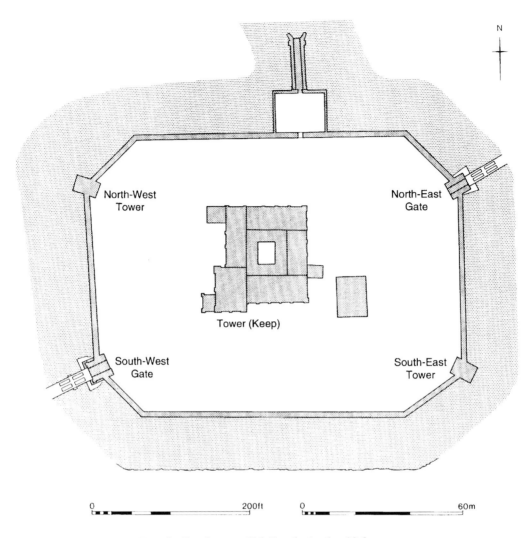

N

North-West
Tower

North-East
Gate

Tower (Keep)

South-West
Gate

South-East
Tower

0   200ft   0   60m

Fig. 3 Sherborne Old Castle in the 12th century

tower keeps were not at all common in Wales and the Marches. Some have already been noticed, and in addition there was Manorbier, while Moreton Corbet (Shropshire)[24] and Usk (Monmouthshire)[25] are almost certainly of the later 12th century. The much more common strong point was the motte or mound, of which numerous examples survive. Such a feature, on a large scale, provided the focus for the major lordly castles at Shrewsbury, Hereford[26], and Brecon, for example. Among these three major castles, we also know that Shrewsbury had a masonry gatehouse, because it survives, though altered. So the concept of Ludlow, with its masonry tower providing both gate passage and

substantial chamber above, and forming part of an integrated defensive system with four other mural towers, is unusual.

That having been said, there is no evidence to suggest that the original structure had more than roof space above a gate passage. Originally, the external elevation seems likely to have been flush with the curtain wall, and was only later extended beyond this defensive line. This arrangement is common in principle to other surviving contemporary gatehouses, although at Ludlow the projection was by no means as pronounced. It was indeed more common for up to half the plan area of the gatehouse to be thrown forward beyond the curtain wall line. The particular effect

142

of this extension at Ludlow was to increase the potential floor area of the chamber over the gate by about a fifth.

Within the gate passage, early 12th-century gatehouses generally depended on stout timber gates hung within; neither the drawbridge nor the portcullis was common at this time. At Sherborne the remains of the surviving masonry bridge remains suggest that a removable timber deck may have provided a line of protection before the gate passage was reached.[27] No bridge survives at Ludlow, and Renn (see chapter XIII) suggests a timber bridge originally. The point is, however, that there would have been no call for a machinery room above the gate passage as part of the original design, and indeed there is no indication of the presence of machinery at any stage during the period of the building's use as a gatehouse. Some evidence for the location of gates within the vaulted passage is, however, still to be seen.

Shortly after the completion of this forward extension, the structure was heightened, so realising its development into something more than a gatehouse. A large space was now formed over the whole area of the upper floor. Access was provided from a straight stair rising in the thickness of the east wall in a manner imitating a forebuilding. From the top of this stair, the chamber could be entered through a vaulted vestibule, or access could be gained to the eastern wall walk. A similar vestibule on the opposite side of the chamber gave access to the western wall walk beyond the gatehouse. This development therefore immediately introduced features which are commonly found in tower keeps.

It has already been noticed that tower keeps were not a common feature of Wales and the Marches. They required heavy investment, using highly skilled workmen and, of some considerable importance in a border area, they took time to construct. By contrast, a mound could be raised quickly with unskilled labour. But wherever they were located, the tower keeps of this period shared some common characteristics, among them the segregation of the ground from the first floors, often, but not always, by stone vaulting,

and access to the main part of the building generally by an entrance at first floor level. In some cases, the access stair may have been of timber, as at Goodrich. However, because a keep, by its nature, was an imposing and high status building within a castle, a stone stair, enclosed within a forebuilding, is common. This arrangement provided at the same time for a more impressive entrance and for one that did not compromise the integrity of the tower's defence. So the arrangements at Ludlow align with the grander keeps in this regard. By comparison, or perhaps in contrast, gatehouses tended to provide upper floor access from the wall walk, an open adjacent stair ramp, or a stair vice or a combination of these arrangements. The presence at Ludlow of an arrangement which can be regarded as a forebuilding would seem to indicate a high status use, similar to that of the upper floors of a tower keep.

In considering Ludlow's use as a hybrid keep, it is also necessary to look at its location. Its position astride the defensive wall would not have been seen as unusual or adding to its vulnerability. Both keeps and mounds are frequently so located, in order to combine the virtues of strong defence with the possibility of escape or relief. Exceptions to this rule seem to be found largely where the emphasis was on the domestic and palatial, rather than the defensive, except possibly in London, where the White Tower attempts to fulfil all three requirements. In a more provincial context, at Bishop Roger's palace at Sherborne, the strong tower is not only near the centre of the bailey, it also forms part of a complex of other domestic buildings, including a large, ground floor hall.[28]

On the other hand, the same patron's contemporary work at Sarum displays a much more rigorous distinction between the domestic and the defensive. The town is dominated by the castle, where the 'keep' (significantly called the postern tower) is located astride the curtain wall, and defends a sally port. The domestic buildings are detached, surrounding a courtyard.

If the Ludlow structure was indeed always intended to combine the characteristics of a strong gate house with those of a tower keep, what of the other high status accommodation in the substantial bailey? At Sarum, the existence of both a hall and a 'keep' has been noticed, but in the early years of the 12th century, the free standing stone-built hall in a castle bailey was rare. Chepstow, one of the earliest examples, may date from as early as 1070;[29] Sarum and Sherborne from the 1120s; Oakham (Rutland) from the 1190s.[30] At Ludlow, Derek Renn ventures domestic buildings of quality in the north-west sector of the bailey, perhaps following the example of Bishop Henry of Blois' palace at Winchester;[31] but that was a good generation later. At least as strong a tradition, and much more appealing where defence was at a premium had been derived from Normandy. The hall was securely located within a keep or *donjon*, as at Loches and Langeais. One interesting English example, at this period, is at Lincoln, where the episcopal hall was located within a strong tower incorporated in the west end of the cathedral, facing the Royal castle further to the west along the ridge.[32]

Against all this background, two matters are of particular note at Ludlow. The first is that for the early 12th century the building was unusually designed, built and extended apparently with the purpose of functioning as a keep-gatehouse. In this regard, it could be argued that Ludlow is a true precursor of a form which came back into vogue in the later 13th century notably at Caerphilly (Glamorgan),[33] Harlech (Gwynedd)[34] and Tonbridge (Kent).[35]

Secondly, there is a question: why did the original concept fail? Among the reasons must have been the conflict between satisfactory domestic arrangements and the use of the structure as the only vehicular access to the heart of the castle. This conflict came to a head with the early 13th century creation of the inmost bailey, which cut off the access completely. By moving the castle gateway to the east, immediate relief was provided. The eastern part of the inmost bailey could then function as a polite entrance to the tower stair, segregated from the traffic wishing to go beyond into the bailey proper. The change would not have been seen by contemporaries as compromising the defensive arrangements; on the contrary, it is known that a whole group of castles, including some nearby, were being newly constructed with gateways arranged in exactly this manner.

CHAPTER XV

The Round Chapel of St. Mary Magdalene

by Glyn Coppack

The circular chapel in the inner bailey of Ludlow Castle is a building seemingly unique in Britain which has been remarkably little studied and even less understood. It is virtually undocumented until the 16th century, and its dedication is known only from the 13th century *Romance of Fulk fitzWarin*,[1] the only partially reliable account of events at Ludlow during the Anarchy. Surveyed and partially excavated by Sir William St. John Hope and Sir Harold Brakspear between September 1904 and Easter 1908 as part of their more general survey of the castle,[2] its nave survives to full height as a roofless shell, and its chancel can still be traced as low walling. It is essentially a Romanesque building which appears to have survived little altered into the 16th century, and its construction was dated by Hope to 'not much after about 1080-90' but not completed until about 1120 on the evidence of its west door and chancel arch, a date which is clearly a little too early for its architectural detailing. It was remodelled by Sir Henry Sidney some time between 1560 and 1586 to serve the Council in the Marches, and it remained roofed as late as 1774, when its woodwork was described as 'wonderfully preserved', but it was ruinous by 1800.[3]

Detached stone-built chapels in English castles are rare in the early Middle Ages, and the only other known examples to be identified are at Pevensey,[4] Hereford[5] and Castle Rising.[6] The first was a two-cell rectangular structure with a north aisle which appears to have been an original feature. Standing in the inner bailey close to the Hall, its placing if not its plan is closely analogous with the building considered here. It was demolished in 1250 when a new chapel was built in the outer bailey. The chapel of St. Martin *in castello de Herefordia* is identified as a three-cell building from limited excavations and the parchmarks occasionally visible on Castle Green. It was built in the later 11th century to replace a timber church as part of St. Guthlac's minster and left standing to serve the castle when the religious site in the bailey was abandoned in favour of a new location east of the city after 1140 but before 1148. It survived perhaps into the early years of the 18th century, but had been supplanted as the principal castle chapel in 1233 by a new chapel in Henry III's great tower there. The three-cell church or chapel at Castle Rising, like the chapel at Hereford, was in fact a chapelry established before the building of the castle but which survived in religious use only until it was replaced in the later 12th century by a chapel within the keep. The chapel at Ludlow is therefore an exception from the first. Apart from the gatehouse-keep and curtain wall of the inner bailey it is the earliest stone building within Ludlow Castle, and appears to have been intended to serve adjacent timber domestic ranges which have not as yet been traced.

As originally built, the chapel comprised a circular nave 8.30m (27ft 3in) in diameter inter-

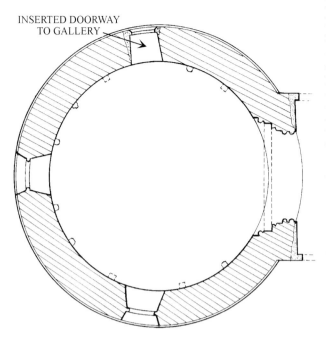

Fig. 1 Plan of the chapel at
ground floor (lower)
and first floor level (upper)
showing features of all periods

nally, a presbytery 3.80m (12ft 6in) square, and a faceted apsidal chancel (Fig. 1). Its tripartite form has a good 11th-century pedigree, and is seen in an immediately post-conquest context at Barton on Humber[7] or before the conquest at St. Bride's, Fleet Street, London,[8] Hereford, and Castle Rising. The nave stands virtually to full height, the presbytery has been reduced to contemporary floor level some 0.36m (14in) above its chamfered plinth with the exception of the stubs of its side walls adjoining the nave which remain to full height, and the chancel which is now covered with turf survives a few courses higher. The weathering of the presbytery roof survives in the external wall-face of the nave, showing that it oversailed the walls by almost 0.5m, and below it above the chancel arch is the scar of a round barrel vault. There is no evidence for the original form of the nave roof, but it probably matched the presbytery roof in pitch and similarly oversailed the building. The nave walls are 1.24m (4ft 1in) thick, and the presbytery, of lesser height, 1.10m (3ft 7½in) wide. A plain chamfered plinth runs all the way round the structure, returning onto the presbytery

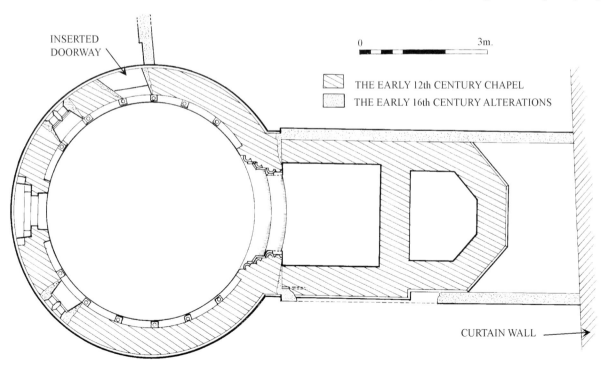

0   3m.

THE EARLY 12th CENTURY CHAPEL

THE EARLY 16th CENTURY ALTERATIONS

Fig. 2 The Chapel seen from the south-west

the ashlar of the head. The capitals match those of the chancel arch, which Hope considered also to be an insertion, though there is no evidence of that in the structure, but more important, the whole of the door-head is *en suite* with the detailing of the internal wall arcade that Hope considered to be primary and which he dated to the 1090s. The hood-mould of the door-case and chancel arch match the billet stringcourse that runs around the exterior of the building at the level of its window cills and which must be primary as there is no evidence for its insertion, a fact that Hope chose to ignore. If the alteration to the door-case is accepted as a variation in the course of building, upgrading a plain rebated door to a decorative one more in keeping with the interior of the chapel, then there is no case to suppose that the building is not of a single phase, which makes much more sense of its architecture. Hope's dating is therefore questionable. All of the

wall on the north side, but not on the south where the presbytery plinth is simply butted against that of the nave. There is just the slightest hint of a break in build at this point and the south wall of the presbytery bonds rather poorly with the outer face of the nave, thus very much unlike the north wall.

The building (Fig. 2) is of roughly dressed but well coursed sandstone rubble with dressings of a finer ashlar sandstone. St. John Hope was convinced that the building had two phases of construction which were based on his interpretation of the west door (Fig. 3). This is a door of two shafted orders with a chevron-moulded head below a hood-mould of bold billet decoration. The bases of the shafts do not bond with the rebated door-case and the top four courses of the door-case which support the scalloped capitals and abaci that carry the arch appear to be inserted. They are certainly better cut stones and are slightly lighter in colour than the lower courses of the door case, but match

Fig. 3 The west door, showing the alterations to the upper part of the jambs that convinced Hope that the building had two periods of construction

Fig. 4 The wall arcade on the south side of the nave, showing the alternating moulded and chevron arches and the relationship with the west door case

original building was laid in a soft orange-brown mortar with coarse aggregate, which contains frequent brick fragments—another indicator that the building is of a single phase and was not built in two campaigns. Some internal plaster in the southern wall arcade of the nave is also primary, having the same base as the bedding mortar.

The nave was lit by three double-splayed round-headed windows set high in its north, west and south walls—originally unglazed and with a half-round nosing at the junction of the inner and outer splays, but altered later by the insertion of glazing grooves and saddle bar holes for windows set into the face of the nosing. Only the west window is relieved externally by attached jamb-shafts on the outer edge of the splay that run around the head without the interruption of a capital, a feature which is repeated on the inner splays of all the windows. Exceptionally the west window also had an external hood-mould which has been dressed back to the wall face. The north and south windows are not set to the cardinal points as might be expected, but are slightly

offset to the west, being placed mid-way between the internal splays of the entrance door and the outer order of the chancel arch. They do not align perfectly with the wall arcades below. However, this does not appear to affect the symmetry of the building inside or out.

Internally, the nave wall is relieved by deep wall arcades of seven bays on each side above a wall-bench with a reeded edge. The ends of the arcade spring from plain responds which are essentially the interior wall face that bonds with both the western door-case and the responds of the chancel arch, but the arcade of alternating chevron and moulded arches is carried on detached shafts with moulded bases and scalloped capitals (Fig. 4). While the arcade on the south side is regularly laid out with equal spacing between the arcade bases, there is some evidence that the northern arcade was less carefully planned, for the three western bays are wider than the four to the east, an irregularity made up by the slight reworking of the voussoirs (shown notably in a curious faceted appearance on the soffit) of the eastern arches to

Fig. 5 The chancel arch as seen from the nave

fit a tighter radius. The chancel arch (Fig. 5) is a tall and elegant composition of three shafted orders, again with scalloped capitals of high quality standing on plain chamfered plinths. The inner order of the arch is carried on paired attached shafts. All the capitals are scalloped and are *en suite* with the entrance door and the nave wall arcade. The arch of the outer order is cut with bold chevrons with a single row of square star decoration on the soffit. The second order is moulded, again with star decoration on the soffit, while the inner order has star decoration on both the outer face and the soffit (Fig. 6). The loss of any evidence of paint to a certain extent mutes the quality of the composition which is exceptional in the context of a chapel.

Little can be said about the internal form of the presbytery and chancel. The relative thinness of their walls would suggest that the wall seats of the nave were not repeated in the presbytery as Hope suggested, because its walls would have been required to carry the weight of a vault (Fig. 7).

However, blind arcading on the wall-face is a distinct possibility. It was screened from the nave from the first, for the plinth of the outer order was cut out for a screen, 0.12m (4³/₄in) thick, that sat on the outer edge of the first of two curving steps that led to the higher level of the presbytery. The rebates appear to be primary to the construction of the chancel arch and not an afterthought. The chancel was probably one step higher than the presbytery.

The circular form of the chapel falls into a class of circular churches that took their inspiration from the *anastasis* (the shrine that contained

Fig. 6 Detail of carvings on the chancel arch

the physical remains of the actual tomb of Christ) of the Church of the Holy Sepulchre in Jerusalem—a building that was not available as a model for western Christians until the capture of Jerusalem in July 1099 at the culmination of the First Crusade. It was a form which was adopted by the knightly orders of Templars and Hospitallers and which is known locally at Garway and Hereford,[9] itself an unaisled building which may well copy the chapel at Ludlow, but more rarely for parish churches such as the Holy Sepulchre churches in Cambridge and Northampton. The Knights Templar did not arrive in England before 1128 when their first house was established in London, and while the church of the Holy Sepulchre in Cambridge is unlikely to pre-date *c*.1130,[10] the round church at Northampton was begun by Simon de Senlis in about 1110 after his return from the First Crusade.[11] The chapel at Ludlow is therefore one of the earliest surviving manifestations of this plan-form in Britain, and its architectural detailing suggests that it was built no earlier than the 1120s or 30s. This in turn would suggest that it was built by Gilbert I de Lacy who, significantly, joined the Templars in his later life after a pilgrimage to the Holy Land, becoming preceptor of the order in the county of Tripoli.

During the presidency of the Council in the March of Sir Henry Sidney (1560-86) the chapel was remodelled to serve the Council, most probably between 1571 and 1575 when he was most regularly resident.[12] A description of his works has survived:

> Item for for [sic] making, rep'ing, and amending of the Chappell w[th]in the said Castle, syling, glazing, and Tyling of the same with ffaire and lardg windowes, wainscotting, benching, and making of seates and Kneling places and putting upp of her Ma[ties] Armes w[th] divers noble mens Armes together w[th] all the L Presidentes and Counsailles rounde about the same.[13]

To this should be added an early 18th century description provided by R. Perkes, town clerk of Ludlow from 1719 to 1751, which is contained

Fig. 7 The evidence for the presbytery vault can be seen immediately above the chancel arch, carefully cut back to the wall face in the late 16th century. The weathering of the 12th-century presbytery roof can clearly be seen on the nave wall

within his collections that formed the Blakeway manuscript:

> and then to the Chappell in which Stalls and a seat raised high for the Prince and nobility (NB y[s] is not in y[e] Chappell but comes out of another room and so jutts into the Chappell) in which Chappell are y[e] Coats of Arms of y[e] Presidents and those y[t] practiced in y[t] Court 1672, & a passage from thence leads to the Council Chamber ...'[14]

Because the site was so thoroughly excavated by Hope, it is necessary to first consider his interpretation of the structure. He wrote in 1908:

The chapel has been so completely gutted, and all remains of the chancel destroyed, that it is difficult at first to follow Sir Henry Sidney's changes, but our excavations have helped make all clear. The Norman chancel was taken down to its plinths and replaced by a new one of half-timbered construction extending from the round nave right up to the curtain wall, against which its abbutal is traceable. The sides were much higher than the old building, no doubt by reason of the "ffayre and lardg windowes" and the roof was a nearly flat one covered with lead. The floor was of tiles, and some traces of the fittings survived, which took up a space of about $3\frac{1}{2}$ feet wide on each side. The altar seems to have stood detached from the east wall and was probably surrounded, puritan fashion, by a railing with kneeling places.

In the case of the nave, a floor, carried by old carved corbels of various dates, was inserted at the window level, $10\frac{1}{2}$ feet from the pavement, to form an upper chapel for the quality while the ground storey continued to serve for the household. Access to this upper chapel was by a wooden gallery from the buildings on the north to the north window of the chapel, into which a doorway was intruded. A doorway was also made from the lower gallery by cutting out the back of one of the wall-arches. The upper chapel continued to be lighted by the original south and west windows, but the putting in of the new floor necessitated the lighting of the lower chapel by two large square-headed two-light windows inserted on each side in the back of the second arch from the door. The raising of the nave walls and the flattening of the roof may have taken place at the same time.[15]

Hope appears to have oversimplified the interpretation of this remodelling by trying to fit all of the available evidence provided by the account of Sir Henry Sidney's works with the evidence which survives within the structure. It is also apparent that the walling of the later 'chancel' recorded on his plan does not accord exactly with what can still be seen *in situ*. While there is good evidence that Hope's observations were normally acute, experience of re-excavation of sites studied by Hope has shown that his excavation techniques were often superficial and inconsistent.[16] His plan was almost certainly drawn up by Sir Harold Brakspear after the event and was unlikely to be contemporary with the actual excavation of the chapel's footings. This would explain, for instance, why Hope and Brakspear show the 16th-century chapel with an eastern gable wall against the curtain wall of the inner bailey while the surviving side walls simply butt against the curtain and provide no evidence whatsoever for an east wall as their inner faces are unbroken. It also explains the inaccuracy of the precise dimensions that Hope published for the 12th-century chapel.

Hope assumed that the round nave was still a part of the chapel in the late 16th century, while neither the 16th-century description nor the Blakeway manuscript suggest this. Indeed, the Blakeway document goes so far as to say that the round nave was specifically not a part of the later building but comprised 'another room' and the description of Sidney's works, normally so inclusive, makes no mention whatsoever of new doors, windows, floors, or a gallery from the Chamber block, all of which are apparent in the surviving structure.

Fig. 8 Corbel in the nave

First, it is necessary to consider the structural evidence that survives for the Sidney chapel. All of its north wall survives, largely to plinth level, carrying a stone superstructure 0.36m (1ft 2in) wide on a footing 0.42m (1ft 4½in) wide. The eastern 5.4m (17ft 8½in) of the south wall survives at just below plinth level and is typically 0.44m (1ft 5¼in) wide, 5.60m (18ft 4½in) from the north wall. The junction of the new work and the stubs of the 12th-century presbytery also survive, and these are very informative, particularly on the south side. The stubs of the 12th-century walls were refaced roughly square to the chapel side walls, and toothed into them 0.90m (2ft 11½in) above plinth level is a thin screen wall only 0.32m (12½in) wide, which rises the full height of the new chapel. As the footings and lower plinth of the new building are some 0.20m (8in) wider on each side than the old work, the wall above plinth level must have been reduced in width by further offsets or a moulded plinth until it was flush with the exterior face of the old work, and from that level, as Hope correctly observed, the walls were carried up in timber. The facing up of the broken presbytery wall stubs was carried up through the 12th-century roof weathering, showing that the new building was taller than its predecessor, and within the building both the evidence of the barrel vault and the roof weathering was carefully cut back to the wall-face where they could have been concealed by plaster (Fig. 7). There is no indication of the roof pitch of the new building on the wall of the nave, or against the curtain wall, although a vague ghosting of the building can still be seen. Within the new building, the 12th-century presbytery and chancel were reduced to a little below its floor level, and what is currently visible indicates the extent of Hope's removal of the 16th-century floor.

The exterior appearance of this new chapel is known from a drawing of 1684 by Thomas Dinely (see Fig.9), a drawing which when compared with the surviving ruins might appear generally to be accurate.[17] There are two prob-

Fig. 9 Dinely's drawing of the Round Chapel in 1684

lems with this drawing, which Hope was obviously not aware of: it shows the tiled or slated roof of the chapel with a fairly steep pitch and a dormer window, and it shows the side walls as masonry to full height. As the chapel is drawn in isolation, it does not show the curtain wall against which the building is butted. While the roof line is not a problem so far as the surviving structural evidence is concerned, the use of masonry for the walls most certainly is, and the drawing cannot be accurate in this regard. It is, however, possible that the walls were plastered externally, as was the circular nave to the height of its string course, though this is not shown on the drawing. Dinely shows that the new building had two two-light windows in its south wall, with a single dormer above the western window, so placed because it lit the pew that projected from the nave through the chancel arch. The fenestration on the north side probably matched that on the south.

The extent of Sir Henry Sidney's new work is very specific; he made, repaired and amended the chapel and ceiled, glazed, and tiled the same, with fair and large windows, panelling, benches, stalls and seats, and set up the altar. He also hung within it, as required by law, the Queen's arms, and those of the Council whose chapel it was—a typical Tudor scheme of decoration. Hope found evidence for a tiled floor, and for the fitting of stalls against the side walls, which were clearly carried up in masonry to their height. What the description does not do is describe any works to the nave, and this is probably because Sidney did not do any work there.

Indeed, the modifications to the nave appear to be earlier than Sidney's work, in particular the first floor door inserted in the north wall which gives every indication of being late-medieval in date and not reused from elsewhere in the castle. The door clearly goes with the insertion of the upper floor that Hope describes and the gallery from the Chamber block to the north which respects its location precisely, and it must also relate to the square-headed two-light windows inserted into the nave to light the ground floor when the floor was inserted. The insertion of the southern of these windows is sealed by surviving external render that implies a thorough repair of the round nave, and probably the provision of the castellated parapet that concealed a new roof. The plaster only extended as high as the external stringcourse, a feature confirmed by early photographs.[18] There is only one likely context for this work, the installation of Arthur, Prince of Wales, and his bride Katherine of Aragon at Ludlow in January 1502. Indeed, Dinely's drawing is captioned 'Prince Arthurs Chappel' and the Blakeway manuscript describes the first floor pew that projected through the 12th-century chancel arch as 'a seat raised high for the Prince and nobility'. Arthur was, in fact, the last Prince of Wales to hold court at Ludlow, and it would appear that folk memory associated the chapel with his short residence there. There is no reason to suppose that the two square-headed windows inserted into the nave could not have

been as early as 1500. Indeed, they lack the hood-moulds that are typical of later Tudor windows and which appear in the chancel of Dinely's drawing.

The remodelling of the nave has left a great deal of evidence in the structure that suggests it was carefully considered and that it happened at a time when other work was being carried out elsewhere. The new upper floor was carried on a series of ten corbels, five of which survive. One was later replaced by an undressed block of stone, indicating a later repair, and four carefully blocked holes indicate the location of those which have since been removed. Their tops are at a consistent height of 3.20m (10ft 6in) above the stone-paved floor of the nave which itself dates from the same period. At the same level, a timber beam was inserted across the opening into the chancel just to the east of the attached shafts of the outer order. Because the placing of the corbels is slightly irregular it is unlikely that they carried beams across the building, but that they carried radiating beams carried on a central post, no trace of which survives. The corbels are derived from at least two other buildings—one is an early 13th-century mask corbel, one the capital from a triple wall-shaft of like date, and three come from a series of late 14th-century portrait corbels.

The insertion of the two-light windows into the ground floor of the nave was coupled with the removal of the wall-bench in the first bay of the arcade to the west, for what purpose it is not immediately obvious. The bench was subsequently replaced somewhat roughly, and its lowest courses sit directly on the paving of the floor. A door was cut at an angle through the north wall, its alignment controlled by the internal arcade and the line required for the connecting corridor and door in the north wall of the chapel. Strangely, this door was not provided with a door-case. That it was not an afterthought is confirmed by the paving of the nave floor extending slightly into the opening. It is now blocked, presumably at the same time that the wall-benches were repaired. The inserted windows and the lining of the door were all set in a brown mortar, visually similar to that of the original build, but much harder and with finer aggregate.

At first floor level, the principal modification was the insertion of the door into the north window, reusing the eastern internal splay as the eastern splay of the door and cutting back the western splay, again to align the door-case on the external wall face with the passage from the Chamber block. Above the door, the upper part of the original window was retained. Seats were inserted at cill-level in the internal splays of the west and south windows, set in deep grooves cut into the face of the splays and cutting the nook shafts. There is some slight indication of the form of the pew which extended into the presbytery at first floor level. The eastern 340mm (13$\frac{1}{2}$in) of the chancel arch plinth was cut out to accept a cill beam at the level of the second step that carried a screen that separated the nave from the presbytery. This was, in plan, 0.55m to the east of the joist inserted into the chancel arch to carry the first floor in the nave, and joists morticed into this beam and cantilevered over the screen could have comfortably extended to provide a pew, the front of which could have followed the curve of the nave wall. When the west wall of the new chapel was squared up, the new masonry extended only from the side walls to the springing of the arch,

unaccountably leaving the curving wall of the nave visible above it. This in itself argues for a curved front to the pew which was retained from the early 16th-century chapel.

The wall of the nave was raised about by about a metre, with a castellated parapet above this, removing any evidence for the original form of the roof. Only one feature appears to relate to the 12th-century roof, a tiebeam set centrally and still surviving in the south wall. No trace has survived on the north side of the chapel, where the wall has been conserved and perhaps rebuilt, but on the south side the beam still remains embedded in the full thickness of the wall. No trace remains, either, of the 16th-century roof, probably because it was set directly onto the wall-head. A single apparent beam socket and a corbel slightly north of centre of the chancel arch are the only features in the upper wall and occur in an area which appears to have been heavily conserved. The form of the roof is known from Thomas Dinely's drawing of 1684, a pitched roof aligned east to west surrounded by a flat parapet gutter which was drained by two lead spouts on the west side and two on the east. Its construction would have required two tie-beams across the nave from north to south that carried the gable walls and most of the remainder of the roof could be framed from them.

CHAPTER XVI

The Solar Block

by Richard K. Morriss

The Solar block, attached to the western end of the Great Hall, seems, at first sight, to be one of the less complicated elements of Ludlow Castle. Appearances are deceptive and the Solar block is not only a fairly complex structure, but also one in which several important phases of the castle's development have left an indelible mark.

The new Solar block was, like the Great Hall it served, built against the inside of the northern section of the Norman curtain wall. Its apartments also colonised the shell of the projecting North-West Tower of this original defensive circuit. The tower was probably once the same height as the curtain wall. However, it was evidently more than a simple defensive tower and contained a first floor—the blocked joist holes of which are still visible between the corbels of the later inserted floor levels.

At the original first-floor level the wall contained a mural passage, lit by ashlar framed semicircular headed loops and reached by a convoluted system of stepped passages and vices (spiral staircases) accessed from opposing ground-floor doorways at the southern ends of its west and east walls (see Figs. 7 & 8, pp.162 & 3). At first-floor level one of the tunnel-vaulted passages contained a finely wrought ashlared garderobe between the east side of the tower and the curtain wall, supported by a squinch arch across the angle between them; another passage led to a second garderobe projecting out from the curtain wall to the west (see chapter XIII).

This evidence suggests that the tower was used, at least in part, for domestic purposes. There is no indication of any masonry or timber-framed back to the tower, and the absence of any structural scars on the internal sides of the curtain wall could indicate that a missing building, probably timber-framed, abutted the open backed stonework. It certainly seems likely that the tower formed part of a larger apartment that occupied at least some of the area now covered by the Solar block. Its function is unknown, but the tower seems to have been the most important of all of the original ones in the Norman defensive circuit after the keep itself.

When construction work on the present Solar block was begun the tower was totally gutted and any building attached to it would have been demolished. The new building was the main element in a completely new suite of rooms at this end of the Great Hall, one which reused the refloored shell of the tower and a new extension—the 'Closet Tower'—built in the angle between the tower's west wall and the curtain. As a result, part of the original mural passage system became redundant whilst other sections were incorporated into the new layout.

The Solar

As completed, the Solar block was a three-storey building constructed of coursed, partly worked, local rubble stone of the same height as the adjacent Great Hall. In this same broad campaign of

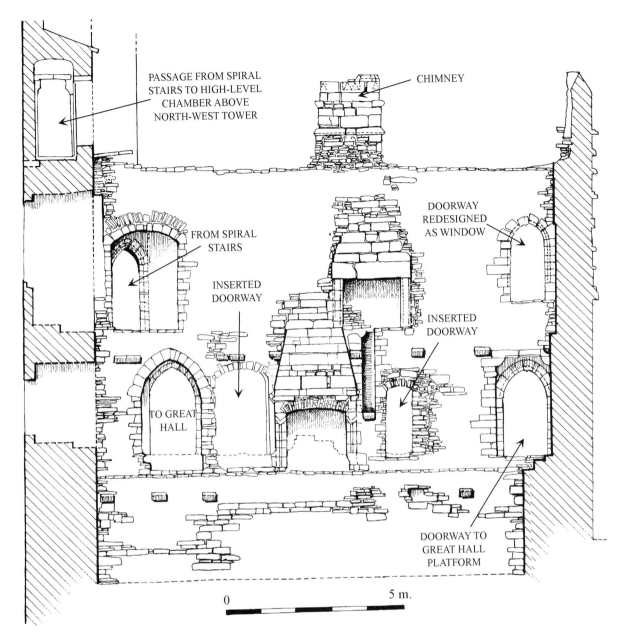

Fig. 1 The east internal wall of the Solar, showing the various doorways to the Great Hall

work the North-West Tower was raised and the new Closet Tower was added.

On its east side the Solar is separated from the Hall range by a substantial masonry wall. In order to accommodate the faceted curve of the curtain wall, and to retain the rectangular shape in each, the cross-wall between the two is wider at the north end than it is at the south. It is pierced by a series of openings at first-floor level, only one of those from the first-floor Hall (at the north end) being primary. At the south end there is a second primary doorway through the wall that leads from the landing above the steps that lead up to the main entrance to the Hall. Both of these doorways have plain-chamfered two-centred heads and both are rebated on the Solar side. The Hall doorway has similar heads on each side and in the thickness of its reveal there was an opening leading into a vaulted alcove off the Great Hall; the reveal of the external doorway to the south is primary rerarch and inner reveal. There are no more visible openings at this level apart from the wide one that leads into the North-West Tower. However, there is a vertical construction break at the south end of the west wall (more visible on the exterior than the interior) that could relate to a blocked doorway of unknown date, and the rougher quality masonry at the north end of the east wall may indicate some rebuilding in this area.

At first-floor level in the main elevation there is a pair of original windows. These have, internally, the same sized reveals under matching two-centred rerarches, but rather oddly are not the same externally. The single light western window is only half the width of the eastern one—which was presumably of two lights. Each had a moulded two-centred hood mould and moulded jambs and in the outer arch the moulding consists of a pair of sunk chamfers separated by a triangular groove. The

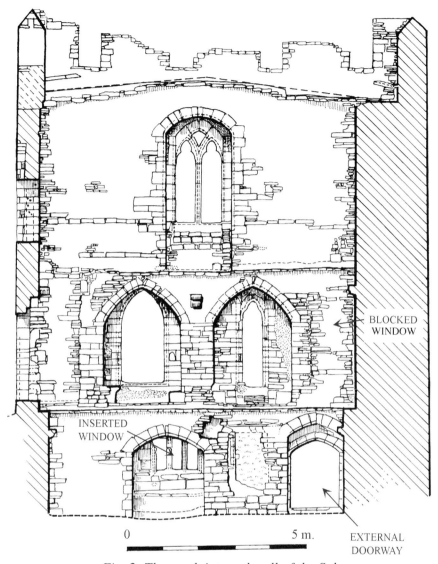

BLOCKED WINDOW

INSERTED WINDOW

0   5 m.   EXTERNAL DOORWAY

Fig. 2 The south internal wall of the Solar

topped by a shouldered lintel—or 'Caernarfon' arch. Its position meant that the door within it opened into the Solar and into a primary recess in the south wall.

On the south, elevation of the Solar there is a primary ground-floor doorway at the western end with a plain chamfered ashlared surround under a fairly shallow, almost triangular, two-centred head matched by its slightly higher rerarch. The five-light stone mullioned window at this level is evidently associated with the remodelling—probably of the late-16th century—of an earlier primary opening, as shown by its surviving

rerarches have a single sunk chamfer but the jambs beneath them are plain. Externally, the larger window has an additional outer order of a hollow roll. It is likely that this window originally had the same type of 'Y' tracery seen in the windows of the Great Hall, though without the transom. Each of its lights, and that of the smaller window, possibly have the remnants of trefoiled heads. To the west of these windows are the construction breaks of a rectangular inserted opening that has since been blocked. This is shown on Pritchard's plan of 1765 as lighting a narrow closet (see Fig. 4 p.183).

A window which was cut into the section of curtain wall to the east of the North-West Tower at this level, has a slightly unusual design. Externally it has a square head but its rear-arch is two-centred and plain, the recess oddly formed, but lined with ashlar. It is possible that the window was the remodelling of an original Norman loop that lit the mural passage and was close to the head of a stone vice reached by the eastern stepped passage from the ground floor. Once inserted, the window effectively blocked the mural passage and the lower stepped section was probably abandoned.

At second-floor level the Solar has single windows in the both south and west walls, similar in style to the two-light window on the first floor but retaining their 'Y' tracery and trefoiled heads. A square-headed window at the north end of the west wall is clearly a later insertion. In the short east return wall that juts out in front of the Hall there is a third window that contains a single light in an original opening—rather odd but certainly medieval (see below).

Internally, each of the three floors of the Solar extended into the remodelled North-West Tower and each was linked to a room in the new Closet Tower. There are no obvious traces of any original partitions in the main rooms, though some were added later. The basement was not a simple

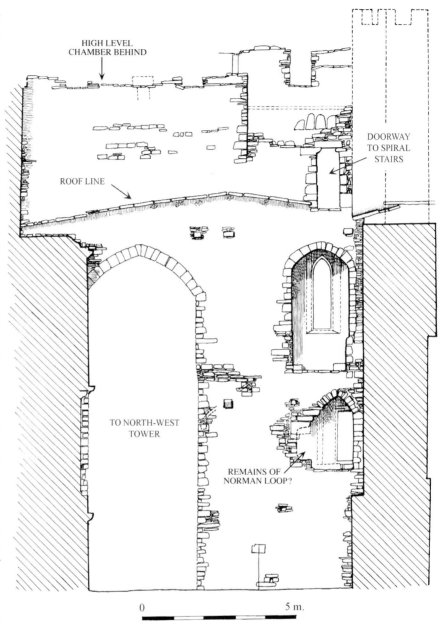

Fig. 3 *The north internal wall of the Solar*

undercroft for it has in its west wall the remains of a primary fireplace that originally had a stone hood. There are no indications of any direct access to the basement of the Great Hall, nor any suggestions as to how, or if, this level was linked to the floor above it.

The first floor was of timber construction with large lateral balks of timber on the west and east

158

walls supported by quadrant moulded stone corbels. These presumably supported the ends of cross-beams that continued onto the masonry set-backs at this level. The new floor level was continued into the North-West Tower, where corbels were inserted into its side walls to take a floor of similar design. The main room at this level was well lit and had direct accesses into the Great Hall, the North-West Tower and the Closet Tower, as well as the outside. It was heated by a fine hooded fireplace in the centre of the east wall, decorated with broad sunk chamfers on nearly triangular-sectioned jambs and was clearly a room of some status.

The second floor construction was very similar to the first, with corbels along the west and east walls and an internal set-back on the south and partly on the north supporting its main timbers. The second floor room was reached by the spiral stair from the north-west corner of the Hall and it also had access to the Closet Tower. It was also reasonably well-lit and had a slightly plainer hooded fireplace in the east wall.

A roof string is clearly visible in the south side of the raised section of the North-West Tower, showing the final solar roof to have had a very shallow pitch, its ridge aligned north-south. The roof was hidden by the embattled parapet and was presumably of lead sheeted timber boards. The precise design of the roof structure is unclear, but it may simply have consisted of a series of cambered tie-beams bearing on the broad wall tops.

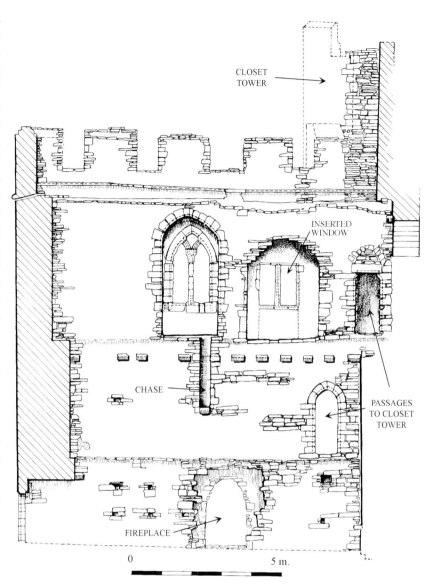

Fig. 4 The west internal wall of the Solar

The Remodelling of the North-West Tower

When the Solar was built, the North-West Tower was given new corbel-mounted floors and it was raised in height. No new openings were created on the ground floor, though the doorway to the redundant eastern stepped passage was probably blocked. At the new first-floor level a new window was created in the north wall by breaking through the walls of the mural passage. Because of the higher level of the original first floor, the threshold of this new opening would have had to be reached by timber steps. The new opening

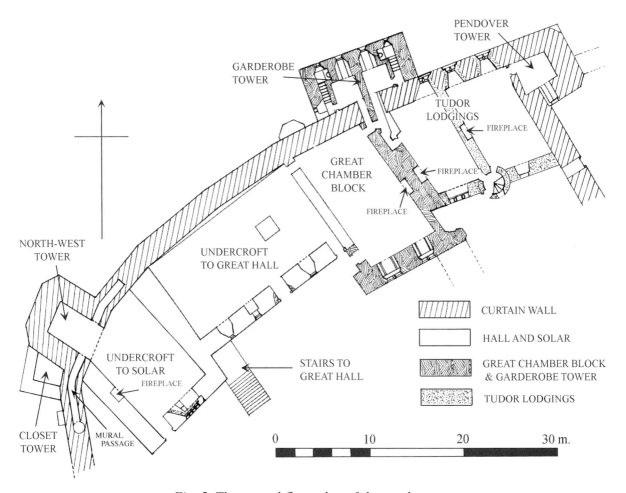

GARDEROBE
TOWER

PENDOVER
TOWER

TUDOR
LODGINGS

FIREPLACE

GREAT
CHAMBER
BLOCK

FIREPLACE

FIREPLACE

FIREPLACE

NORTH-WEST
TOWER

UNDERCROFT
TO GREAT HALL

UNDERCROFT
TO SOLAR

FIREPLACE

STAIRS TO
GREAT HALL

CLOSET
TOWER

MURAL
PASSAGE

///// CURTAIN WALL

HALL AND SOLAR

GREAT CHAMBER BLOCK
& GARDEROBE TOWER

TUDOR LODGINGS

0   10   20   30 m.

Fig. 5 The ground-floor plan of the north range

would have lit this section of the tower and also
provided direct access to the mural passage for
defence—and to reach the garderobe to the east.

Because of the height of the new Solar, the
tower had to be raised. The new work had walls
slightly thinner than the old, slightly smaller in
plan, and more regular. The junction between the
two phases is quite distinct, and there is a set-
back between the new build and the faceted curve
of the original. The new section also did not have
the chamfered corners of the lower sections,
resulting in a rather unusual set-back externally at
the junction between the two builds. The open
back of the tower was retained in the raised
masonry at second-floor level and topped with a
two-centred arch below the roof of the new Solar;
above this the raised tower had, necessarily, a
closed back because it was higher.

The only window in the tower at second-floor
level was built into the raised portion of the east
wall. This was a large window with wide splayed
recess and window seats, though with only one
trefoiled headed light. The base of the opening
was rather high compared to the floor level.

At the top of the tower is a third floor, not
linked to the Solar but reached by a continuation
of the vice from the corner of the Great Hall, and
a short passage. This floor level was supported on
lodged beams resting on setbacks in the walls and
was linked to the upper room in the adjacent
Closet Tower. The passage has the remains of a
stone-vaulted lean-to roof and is reached through
a doorway with a shouldered lintel from the spiral
stair; a similar doorway from the passage gave
access to the leads of the Solar roof. The main
room is lit by single-light windows in the north

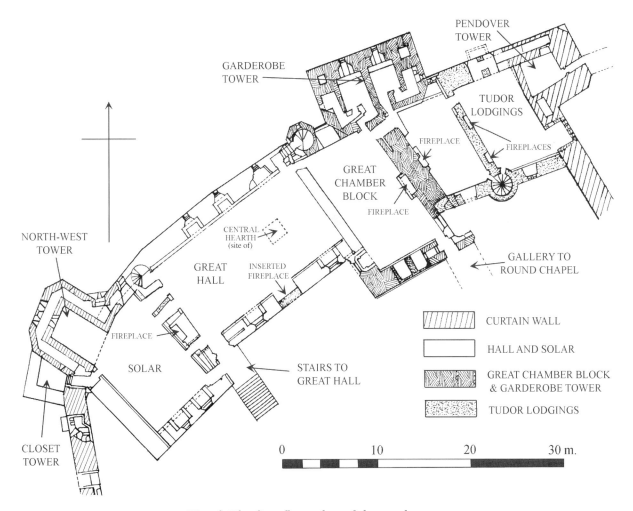

GARDEROBE
TOWER

PENDOVER
TOWER

TUDOR
LODGINGS

FIREPLACE

FIREPLACES

GREAT
CHAMBER
BLOCK

FIREPLACE

NORTH-WEST
TOWER

CENTRAL
HEARTH
(site of)

GREAT
HALL

INSERTED
FIREPLACE

GALLERY TO
ROUND CHAPEL

FIREPLACE

SOLAR

STAIRS TO
GREAT HALL

CLOSET
TOWER

CURTAIN WALL

HALL AND SOLAR

GREAT CHAMBER BLOCK
& GARDEROBE TOWER

TUDOR LODGINGS

0   10   20   30 m.

Fig. 6 The first-floor plan of the north range

and east walls, with shouldered lintel outer heads and two-centred rearrches; originally barred and shuttered, their reveals had window seats. The room was heated by an ornate hooded fireplace against the south wall and was evidently a fairly important one despite its size.

The roof of the raised tower had wall-plates supported on corbels on the north and south walls and was of a very shallow pitch, presumably boarded and leaded. Behind the embattled parapet there was sufficient room for a roof walk.

The Closet Tower

The four-storey Closet Tower was built in the angle between the outer face of the curtain wall and the west side of the tower in a single phase. It is of the same type of masonry as the raised

section of the North-West Tower, mainly a grey rubblestone with redder sandstone used for quoins and window surrounds. The putlog holes for the timber scaffolding used during its construction are now quite obvious.

Its narrow plan form is rather odd, but this seems entirely due to its position in relation to the curtain and tower. When it was built, the loops of the mural passage that ran around the North-West Tower at first-floor level were blocked. It has square-headed windows in the west wall at first- and second-floor levels and in the north wall at second- and third-floor levels.

The first three floors of the tower were linked to the Solar block. At ground-floor level the access was off the stepped Norman mural passageway in the curtain wall through an inserted, and now

Fig. 7 The first-floor mural passage in the north wall of the North-West Tower

two; it was presumably leaded, and virtually flat with only a gentle outwards slope to the projecting chutes on the north side. The tower was topped by battlements with capped merlons and in the post-medieval period two of the embrasures on the west elevation were infilled and converted to gun loops.

Although this has been regarded simply as a garderobe tower it has few of the obvious features that would be expected of such a structure. There is only one drain outlet at the base of the tower and this seems incapable of serving a full-height chute within. The rooms, although small, are larger than the normal garderobe chambers—larger, for example, than those in the slightly later garderobe tower in the Great Chamber block on the opposite side of the Great Hall. It is more likely that each of its floors was used as a closet as part of the suite of rooms on each floor in the Solar and similarly for the chamber at the top of the North-West Tower.

Internal Usage

As originally completed, the interpretation of the new arrangements at the west end of the Great Hall seem to be plain enough. There is no doubt that these arrangements predate the later Great Chamber block at the opposite end of the Hall range. It is possible that the ground-floor of the Solar contained the traditional services—buttery and pantry—at the 'low' end of a medieval hall, but the position of these is considered in the chapter on the Great Hall. The ground floor of the Solar did extend into the North-West Tower and had access into the base of the Closet Tower. The possibility of access between it and the Great Hall—perhaps in a carefully blocked or removed vice in the wall between them—cannot be completely eliminated.

At first- and second-floor levels the large heated rooms in the Solar were the principal elements of separate domestic suites of rooms that included a large 'alcove' in the North-West Tower (possibly partitioned off from the rest, perhaps as a bed chamber) and a closet in the Closet Tower. Both levels had direct access to the Great Hall, either through a primary doorway or

blocked, doorway close to its entrance. The position chosen was probably that of an original loop in the wall, which would have been relatively easy to enlarge into a doorway. At first- and second-floor levels the access was more direct and at first-floor level cut through the mural passage in the curtain wall, severing its link with the section around the tower. At the top of the Closet Tower the third-floor room is connected to the chamber at the top of the North-West Tower.

The roof was supported by corbels in the north and south walls and offsets on the other by way of a spiral stair. The first-floor room had its own independent access from the outside. Significantly, the rebates on the doorways from the Hall or spiral were on the room side, and, typically, the doorways to the closets were rebated on the closet side.

The heated room at the top of the raised North-West Tower was the centre of a smaller suite, reached by the same main spiral stair from the Great Hall. The rebates of its door from the passage are on the room side and the rebates of the doorway to the closet on the closet side. The new build therefore created three separate high status suites of rooms on the upper floors—or four if the ground-floor rooms were not used as part of the services—and all associated with the adjacent Great Hall.

One Phase - or Three?

The differences between the original Norman work and the later Solar complex are quite obvious. Equally obvious is that the Solar and the Great Hall next to it were built at the same time. Less clear are some anomalies within the later work, anomalies that could indicate that there were as many as three separate, but closely related, construction phases.

In the first instance there is some evidence to suggest that the new Solar was originally designed to be just two storeys high. At the second-floor level in the south and west walls there are distinct courses of red sandstone ashlar in what is otherwise a grey rubblestone wall. Taken alone they are of no obvious significance. However, above this level and at the extreme east end of the south elevation is a primary series of projecting bonding stones, or 'tushes', about 1.2m wide and respected by the string course below the present parapet.

These would only have been incorporated into the masonry in order to key in another masonry wall set at right angles to this face of the Solar, and a logical purpose for such a wall would have been as part of a grand porch to protect the main entrance into the Great Hall. The east wall of the porch would have joined the wall of the Great Hall and, indeed, in its upper section there are

Fig. 8 The western stepped mural passage in the curtain wall, rising from the ground floor doorway of the North-West Tower

again the distinct remains of the tushes for such a wall, though these have been cut back flush with the masonry.

Such a porch would also explain the odd second-floor window in the short east return wall of the Solar. This has straight reveals and was quite clearly designed as a doorway and not as a window; as a doorway, its rebates are on the outside, as is its rearch, so it was clearly intended to open outwards—and into the projected porch. The porch was apparently never built, but the significance of this structural evidence is that there

Fig. 9 A typical section of sunk-chamfer moulding,
part of the jamb of the larger first floor window of the Solar block

are no signs of tushes in the lower part of the walls of the Solar and the Great Hall. The porch was either decided upon after construction of the Solar and Great Hall was well under-way, or as part of a separate campaign altogether. There is no obvious evidence that the Hall was raised—but it is possible that in the south wall its windows may have originally been designed to be topped by gables (like the Hall of Winchester Castle in the 1230s). To accommodate the projected porch it would have then been necessary to build up the masonry between the gables.

Given the possibility of two phases—or an original phase modified during construction—there are a few other structural elements that warrant further investigation. In this light, the ashlared coursing at second-floor level could either be interpreted as the finer work at the base of a parapet, or perhaps levelling courses below new build. Internally, one of the oddities of the second floor construction is the evidence for a matching pair of corbel mounted wall-posts chased into the wall that hint at one of the main second floor beams being braced in some way. Another possible interpretation of these, if the Solar was planned originally to be of two storeys, would be that they supported the main intermediate truss of a two-bay roof.

There are some differences in decoration between the first and second floors of the Solar, but some similarities too, including the use of the sunk chamfers for the window moulding and the use of 'Y' tracery. The main differences are in the treatment of the inner jambs of the window reveals, and of their rearches, and this evidence suggests another possible phase. At first-floor level the rearches are two-centred and have sunk chamfers, whilst the jambs are plain ashlar. At second floor level the rearches and jambs have a continuous quadrant moulding and the rearches are very clumsy and partly deformed shallow two-centred arches.

Fig. 10 Detail of the inside of the southern second-floor window of the Solar Block, showing the unfinished masonry inner jambs on either side of the opening and the deformed rearach

In both the west and south windows the inner jambs of the second-floor window openings, which are a carried up into the arches on the first floor, are unfinished, stopping at the springing of the rearach. The west window, recently repaired, was made up of several different sections of moulded stone that did not quite match. The mullion had no sunk chamfers and only one part of the head had this decoration. The shutter rebate of the mullion was also nearly 20mm deeper than that of the head and it appeared that the window had been rather hurriedly finished. This then leads to another question. Was the work finished in a hurry or had it been stopped before being finished off as quickly and as cheaply as possible at a later date?

It is always rather dangerous to try and allow historical theories to explain archaeological fact, but such an approach could be valid in the Solar complex. Dating the construction of the building on stylistic evidence is equally problematic, but at least the castle was a very high status building and owned by men of importance likely to be aware of—and to use—the latest architectural fashions.

The distinctive feature of both Hall and Solar is the use of 'Y' tracery, a style that had been abandoned by the time the Great Chamber block was built. This type of tracery is subtly different from other forms in that the arches of the lights are drawn with the same aperture of compass as the overall window head, creating acutely pointed two-light windows and a distinct profile. This form, developed in eastern France—in Picardy, Burgundy and Champagne—was, for a relatively brief period in the 1280s and early 1290s, an important element in the English Court style.[1] Geoffrey de Geneville came from Joinville—a town on the Marne in Champagne—and was a close friend and supporter of Edward I.

Another close friend of the king was his chancellor, Robert Burnell, bishop of Bath and Wells, a man clearly interested in architectural fashions. His fortified mansion at Acton Burnell was started in the early 1280s and had cinque-cusped lights with cusped curve-sided triangles in the two-centred heads. By the end of the decade his new palace at Wells was built with 'Y-tracery' windows. This fashion for 'Y' tracery was relatively short in Court circles but it did, like so many, continue elsewhere for a few decades afterwards. Indeed, it appears in the outer bailey of Ludlow in St. Peter's chapel, said to have been built in the 1320s (see chapter XXII).

The other main architectural feature in the Hall and Solar is the use of the sunk-chamfer, a distinctive moulding of the Decorated period particularly in the 1320s and 40s.[2] However, the earliest cited example of its use in Britain is in the Queen's Gate of Caernarfon Castle, Gwynedd, dated to between 1283 and 1292 but probably finished by 1287.[3] One of the supervisors at Caernarfon, incidentally, was a Master Manasser of Vaucouleurs, a small town in Champagne near Joinville of which one of the de Genevilles was the lord in the 13th century, but the significance of this is unclear. Other features used at Caernarfon—the famous shouldered lintel (or 'Caernarfon' arch), the octagonal stair towers and the very low pitched roof of the Hall—are also found in this phase of work at Ludlow.

On balance, the evidence suggests that the Great Hall and Solar was begun during the 1280s or 90s (though Michael Thompson in chapter XVII argues for a date between 1250 and 1280 for the Great Hall) when the castle was held by the de Genevilles, rather than the early 14th century when it was held by Mortimer. The reasons for the apparent change in plan from a simple two-storey Solar to a two-storey block with grand porch to the Great Hall could have been a whim of the owner or, possibly, have occurred after the death of Peter de Geneville and the re-acquisition of the castle by his father, Geoffrey. It is presumed that the first phase had not, at that stage, been quite finished.

The reason for the rather hurried execution of the finished building could also have been associated with a change of ownership—perhaps the arrival in 1308 of the young Roger Mortimer. This may have been due to de Geneville trying to finish off the building for his grandson-in-law or Mortimer swiftly finishing off a nearly finished building before setting out to plan the future expansion of his new palace.

Later Changes

The status of the Solar block would have changed soon after Mortimer's plans were executed in the 1308-1322 period or between his return from exile in 1327 and his own execution in 1330. Significantly, the main decorative motif in the new Great Chamber block—and one also found at his Wigmore Castle—is the ogee arch, a feature fashionable in the 1320s but not before. Once the new chamber suites were available the status of the older ones in the Solar would have presumably been downgraded. However, no obvious structural alterations to them appear to have occurred in this period.

Some changes were made in the later medieval period when a two storey range was built along the inner face of the curtain wall to the west of the Solar, infilling the section between the wall and the west wall of the Solar. This had floors supported on corbels not dissimilar to those within the Solar and North-West Tower, and it also made use of part of the dislocated mural passages in the curtain. The probable door inserted into the ground floor of the Solar could have been directly related to this now lost range.

Other changes made—the inserted windows, the knocking through of relatively crude doorways from the Hall, and the addition of gunloops in the parapets—were later, probably of the later 16th or early 17th century and thus associated with the Council in the Marches. On Pritchard's plan of 1765, the partitioning shown at first-floor level explains some of the inserted openings. To the south of the original door from the Hall another was cut through the former vaulted alcove to lead to a spiral stair (presumably timber) down to the basement. Further south, the second inserted doorway was needed to access the south half of the Solar after this was separated from the rest by a new partition. On the west side was the long closet lit by an inserted (and now blocked) window in the south wall. At this level the accommodation had clearly been modernised, possibly as early as the 16th century.

CHAPTER XVII

The Great Hall & Great Chamber Block

by Michael Thompson

In the middle ages domestic arrangements, particularly for those of the higher social levels, were so different from what it is today that a few words of explanation are necessary.

The kernel of a medieval house was the hall (*aula* in Latin), a large communal building used primarily for formal meals but also serving several other functions. Its origins go back to early medieval times and, although it started off being free-standing, gradually buildings serving other purposes were tacked on to it at either end creating the sort of flanking wings that are so well displayed at Ludlow Castle. The hall, however, remained the primary element in domestic design throughout the middle ages and beyond, all other buildings being in varying degrees subordinate to, and in a sense serving it.

At Ludlow Castle, as indeed in all castles, the problem facing the designer was to fit this arrangement into a heavily fortified site. Usually this was done by stringing the hall with its attendant buildings against and along the curtain wall. The open area in front of the hall formed an open courtyard within the ward or bailey. Such was the 13th century arrangement at Ludlow, where the well-preserved stone buildings may well have succeeded wooden ones and where there is also some hint of an earlier stone hall in this position.

The main domestic buildings are grouped in the least vulnerable part of the castle—on the north side of the inner bailey where the curtain overlooks a precipitous slope down to the river; any form of attack or bombardment from this side was virtually impossible. The security thus provided allowed apertures for windows to be made in the main curtain wall even as early as the 13th century, albeit smaller than those facing the courtyard. Another factor influencing the choice of site for the Hall was its southern aspect inside the castle so that the Hall enjoyed sunshine most of the day.

Approaching the Hall from the courtyard, the steps that lead up to the first floor—the Hall proper—are on the left at its west end. These now lead on to a timber 'gallery' that gives the impression of the Hall floor level and the room underneath. To the right of the door were three two-light windows with transoms, the central one since blocked to allow for a fireplace inside. Internally the building measures 18m (60ft) long by 9m (30ft) wide, being twice as long as it was wide, a ratio that is quite usual for medieval halls (for instance Kenilworth and Goodrich, the latter 18m x 8.4m). The basement below was lit by three rectangular windows, with entries from the courtyard through doorways at its eastern end and in the middle.

The unusual feature that emerges from this description of the Hall's elevation is that it was two-storeyed, the basement with windows being considerably more than a mere cellar. It is possible that the ground level sloped steeply to

*Fig. 1 The Great Hall in the centre of the picture,
with the Solar block to the left, and Great Chamber block to the right*

the north before the Hall was constructed which made this arrangement more convenient—such was the case with the earlier hall at Chepstow. However, this feature tends to link it with the usual practice with halls in the Welsh March where they (probably for defensive reasons) were usually on the first floor. It may be contrasted with the beautifully preserved hall at Stokesay, near Craven Arms, where, like those in southern England, by the 13th century the ground floor was preferred.

The basement was not roofed with a stone vault—a medieval form of fire protection often employed in this type of building. Instead it was covered by a wooden ceiling that formed the floor of the Hall over it. The corbels projecting from the walls supported the transverse beams for this floor which was also carried on a longitudinal beam itself supported by two stone pillars in the centre of the building. The stone footings survived early

in this century—the eastern one, being two metres square, probably also providing a stone fireproof platform for the central hearth in the hall above. Halls of this period were warmed by a central fire the smoke of which escaped through an outlet in the roof. The basement was probably originally subdivided and used for storage and perhaps also as servants' accommodation.

The new timber 'gallery' allows visitors to stand at the original level of the vanished floor of the Hall. The three windows on either side of the Hall originally had stone seats facing each other in the embrasures, now partly hacked off. The central window converted to a fireplace has already been mentioned. The windows were not originally glazed but the openings closed with wooden shutters, the rebates for which are still visible. Similar shutters can still be seen at Stokesay Castle where the hall windows were never glazed. The moulded main doorway is

168

Fig. 2 The three doors in the wall at the west or 'service' end of the Hall

upper end was the place for the high table where the lord ate, with his private chamber in the adjoining building usually on the first floor. One entered the main door into a passage with a screen dividing it from the hall on one side and the gable wall of the hall on the other. The screen at Ludlow stood to the right of the door creating a sort of passage. In a normal hall the passage passed right through the building to a door in the opposing wall, but in a castle this was blocked off by its main curtain wall. There were openings in the wooden screen to allow entry to the hall. On the other side of the passage, the main wall would normally be pierced by three doorways: a large central one opening into a passage that led to an outside kitchen, which was flanked by doors into a pantry (for bread) and a buttery (for liquor) on either side. But at Ludlow the three doorways (Fig. 2) are not placed centrally but towards the north end. There had been a pre-existing kitchen in the courtyard which continued in use, so no kitchen door was necessary. The corner doorway at the north end gives on to a spiral staircase leading to a chamber on the second floor of the adjoining block. The next doorway leads through into the adjoining block. The third, larger, doorway led to an L-shaped passage in the thickness of the wall turning right into the passage of the middle door. It has been subsequently carried straight through the wall into the next block. Possibly the middle door was more in the nature of a service hatch for the pantry and buttery wherever they may have been located. In the south end of the gable wall is yet another inserted doorway with a flattened head leading into the west wing. The arrangements at the service end of the Ludlow Hall are

original, but not the fragment of wooden door. It was closed by a drawbar—the socket in the wall shows that it was about 19cm (7in) square in section.

The form of roof may be inferred from the corbels projecting from the walls. The lower large corbels supported braces against the wall securing the main tie or transverse beams from which crown posts rose up to collars holding the principal rafters. The intermediate ordinary rafters were set on wall plates resting on the upper level of smaller corbels. The closeness of the two large corbels to the east was to provide extra support for the *louver*, a large and elaborate cagelike structure that let the smoke out without letting the rain in. The roof cover can only be guessed at, possibly shingles at first, and later stone tiles.

But how did this Hall differ from others? From the late 12th century the functions served by the two gable ends of the hall differed markedly. The main entry door was at the lower or service end of the hall while its opposite or quite different from those of a normal hall. This is partly due to the unusual position of the kitchen in the courtyard, but mainly as a consequence of the decision to create a three-storey Chamber block adjoining the gable end of the Hall. The extra accommodation afforded by the earlier Norman wall tower may have influenced this decision. As meals were taken increasingly in private during the later middle ages proximity to the kitchen had advantages. The west wing must be more or less contemporary with the main Hall but being thrust forward from the Hall frontage suggests that a symmetrical design with a similar wing the other end of the Hall was envisaged from the beginning.

Turning now to the upper (east) end of the Hall, there is another arrangement that differs from the normal. The first point is that the east

Fig. 3 Two windows looking north from the Hall with corbels for roof timbers and wall-walk door above

wall is only 1m (3ft 3in) thick as opposed to the 2m (6ft 6in) for the other walls and is of rougher construction; it seems likely that it had been retained from an earlier building. It was evidently left unaltered when the eastern wing was built. The elaborate three-storeyed Great Chamber block with the new latrine tower was erected almost without reference to the earlier Hall, the links being late and not very close. There are two later doors at the north end of the east wall of the Hall giving access to the wing, one at Hall-floor level and another of more elaborate 15th-century form apparently connected by wooden stairs to the Hall floor below. The east block seems to have been conceived as independent chambers, only related to the Hall to complete a symmetrical elevation.

The defensive wall walk of the curtain wall was reached by a door in the turret of the east wing as can be seen from below. The doorway has a shouldered head or 'Caernarfon arch' as it is called from its use in Edward I's work at the Welsh castle and is a fair indication of the later date of the eastern block than the Hall. The wall

walk continued above the wall-plate level of the Hall. On the opposite side the top of the Hall was finished with a moulded cornice surmounted by a battlemented parapet.

As with most parts of the castle erected before Tudor times there are no written records to provide firm evidence for dates of building, so it is necessary to use comparative architectural material from elsewhere to give rough dates and then try to relate these to the known owner of the castle at the time in question. For the Hall the window tracery and the mouldings of the doorway are the most significant, indicating that it was constructed somewhere between 1250 and 1280. The likely builder seems to have been Geoffrey de Geneville, husband to Maud de Lacy who controlled the castle at this time. Building was almost certainly not continuous and the Great Chamber block was probably erected by Roger de Mortimer of Wigmore who was joint owner of the castle from 1314 and who built St. Peter's chapel in the 1320s in the outer bailey.

The Great Chamber Block

The three-storeyed Great Chamber block to the east of the Great Hall, which St. John Hope refers to as the Edwardian block, was added in *c*.1320 to balance the three-storied Solar block, to the west of the Hall. From the surviving corbels and fireplaces it clearly contained several imposing rooms and was associated with other domestic buildings to the east and with a large chamber and garderobe tower built through a breach made in the Norman curtain wall. At a later date its first-floor was linked by a gallery to the round chapel, and two groups of Elizabethan lodgings replaced the eastern buildings in the eastern corner of the curtain wall.

The block measures 14 m (46 ft) by 8 m (26 ft) internally. The ground floor—effectively an undercroft—is entered from the inner bailey by a small recessed doorway in its south-west corner (Fig. 4). The only other doorway in the rather bleak walls of this room is in the north-east corner leading to the garderobe tower and, through a twisting passage to the eastern

building. At the northern end of the west wall there is evidence of a blocked opening which would have led into the Great Hall's undercroft. For all its bleak appearance, this undercroft was not simply used for storage for there is a fireplace in the east wall and two fine two-light windows with stone side seats in the south wall. These have rebates and hinges that provide evidence for the presence of shutters. St. John Hope mentions that the window tracery was lying about when he visited in the early 20th century and could 'easily be replaced', but this has not occurred and the pieces have since been removed. St. John Hope also suggested that the room may have been a guard-chamber, but perhaps a more probable use was as offices or rooms used by servants.

The ceiling of the undercroft was supported by a series of close set corbels on the east and west walls, with added support on the north and south walls provided by curved braces with verticals set into the walls. There may have also been central pillars to support the spine beam, and to support similar pillars at the first-floor level.

Fig. 4 *Looking east along the front of the Solar block, Great Hall and Great Chamber block showing the recessed door in the south-west corner. The round chapel is on the right*

The first-floor room may have been reached at a later date by a wooden staircase in the north-west corner, where two of the corbels in the west wall have been broken back, the broken surface of one of them still showing signs of having been plastered over. This was a much grander room in all ways than the undercroft. Its east wall contains a grand hooded fireplace carried on a fourfold series of corbels with, to either sides, large carved corbels containing heads with leafwork (Figs. 5 and 6). 'The heads ... are believed to represent Edward II, himself and his wife Queen Isabella, the She wolf of France, whose liaison with Roger Mortimer is a matter of history. The chimney of this fire-place has been re-built, stone by stone, and represents exactly the old 14th century one.'[1] In the southern end of the west wall there is a two-light window with tracery, again showing evidence of having been shuttered and with side stone seats. Opposite is a similar two-light window in the southern end of the east wall. The Tudor transomed and mullioned window in the south wall is a later insertion, presumably replacing an earlier window, though no evidence for such a window remains. Evidence which was visible at the time of St. John Hope's work has perhaps been obscured by subsequent repairs.

Towards the northern end of the room there are several openings—an Edwardian window that was replaced in Tudor or perhaps Stuart times and since narrowed to provide additional support to the wall above; a doorway into the garderobe tower; and doors into a since demolished room on the east side and into the Hall on the west. The doorway to the quarters on the east side leads through a passage almost 5ft wide, the door being secured on the passage side as demonstrated by holes for a drawbar.

The access to the Great Chamber would not have been merely by a staircase from the far corner of the undercroft. There must have been a staircase at the front of the building. Traces of this remain in the blocked openings in the east wall of the Great Chamber (best seen from the eastern side) which would have led into wall passages and thence into the Great Chamber itself. There would

Fig. 5 The fireplaces in the undercroft and Great Chamber, showing the carved corbels to either side of the hood. Two of the corbels which supported the floor of the great chamber can be seen, one to either side of the fireplace

have been a similar arrangement on the floor above. This access was destroyed when the buildings to the east where demolished to make way for the present Tudor Lodgings, which had their own spiral staircase that replaced the earlier one in a slightly different position.

It would appear that the Great Chamber was initially roofed over, the roof being carried on corbels with carved heads, forming a structure of three and a half bays, the half bay being closest to the north wall. However, these supports seem to be excessively flimsy to have supported a roof and the possibility of this range having been built a full three stories high from the beginning must be considered.

The first-floor room was clearly important and is in the position of a traditional 'parlour' as found at the upper end of great halls from the 14th century onwards. As such, it would have been for the use of senior members of the household and important guests.

Accepting that this was the full height of the original building, at a later date the roof was replaced by a floor and another storey was added. There is no indication of a spine beam running north/south to support the second floor, so the east/west timbers must have been massive in order to take the north/south joists, which would have also been supported on slight shelves in the north and south walls. The access to this room from the Great Hall is problematic. There is a doorway inserted into the east wall of the Hall, which appears to be at the mid-point of the roof level (see Fig. 6). To function, there would have had to be a flight of steps within the Hall, probably rising from the eastern gallery or dais. On the Hall side, the lower half has been blocked up, perhaps changing the nature of the opening to that of a window which would have provided extra light into the room over the Great Chamber. This may suggest that, when the blocking was introduced, the Great Hall had largely lost its ceremonial function and that the room above the Great Chamber was no longer a retiring room. Accepting this, the entrance to the chamber from the Hall was via a spiral staircase in the turret attached to the Norman curtain wall, opening into the room via a doorway in the north wall over which is a label ending in carved heads. The date of this addition is uncertain, but the constructional details appear to be similar to those of the garderobe tower and it could well be of the same date, or perhaps slightly later.

Adjacent to this entrance the room had a tall single-light, recessed window with a stone seat

Fig. 6 Drawings of 1852 showing the fireplace in the Great Chamber and doorway entrance to the room above

constructed within the thickness of the curtain wall. Further east again was an entrance into the garderobe tower. This is alongside a door in the east wall that led into the chambers beyond, more or less replicating the layout of the Great Chamber floor below. The room was lit mainly by windows at its southern end—an inserted 15th-century window in the south end of the west wall; a two-light window in the south wall; and a window in the west wall with side seats and a label over finishing, once more, in carved heads. The west wall also contains the room's fireplace with a projecting hood—a fireplace that is even larger than the one in the Great Chamber below. The roof of this block was also three and a half bays in length, supported on massive corbels and inset wall posts of a much greater size than those on the second floor. The roof was almost flat and its apex probably ran north/south. It has been suggested that the room was originally used by the ladies of the household, but it would doubtless have had a different function when the Council in the Marches was using the building.

The garderobe tower which leads off the north-eastern corner of this block was probably constructed at the same time, but is built outside the line of the curtain wall, and was clearly intended to serve both the Great Chamber block and the adjoining rooms to the east. Oblong in shape, its longest side resting against the curtain wall, it contains four storeys. The rooms of all but the top storey are reached both from the Great Chamber block and from the accommodation to its east. The first two storeys are divided into two sections, each further subdivided into two compartments. The larger rooms were presumably bedrooms, with single-light windows whilst the outer compartment in each case contained a short flight of steps leading up to a single latrine set in a recess at the northern end. These small, narrow rooms were illuminated by small windows that were little more than arrow slits. These garderobes followed the normal arrangement at this date by discharging down a chute into the surrounding undergrowth. It would appear that the tower was designed both to provide a necessary facility and to contribute to the defences of the castle.

A spiral stair continues up to a third storey in the garderobe tower which contained a single room with windows and fireplace. On its east and west walls were doorways to garderobes. The fourth floor also contained a single room, this time reached by a passage from the top of the vice.

Fig. 7 Chute outlets from the garderobe tower

CHAPTER XVIII

The Tudor Lodgings & use of the North-East Range *by* Ron Shoesmith

The Tudor Lodgings fill the space between the Great Chamber block and the east curtain wall of the inner bailey and incorporate the Norman Pendover Tower. They replace an earlier building of which traces remain in the curtain wall and on the western side, notably at the southern end. The Elizabethan south wall cuts across blocked openings in the east wall of the Great Chamber block, which probably represent a stair turret on the south-west corner. The earlier block was presumably of the same date as the Great Chamber block—the reason for demolition and replacement by the Tudor Lodgings is unknown, but it may be that there was a need for additional rooms involving an additional storey and attics.

The 16th-century work consists of two almost identical sets of lodgings, each a full three stories high with attics above. The south wall has, at its centre, a circular vice that protrudes out into the courtyard and also forms the southern end of the cross wall that divides the lodgings. It serves all three main floors, but not the attic level. The vice has an external entry from the inner bailey on the western side with a small square window facing south. It provided the main access to each floor of the two sets of lodgings by means of diagonally-set doorways. This form of shared entry to lodgings has a long history, first appearing at places such as Dartington Hall in Devon and in various episcopal palaces.[1] When the lodgings at Ludlow were built in the 16th century, they were probably designed as independent chambers—at least two

lodgings to each floor—providing the necessary permanent quarters for the more important officials. Each chamber would have been suitably partitioned off from the others and from the access corridors and would have provided a combination of bed-sitting room and office—a room in which to work and sleep. The upper attic rooms would have contained accommodation for the squires, yeomen etc. who would have been expected to share rooms and, as necessary, beds. The modifications that created two major lodgings, each with several rooms, was probably part of the 17th century alterations.

The cross wall between the pair of lodgings was built to be parallel with the east curtain wall, which left the western lodging as an irregular shape, narrowing slightly to the south. The south wall of the western lodging contains a square-headed window of three lights set into a deep recess—the splay of an earlier 16th-century window which effectively dates the rebuilding here. The northern side of that room is mainly taken up with the eastern half of the garderobe tower so that on the ground floor the pointed 16th-century window had to be inserted within a skewed opening. The entrance to the garderobe tower from the western ground floor room is through a doorway in the earlier west wall and along a short passageway that also provides a tortuous route to the ground floor of the Great Chamber block. To the south of this doorway is a plain fireplace with a curved and chamfered head. Towards the northern end of the east wall there is an inserted timber-headed doorway, presumably to provide an access passage from the eastern lodging to the garderobe tower. A timber partition would have separated the passage from the main room to the south. Corbels set into the north wall and a shelf in part of the south wall above the window opening would have supported large timber beams. There are two pairs of large holes in the east and west walls that would also have taken two massive cross beams. The joists that supported the floorboards ran north/south and would have been set into these major beams.

The curtain wall at first-floor level was totally demolished when the garderobe tower was built and a small doorway leads from the lodging directly into the main room of the eastern part of that tower. To the east of the doorway is a skewed opening somewhat smaller than the one on the ground floor with a four-centred reararch and a square-headed window. Adjoining the garderobe entry, but in the west wall, is a segmental-headed doorway that led into the Great Chamber. This is matched by a square-headed doorway inserted into the northern end of the spine wall. The 1765 plan shows a timber partition separating the north passage that joined these two doorways from the room to the south, but no trace remains. The southern room contained a square-headed fireplace supported on a double row of corbels in the centre of the west wall. At the south end of that wall is the chamfered jamb of an original opening from the turret that was destroyed when the Elizabethan lodgings were built. The south wall contained a rectangular opening, now blocked, that once contained a mullioned and transomed window of three lights. Most of the east wall at this level is slightly corbelled out to take the fireplaces and chimneys of the eastern lodgings. There is again a diagonal opening from the vice and adjacent to it, but in the spine wall, there is a sealed doorway with an arched head, presumably blocked when a fireplace was inserted on the other side of the wall.

The pattern of the second floor was similar to that of the floor below, being supported on large timber beams at each end, one resting on the shelf

in the south wall, and the other on two corbels on the east end of the north wall, and a single corbel at the west end. Two central beams were supported in an identical fashion to the floor below.

The second floor must have had a similar design to the one below with an original doorway in the northern part of the west wall, smaller but matching in design the one on the first floor, and an inserted square-headed doorway in the spine wall, again smaller than the one on the first floor. A small door in the north wall led into a passage in the garederobe tower that turned east and then led to a single garderobe. There was no direct access at this level to the other rooms in the garderobe tower, the only approach being from the Great Chamber block. The north wall extends above the original line of the curtain and contains

Fig. 1 The external view of the south-west corner of the Tudor Lodgings, showing the corner of the destroyed turret to the Great Chamber block on the left, and, on the right, the vice that served both sides of the Tudor Lodgings

a square-headed window at its eastern end, with a four-centred rearrach partially blocked by the spine wall, suggesting an earlier opening. In the west wall are a square-headed fireplace with a relieving arch above and a blocked turret doorway above that on the floor below. The south wall contained a large square-headed window of four long lights with round heads. It was blocked in the early 20th century to preserve the surviving features. In the west wall, the two grand fireplaces on the first and second floors are each stepped slightly further to the north of the one on the ground floor to allow room for the flues.

A small two-light window in the south wall provides some evidence for an attic floor, but the central vice does not reach to this level. Apart from an internal wooden stair that has left no visible trace, the only apparent access was from the spiral vice in the north-west corner of the Great Chamber block leading first into the garderobe tower and thence to the attic floor. There is little indication of the design of the roof, but the lack of gables leads to the presumption that it was almost flat.

The easternmost section of the Tudor Lodgings was of a similar size to the western block, but was enclosed on the north and east by the curtain wall and thus included the Norman Pendover Tower. Several openings were made in the tower walls so that it could be used as an entrance to the Tudor Lodgings from the outer bailey. At ground and first floor levels it also contained a main staircase, which is shown on the 1765 plan (Fig. 4). The entrance into the tower from the outer bailey was in the south wall (now blocked), with a second entry at first-floor level from the wall walk of the outer bailey defences. The Norman curtain wall originally contained wall passages leading from the tower and remains of the doorways and small sections of the passageways survive. At the second-floor level there were openings in the north wall (leading west) and through the south wall on to the inner bailey wall walk.

The wall built across the open end of the tower includes a high level arch that was blocked at an early date. This wall now contains an open doorway at ground level and a blocked timber-framed opening at first-floor level. There are also traces of another stone-sided opening at second-floor level, which was blocked at an early date, for it is partially covered by plaster. Central to the main arch blocking are the head and southern splay of a narrow single-light Norman window, visible only on the western face. The ground and first floors were taken up with the inserted winding wooden staircase, poorly illuminated by a single window introduced into the north wall at second-floor level. The stairs and associated landings, with traces of painted plaster still surviving on the walls, led into the high second floor of the tower (at the same level as the third floor in the lodgings), which was used as a private chamber. It was illuminated by a rather fine square-headed window of four transomed-lights inserted into the east wall, now blocked, and heated by a fireplace in the south wall. The tower was heightened, probably in the 14th century, and a third/fourth floor room was introduced in the Elizabethan renovation. It had a two-light window in the east wall and was approached by a doorway in the west wall, the access being across the roof leads of the Tudor Lodgings. Such a means of access was quite fashionable in the latter part of the 16th century. The tower thus provided an alternative means of access to the main floors of the eastern block of the Tudor Lodgings as well as two upper chambers.

The ground floor of the eastern block was heated by a fireplace with a corbelled-out head and mantleshelf set in the west wall and was illuminated by two two-light windows in the north wall, identical in appearance to the one in the western block, but without the skewed opening, and a square-headed window with a two-centred rearrach in the south wall. There is no indication of any partitions at this level and the room may well have been completely open. The first floor was partly supported on ledges on the north and south walls, together with the massive beam holes that continue through the spine wall from the western lodgings. However, there is no trace of any corresponding holes in the east wall, so the complete design of the floor remains somewhat of a mystery. It may be that vertical timbers were set against the original east wall to support the beams, rather than taking the risk of weakening the wall by inserting new holes.

The first floor was entered from the vice in the south-west corner and from the eastern stair tower, although the latter doorway is now blocked. There was also a door leading through the spine wall into the passage on the north side of the western lodging, providing access to the lavatory and to the Great Chamber. The 1765 plan shows that this floor was partitioned into three rooms—two small ones on the south and a larger one to the north. The larger room was illuminated by an enormous four-bay square-headed window that was corbelled out from the wall allowing single lights on each side of the bay. This Elizabethan bay window replaced a pair of narrow lights of which parts of the jambs and a segmental rearch survive. The room was heated by a square-headed stone fireplace in the west wall. The smaller room next to the vice also had a fireplace in the west wall. With its chamfered and stopped wooden lintel, this fireplace is obviously inserted. The room was lit by a square-headed two-light transomed window complete with side seats and set in the south wall. To the east of this was a second smaller chamber that had been enlarged by a large recess cut into the Norman curtain wall. This recess contained a square-headed and transomed four-light window which included a small cupboard in the north reveal.

The floor above was supported on a series of corbels in the south wall and a shelf and some corbels in the north wall. The two massive beam holes continued through the spine wall providing some evidence for a similar floor design to the western lodgings. One of the beams could have continued into the curtain wall, the other may, once again, have been supported on a vertical timber.

The second floor was probably divided in a similar way to the first. The principal room contained a square-headed four-light transomed window in the north wall and was heated by a re-used fireplace, set slightly to the south of the fireplaces below, which Hope describes as being of the time of Edward IV.[2] There was a small doorway in the northern end of the west wall leading into the western half of the Tudor Lodgings, but, in the final phase, no access from the Norman Pendover Tower. The small room at the south-west corner has a small inserted fireplace in the west wall adjoining the doorway leading to the vice. This room was illuminated by a window in the south wall identical but slightly narrower to that in the room below. The south-eastern room had a very small fireplace that was corbelled out from the south wall and, as with the floor below, included a deep recess on the eastern side that would originally have been part of the wall walk. A doorway in the south wall of the alcove led to the remaining part of that wall walk. Light for the room was provided by a small single-light window in the east wall. However, most of the space in the alcove was taken up with

Fig. 2 The northern walls of the inner bailey, at a time when the surrounding trees less obscured the building. The huge window opening on the first floor of the eastern section of the Tudor Lodgings can be clearly seen to the left of the garderobe tower

a spiral staircase set on the wall walk level in the north-east corner. This would have provided access to the attic rooms and to the leads above the lodgings.

Only slight traces remain of the attic floor, including a fireplace with a wooden head in the west wall and a small two-light window in the south wall overlooking the inner bailey. To the east there is a single-light opening providing illumination for the upper staircase room. The roof was almost flat and had a battlemented parapet.

The spine wall between the two sets of lodgings was built with the ability to take the weight of the main three fireplaces that heated the eastern block. To achieve this it was corbelled out at first-floor level on the western side. The three flues ran up to a stack which has since collapsed. The three inserted fireplaces and flues in the southern part of this wall lead up to an almost perfect stack made of brick with star-shaped chimneys.

Fig. 3 Close up of the windows in the north wall of the Tudor Lodgings, with the Pendover Tower to the left and garderobe tower to the right

The use of the North-East Range

The long range of buildings that completely filled the northern side of the inner bailey had totally different functions as the use of castle changed from having a mostly defensive purpose, through a long period when it was mainly residential, becoming almost a small palace, to its final use as ceremonial/official and residential accommodation associated with the Council in the Marches. Each change of use led to considerable alterations and, in some places, total rebuilding. Although many of the changes have been described in the previous chapters, this section attempts to look at the north-east range and establish how the various parts related to each other.

The earliest period represented is the 12th-century castle with its eastern corner tower (the Pendover Tower) and the North-West Tower as the main features. The spine wall between the Great Hall and the Great Chamber block may also be of this period. There were passages within the walls associated with one or more garderobes, suggesting that buildings were erected against the curtain wall. Certainly a building in the position of the present Solar block is probable, and one is also likely against the open gorge of the Pendover Tower. It is quite possible that some of these buildings were of timber, possibly of a lean-to nature, leaving little trace in the surviving stone curtain walls. However, the chapel was of stone and the suggested end wall of a possible hall was also of stone, so stone buildings are a distinct possibility. Other buildings of timber, whilst providing the required accommodation, may well have been seen as being of a temporary nature, to be replaced in stone when the occasion arose.

Such a change could well have occured with the arrival of Geoffrey de Geneville, and following the Edwardian conquest of Wales which brought peace and an increasing degree of prosperity to the border regions. Following his marriage to Maud de Lacy, de Geneville was granted vast estates in Ireland and joined Edward I in a Crusade. The various conquests made him extremely rich so he was well able to carry out extensive renovations. It was also very fashionable to rebuild domestic ranges on a larger and more elaborate scale at this date. Only a short distance to the north of Ludlow, Stokesay Castle was rebuilt in 1294.

The first buildings to be completed were the Great Hall and its associated Solar block. Both were initially two stories high (the ground floor in both cases being rather superior undercrofts for the use of servants) with the Solar having a second floor added at a slightly later date. It has been suggested that the main construction period took place some time before Peter de Geneville's sudden death in 1292[3] and that the second floor was added shortly afterwards, perhaps by Geoffrey de Geneville, who outlived his son by some 22 years. Alternatively, the work could have been done by Roger de Mortimer who, after he married Joan, a daughter of Peter de Geneville, took over the castle. The largely blank wall on the eastern side of the Great Hall (possibly retained from an earlier essentially lean-to building) strongly suggests that this was the limit of the residential buildings at this time. Even so, the first-floor Great Hall, some 18m (60ft) long and 9m (30ft) wide, compared well with others of the same period along the Welsh Border. It still depended for heating on a central hearth—a feature that was still *de riguer* in halls of this nature and did not go out of fashion until much later in the 14th century. The Solar block presumably served a dual purpose, with pantry and buttery having direct entrances from the Hall at first-floor level whilst the private chamber above had an access from a vice in the north-west corner of the Hall.

It is suggested that the Closet Tower (in the angle between the Norman North-West Tower and the curtain wall) was built and the North-West Tower was heightened at the same time as the Solar block was heightened. This would accord with the access from the spiral stair via a passageway into the upper room in the North-West Tower. These additions provided an additional private chamber in the North-West Tower and closets opening off both chambers possibly for the use of bed-servants.

The accommodation that Roger de Mortimer found, or completed, was of a reasonably high stature and was doubtless accompanied with other buildings in the inner bailey including a detached kitchen, but the main range was still far from sufficient for his needs. More palatial accommodation was required and a new block was built onto the eastern side of the Great Hall. This, the Great Chamber block, was a magnificant suite of rooms, probably three stories high, balancing the old Solar range, which could then become a service wing, with the chambers above being used by important visitors. The new building had to have the finest services, and a section of the old curtain wall was demolished to make way for a complex five-storey high closet and garderobe tower, extending out from the wall line. The design of the garderobe tower indicates that additional accommodation was built to the east of the Great Chamber block.

The new Great Chamber block was probably designed to provide high quality accommodation for the Lord and Lady of the castle. The ground floor or undercroft was doubtless the province of the servants whilst the first and second floors provided the private chambers with an independent access from a since demolished stair tower next to the south-east corner as well as from a gallery in the Great Hall. Both private chambers had large and ornate fireplaces, the parlour for the reception of important guests and a retiring room or chamber of state on the floor above, approached by a spiral staircase in a small semi-octagonal tower added to the curtain wall at the north-west corner. Servants may have used the smaller rooms in the garderobe tower that led off the principal rooms whilst visitors would have the upper rooms associated with the Solar block as well as the upper floors of the garderobe tower.

This then was the palatial 'palace' of Roger de Mortimer and his heirs and eventually the home of Richard Plantagenet, duke of York and his son, the future Edward IV. When he became king, Edward sent his son, eventually to become the ill-fated Edward V, with his younger brother and court to live in Ludlow Castle, well away from the intrigues of London. This was the beginning of the Council in the Marches, for it really began as a prince's Council, gradually gathering more power. This was the time when some parts of the castle were given names—the rooms to the east of the Great Chamber block are reputed to have been the home of the young princes and the upper chamber in the Solar block is known as Prince Arthur's Chamber. Arthur, the eldest son of the Tudor king, Henry VII, and first husband of Catherine of Aragon, stayed there in the winter of 1501 and died in Ludlow. After Arthur's death Catherine became the first of the unfortunate wives of his brother, Henry VIII.

The Council gradually expanded until the 1530s when Rowland Lee, Bishop of Coventry, extended its authority throughout Wales and the Border counties. For over a hundred years Ludlow was the administrative capital of Wales, trying ecclesiastical as well as civil and criminal cases. Accommodation that had been suitable for a prince, and even a king, was insufficient for the large number of officials that were needed to administer the Council and many changes had to be made. Facilities were needed for the Lord President of the Council himself, the vice-President, and the various bishops, Welsh circuit judges and paid officers in attendance on or employed by the Council. The latter included the Secretary to the Council, the Clerk, the Prosecuting Attorney(s) and the Porter, who would also be responsible for the prison and the prisoners.

Accommodation for the judges had to be separate from the rest and they eventually had their own lodgings, built by Sir Henry Sidney in 1581. This building, just within and extending above the main gate to the inner bailey, gives a good impression of the extent and quality of the buildings being converted and erected in the castle at that time.

The lodgings for the minor officers of the Council were probably of timber and their most likely positions have been recorded by St. John Hope against the west wall of the inner bailey. Other lodgings were scattered around the castle such as those in the upper part of the Oven Tower and in Mortimer's Tower. The upper floors of the old Gatehouse also provided additional rooms, although some may have been connected with

and used as part of the Judges Lodgings. This left the north range, the old royal palace, available to accommodate the most important officers and to provide the business rooms.

The Great Hall was modernised about 1580 when the central hearth was finally abandoned and a fireplace with an elaborate double flue was inserted in place of a window in the south wall. The Hall was apparently kept mainly for public occasions, ceremonial meals and entertaining important guests—indeed its use changed relatively little throughout its life. Its ceremonial nature is perhaps emphasised by the fact that it suffered less alterations than any of the other rooms in the north range, keeping most of its late 13th-century windows and door openings. In 1634 it was used for the first performance of Milton's *Comus* before the then lord president, the earl of Bridgewater. The Solar block together with the North-West Tower also required relatively little work, the main change being the insertion of a rectangular window in the ground floor of the south wall. However, there were other changes that are not now obvious, but which show on the 1765 plans and which probably existed in the 16th century. These plans also help in establishing the use of the various rooms.

The plans indicate that the ground-floor room underneath the Great Hall was in use as a cellar and offices and that it still contained the column that had supported the central hearth. No use is given for the ground-floor room in the Solar block, but the base of a spiral staircase is shown set against the east wall. The first-floor plan shows the Hall as a single open space, without even a screen, and with the three openings leading into the Solar block. The spiral stair rising from the basement apparently led out towards the central opening, whilst the first floor of the Solar was partitioned into several rooms. On the west was a long passage leading from the now-blocked opening in the south wall to the closet tower. The passage provided access to two rooms, a southern one that included the fireplace, and an irregularly-shaped northern one extending into the North-West Tower. These partitions and stair may well represent the earlier arrangement of pantry and buttery with the stair providing access from a kitchen or food preparation room in the ground floor. There were few changes to the upper floors in this block and in the North-West and Closet towers which must have continued in domestic use, possibly for the principal officers of the Council.

The Great Chamber block required substantial modernisation, with several new windows inserted to provide increased illumination. The 1765 plans do not indicate the use of the ground floor, but do show a flight of stairs rising against the east wall. These provided access to the first floor which is shown as the Council Chamber. This was obviously a palatial room which had most of its fenestration modernised in the 16th century to suit its new importance. A doorway, inserted into the south wall, provided access to the chapel along a first-floor gallery. The palatial room above the Council Chamber, approached by the vice in the north-west corner, may have been part of the accommodation belonging to the Lord President of the Council.

The building to the east of the Great Chamber block, possibly used by the Royal Princes, was demolished and replaced by the Tudor Lodgings. The earlier building may have been of similar size to the present one and probably included some of the windows inserted in the curtain wall. Originally possibly the wardrobe, built against the garderobe tower, it may have been extended as a two-storey block built as a lean-to against the curtain wall. Pressure for additional accommodation would have demanded that as many floors and rooms as possible should be built within this prime site, next to the Council Chamber. The Tudor Lodgings were the result. In their final state they comprised two almost identical suites, each three stories high with independent attic rooms above. When built, they were probably designed as separate chambers built on a college style with a common access. The individual rooms and eventually the suites were accessed from a vice in the centre of the south wall, and the 18th century plans indicate a degree of parititioning into smaller rooms. The rooms thus

provided, together with the rooms in the upper part of the Pendover Tower (above a winding wooden staircase to the first floor) and the various rooms in the Garderobe Tower, must have provided the accommodation for the more senior visitors—the various bishops, landed gentry and others—who had business with the Council.

The Rooms of the North-East Range

Several visitors to the castle between the 17th and the 19th centuries have left descriptions of the rooms in the north range to the east of the Great Hall. The varying usages and different approaches make it a rather fascinating puzzle to determine the names, and thus the uses, of the various rooms.

The earliest indication is given in a letter written by the then Steward, George Betts, in 1634, before the Civil War. He describes:

> ... my Lord's Lodging, I mean that part of the castle, the Council chamber below the stairs, the drawing Chamber to that, beyond that my lord's Lodging Chamber with a Chamber within that, these are furnished, the Chief Justice now lies there. Above the stairs over these rooms the great Chamber, the drawing Chamber, my lady's bed Chamber, these three rooms for the most part were hanged, for two of them there is necessity, the drawing Chamber and my lady's and the great Chamber as occasions were, and my lady's Closet at the end of the great Chamber, was always hanged, one little Chamber within my lady's Chamber, and a Chamber up one pair of stairs here, where my lady's gentlewoman did lie; one chamber next to the top of the leads, one Chamber under the Lower drawing chamber where Mr Goodwin and his wife did lodge; and a Closet to that and one Chamber within it for servants, these are at that end of the castle.

The 1650 Inventory, taken during the Commonwealth, lists many of the rooms. What appear to be the relevant ones in the north range comprise:

> the hall
> a withdrawing room
> a chamber called Lord Berkley's Chamber
> a chamber called Lady Alice's Chamber

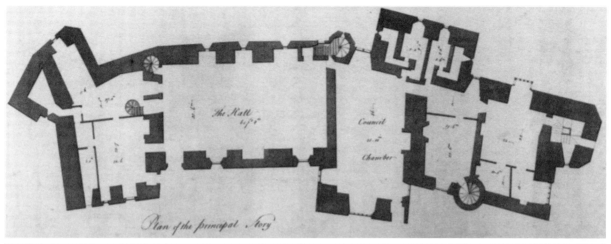

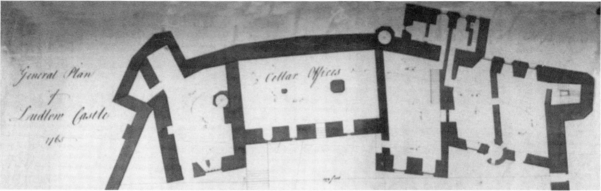

Figs. 4 & 5 Pritchard's plans of 1765 of the ground (lower) and first floor (top) of the Northern Range

a room adjoining it
a chamber called the Constable's
Mr Houghton's room
a low room near it[4]

This list was made with little reference to the use of the various chambers, as the main purpose was to sell the furniture.

The Civil War doubtless caused considerable problems within the castle and its administration as is hinted by Dinely when he visited in 1684 after the Restoration. He wrote:

> The Castle Hall is very fair, having neer those arms this inscription in Letters of Gold in Roman Character:
>
> 'Richard, Lord Vaughan Earle of Carbery Lord President of Wales and the marches'
>
> Walter de Lacy is deemed founder of this Castle, this appears by an Inscription in the Chappel with his Arms ...

Next ye Great Hall of the Rooms below stairs are The Council Chamber where ye Judges dine hath now Inscriptions and Arms of the Lords Presidents that hath been.

Near this is the repository for the King's plate belonging to this Castle. Then a fair room.

The President's Bed Chamber with stone Walls of a foot in thickness with a drawing Room for privacy.

Above stairs are A large Dineing Room famous for its Roof of large Timber. Near this is Prince Arthur's Bedchamber who was sd. to have a double heart according to this device seen therein, painted and guilded against ye Wainscot. [Here is a picture of double heart].

Next above stairs to be considered is the Lord President's Ladys Drawing Room And her Bedchamber furnished by his Majestie & hung with Lemon coloured Damask in ye window is painted an escutcheon passed with a Garter, inscribed in Church text 'qui man pente'.

The king's Kitchen is below stairs very fair.[5]

Next there is the description provided by Mr. Perkes, who was the Town Clerk of Ludlow between 1719 and 1751.[6] Following a description of the buildings in the outer bailey, the Judges' Lodgings and the chapel he goes on to write:

... a passage from thence [the chapel] leads to the Council Chamber where ye Prince is present Lord President Judges and Head offices determine the affaires belonging to the Principality of Wales, in which are ye names of ye Lords Presidents on ye wall; from which room eastward ye go to ye Kings Chamber and Dining Room out of which place there is Wigmore Hole and thence on to the walls which once might have been walked round, but now by reason of more Building near the wall cannot ...

The plans of 1765 (Figs. 4 & 5) indicate that the rooms on the first floor in the Tudor Lodgings were partitioned and that there was an internal flight of steps from the ground floor in the first floor of the western lodging.

It would seem almost certain that the first floor contained the principal rooms and that the servants offices, cellarage and kitchen were in the ground floor. Assuming that the kitchen mentioned by Dinely was below the Council Chamber, then the stairs shown on the plan would help to bear out his comment that the judges dine in the Council Chamber. The food could be delivered with the greatest of convenience.

It is suggested that the whole of the first floor of the Tudor Lodgings was given over to providing the President's accommodation. Dinely's repository for the king's plate could well have been in the garderobe chamber, leaving the two main first-floor rooms as his drawing room and bed chamber. This agrees with the 1634 description and could well be the 'Kings Chamber and Dining Room' of the 18th century. Wigmore Hole could only be the Pendover Tower where there was access to the wall walks.

The second floor—Dinely's 'above stairs'—follows the same pattern. The room above the Council Chamber must be the large dining room. Here Dinely also has Prince Arthur's Bedchamber, which other writers have considered to be on the top floor of the Solar block.[7] This could be the name for the western room in the Tudor Lodgings leaving the eastern room, doubtless partitioned as the President's Lady's Drawing Room and Bedchamber. The 1634 description is more detailed but starts with a Great Chamber—surely the famous Dining Room of Dinely—which had 'my lady's closet' at the end. On the same floor were the drawing room and 'my lady's bed chamber,' the latter with a little chamber within—a fair description of the second floor of the Tudor Lodgings. Betts goes on to describe a chamber up a pair of stairs—was this a room in the east tower? There was also a room that was apparently approached across the leads—presumably the top room in the east tower or the one in the garderobe tower.

Mr & Mrs Godwin lived in accommodation comprising a chamber, a closet and a second chamber within. under the lower drawing room. As this accommodation was at the end of the castle it was presumably in the ground floor underneath the Lord President's lodgings and next to the kitchen.

Alternative plans can be made and different uses can be proposed. This short section is offered as an indicative picture of the varied use of this part of the castle—a mixture of state and private rooms—during the later years of the Council in the Marches.

CHAPTER XIX

The Judges' Lodgings

by Anthony Fleming

On entering the castle gateway into the wide outer bailey, ahead rises the massive square 12th-century Entrance Tower and later Keep. To the right of the Keep is the initial view of the subject of this chapter—two ruined gables, a pointed gateway and an array of large windows that create a strangely domestic character within the severe expanses of the medieval curtain walls. It appears to be a house, in fact the former Judges' Lodgings, a building apparently struggling to assert itself from the uniform integrity of a great encircling castle defence (Fig. 1).

The presence of such gables rather than crenellations topping a castle curtain immediately signals peaceful conditions at the time of building and with it, a fundamental change in the whole function of the castle. This impression is confirmed by the large windows at a low and therefore indefensible level. This then is the archaeology of peace. Peace in the Marches expressed in similar archaeology may be seen much earlier at nearby Stokesay Castle. There, in the very aftermath of Edward I's campaign against the Welsh, leading local wool merchant Laurence of Ludlow felt sufficiently confident to build his castle-like house with undefendable ranks of tall gabled windows piercing the curtain facing out towards Wales.

Architecturally then, this façade as it survives is uncomfortable, ambiguous. The lowest part of the rubble walls clearly show the short straight lengths of primary castle construction joined at

the shallow angles by larger blocks of inter-locking red sandstone. The upper part of the curtain's fabric continues in the same character of rubble walling as below, but lacks the red stone angle binders. Then above, walling of small, well-coursed, slightly redder rubble forms twin tall attic gables set wide apart, each containing four bay mullion and transomed windows, square-headed with drip mouldings. This small rubble walling forms much of the wall at first-floor level on the left, southern side of the façade and a diagonal line up to the right, northern gable shows the division with the earlier, larger rubble work. There is sufficient space between the gables, set as they are at the extreme ends of their building, for a third, central gable. However, a string course which unites the ashlar surrounds of the two gables, crosses the intervening space at too high a level to admit to a third gable in the design. This string moulding appears likely to have continued north-easterly to join the ashlar surround of the gable of the end wall of the building which survives to a height just visible above the curtain. The twin gables and the windows they contain provide an element of symmetry at attic level.

However, symmetry immediately crumbles at the middle level below. An elegant monument sits below the south-westerly gable, whilst a window below the south-easterly gable is merely nearly in vertical alignment with the attic window above. It is also slightly smaller and the

Fig. 1 The southern façade of the Judges' Lodgings

visual to hold the building together, it simply dissolves into the stone curtain. Visual ambiguities persist —while the upper part of the left gable reads across with the supposedly domestic symmetry of gables and windows, the same gable reads downwards, via the mediation of a grandly elegant renaissance monument, to the sturdy gothic arched main entrance to the inner bailey.

This entrance is approached across the rock-cut ditch by a stone revetted causeway cut through by two round arches (Fig. 3). The pale limestone monument blazoned above the entrance is carved in high relief of the finest quality work, akin to the best church memorials surviving from the renaissance. Here, outside, the weather and time have left their ravages. The canopy is supported by square fluted classical columns carved in high

transom is halfway rather than two-thirds of the way up the mullions. At this middle level two irregularly placed much smaller windows totally confuse any further symmetry. Below, but set quite high above even the present ditch level, a single off-centre window provides light from the outer bailey. Such symmetry as there is derives from the gables and is not sustained as a conventional architectural façade. However, the design implies a façade, but as it survives it is uncontained by the normal expectations of domestic architecture, though the uppermost rectangular mass when roofed would have added significantly greater shape and coherence to the whole.

To the left the building abuts the Keep. To the right, the building is alarmingly neither defined by a designed edge, nor a quoin, nor even an implied quoin. With nothing

Fig. 1 The northern façade of the Judges' Lodgings

relief. The crowned royal arms with dragon supporters are encircled by the garter and the whole surmounts a rectangular tablet. Below, arms also carrying the garter are denoted above to left and right, 'H' and 'S'.

The arms are topped by a chained beast and fixing holes either side imply the former presence of heraldic supporters. The inscription below may be read as follows:

Huminibus. Ingratis. Loquimini. Lapides. In-regni. Reginae. Alyzabethae. (Next two figures illegible) The. 22. Year coplet. Of. The. Presidenc. Of .Sir. Henri. Sidney. Knight. Of. The. Most. Noble. Order. Of. The. Garter. Et. C. 1581.

Fig. 3 The entrance to the inner bailey showing the arms of 1581 above the entrance. (see also Dinely's illustration p.77)

Despite the overall quality of the work, the last figure '1' is carved on the frame of the inscription owing to lack of space in setting out.

This building was indeed erected by Sir Henry Sidney in 1581 who was president of the Council in the Marches from 1560, and is one of the relics of his attempt to firm up and centralise the political, judicial and administrative control of the Marches. He also provided permanent purpose-built accommodation for the judges meting out royal justice in the Council Chamber on the opposite side of the inner bailey. Such stabilisation of a court and such permanent provision expressed in these buildings is a clear indication of the confident consolidation and exercise of Tudor power.

Passing through the gateway beneath Sir Henry's monument there is, on the right, a window, interpretable as a porter's hatch from which visitors could have been accosted, reasons given and directions taken. It is on the opening side of the great double door to the inner bailey in which side was formerly a wicket and so more immediately accessible to those entering and leaving. North of the hatch is a door and the arrangement seems to point to porterage and court management functions rather than domestic use. However, the accommodation behind the window and door is the width of the lodging, it is well lit and well heated by a large fireplace with moulded jamb (Fig. 3). The overall character of the space and the 18th century plan showing access to the north-eastern room beyond, point to it being part of the lodgings and indeed the main access to the ground floor. So, the small dark room built for the medieval porter surviving on the opposite side of the gate-passage may well have continued in use.

Entering the inner courtyard and stepping back to view the Judges' Lodgings, the regular, orderly, domestic appearance provides a pleasing contrast with the rather clumsy outer bailey façade. Eighteenth-century prints show that the pattern of two widely spaced attic gables with their stone surrounds and string courses uniting the design, was matched on the inner bailey. The intervening space was occupied by two bays, one

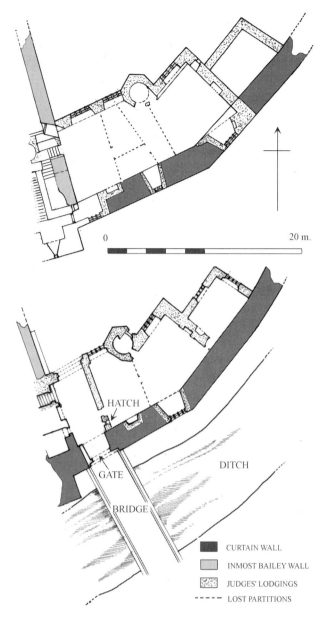

Fig. 4 Plans of the Judges' Lodgings, ground
floor (below), first floor (above), incorporating
information from Pritchard's plans of 1765
(see p.92)

containing a spiral stair and the other a pair of
windows (Fig. 5).

Sir Henry's lodgings for the judges neatly
dated to 1581 consist of range set against the
inner bailey wall. Its plan, as indicated from the
outside, follows the curve of the curtain. Face on,
the inner bailey façade contrives to appear

normal. This was achieved by the device of the
stair tower masking the angle forced upon the
building (Fig. 2). Viewed aslant from east of the
round church the smart façade deconstructs into
a mass of receding angles. It is a clever and
stylish design. The walls rise from a wider foundation plinth with a moulded offset which unites
the elevations. The ashlar stonework of the walls
is of good quality, especially on the ground floor
both inside and out but the higher work tends to
decline in quality.

Architecturally, the lodgings consist of four
bays each of different elevation. Two sets of lodgings accessed by separate stairs form the accommodation. On the east, a set of lodgings on three
floors were lit by equal-sized four-bay mullioned
windows each with a central transom. The
window mouldings of bold recessed chamfer are
consistent throughout. Each eastern room was
heated by fireplaces in the gable. Entrance is by
the door at the foot of the polygonal stair tower
which occupies the second bay from the east and
is lit by rectangular helicoidally arranged
windows. Originally the stair tower stood to
above gable top, perhaps providing access to the
leads and to a small chamber at the summit. It
was capped by a polygonal lead roof. The third
bay flanks the gate passage on the ground floor.
The gate-passage to the inner bailey forms the
ground floor of the fourth bay and above it are
windows to rooms on the two upper floors, those
to the top floor now being blocked on both the
north and south walls. The lodgings above the
gate-passage appear to have been accessed from
the inner bailey by the quite grandly embellished
doorway just inside the gate-passage on the west
opening onto stairs which also lead up to lodgings in the Keep (Fig. 6). This arrangement of
lodgings on three floors was traditional and may
be seen on a more sumptuous scale in the planning of the Tudor Lodgings attached to the Great
Chamber block on the opposite side of the inner
bailey. There too, a set-piece stair tower for one
set of lodgings is complemented by less obvious
access to the adjacent quarters.

It is possible to discern in the ruins the broad
pattern of the internal arrangement of floors and

Fig. 5 Pritchard's drawings of 1765 of the Judges' Lodgings as seen from the outer bailey (left) and inner bailey (right)

partitions from beam and joist holes. However, details essential to comfort and the character of the living accommodation, as for example internal timber screens; draught excluding internal porches; and wall panelling (whether plain, carved or painted); not to mention wall hangings and fixed furnishings; are all lost.

Externally the architecture of the Judges' Lodgings was not modified, and the extensive survival of the design of 1581 makes the building of importance among the body of precisely dated 16th-century buildings. Here are seen elements which look backward to the communal life of a great institution, in this case the Council, and forward to new standards of space, light, comfort and privacy for the conduct of professional life. The only obvious modification to the building is a low extension to the end gable. It is of a single bay accessed from a doorway by the ground floor fireplace and consists of an upper and lower room both heated, the former presumably reached by a box stair set in a corner. The brick surrounds of the windows with remains of drip moulding suggests a 17th-century origin for what appears to be additional lodgings, perhaps for a servant. Reused carpentry forms the surviving window

lintel, and it is possible that this extension post-dates the use of the building by the judges.

The lodgings ceased to serve their original function in 1689 and the castle passed out of royal hands. When in 1721 William Stukeley sketched the lodgings from the outer bailey, triple–chimneys still rose above the bay adjacent to the gateway and above the end gable, but the roofs were beginning to look skeletal. The chimneys had all gone by the time the elevations are recorded in prints.

However, of far superior quality to the elevation drawings are measured plans of the internal arrangement of the ground floor and first or chamber storey. The ground floor appears on a plan of the inner bailey dated 1765. It confirms the interpretation from the fabric that the eastern room accessed via the door to the stair-tower

Fig. 4 Stukeley's sketch of the Judges' Lodgings from the outer bailey

189

Fig. 6   The doorway in the Keep that led to rooms above the gateway in the Judges' Lodgings

were divided from the western room by a timber partition with an inter-connecting door. This plan also confirms the tenuous surviving evidence visible in the gable wall of the small extension that there existed a window but no external door.

At first floor, or as stated on another 18th-century measured drawing—'Plan of the Chamber Story of the Gatehouse'—accommodation is shown in both the Judges' Lodgings *per se* and in the adjacent Keep. It is possible that the Keep also offered quarters to supplement the lack of ground-floor accommodation for the second set of lodgings owing to the space occupied by the gate passage. If this was so, this second set of lodgings are notable for their passages, stairs and sheer inconvenience. The relationship between the two sets of lodgings at first-floor level is also marked by the odd joggling of space in the bay to the west of the stair in order to share space and light, thereby creating long thin gloomy rooms, one with a small closet off, lit by a now blocked window onto the outer bailey. Given the relative ease of re-arranging partitions, there would seem to be little way of confirming whether this arrangement reflects usage during the judges' occupation. Nevertheless, these substantial lodgings when well heated and serviced would have been convenient and comfortable quarters for maintaining the judicial process, so much more so than tolerating long periods at inns or other indifferent accommodation. Indeed, purpose-built judges' lodgings increasingly became the norm. Where courts met within castle halls, there are several later instances of lodgings located next to the castle gates. Thus the courts in the great romanesque hall of Leicester Castle, only recently ceasing to house the administration of justice, were served by judges accommodated in lodgings just inside the castle gate. At Lincoln the judges' lodgings were just outside the main gate of the castle. Elsewhere, when new courts were set up apart from castles, as for example at Northampton after the town fire of 1675, the lodgings were alongside the courts. A fine 19th-century example in the Marches at Presteigne has recently been meticulously conserved and is now on public display.

The proper administration of the law affects each of us and yet while the prerogative court of the Council in the Marches is long dead, Sir Henry Sidney showed early enlightenment in ensuring that those charged with the law's just administration were properly accommodated to carry out their duties efficiently.

CHAPTER XX

The Outer Bailey

by Derek Renn & Ron Shoesmith

This brief chapter serves as an introduction to the following chapters which deal with some of the individual buildings in greater detail.

The small Norman castle, on the edge of the escarpment overlooking the river Teme and cut off from the town by a reasonably wide dry rock-cut ditch, was well defended by its towers. There would probably have been a timber bridge across the ditch that could have been removed in times of trouble. But it would not have been long before it was realised that the small bailey was impractical for everyday life in peacetime. There was little room for exercising man and horse, for buying and storing necessities, for feeding and accommo-dating extra numbers. Whilst the original bailey may have been fit for a small baronial castle such as Goodrich, which never expanded outside its early defences, it was far from being adequate for what was rapidly becoming a major power base.

The original Entrance Tower faced south, but this was changed when the defences were extended and the new castle entrance was re-orientated towards the east. The south-facing entrance indicates that, when it was in use, the main focus was towards the south-west and a crossing of the river at Dinham. It may well be that a market and working area would have developed organically outside the castle defences, at some stage becoming defined by a fence or informal boundary, but which may then have become formalised as an enclosure of earth and timber. The imposition of a boundary may

well have created a degree of order to this area just outside the castle gate. Presumably the ridge to the east of the castle leading towards the north-south road was also being developed with the construction of St. Laurence's Church and a road joining castle and church.

The outer bailey, constructed to the south and east of the original stronghold, quadrupled the area of the castle, providing a vast open space within a well-defended enclosure. On both south and east the wall seals the original ditch line and butts against the corner towers of the inner bailey providing conclusive evidence that it was not part of the first castle. The extended defence was orig-inally surrounded by an external ditch on the east and south, but this has since been filled in and is now a public garden and open space for most of its length.

The main approach to the new outer bailey was on the east side, facing what is now the main market area. The entrance was through a two-storey shallow gatehouse, with pointed arches front and rear and a pointed vault which Hope describes as belonging to the end of the 12th century.[1] The gatehouse projected from the curtain wall with buttresses which probably flanked the end of a bridge over the ditch. There is a rebuilt round-headed opening above a plain string course over the outer arch. An altered wall on the south side within the gate passage may be part of an inner square barrel-vaulted bay, being of the same thickness and alignment as the outer wall on this side. Internally, the gate faces across the outer bailey towards the Entrance Tower and echoes both its likely appearance after the Transitional alterations and the 'arch within an arch' of the present inner entrance. On the outside of the gatehouse there may originally have been some form of barbican, but included in the works attributed to Sir Henry Sidney was the 'making of a fayre lardge stone bridge into the said Castle, wthe one greate arche in the myddest and twoe at both ends conteyning in leinght about xxx or xl yardes and in height upon both sydes with ffyne stone a yard and a half'.[2]

All traces of this bridge were either demolished or buried when the ditch was infilled as part of the landscaping.

From the gate, the straight outer bailey wall running north is on the same alignment as the gate as far as a square tower with offsets only on the east side. This tower is now incorporated within the early 19th century Castle Flats which are private property. Clark's 1877 plan[3] shows that the tower was entered at ground floor level at the north end of the west wall. Beyond here the curtain wall is missing for some distance, but earlier plans and existing property boundaries indicate that it curved round to the west where it met the town wall at right angles as a re-entrant. It then continued past a rebuilt postern door (plated in sandstone slabs)[4] to abut against the East Tower of the inner bailey, with a door at wall walk level.

South of the gatehouse, the curtain wall runs in a south-south-west direction, at a slightly different alignment to the gate. The Elizabethan Porter's Lodge, Prison and Stables are attached to the inside face of this straight stretch

of wall. Formerly there was a round-fronted tower projecting eastwards near the south-east corner.[5] This or another lost tower may well have been associated with the quoin stones set in wall at the south-east angle, observed and recorded by archaeologists both before and after this section of wall collapsed on Saturday 10 February 1990.[6] The investigation demonstrated that the orientation of the wall changed at each of the two sets of quoin stones, especially in the lower parts of the wall. There were few quoin stones in the upper parts of the wall, and none in the parapet. This section of wall has since been rebuilt, incorporating details from earlier drawings and a photogrammetric survey and reusing as much of the fallen masonry as possible. This has allowed the quoins to be replaced with considerable accuracy. The extent of the rebuild is indicated by a deliberate and visible break in the wall construction. There was no indi-

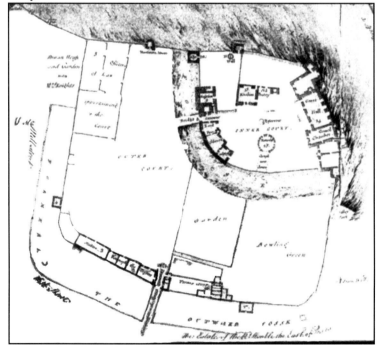

Fig. 1 The plan of 1771, showing the since disappeared square tower on the south wall of the outer bailey

Fig. 2 An aerial view of the castle showing the extensive outer bailey. The private flats lie to the left, beyond which is the new roof of the castle entrance in the converted Porter's Lodge and Prison. Beyond them again lie the roofless Stable Block. In the top right of the bailey lies the ruined St. Peter's Chapel and Mortimer's Tower, with the public path created through the corner of the bailey beyond

cation in the wall between the two sets of quoins of any entry from inside the castle into the tower that may once have protected this corner. The masonry and pointing between the two lines of quoins was different to that in adjacent parts of the curtain wall and it has been suggested that the whole of this section of wall was rebuilt following the demolition of a tower. The ground level on the outside of the wall appeared to have been lowered, possibly when the ditch was filled, and is now much lower than that on the inside. The limited excavations on the outside of the wall did not produce any evidence for the extent and width of the ditch, nor did it establish the level of the natural rock. It has been suggested elsewhere (p.12) that, apart from the condition of the wall and the spell of very wet weather before the collapse, this stretch of curtain wall may have been built on top of an early ditch surrounding Dinham.

From the rebuilt section the curtain wall then takes up a westerly course. Until the end of the 18th century a short distance along from the corner a square tower projected southwards from the line of the wall (Fig. 1). There is no indication

of its position on either face of the wall, but plans show it to have been of similar size to the existing tower north of the gatehouse in the east curtain.

From the tower the south curtain wall continued westwards in a straight line. Almost the whole of this stretch of wall and the length as far as the gatehouse survives to full height and includes a parapet walk on the inside. The parapet wall appears to be of a completely different construction to the lower part of the wall, using smaller, more friable stones and much mortar. These sections of wall retain much of their battlements, with relatively few crenels and correspondingly wide merlons. The section of wall that collapsed included three complete loops, each covered with a large capstone with the wall continuing above—they may well have been purely decorative.

At the south-western corner, where the bailey met the town wall, there was no tower at the angle and the earlier public footpath, that was blocked by the grounds of Dinham House, was re-routed through two 18th-century openings in the curtain wall, one placed almost centrally in the south wall and the other a short distance north of the south-west corner. The castle walks were laid out in 1771-2 and this walk, through a walled part of the south-western corner of the outer bailey alongside the remains of the south wall of the chapel of St. Peter, was an integral part. Appropriately an 18th-century inn, on the site of what is now Dinham Hall, was named 'The Hole in the Wall.'

The western wall of the outer bailey was completed by two straight panels, joined by the semi-circular Mortimer's Tower. This originally provided a postern entrance to the outer bailey, possibly replacing the earlier one in the Postern Tower of the inner bailey (see p.129). The northern section of wall ends against the south-west corner of the Oven Tower.

The casual visitor to Ludlow Castle sees the vast open area of the outer bailey leading across to Mortimer's Tower and St. Peter's Chapel at the south-west and to the imposing buildings and main entrance to the inner bailey directly in front. What is not realised is that at least a third of the outer bailey is hidden behind the high wall that runs from near the Gatehouse to the inner bailey curtain wall just to the east of the Judges' Lodgings. This area, now private grounds attached to Castle Flats, in the late 18th and early

19th centuries comprised a Bowling Green and gardens attached to the Castle Inn. At that time much of the present outer bailey was used as timber yards, with an area adjacent to Mortimer's Tower being used as a Fives Court.

Apart from the rounded south-eastern tower and Mortimer's Tower, the outer enclosure—at least its construction in stone—is better dated to the 12th rather than to the 13th century, to judge from the square towers. The repairs and alterations that have been suggested for the inner gateway around 1140-70 (see p.133) may well have included at least the building of the east front of the outer bailey. The outer bailey is likely to have been completed before King Henry II's sequestration of Ludlow in 1177. For some time after that interest grew in the town as an economic asset rather than in the castle. This probably continued at least until the renewed Welsh threat posed by Llywelyn ab Iorwerth shortly after 1200, which culminated in his capture of Shrewsbury in 1215 and led to the abortive Ludlow Conference of 1233 and the founding of the new royal castle at Montgomery in the same year. It may well be that the simple defensive circuit of the outer bailey was completed by 1177, but that the defensive capability was improved by the addition of Mortimer's Tower and the semi-circular tower near the south-east corner early in the 13th century. These should both be considered as later additions to the defensive works, the one protecting the otherwise poorly defended south-eastern corner and the other providing an additional and well-defended means of access. The construction of the town defences, built against the curtain from 1233, provides a *terminus ante quem* for the completion of the outer bailey wall.

Fig. 3 Sheep grazing in the outer bailey in the early 20th century

194

CHAPTER XXI

Mortimer's Tower

by Peter E. Curnow and John R. Kenyon

> 'He made also a goodly wardrope underneath the
> new parlour, and repayred an old tower, called Morty-
> mers tower, to keep the auncient records in the same …'[1]

Fig. 1 Mortimer's Tower from the outer ward

Thomas Churchyard's poem *The Worthines of Wales*, first published in 1587, includes several pages on the town and castle of Ludlow, and his description of the works undertaken by Sir Henry Sidney informs us that in the late 16th century Mortimer's Tower had become a record repository. This highlights the problem that faces anyone examining the medieval features of the building: late medieval and post-medieval occupancy has altered the appearance of the tower radically, which is not surprising considering that the castle functioned until the late 17th century.

Mortimer's Tower is situated mid-way along the western side of the mid to late 12th-century curtain wall of the outer ward. Its original function as a gateway was largely overlooked by scholars such as Clark, and St. John Hope does not go into much detail other than noting that the front of the tower 'was originally pierced by a depressed arch of entry'.[2] This oversight was possibly because the remains of the portcullis slot and gate rebates were obscured by this time. It was left to others to emphasise the purpose of the tower and the role it played. It overlooks the river Teme and one of the main approaches to the town and castle, from the border with Wales; indeed, it

Fig. 2 Mortimer's Tower from the south-west

Description

would have had a commanding view of the medieval Dinham Bridge.[3]

Mortimer's Tower is D-shaped, with a shallow, chamfer-angled projection into the outer ward, and is rubble built with sandstone quoins inserted into the curtain wall (Figs. 1 & 2). When built, possibly in the early 13th century, the tower consisted of a ground-floor entrance passage, with two floors above. However, later, and probably in the 16th century, a further floor was inserted between the first and the second floors; this was made possible by the height of the medieval first floor. The tower ceased to be a gateway certainly by the 15th century when a fine ribbed vault was inserted, and the passage became a chamber. The main openings on the outer face of the tower are 'modern' windows, in

Gothic style and now blocked, and are situated at the medieval ground-, first- and second-floor levels. Openings either side of the window on the top floor may be the remains of narrow medieval windows or slits.

Evidence for a possible external door or postern, or entrance to an outbuilding attached later to the tower, is evident on the north side, against the curtain, and clearly seen in Fig. 4 of St. John Hope's paper. If a postern, the passage into the outer ward would have been dog-legged, similar to that in the Norman postern tower to the north. Also on the north side of the tower is the corbelled chimney of the first-floor fireplace, and there are a number of corbels running around the top of the tower, just below the line of the battlements. These corbels probably supported timbers for a hourd (a timber gallery projecting from the battlements enabling defenders to cover the base of the wall below), although its form is not clear due to alterations at this level. There is no evidence as to how the gate was approached from the outside, but there must have been a zig-zag route to the tower ending with a right-angled turn into the gate.

There are four 16th-/17th-century windows in the rear wall of the tower, all of two lights other than that in the inserted second floor; the window in the second floor is blocked, as is one light on the top floor.

Ground Floor

The ground-floor window overlooking the outer ward is situated within the blocking of the medieval gate passage, and to its north is the doorway to the newel stair, with alterations made to provide access to the ground-floor chamber when the entrance passage was blocked. Access to the upper floors is from the staircase or via the doors that opened onto the battlements to the north and south.

The remains of the portcullis chase and the door rebates at the west end of the ground-floor chamber (Fig. 4) indicate that the entrance passage was 1.68m (5ft 6in) wide; there was also

Fig. 4 Mortimer's Tower:
the remains of the portcullis chase

a murder hole in the roof at this point. This was a narrow entrance by medieval gatehouse standards; nevertheless, Mortimer's Tower was no mere postern, but one of the main entrances into the castle and the principal entrance from the field. Evidence for the form of the original roof to the passage has been lost through the construction of the 15th-century vault, making a handsome chamber. The square hole in the centre of the vault would have taken a roof boss, possibly carved wood.

A recess on the north side of the room may have been the site of the original 'porter's lodge' or led to a postern which was later blocked (see above); in the early part of this century it was a coal store. The floor slabs in this area are similar in appearance to those framing the portcullis

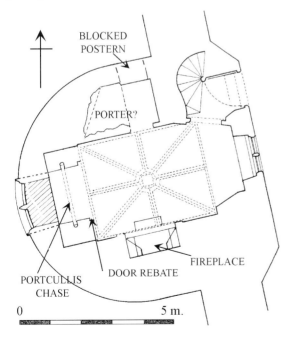

Fig. 3 Mortimer's Tower: ground floor

chase. The main feature of the room, besides the vault, is the fine 17th-century fireplace on the south side, with a drain in front of it. It is possible that this room was then a kitchen for the use of the occupants of the tower, perhaps when the courthouse was in use. The inventory of the castle in 1650 mentions after the 'Court House of Justice', housed in St. Peter's chapel, the 'Secretary's Chamber', together with the Secretary's study' and the 'Scullery', and it is possible that these were the main rooms in Mortimer's Tower.[4] The smoke must have escaped by the medieval garderobe chute still visible and so out through the top of the tower, presumably through a chimney that is no longer evident.

First Floor

The remaining floors are open to the sky, although there was a roof at the top in the time of St. John Hope's visit, and there were plans drawn up in the 1960s to re-roof the tower. The medieval first floor was a tall chamber, presumably to allow room for the portcullis and its mechanism. However, the alterations and blocking at the upper levels on the west side make interpretation

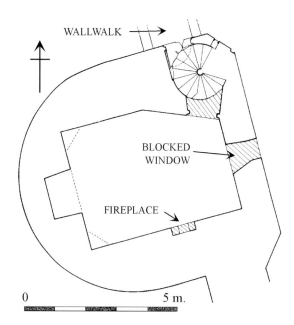

Fig. 6 Mortimer's Tower: second floor

impossible; all evidence for the portcullis chase has disappeared other than the slot in the floor. It is possible that the portcullis mechanism may have operated from the top floor, the portcullis resting between the first and second floors when raised.

On the south side of the chamber is the original garderobe, entered through a narrow asymmetrical shouldered doorway, similar to that leading off the newel staircase. A fireplace with later repairs is situated in the north wall.

Second Floor

This floor is a post-medieval addition to the tower, seemingly in the Tudor period. It must have been a dark room, for the only natural light came from the east window (now blocked), as there does not appear ever to have been a west window. The door that led from the newel stair into the new room is also blocked, although the wooden lintel survives. In the south wall there is a small fireplace.

The only other feature of this chamber is the corbelling to strengthen the west face of the tower associated with the medieval first-floor room.

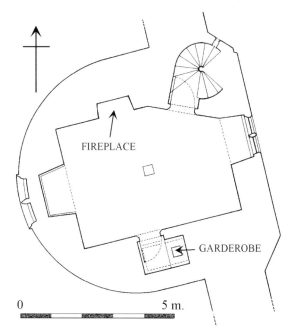

Fig. 5 Mortimer's Tower: first floor

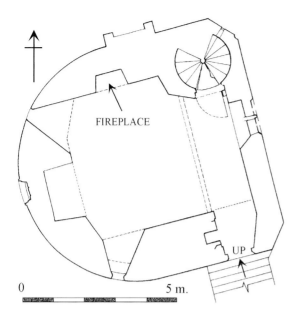

Fig. 7 Mortimer's Tower: third floor

Third Floor

Approaching the upper floor, which was originally the medieval second-floor chamber, a door
leads out to the wall-walk to the north. A feature
of the wall-walk is that a section of the crenel-
lated wall is much higher than the rest of the
battlements, and Renn has suggested that its
purpose may have been to give the impression
from a distance that Mortimer's Tower was in fact
a twin-towered gatehouse.[5] The difference in the
masonry would suggest that the raised section is
much later in date, perhaps associated with a
feature in the outer ward in the 16th century or
later. It is worth noting that in the quite accurate
painting by William Marlowe (d.1813) of the
west side of the castle, depicted in the current
guidebook, there is no evidence for a merlon at
all; just a gap in the battlements.

An offset and sockets for the main beam mark
the level of the third floor. Entering the room
there is an equivalent doorway on the south side,
steps from which dropped down to the south
wall-walk. Presumably a passage connected these
two doors which ran across the east side of the
tower, divided from the upper chamber by a
timber screen. The remains of a fireplace are

apparent on the north side, but there has been
much repair work at this level.

The Gateway and its Parallels

An entrance through a single tower is a common,
indeed normal, feature in medieval castles,
ranging from 11th-century Exeter through to
15th-century Coity in Glamorgan, and of course
the original entrance to what became the inner
ward at Ludlow was through such a tower.[6]
However, such gateways tended to be square or
rectangular towers. What is unusual is to find
such an entrance through a D-shaped or semi-
circular tower. There are few parallels to
Mortimer's Tower, although a number of late
medieval circular gate towers exist in France.[7]
One of the French castles cited by Mesqui was
the subject of a paper by one of the present
writers.[8] Le Coudray-Salbart in Poitou, built in
the early 13th century, has a circular tower mid-
way along the west curtain, originally provided
with a drawbridge, a full-width of passage
murder hole, but no portcullis, and there are other
parallels nearby, such as Bressuire.

In Britain the closest parallel is the north-west
gate of the inner ward of Edward I's Aberystwyth
Castle, begun in 1277,[9] although at both Pembroke
and Caldicot there are early 13th-century gateways
pierced through the sides of D-shaped towers.[10]
The early 13th-century gatehouse at Grosmont is
basically rectangular, although traces survive of its
curved front. However, there may be an even
closer parallel, and one contemporary with
Mortimer's Tower, namely the tower built by King
John that is now part of the Constable's Gate at
Dover. John's tower here is larger than the others
he built on the outer curtain, and it may be that the
entrance passage through it formed part of the
original structure, and was not forced through
when the fore- and flanking towers were added by
Henry III.[11]

Although not identical in plan, perhaps one
should not look any further than from one great
de Lacy castle (Ludlow) across the Irish Sea to
another. At Trim in County Meath[12] the early
13th-century southern curtain wall with its five

Fig. 8 The south-east gate at Trim Castle, Co. Meath

D-shaped towers and round south-east or Dublin gate is one of the most impressive frontages of any European castle. The gatehouse (Fig. 8) is more sophisticated that Mortimer's Tower; in fact one could argue that the defences of the Trim gate are more sophisticated than the French examples cited for it had a rectangular barbican extending out from it, and the tower has a series of arrowslits, besides a portcullis. Although Mortimer's Tower had a portcullis, there is no evidence for any arrowslits; even allowing for the alterations to the front of the tower, the flanks bear no evidence for slits. The main defence of the gateway must have been from the roof-top hourd, therefore.

The other gatehouse at Trim, on the west side, is rectangular, and so the entrance arrangements at the castle almost mirror those to the outer ward at Ludlow. Although by the early 13th century twin-towered gatehouses with rounded fronts were becoming increasingly common in France and Britain,[13] the de Lacy family presumably considered that Ludlow's east gate was sufficient. The entrance to the castle from Dinham, in a strong position topographically but of less stature perhaps than the east gatehouse, merited no more than a single tower.[14]

CHAPTER XXII

St. Peter's Chapel & the Court House

by Paul Remfry & Peter Halliwell

'... there is also the Wood Yard, and next to that the Court House of the Marches of Wales, in which sate the four Welsh Judges with all other officers belonging to this Court, to try and determine Causes, a place once of great Request, in which all the Records belonging to the Court of the Marches were kept, but since the Revolution has been utterly ruined, and the records have been taken out by the Dragoons and people of the Town for their own use, or sold by the Dragoons to them'.[1]

In 1321 Roger Mortimer of Wigmore and Ludlow, together with his uncle, Roger Mortimer of Chirk, rebelled against Edward II. In a short campaign, the Mortimers repulsed Edward's attempt to cross the river Severn at Bridgnorth, but then agreed to surrender to a false offer of royal clemency when they appreciated that royal forces had separated them from their ally, Earl Henry of Lancaster. For their troubles they were incarcerated in the Tower of London, where Roger Mortimer's uncle died in 1326. However, on 1 August 1323, the feast of the liberation of St. Peter, Roger Mortimer escaped from the Tower after drugging his guards at a banquet.

After the deposition and murder of Edward II (see pp. 47-9) Edward's eldest son was crowned King Edward III on 1 February 1327. But for the first three years of his reign, rule was exercised by Roger Mortimer and the queen mother, Isabella. Mortimer had himself made earl of March in October 1328 and soon afterwards he followed the example of his grandfather and held a courtly gathering at a round table, probably as a reminder of the Mortimer claim of descent from Arthur and Brutus through his grandmother, Gladwse Ddu, a daughter of Prince Llywelyn

Fawr. A few months later Mortimer entertained both Edward III and Isabella at Ludlow.

This was not long after the start of the building of St. Peter's Chapel, founded to celebrate Mortimer's escape from the Tower, with 'for alienation in mortmain of a rent of 10 marks to two chaplains, to celebrate divine service daily in the chapel of St. Peter in Ludlow Castle, for the souls of the king, queens Isabel and Philippa, Henry, bishop of Lincoln and the said Roger and Joan his wife'.

The whole of the south-western corner of Ludlow Castle is now separated from the rest of the outer bailey by a modern wall that curves to meet what was the south-eastern corner of the chapel. From this point the eastern and northern walls of the chapel / courtroom complex form the present boundary, returning to the curtain wall a short distance south of Mortimer's Tower. The section so cut off from the bailey now forms part of the scenic walk around the whole castle, by means of two gateways constructed through the curtain wall. From the castle side only the external north and east walls of the building complex are visible; the internal parts can only be examined from the public walk.

The chapel was initially a free standing rectangular structure about 15.3m long and 7.65m wide, built towards the south-west corner of the castle's outer bailey. To its west are the attached remains of a second building, which, together with the chapel, formed the Court House of the Council in the Marches. The building was redesigned to provide a courtroom above an undercroft.

The chapel building

Externally the chapel consisted of an east to west orientated nave with a single central buttress to north and south. The walls to the east, south and west have been largely destroyed to foundation level and consequently little detail survives.

The walls of the chapel were built with a double plinth, visible on the south and west walls. The stones forming the plinth vary in size from 0.6m to 1m in length. Towards the middle of the south wall there is the base of a buttress. A cut back to its east, 1.1m wide, in which the walls have been carefully faced off on all three sides of the alcove so created. It appears to serve no apparent purpose, though a further entrance to the chapel is a possible explanation.

Towards the west end of the south wall the plinth's chamfer is broken for a width of 2m and there is a rubble stone infill. There are no signs of door jambs and the wall face to the west is lost, but this was presumably the main entrance to the chapel. There is an additional inserted doorway towards the east end of the south wall, with a splayed west side and straight east side. The jambs are formed of large boulders and the door opened outwards.

At the south-west corner of the chapel, the wall appears to go behind the out jutting wall of the Court House extension. The break is not as apparent on the outside face due to a complete rebuild of that corner, the chamfer course being absent for about 1m. The rebuild was presumably to support the the jamb of a large window in the first floor courtroom.

The west wall stands about 0.7m above ground level with core work above it to the north and south.

The north wall of the chapel stands about 6m high. Towards the west end there is an inserted doorway with four steps leading up to an opening 1.1m wide with a four-centred internal arch and

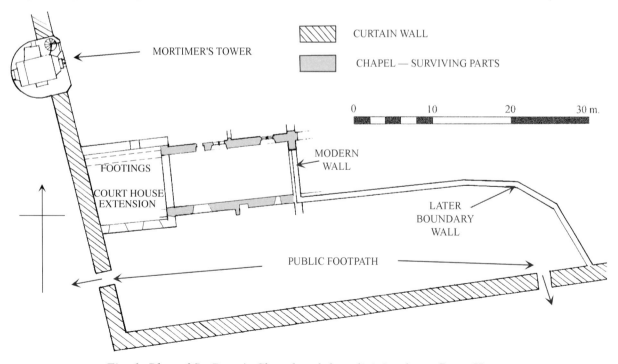

Fig. 1 Plan of St. Peter's Chapel and the adjoining later Court House

Fig. 2 Blocked window in the north wall

two re-used timber beams supporting the wall above. One metre further east is a blocked window, better seen from the north side (see Fig. 2). It was originally a two-light opening, but, presumably when a floor was inserted in the chapel at roughly the level of the head of the doorway to its west, a transom was inserted, the upper part blocked, and two small windows created below illuminating the undercroft.

Towards the eastern end is a second original window now containing a first-floor blocked doorway. This window was probably similar to the western one, about 1.95m wide internally, in which case it would have had two lights with plain tracery and a pointed head. The inserted door is 0.9m wide, and its cill level some 2.6m above the present internal ground level. Again this opening is better examined on the north side where the door jambs and head are clearly seen. Protruding stonework below the door's cill presumably formed the base for a timber stair, of which the 'putlog' holes may still be seen,

leading from the outer bailey to a door which was hinged on the west and opened outwards. This north door bears comparison with apparently Elizabethan work at Brampton Bryan Castle, some 10 miles due west from Ludlow.[2]

The east wall of the chapel survives mainly as footings; the north-east corner has been rebuilt as a buttress on top of the footings as has the 18th-century boundary wall which continues to the south-east. It is possible that the chapel continued to the east with a chancel, demolished as unnecessary when the Court House was built.

There are only slight indications of the inserted floor, apart from the level of the blocked inserted doorway. However, there are four small holes in the north wall and two in the west end of the southern wall, some 1.2 to 1.5m above present ground level. These are too low for the floor, but could be for undercroft fittings. There is one definite joist hole in the extreme west end of the south wall, some 2.8m above the present ground level.

Seen from the outer bailey it is apparent that the ground level is about 1m higher than that in the chapel, and thus there is no sign of any plinth on the north side. However, the steps in the inserted door leading down into the chapel, indicate that the current level of the outer bailey has existed for some centuries.

The north-east exterior corner of the chapel shows rough stonework—evidence for a wall continuing to the north. Did this form the back wall of the later Fives Court? Next to the blocked window there is an indication of another stone wall extending northwards which may have formed a small lean-to.

The Court House

Sometime, apparently under the supervision of Sir Henry Sidney, a rectangular building was added to the west wall of the chapel: 'Item from making of a corte howse and twoe offices under the same for keping of the recordes and for syling tyling and glasing thereof'. The first floor courtroom continued through the whole length of the chapel and was well illuminated, unlike the record rooms underneath—the difficulty of retrieving records in the near dark must have been considerable.

Seen from the south, the south wall butts against the curtain wall and contains a slight step in the masonry about 0.9m above present ground level. The south-east corner has well-made ashlar blocks above the step. The wall contains the outlines of two large windows at first-floor level, each about 2.8m wide internally. (The width of the western one can be ascertained, and a similar dimension for the eastern one would conform to the dimensions of the building.) At the west end of the wall inside the Court House, well-cut ashlar blocks contained within the core of the curtain wall must represent an earlier feature of which no other traces survive.

The south wall is the only wall where joist holes are visible and indicate a floor at about 2.8m above present ground level in the chapel, or 2.5m above that in the Court House. At first-floor level the chapel wall joins into the Court House at an angle indicating that the two buildings were at least partly contiguous at this level and did not have a separating wall.

The west curtain wall contains the remains of a simple fireplace at first-floor level.

The western end of the north wall butts against the remains of the curtain wall and over-sails it with a crude blocked opening that presumably followed the wall walk. Seen from the outer bailey this appears as a very inconvenient form of access to the wall walk and Mortimer's Tower. However, there is a parapet wall well-finished on the inside adjacent to the opening. Some form of stairs or even a ladder must be a possibility to provide access to the doorway on the third floor of Mortimer's Tower (see Fig. 7 p.199). An alternative is that the curtain wall was subsequently heightened and the opening then blocked.

The north wall sits on a double-stepped foundation which extends into the Court House for 1.4m, the reasons for which are unclear.

Seen from the inside, some 1.6m from the west wall, there is a 1.8m wide blocked opening in the north wall at first-floor level with a timber lintel. From the outside the opening measures 1.3m and indicates a fairly grand splayed entrance to the Court House.

To the east of the opening on the inside face are two horizontal timbers, one approximately at first-floor level and one a little higher that may have been associated with internal fittings. Some 2.9m from the north-east corner is a blocked ground-floor opening 1.55m wide with a recently lost timber lintel 2.15m above what appears to be the step. The wall also contains traces of a central blocked opening at first-floor level, and also a window opening 2.7m wide with a cill level similar to that of the other blocked window in the wall. This latter window roughly matches the western window in the south wall, and is about 2m wide.

Seen from the outer bailey, the Court House extends out from the chapel by 1.2m, and has a chamfer course along part of its length just above ground level. The north wall has three blocked openings. These were presumably windows to illuminate the ground floor. The old timber frames are generally crude with no indications of peg holes (one lintel has recently been replaced). However, the upper opening has a set back fill which allows more of the timber to be seen, the lintel having a square mortice centrally and two holes for bars.

The Public Path

It is possible that the priest's and chaplain's lodgings were situated along the south wall of the outer bailey within easy reach of the chapel. Any possible trace of these has now disappeared with the creation of the Georgian panoramic walk.

This has been set in a man-made cutting. It is apparent that the previous ground level adjacent to the south wall of both buildings has been reduced from the level of the step on the Court House to create a flattened area. This reduction in the ground level would have exposed the foundation of the south wall of the chapel, and it would appear that the ground level within the chapel would also have been reduced, though left largely undisturbed in the Court House.

CHAPTER XXIII

The Porter's Lodge, Prison and Stable Block

by Richard Stone

There has recently been a trend away from the study of castles as purely military structures towards a more rounded view of the whole range of activities that took place within the walls.[1] The concept of a 'hierarchy of space' to describe and interpret the use of various buildings is often used. Such studies consider all aspects of the castle, yet it remains easy to focus on the higher status areas, which are in general larger, more architecturally interesting and more long lived. Within any self-contained complex, however, there are many ancillary buildings that play an important role in the daily life of the community and which are worthy of some study. The porter's lodge and stables are such a case, dismissed in former times as 'not of much importance'.[2]

The range lies directly south of the gateway into the outer bailey of the castle. There are no medieval buildings visible, the whole range dating from the Elizabethan era when the castle was headquarters of the Council in the Marches. The range consists of three separate buildings extending southwards along the inside face of the medieval curtain wall. During the 19th century the range was in partial use as stabling and was associated with stone and timber yards (see Fig. 1), but stabling was clearly not the sole original use of the range and St. John Hope, drawing on documentary evidence as well as an architectural interpretation, identified the block adjacent to the gatehouse as the porter's lodge, the next block being a prison, with stabling beyond.[3]

Small scale archaeological excavations were carried out on the northern part of this range in 1992 and 1993 by the City of Hereford Archaeology Unit prior to its adaptation for use as a shop and toilet.[4] This work added considerably to a detailed understanding of the development of this part of the castle both in the medieval period and since the construction of the present range.

To complement the archaeological work a study of the standing structures was carried out together with research into historic plans and documents. As well as contemporary documentary evidence referring to the porter's lodge and prison there are later plans and descriptions of the castle which include references to the area. From these it is possible to build up an understanding of the use of this part of the outer bailey from the construction of the curtain wall to the present day.

The excavation consisted of a shallow reduction of the general ground level within the two bays of the northern building and the northern bay of the central building. A deeper drainage trench falling to the north was then excavated through the length of the building and continued below the gate passage where it was 1.6m deep. At the south it was only 0.25m deep. In the gate passage there was an opportunity to investigate the earliest levels of this part of the castle, but to the south the medieval deposits were not disturbed. Numbers in square brackets refer to Fig. 2.

The earliest layer seen was within the gate passage and consisted of a stony clay layer which produced 12th-century pottery and which may pre-date the construction of the curtain wall. Alternatively it could have been laid as hard-core for the stone surface which sealed it. This surface was presumably part of the gatehouse and survived sufficiently long to become worn to the extent that it was replaced by a surface of large flat stones. Above these was a further build up of post-medieval deposits associated with the continuing use of the gate passage.

To the south of the gatehouse the earliest deposit seen was a dark soil [141] dated by pottery to the 12th or 13th century. This layer contained small amounts of mortar which was presumably derived from nearby building work. Above this soil layer was a spread of rubble [136] at the foot of the curtain wall which was probably building debris. A similar spread overlay this at the foot of the gatehouse wall and is thought to be associated with its construction. It is therefore quite likely that the earlier soil [141] is contemporary with the building of the curtain wall.

Further south were traces of two parallel stone walls [132 and 134] aligned at a right angle to the curtain wall. These were only 300mm wide and were either internal cross walls of a larger building or, more likely, they carried timber cills for a timber structure set against the curtain wall. The area between the walls was a rough floor of gravel and fragments of stone [139]. This was the only indication of land use in this part of the bailey during the medieval period. However, to the south, 16th-century demolition debris consisting of a layer of burning [161] and a layer of stone [84] suggest the presence of structures that predate the present buildings.

During the course of the 16th century the present range of buildings was erected. In its primary form the range consisted of two adjacent two-storey buildings of local sandstone and built in good ashlar. The southern building projects slightly to the west of the northern one. Their east wall is formed by the curtain wall, the gatehouse forms the end wall at the north, the remaining

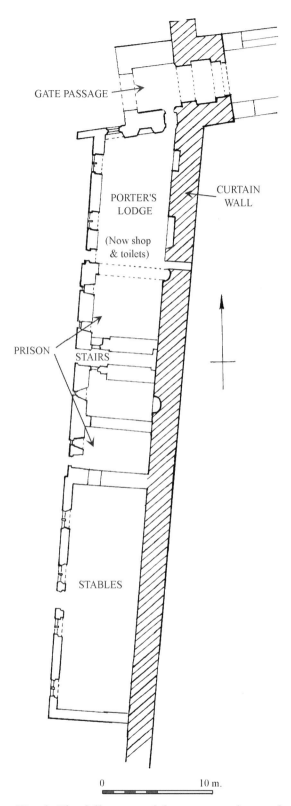

Fig. 1 The full extent of the range to the south of the main gateway

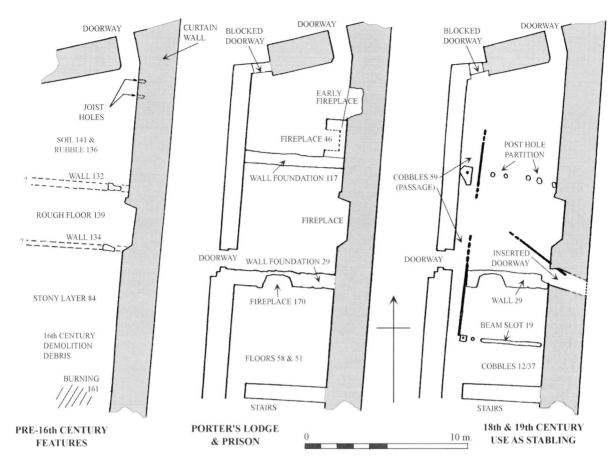

DOORWAY   CURTAIN WALL   BLOCKED DOORWAY   DOORWAY   BLOCKED DOORWAY   DOORWAY

JOIST HOLES

EARLY FIREPLACE

SOIL 141 & RUBBLE 136

FIREPLACE 46

POST HOLE PARTITION

? – – WALL 132

WALL FOUNDATION 117

COBBLES 59 (PASSAGE)

ROUGH FLOOR 139

FIREPLACE

? – – WALL 134

INSERTED DOORWAY

DOORWAY   WALL FOUNDATION 29

DOORWAY

STONY LAYER 84

WALL FOUNDATION 29

WALL 29

FIREPLACE 170

BEAM SLOT 19

16th CENTURY DEMOLITION DEBRIS

COBBLES 12/37

FLOORS 58 & 51

BURNING 161

STAIRS

STAIRS

PRE-16th CENTURY FEATURES

PORTER'S LODGE & PRISON

0   10 m.

18th & 19th CENTURY USE AS STABLING

Fig. 2 Three stages in the excavation of the Porter's Lodge and north room of the Prison, showing the main features described in the text

walls being of one build. The west wall, fronting onto the outer bailey, has a chamfered plinth. The internal cross wall separating the two parts of the building has since decayed and been demolished, but its foundations [29] were identified in the excavation. The coursing of the west wall shows that the two parts of the building were of one date and that the architectural differences between them reflect their different functions. The southern building has been identified as the prison and the northern one, adjacent to the gate-house, was the porter's lodge.

The porter's lodge was of two bays forming two rooms on each floor, separated by a timber partition [117], traces of which can still be seen internally in the west wall. Both ground floor rooms had fire-places with stacks built into the curtain wall. There were two four-centred entrances from the gate-house into the northern room and another from the

outer bailey leading into the southern room. The only windows were in the west wall, giving onto the outer bailey. These were also four centred with horizontal hood-moulds. The arrangement of the first floor was similar. The upper rooms were supported by beams set on corbels and accessed by a low flat-headed doorway from the mural stair in the gate passage. The windows had small stone seats and it is likely that both rooms had a fireplace, though the evidence for this is now lost due to the collapse of the inside face of the upper part of the east curtain wall.

Externally the hood-moulds of the first-floor windows of the porter's lodge continue as a string course. The top of the wall is defined by a second cornice punctuated with gargoyle water spouts and the remains of an embattled parapet above. This arrangement at the top of the walls was continued through into the prison block.

207

Fig. 3 The excavation from the south, showing cobbling and partitions

The architectural detailing of the prison block is somewhat varied. In plan there is a central entrance from the bailey to a small lobby with plain flat-headed doors to left and right. Above the main entrance is an area of core masonry from which the face has been removed. This is presumably the position of the coats of arms of Henry, earl of Pembroke and of Queen Elizabeth I, which numerous writers have described[5] and which is thought to have been added during the earl's Lord Presidency (1586-1601). Beyond the lobby is a staircase which has in the past been limewashed. At the top of the staircase are four-centred doors to left and right. There is no evidence of any division in the two-bay room to the north of the lobby. The ground-floor room had plain high set windows with deeply splayed sills and corbelled lintels, such that prisoners could only see the sky. The windows were barred both horizontally and vertically. The excavation revealed that there was a fireplace [170] in the northern dividing wall between the prison and the porter's lodge. The earliest floor was of beaten clay [58]. This was replaced in the first half of the 17th century by a floor of compacted crushed mortar [51]. The first floor was supported on a cross beam with longitudinal joists and the barred upper windows are slightly larger with less deeply splayed sills. It is likely that this room also had a fireplace.

To the south of the lobby the remaining part of the building was divided into two rooms on each floor, each with a single window corresponding to those to the north of the lobby. The northern rooms on both floors had fireplaces set into the curtain wall. A doorway at the southern end of the west wall gave onto the outer bailey from this unheated room. An interesting survival is a late medieval cornice reused as the lintel of the ground-floor window south of the main entrance.

Externally the windows of the rooms to the south of the lobby all have separate hood-moulds, suggesting that these were of higher status than those to the north. Their floors were carried on longitudinal joists, recessed into the wall at the north and laid on an offset at the south. The upper rooms all have larger windows and better fashioned entrances. The upper room directly south of the lobby was presumably the highest status as it also had a fireplace. The room south of this had internal corbelling at ceiling height, which is again commensurate with a high status. It may be that the room below this, the southernmost ground-floor room, unheated and with its own entrance to the bailey, was the lowest status.

Fig. 4 The range of buildings seen from the outer bailey, indicating that the Prison (centre) projects beyond the Porter's Lodge to the left, and likewise the later Stable block on the right projects beyond the Prison

The date for the construction of the porter's lodge and prison has been given as 1552.[6] There is a bill of quantities for works by Henry Sidney (Lord President 1560-1586) referring to works in this area, and indicating their extent:

> Item for making and repairing of two chambers and divers other houses of offices as kitchen, larder and buttery at the gate over the Porter's lodge at the Castle of Ludlow and for tiling and glazing thereof.
> Item for making of two walls of lime and stone of forty yards in length at the entry into the said gate.
> Item for making of a wall of lime and stone at the Porter's lodge to enclose in the prisoners of about two hundred yards compass within which place the prisoners in the day time use to walk.

The two 'chambers' referred to were the presumably the upper storey of the building adjoining the gatehouse and comprise the principal dwelling of the porter. The size of the fireplace in the southern ground floor room of the porter's lodge is appropriate for a large kitchen, though the inventory suggests this was in the gatehouse itself, which is seen as part of the porter's lodge. Whether this constituted completion of a scheme already started or new work ordered by Sidney is not certain.

The various enclosing walls are now all lost and are not shown on any historic plan indicating that they had disappeared by the later 18th century. There is, however, a series of inserted joist holes at first floor level in the western elevation of the prison, which continue as far as the south window of the porter's lodge. Although it is not clear what structure these are associated with the northern end could reflect the northern end of the prison yard. In this case the door at the south of the porter's lodge would have opened into the prison yard, rather than into the outer bailey proper. The same would be the case for the doorways from the prison block.

A document setting out the fees due to the Porter and the Lodge dated 24 March 1576 gives further useful information.[7] In addition to detailing some of the rules it relates to the treatment of the prisoners. Emphasis is primarily on ensuring that the prisoners do not escape and, once that criterion was satisfied, on ensuring that they were adequately fed—provided they paid for their meals. The detail confirms that the prison was considered to be within 'the circuit of the porter's lodge' and it is beyond reasonable doubt that this document refers to the present buildings.

The Porter's Fees

First to take and receive as the ordinary fee, of every person committed for a single contempt, and not above except for his diet, 2s 6d
Item for every person of the degree of an esquire, or above, for offence, to wear irons,

for the contempt, 2s 6d and for the discharge of the irons, if he seek to be discharged, the sum of 2s 6d.

Item for commitment in cases next before and under the degree of an esquire, 2s 6d

Item for the diet at the choice of two tables, the one at 8d the meal, and the other at 6d the meal.

For the Porter's Lodge

First that every person committed to the charge of the porter, shall there be detained as a prisoner, according to the quality of the offence, and not to depart out of the circuit of the porter's lodge, without the special licence of this council, and to take and receive of them such fees as hereafter ensueth.

First For Treason, Murder, or Felonies, to be detained in irons, during the council's pleasure, and not to depart out of the circuit of the porter's lodge.

Item all persons committed for contempts, or any misdemeanours, or offences where the Queen is to have a fine for the same; they likewise to be detained in prison, without sufferance to go abroad, without the special licence of this council.

Item, to take and receive as their ordinary fees, of every person committed for contempt 2s 6d. and not above, except for his diet.

Item, to take and receive of every person being of the degree of an esquire, and above, and committed for any offence for which he is to wear irons, to take for his commitment 2s 6d and for every person being committed as is aforesaid and under the degree of an esquire 2s 6d for his fee.

Item, it is further ordered that the porter shall continually have in readiness for the entertainment of the prisoners, two tables for diet; to be in this sort kept, viz: The best and first table at eight-pence the meal; the second at six-pence the meal; and the same to be with meat and drink so furnished as the parties may according to their payment have therein competent and convenient; and the party committed to choose at his commitment at which of these tables he will remain; and if he fail to make payment of his fees of commitment and the ordinary charges of the diet after every week's end; then the porter to take bonds for due payment thereof.

Item, it is further ordered that if any person be committed to remain in ward until he should pay the Queen's Majesty any sums for a fine, or to any person, or any sum of money to the same party by this council ordered, or for the not accomplishing of any order taken by this council, and shall not conform him to perform the order, discharge the fine, and make payment to the parties, within one month after the time of his commitment; then the porter at the end of the said month, to give knowledge to the council thereof to the end order thereupon may be taken, that the party may be removed to Wigmore, or such other place as this council shall think meet.

And when any person is or shall be committed to ward, there to remain until he shall pay fine or other debt to the Queen, or any sum of money for costs, or other causes to the party to detain him as a prisoner in manner aforesaid, until the attorney of the party and the clerk of the fines, by a note in writing subscribed by their names upon the copy of the submission, shall acknowledge to have received the said sum, wherein he is chargeable as well to the Queen as the party. At the Court of Westminster the 24th Day March 1576.

In 1597 a stable block was added at the southern end of the range at a cost of £74 4s 4d.[8] Its local sandstone walls are of ashlar externally, but of less well-finished, roughly-coursed stonework internally. The walls are thinner than those of the porter's lodge and prison and it is less architecturally ornate, belonging to a late medieval tradition. It has a chamfered plinth but no ground-floor hood-moulds to the windows and no ground-floor string course. Its central four-centred doorway, now blocked, was flanked by pairs of square-headed two-light windows with plain chamfered stone mullions. The upper storey had windows over the north and south windows of the ground floor but not over the inner windows. This upper part is in a ruined state from about sill level and the southern gable end has been largely rebuilt, probably in the 18th century. The stables are doubtless the building described in the 1650 inventory as a riding house.[9]

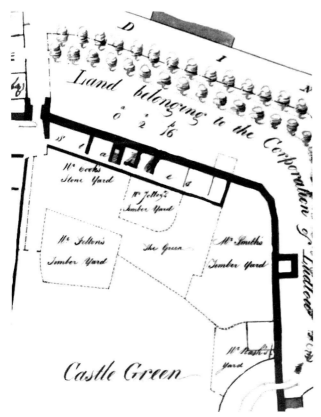

Fig. 5 Plan showing the later timber yards adjacent to this range of buildings, all marked as stables (see p.212)

The excavation revealed evidence of changes to the internal arrangements of the porter's lodge in the 17th century. The base of another stack [46] projecting into the southern room from the curtain wall was found, perhaps suggesting that the larger, earlier, fireplace in this room had been disused. The foundations of a stone cross wall [117] replacing the original timber partition were also found. As no evidence of this survives above ground it is not clear whether this divided only the ground floor or both storeys.

Though of no direct bearing on the buildings, an indication of the potential impact of the porter on the security of the castle, is given by a 17th century 'Remonstrance of the Justice in Ordinary at the Council, in the Marches of Wales &c'.[10]

Again, we have a common Drunkard our Porter, at the Castle Gate, which is encouraged to be saucy with us, and speak scornfully of us,

saying he is no servant of ours: But besides, this Fellow was a Captain under the Rebels, and was known by the name of Captain Cow-driver, because he purveyed for the Rebels the Cattle of the King's good Subjects. Upon what Terms my Lord President accepted him we know not, but if there should be an Insurrection, we shall be afraid of his Partnership, least he should let in upon us his old Masters, and that pity it were fit he were removed; and an honest Man put in his room.

The excavation of the northern bay of the prison revealed a series of mixed layers of soil and loose broken stone which included pottery of late 17th and 18th century date. This tends to suggest that this range of buildings fell into neglect almost as soon as the Council was abolished in 1689. Some later reuse of the area is shown by the insertion of a doorway in the curtain wall at the southern end of porter's lodge some 15 metres from the gatehouse, giving direct access to the building from outside the castle. This has an insubstantial timber lintel and is thought to be of 18th century date. It has since been blocked.

William Stukeley, who described so many ancient monuments in the middle years of the 18th century, described the outer bailey as follows:[11]

The Green takes in a large compass of ground, wherein was formerly the Court of Judicature and Records, the Stables, Garden, Bowling-green and other offices all which now lie in ruins etc.

A slightly later account confirmed that in 1771 the prison was ruinous 'the Cross walls are almost down without Roof or Walls'.[12] The stables were in a slightly better state but still 'in bad condition half Thatched, half slated'. They were still in use as stables at this time by the tenant who lived at Bowling Green House.

According to an 1811 report part of the range was still in use as stables, but the whole area required repair or conversion.[13] The excavation in the northern bay of the prison uncovered two areas of cobbles [12 and 37] and a layer of paving slabs of late 18th or early 19th century date suggesting that there was some reuse of this area around this period. The nature of the reoccupation is unclear, but the makeshift nature of these surfaces suggest that it was patching rather than restoration.

The various plans of the castle that were reproduced throughout much of the 19th century refer to the whole of this range as stables and indeed the texts of authors of this period indicate that they wrongly believed this had always been the case.[14] The reason for this interpretation was shown by the excavation which revealed, above the earlier patchy cobbles, a 1.5m wide passage along the west of the Porter's Lodge and the northern bay of the prison. The passage consisted of flat paving slabs at the west with sloping cobbles leading into an open brick drain at the east [59]. To the east of this passage along the length of the building were at least three partitions. This arrangement is typical of early 19th century stabling, and it is likely that there were more divisions which have left no trace in the archaeological record.

St. John Hope noted that in the early 20th century the central bay of the prison was in use by the local Volunteers as an ammunition store.[15] There is also a reference to one of these buildings having been rebuilt by the Powis family as a museum for fossils and rocks. However, for the majority of the 20th century the range continued to decay and it was only in the 1990s that the decay was reversed, restoring the function of at least part of the range to its original purpose, that of controlling access to the castle.

Appendices

APPENDIX I

The Lands appertaining to Payn fitzJohn's marriage contract

First among these was the lands of the old pre-Conquest church at Bromfield, which Payn probably suppressed preparatory to an intended refounding of it.[1] The prebends of this church lay at Dinchope and Halford near Craven Arms, at Lady Halton, Hill Halton, Prior's Halton, Felton and Burway in Bromfield, and at Lower Ledwyche in Ludford and Ashford Bowdler, besides Bromfield itself. Together with the four Lacy demesne manors these lands effectively completed and extended a compact lordship around Ludlow.

Subsequently Payn acquired a lost *Wilfrescota* in Wistanstow, which was a prebend of the canons of St. Alkmund's church at Shrewsbury whose possession the canons were currently disputing with a certain Gilbert of Condover. When the canons called on him as sheriff to adjudicate in the matter, he merely forced them to 'make a chirograph' in which they conceded the manor to him for life. It was a valuable acquisition, for although it had been valued at only £1 in 1086, when he gained it it was said to be worth £20 per annum. The displaced Gilbert he compensated with the tenancy of the Lacy manor of Waters Upton, which had been valued at just over £1 10s in 1086.

A little later Payn exchanged his overlordship of this manor for five manors belonging to William Pantulf, lord of Wem, which lay adjacent or close to Ludlow. These were at Little Sutton, Upper Ledwyche and Middleton on the border of his lordship and at Monkhall (*Buchehale* in *Domesday Book*) and Ingardine further to the east. In Payn's day these five manors, plus two Lacy manors at Plaish and Higford, were held from him by Walter of Higford and Roger of Ledwyche.

Great Sutton (including Witchcot) and Steventon he obtained from Herbert of Castle Holdgate. The first of these he gave to Hugh de Chanceaux and the second to Roger son of Grent, both in return for knight-service at his castle of Ludlow. Steventon eventually reverted to the barony of Castle Holdgate.

Lands at Shelderton, Tately and Weo were represented in 1086 by 2 hides in Clungunford held by Reginald de Balliol, sheriff of Shropshire, who was also lord of Henley in Bitterley. Payn seems to have to used his position as sheriff to obtain these four places, although all but Henley, which he seems to have given to William de Clinton, younger son of Geoffrey de Clinton, treasurer to Henry I, eventually reverted to sheriff Reginald's heir, William fitzAlan of Oswestry.

Another part of Ashford Bowdler (apart from the one belonging to Bromfield Priory) had been part of the lordship of Richard's Castle in 1086, but this manor Payn acquired from its current lord, Hugh fitz Osbern.

Finally, Payn brought into hand the fief Robert, butler to Roger de Montgomery, earl of Shrewsbury, had held in 1086. This consisted of manors at Stanwardine-in-the-Fields, Walford, Eyton and Weston Lullingfields (all in Baschurch), Aston and Wootton in Oswestry, Crudgington in Ercall Magna, and Petton. Later the fief owed the service of 1 knight's fee to the king at Montgomery Castle, but Payn made it do service at Ludlow.

At Stokesay, Stoke-on-Tern and Wheathill in Shropshire a family with the name of Say, who may have been related to the family of that name at Clun, had been enfeoffed by the Lacys before the death of Hugh I in about 1115. This family also had the manor of Childrey in Berkshire by knight-service, and as their fees at the three Shropshire manors became appurtenant to Ludlow so did their fee at Childrey.

APPENDIX II

Charter evidence for Sybil's marriage to Joce de Dinan

This evidence is contained in a charter of Sybil's in the cartulary of St. Peter's Priory at Hereford. St. Peter's had been founded by Walter de Lacy, Sybil's grandfather, and had been made a cell of St. Peter's Abbey at Gloucester in 1100 or 1101 by his son Hugh. It was amalgamated with the rival, but much older, priory of St. Guthlac at Hereford in 1143, but it was still a separate house when the charter was issued. It runs as follows:

Sciant tam presentes quam futuri quod ego Sibilla domina de Lodel' ex proprio jure hereditarie mee dedi et concessi dimidiam virgatam terre apud Parvam Fromam deo et sancte Marie matris ejus et sancto Petro et monachis Hereford' pro salute anime mee et parentum meorum in elemosinam perpetualiter tenendam liberam et quietam ab omni consuetudine, et aliam dimidiam virgatam terre similiter solutam et quietam ab omni consuetudine ad perpetuam firmam pro iiii. solidis in eadem villa. Hanc donacionem feci consensu domini mei Gozonis de Dinan pro salute anime ejus sicud pro mea. Et postea dicti monachi Hereford' dederunt unum equum de recognicione hujus donacionis. Testes
sunt Godfridus sacerdos de Stocha, Geldwinus Ginun, Brien Miete, Fugenulfus dyaconus, Pinellus, Turstanus filius Wygeri, Ricardus de Croili, etcetera.[1]

'Parvam Fromam' is Castle Frome in Herefordshire, a Lacy demesne manor. As Sybil, calling herself 'domina de Lodel', makes her grant of land there 'ex proprio jure hereditare mee', it must have been included in the dower she took to both Payn fitzJohn and to Joce, the latter being called 'domini mei' later in the charter. Before this, while she was still married to Payn, Sybil had given to St. Peter's another half-virgate of land and an assart in 'Little Frome'. Then, in the short period between the death of Payn and her marriage to Joce, at a time when she could refer to herself with some legitimacy as 'Sibilla de Laceo', she gave it a whole virgate of land there.[2] The cumulative evidence, therefore, is that Sybil 'de Lacy' was married to Payn fitzJohn before she was married to Joce de Dinan and that when married to Joce she was 'lady of Ludlow'. There could not be clearer testimony that Joce de Dinan had Ludlow by right of his wife, Sybil Talbot (de Lacy).

APPENDIX III

The Knights' Fees appurtenant to Ludlow Castle and their holders

The *servicium debitum* of the whole Lacy fief (that is to say, the number of knights the Lacys were expected to provide in the king's service when called upon) as established in the late 11th century is thought to have been 60 knights. This figure placed the barony among the greatest in the land in terms of numbers of knights owed in the royal service.[1] However, the earliest statement of the number of fees in the barony does not occur until 1162 or 1163 when Hugh II de Lacy succeeded his brother Robert as its overlord. It was then said that Hugh had 52 knights' fees in the barony as a whole, of which $23^{1}/_{2}$ were in Herefordshire, but that the barony was deficient of 10 knights' fees that Cecily, daughter of Payn fitzJohn, had taken to her (third) husband, Walter de Mayenne.[2] This latter statement, however, is not strictly true, since out of the knights' fees that are known to have been part of the *maritagium* in the Lacy barony that Payn fitzJohn provided for his daughter only five (divided between Painswick, Edgeworth & Quenington in Gloucestershire, Blithfield and Walton in Staffordshire, and Shell, Kington Lacy, Staunton, Hill Croome, Himbleton and Spetchley in Worcestershire) were permanently lost by the barony. When Hugh returned the *carta* required for his barony in 1166 he said that nearly 52 knights' fees had been enfeoffed on his barony by the time of King Henry I's death in 1135 (that is, fees of the 'old' enfeoffment).[3] If either the 10 fees said to be missing in 1162 (fees that will certainly have been enfeoffed before 1135) or the 5 that were actually missing at that date are added to this figure, the total for the number of fees in the barony before 1135 comes to around 60. This figure for the possible *servicium debitum* of the barony has belated confirmation in 1285, when it is said that Geoffrey de Geneville's moiety of the barony contained 30 knights' fees. Even if not strictly correct ('moiety' is a somewhat imprecise term), it shows that the barony was then viewed as containing 60 knights' fees, although after Hugh's return of 1166 reached the Exchequer the fief never paid scutage on more than $51^{1}/_{4}$ fees.

If Walter I de Lacy and his sons had intended Ludlow Castle to be the caput of all their lands in England and Wales, then it could be said that all these 60 knights' fees owed their feudal service there at some time, but the evidence for this is very tenuous. From the 12th century onwards, the actual number of fees owing service there was understood to be 10. The earliest evidence for this is in 1186/7 when the Lacy fief was remitted scutage on 10 knights' fees that did their castle-guard service at the royal castle of Shrawardine.[4] Although these were Lacy fees they had done their service at Shrawardine because the crown had the whole barony in its hands at the time.[5] This attachment of Lacy fees to Shrawardine could have happened when Roger de Lacy forfeited his lands in 1096, although it is more likely, because of his known concern with Wales, that Henry I made the arrangement after the death of Hugh I *c*.1115. Henry had conducted a campaign in Wales in 1114 and the dispositions in respect of Shrawardine Castle and the Lacy Shropshire fees may have been made shortly afterwards, after Hugh's death, as part of a general settlement of the border resulting from the campaign. Shrawardine Castle remained in royal hands until it was destroyed by the Welsh in 1215 and in 1229 Henry III annexed all services and castle-guard duties appurtenant to it, including the Lacy fees, to the new castle at Montgomery, which he had just given to Hubert de Burgh, the justiciar.[6] By 1255, however, most of the Lacy fees in Shropshire had reverted to their original service at Ludlow Castle.

The transfer of Lacy castle-guard duties from Shrawardine to Montgomery is highlighted in the hundredal inquisitions for Shropshire in 1255 and 1274. In 1255, for example, although there were said to be 2 knights' fees at Stokesay 'and appurtenances', only one of these fees did service at Ludlow, the other doing ward at the castle of Montgomery for 40 days in time of war. However, as there was only ever one knight's fee at Stokesay, it is likely that the fee owing service at Ludlow was in fact the one at Childrey in Berkshire, which in 1242-3 was held by the lord of Stokesay '*de honore de Lodelawe*'.[7] The service from 1 knight's fee at Corfton, held by the Furches family, was also due at Montgomery in 1255. This is nowhere stated as fact but we can infer that this was the case from the record in that year for one of its members, Patton. Here Hugh of Patton had half the manor from the prior of Wenlock for 1 mark annually and for castle-guard at Montgomery in time of war for 10 days with 2 serjeants and horses and two hauberks (long mail shirts), this service being deemed to be 'in proportion to one-third knight's fee through William de Furches'.[8] In 1274 1 knight's fee at the Lacy manor of Wheathill owed ward at Montgomery Castle for 40 days in time of war, but the record for Stoke-upon-Tern for that year seems a little behind the times. Here it was said

that the manor was held '*de feodo de Ludelow*' for sending one knight to Shrawardine Castle in time of war for 40 days at its own cost.[9] Part of this service had been subinfeudated to Hugh of Eaton (of Eaton-on-Tern in Stoke), whose duty was to provide one horseman at Shrawardine Castle for 40 days at his own cost.[10]

Apart from these fees the remainder of the Lacy knights' fees listed in 1255 and 1274 all owed their service at Ludlow. These were ¼ knight's fee at Wootton, land in Onibury and Walton valued at 20s per annum (said later to be the equivalent of ¼ knight's fee), ¼ fee at Downton, 1 fee at Hopton Cangeford, 1 fee at Bitterley, ½ fee at Rushbury, ½ fee at Henley, 1 fee in Great Sutton and Witchcot, and ¼ fee at Pool (with Ayntree).[11] There were also two virgates of land at Wigley which owed '*custodire turrim de Lud' pro quindecim dies tempore werre*' and which again was said later to be the equivalent of ¼ knight's fee.[12] A further single knight's fee at Middleton had been given to William fitzAlan of Clun in marriage with Walter de Lacy's sister 80 years before. This was one of 5 knights' fees that Payn fitzJohn had added to the strength of his feudal garrison at Ludlow from lands he had acquired, of which 4, including this one, either returned to their original owners or passed out of Lacy possession in some way.

Additional to all these knights' fees mentioned in the hundred rolls were many parcels of land '*quod pertinent a castrum de Lud*'' on which service tied to the castle had been commuted either to a money rent or render, or abolished altogether.[13] In this category were 8 virgates in Rock held by the Hospital of St. John of Ludlow in free alms; 1 virgate in Rock for which 8 silver shillings was paid to Margaret de Lacy in the name of dower and rent of a further 5s for an assart and a meadow called Old Fishpond; 12 acres of land at Wigley that paid 2s annually to Margaret de Lacy's dower; 3s rent for a meadow in Rock; 2 carucates of land in Ludlow held in chief by Margaret de Lacy as dower; the Old Vivary which paid 1lb wax at the castle on St Mary Magdalene's Day; rent of 18d for a messuage; two pairs of tongs (*forces*) for a parcel of land; 4d annually for a smithy; 2lbs of cumin for two shops; a spur for a plot of land and 1lb of pepper for a virgate of land.[14] Most of these have a distinctly non-feudal flavour and probably represent commutation of a duty to supply the castle or its lord with a service. These services were normally held by a kind of non-military serjeanty tenure, such as for providing the lord with hunting dogs, napery, spurs, equipment for the kitchen (the tongs), food (the Old Fishpond) and spices or for providing the castle with its necessary ironwork (the smithy).[15] Since the round-naved chapel in the inner ward of the castle was dedicated to St. Mary Magdalene, the 1lb of wax provided annually by the holder of the 'Old Vivary' was doubtless for lighting this chapel.

The hundred rolls for 1255 and 1274 do not present a complete picture of the feudal services appurtenant to the castle, unfortunately. Omitted altogether from them, but included in the Exchequer assessments for the aid of 1242-3 was 1 fee at Corfton (including Middlehope), $^1/_2$ fee at Upper Hayton, $^1/_2$ fee at Lower Hayton, $^1/_2$ fee at Aldon and $^1/_2$ fee at Wilderhope, this latter fee normally being held with the $^1/_4$ fee at Rushbury recorded in the hundred rolls.[16] There was also $^1/_4$ knight's fee at Cressage that was omitted from both these sources. Taken together these figures show that the total number of knights' fees in Shropshire owing or formerly owing service at Ludlow Castle by the mid-13th century was 11$^3/_4$, to which must be added the fee at Childrey to make a total of 12$^3/_4$ fees within Ludlow's 'barony'. Within this total, however, the 1 knight's fee at Great Sutton & Witchcot, the $^1/_2$ fee at Henley and the $^1/_4$ fee at Cressage were on lands that did not originally belong to the Lacys and when these and the fee in Berkshire are taken away the total number of knights' fees on the Lacy lands in Shropshire in the mid-13th century was 10. This figure coincides exactly with the figure of 10 knights' fees (at Bitterley, Henley, Hopton Cangeford, Downton, Over & Nether Hayton, Stanton Lacy, Pool, Wilderhope, Wootton, Ayntree (in Stanton Lacy), Aldon,

Wigley and Cressage (in Cound)) that Joan, widow of Roger de Mortimer, earl of March, was said to hold of the king by service of $^1/_2$ knight's fee when she died in 1356 and with a list of chief tenants in Shropshire drawn up in the Exchequer in 1202, which accounts for the Lacy fief as 'Walter de Lacy, 10 knights' fees in this county'.[17] As it also coincides with the number of Lacy fees that did service at Shrawardine Castle in 1186/7 and as the fees were owed only on lands that were in Lacy hands in 1086 it can be said with a fair degree of confidence that this figure represents the feudal military service attached by the Lacys to Ludlow Castle from at least the time of Henry I, and possibly earlier.

The earliest statement of the kind of service expected at Ludlow Castle from a knight's fee is given in Hugh II de Lacy's (re)grant of the fee at Wootton in Aldon to William of Wootton, which probably dates to the 1170s. This was for the service of $^1/_2$ knight's fee in the host and in castle-guard and for $^3/_4$ knight's fee when the lord levied an aid on his knights.[18] The terms of this grant can be illuminated thus: a lord normally expected his knights to perform three services for him, *exercitu* (service in his host), *custodia* (guard at one of his castles) and *equitatio* or *chevalchia* (personal escort duty to him). The first two of these correspond to the first two services demanded from William of Wootton above. The third service, 'escort duty', was in practice difficult to distinguish from service in the host and for this reason soon fell into abeyance, as seems to have happened at Wootton (and probably elsewhere in the Lacy barony) by the 1170s. One other duty incumbent on a knight was to pay his lord an 'aid' or tax at certain times, such as for ransoming the lord if he was captured in war or for the knighting of his eldest son. According the grant to William of Wootton, the payment of an aid at Ludlow was at a rate 50% higher than the going rate of commutation for knight-service.

Commutation of personal feudal service to the payment of an agreed fee (scutage), which seems to have happened at Ludlow by the 1170s, had distinct advantages for the lord. With the money provided he could hire professional or mercenary knights who were more useful to him in the field or in his castle than the variable quality of soldier he could by now, after the era of conquest had passed, expect from the men enfeoffed on his lands. Better still, in respect of castle-guard, he could hire mounted or unmounted men-at-arms or serjeants who, being non-feudal in origin and so more open to instruction, were more suited to that kind of service. Additionally, two of these serjeants could be hired for the price of one knight, and although they were armed at a lower level than their feudal counterparts of the 12th century, that level was similar in nature to the standard of armament possessed by a knight at the time of the Conquest, and it was these knights who formed the earliest garrisons at Ludlow and elsewhere.

All told, therefore, commutation of knight-service to the payment of scutage had numerous advantages to the lord of Ludlow. In respect of the amount scutage payable at Ludlow, shortly before 1256 Nicholas of Willey had held the manor of Rushbury appurtenant to the castle of Ludlow 'by military service of $\frac{1}{2}$ knight's fee, that is, he paid 20s when the king levied a scutage of 40s, more when the rate was higher and less when it was lower'.[19]

Both Wootton and Rushbury were held for the service of only $\frac{1}{2}$ knight's fee, that is, their holders would expect to do only half the amount of free knight-service of a man holding a full knight's fee, or pay half the amount of scutage. If the services owed at Shrawardine or Montgomery in 1255 by the Lacy fees at Corfton, Stokesay, Stoke-upon-Tern and Wheathill (together with the evidence for Wootton presented below) represents the kind of service expected of them at Ludlow, as may well be the case, then the amount free knight-service expected from a full knight's fee in the late 12th century and later was 40 days in time of war. After the 40 days free service was over the lord would pay the knight at the going daily rate for as long as he required them. Knights holding fractions of fees would perform that fraction of the full 40-day free service: $\frac{1}{2}$ fee - 20 days, $\frac{1}{4}$ fee - 10 days, etc. However, the story at Ludlow is not quite as simple as that. In 1255, as we have seen, the service of $\frac{1}{4}$ knight's fee at Wigley was for 'fifteen days in time of war in the *turrim* of Ludlow', while the service of one-third knight's fee (*recte* $\frac{1}{4}$) at Patton was also for 15 days. This strongly suggests that at one point 60 days free service was the norm. As has been noted elsewhere, 60 days free service (notionally two months) is quite frequently found as the original service imposed by lords on their knights in this country, although it was common for this to have been reduced to 40 days in the 12th century as times became more settled.[20] Similarly, an early obligation by knights to perform their free service annually became reduced over time to a duty to supply it only in time of war. It seems therefore that the original period of free service Walter I de Lacy and his sons imposed on their knights might have been 60 days annually, subsequently reduced to 40 days in time of war. It is possible, however, that at a border castle like Ludlow reductions in service occurred at a later date than in more settled areas of the country, for obvious reasons, though this must still have been before the 1170s if the grant to William of Wootton mentioned above is to be believed.

Hugh de Lacy's grant of Wootton was made in return for knight-service, although it seems likely that the service he actually received from it was that of a serjeant rather than a knight. It was certainly held by service of a serjeant one hundred years or so later, and it may be possible to project this back to the time of Hugh in view of the fact that he was already willing to accept money from his knights (and so open up the possibility of acquiring serjeants to replace them) in lieu of personal service. The record for Wootton in 1295 states briefly that it was held by service of a 'horseman' at Ludlow Castle in time of war for 40 days at its own cost.[21] As we know from other evidence that it was held for only $\frac{1}{2}$ knight's fee, however, this should have produced the services of a knight for only 20 days rather than 40 stated, and this leads us to suspect that the 'horseman' is in fact a serjeant, two of whose services could be hired for the cost of one knight.[22] The equation '1 knight equals 2 serjeants' was certainly present in the adjacent lordship of Clun in the mid-13th century, when a knight's fee at Edgton provided either 1 knight or 2 serjeants for 40 days ward at Clun Castle in time of war,[23] so it may well have been present at Ludlow at a similar date.

A serjeant or man-at-arms could be mounted or unmounted. Some local examples will serve to show what kind of unmounted service may have been due at Ludlow. When in the 1150s Bishop Gilbert Foliot gave a man land at Linley in his lordship of Bishop's Castle he gave it for a money rent and 'by doing the service of a serjeant for castle-guard at Lydbury North at his own expense for 40 days'.[24] Similarly, in 1295 ¼ knight's fee at Stanage was held for providing a footman with bow and arrows at Stapleton Castle for 40 days in time of war in Wales at its own charges or for payment of ½ mark of scutage,[25] while in 1299 the service of ½ knight's fee at Hergest in Herefordshire was defined as for providing one foot soldier with bow and arrows at Huntington Castle in time of war for 15 days at its own cost.[26]

By contrast with these unmounted services, in the mid-13th century ½ knight's fee at Stowe near Brampton Bryan in Herefordshire was held for the provision of a mounted serjeant at Clun Castle at his own cost for 20 days in time of war.[27] In the reign of Edward III, moreover, 2 knights' fees at Neenton and Sidbury in Shropshire were each held by service of 1 hobelar (mounted serjeant) for keeping Wigmore Castle for 40 days at their own cost when there was war in Wales, although the service of only 1 knight's fee at Overton, Eudon George and Coreley was expected to provide 2 such hobelars at Wigmore for the same period.[28]

Mounted serjeants had been a feature of border warfare as early as the reign of Henry I. Sometime before 1114 Henry gave the manor of Wilton near Ross-on-Wye in Herefordshire to Hugh de Longchamps 'for the service of two mounted serjeants in the wars of Wales'.[29] What was good enough for the king we may suspect was good enough for his barons at a similar date, depending on the circumstances. At Clun at least it seems clear that the service of serjeants at the castle had considerable antiquity. In 1295 the value of the whole knight-service due at the castle there, when commuted to 'ward penny' or 'ward silver', was put at £6 15s in time of war and nothing in time of peace, 'but an esquire [serjeant]' it was said, 'shall take 4½d daily'.[30] Mounted serjeants could be hired at a similar daily rate to this (4d) only in the mid-12th century,[31] before a discernible wage-inflation took place in the reigns of Richard I and John, and this may indicate the antiquity this arrangement.

The kind of equipment these men were to provide for themselves is mentioned several times in connection with lands on the border with Wales. In 1250 land in Dilwyn, Herefordshire, was held by a rent of 3s and for finding the lord 'yearly in war time for 15 days at Dilwyn or Boughrood one man with a horse, doublet, iron cap and lance at the [lord's] cost'; provision also being made for the loss of his horse.[32] At the same date ½ knight's fee at Turnastone, Herefordshire, was expected to provide two footmen, one with lance and the other with bow and arrows, for 40 days at Snodhill Castle at its own cost 'when there shall be war with Wales'.[33] Half a knight's fee at Sandford in Prees, Shropshire, in 1212 was held in 1327 by serjeanty of an armed man with an unbarded (unarmoured) horse at Montgomery Castle for 40 days at its own cost 'in time of Welsh war',[34] this man apparently being the counterpart at Montgomery of the 'horseman' due from Wootton at Ludlow in 1295. In 1272 lands held of Clun Castle for a whole knight's fee were to 'owe in time of war guard at the castle of Clun for 40 days yearly one man with corslet (short mail shirt) and horse'.[35] As with the 'assizes' of arms of 1181 and 1230, where the item is also omitted, it is assumed that all these men will have a sword.

Any garrison at Ludlow Castle—feudal, non-feudal or mixed in composition—will have come under the control of the constable. This officer looked after the military affairs of the castle just as the seneschal or steward looked after the administration of the castle and of the lands dependant on it. The earliest name we have for a man we know for certain was constable is William de Lucy in 1234, by which date the Lacys seem also have combined that officer with the steward of their English lands. Men such at Philip d'Aubigny and Engelard de Cigogné, who held the castle on behalf of King John, and William de Gamages in 1224 for Henry III, may have been considered as constables, although their duties seem to have extended beyond the range of a normal constable to that of governor. John Sturmy of Watmore in Burford was constable at Ludlow at a date before 1274, while in 1286 Richard le Seneschal occupied that office,[36] his name suggesting that the offices of constable and seneschal were still combined as they had been in William de Lucy's day. No other constable's name is known until 1322 when Ralph le Botiller was put in charge of the castle.[37] However, Robert, marshal to Hugh II de Lacy, is mentioned in two charters he gave to St. Guthlac's Priory,[38] which suggests that, as in all great households, the Lacys maintained this officer in addition to their constable to organise their military forces in the field and to make their travel arrangements.

Details of the duties of the constable of Ludlow Castle and of his allowances are given in Walter de Lacy's grant of that office to William de Lucy in 1234. Regarding the allowances, Lucy expected Walter to provide him 'with garments and vestments as for a household knight' and also firewood from nearby woods as previous constables had been wont to receive. As constable he would live in the inner ward of the castle, except when Walter came to the castle, when he would move out to the outer ward. Although he could expect to be at the castle for long periods (if he performed the service in person rather than through a deputy), it is clear nevertheless that he needed to provide little for his own needs during such times. He himself had to provide certain permanent staff as previous constables had—a priest to serve the free chapel of St. Mary Magdalene in the castle, a porter to keep the door

of the castle and two sentinels or watchmen to watch over it. Any repairs or building work Lucy thought necessary would be paid for by Walter provided it had been approved and overseen by two honest men.

This is how the castle would be kept in peacetime. In time of war Lucy would remove himself to the outer ward and give up the inner ward to Walter. Lucy would remain in the outer ward of the castle for as long as Walter kept the castle garrisoned, and it can probably be inferred from this that the defence of the outer ward was his responsibility under Walter. The feudal tenants of the lands dependant on the castle would provide, either personally or via the payment of scutage (from which Walter could hire the equivalent) 10 knights or 20 mounted serjeants for the defence of the castle for a period of 40 days. If they were required for longer than 40 days, then the additional daily cost of was born by Walter. These men would probably have augmented other knights and/or serjeants in a small permanent garrison paid for by Walter out of his own pocket and by archers and footsoldiers hired in the same way or recruited from the surrounding lordship.

The *Romance of Fulk fitzWarin* says that Joce de Dinan left a garrison of '30 knights and 70 serjeants and valets [footsoldiers]' to hold the castle while he went to Devon seeking reinforcements against 'Walter' de Lacy and that while he was away Lacy brought up an army of 'more than a thousand' knights, esquires and men-at-arms to besiege the castle (see chapter IV). These figures probably allude to late 13th century notions of how many men would be required to hold the castle in times of danger and how many to besiege it rather than those of the mid-12th century when the events took place. However, they do provide an 'order of scale' against which the Lacys' known provisions for the manning of the castle can be compared, and also a realistic view of the numbers of men likely to have been involved in the fighting in and around Ludlow in the 12th and 13th centuries.

As indicated the number of knights' fees the Lacys had in the late 12th century on lands in

Shropshire they had retained since 1086 was 10. 12th- and 13th-century evidence provides names for the families enfeoffed on those fees by the time King Henry I's death in 1135, and probably by 1086. In alphabetical order, with, in brackets, the names of the manor(s) in Shropshire they held, they were the families of Bernières (Rushbury and Wilderhope), Cricetot (Over Hayton), Devereux (Nether Hayton), Doville (Wigley), Esketot (Bitterley), Furches (Corfton, Middlehope and Patton), Hopton (Hopton Cangeford), Pirun (Pool and Ayntree), Say (Stokesay, Moreton Say, Stoke-on-Tern and Wheathill) and Wootton (Wootton, Onibury, Walton and Downton). The name of the original holder of the fee at Aldon is unknown and by 1166 it had come into the hands of five joint heirs. Lands not belonging to the Lacys in 1086 whose military service had probably been made appurtenant to Ludlow by Payn fitzJohn were at Great Sutton and Witchcot, held by the Holdgate family, and Henley, held by the Clintons. Cressage became attached to Ludlow after fitzJohn's day but before 1180, and this was given to a junior line of the Lacy family itself. Each of these families is dealt with under the heading of the manor(s) they held.

Rushbury and Wilderhope

The Odo who held the manor of Rushbury (which included Wilderhope) under Roger de Lacy, and the manor of Kenley and other places under Reginald de Balliol the sheriff, in 1086 is probably Odo de Bernières, from Bernières-sur-Mer, on the Channel coast north of Caen (Calvados).[39] Odo de Bernières was a benefactor of Shrewsbury Abbey.[40] In 1166 Roger fitzOdo of Rushbury held 1 'new' fee (probably only 'new' in the sense that he held it on different terms from his father Odo de Bernières) of Hugh de Lacy and a fief of 1 knight and 3 mounted serjeants (*muntatores*) of William fitzAlan, successor to sheriff Reginald.[41] Roger's son, Herbert of Rushbury, died before 1221 leaving as his heir his sister Parnel, who had married Warner of Willey and who had received Kenley from her brother

Thomas.[42] By 1242-3 Parnel 'of Kenley', widow of Warner, and Stephen of Bitterley shared 1 knight's fee at Rushbury and Wilderhope.[43] In 1256 Margery, widow of Walter II de Lacy, claimed the wardship of Andrew, son and heir of Nicholas of Willey, because his father had held a tenement in Rushbury of her (as of her dower in her husband's lands) 'by military service of half a knight's fee, that is, he paid 20 shillings when the king levied a 40-shilling scutage, more when the rate was higher and less when it was lower, and she was seised of such scutages on the day Nicholas was alive and dead. By reason of that forinsec service, Andrew ... a minor ... should ... be in her wardship ...'.[44] Roger of Bitterley sold his share to Hugh Burnel in 1283 and in 1315 Edward Burnel, Hugh's grandson, had a moiety of Rushbury for $1/4$ fee.[45] In 1316 Theobald de Verdun, the chief lord, had $1/2$ fee in Rushbury and $1/2$ in Wilderhope.[46]

Over Hayton (in Stanton Lacy)

The Cricetot family who held this manor under the Lacys came either from Criquetot-sur-Ouville near Yerville (Seine-Inférieure) or Criquetot-sur-Longueville, just east of Bacqueville-en-Caux (probably the home of the Baskervilles, the most important Lacy honourial barons) north of Tôtes (Seine-Inférieure). In 1086 one Gerald (de Cricetot) held Cobhall, Webton and Meer Court, Herefordshire, from Roger de Lacy.[47] In the 1160s Michael de Cricetot had Webton and in 1166 William son of Michael had $1/4$ knight's fee from Hugh de Lacy.[48] In 1242-3 the heirs of Michael de Cricetot had $1/2$ knight's fee at Over Hayton and $1/8$ fee at Cobhall, Webton and Meer Court in Herefordshire.[49] This Michael had witnessed the deed in which Walter de Lacy had granted the constableship of Ludlow to William de Lucy: John, his son and heir, was living in 1265. In 1283 John son of Osbert of Westhope, Agnes his wife and Agnes's sister Alice quitclaimed the manor to William of Stapleton, who had $1/2$ fee at Over Hayton in 1284/5.[50] Robert Brown held it of Theobald de Verdun in 1316 .[51]

Nether Hayton (in Stanton Lacy)

The Devereux family, who were the military subtenants here, were from Evreux (Eure), which belonged to William fitzOsbern, earl of Hereford (1067-71). William son of Walter Devereux married Eloise, a neice of Walter I de Lacy. In 1086 William Devereux held Chanstone, Street, Putley and Grendon Bishop in Herefordshire from Roger de Lacy,[52] as well as other lands in Gloucestershire, and shortly after that date he obtained Lyonshall in Herefordshire. His son Walter I was dead by 1166 when his *feodum* owed the service of 3 knights to Hugh de Lacy.[53] In 1242-3 William III Devereux of Lyonshall owed the service of 1/2 knight's fee for Nether Hayton.[54] William IV Devereux, who had 1/2 fee at Nether Hayton in 1284/5[55] died in 1314 leaving as his heir his nephew, William V, the son of his brother John. William V Devereux had the manor of Nether Hayton of Joan widow of Roger de Mortimer for 1/5 fee at his death in 1338.[56]

Wigley (in Stanton Lacy)

In 1255/6 Robert de Doville had 1/4 fee at Wigley. His fief is possibly derived from one or other of the 11/2-hide holdings, knights called Richard, Roger and Azelin had in Stanton Lacy in 1086.[57] This family probably came from Douville-sur-Andelle, 20 kilometers south-east of Rouen (Eure) in the Norman Vexin, from whence came many of the men who helped William fitzOsbern secure his earldom of Hereford. Robert de Deuville was a juror in the liberty of Stanton Lacy in 1256 and, with Elias of Sutton, accounted for 20s of an amercement.[58] In 1274 a Hugh de Doville was constable of Bridgnorth Castle and when Theobald de Verdun died in 1316 Robert son of Robert de Doville had 1/4 fee at Wigley.[59]

Bitterley

Loyd suggests that the family of Esketot, who held this and other manors from the Lacys, were from St.-Germain-d'Ectot mid-way between Lassy and Bayeux (Calvados).[60] However, the presence of other men from the Pays-de-Caux (Seine-Inférieure) among the Lacy feoffees in

Shropshire favours either Ectot-l'Auber or Ectot-les-Baons, both near Yerville in that district. In 1085 a Richard de Esketot witnessed on behalf of Roger de Lacy the agreement between Roger and the bishop of Hereford in respect of the manor of Holme Lacy, Herefordshire.[61] Gilbert de Esketot held a manor of 2 hides at Duntisborne Abbotts in Gloucestershire from Roger in 1086 and in 1100, with the permission of his wife and of Robert his son, he gave this land to Gloucester Abbey.[62] A Gerard de Esketot who held lands in Clehonger, Herefordshire, in 1086 under Ansfrid de Cormeilles of Tarrington,[63] may have been related to Richard and Gilbert. By 1135 (and probably by 1100, or else Gilbert would not have been willing to relinquish his hold on his only *Domesday Book* estate in that year) they had acquired 3 knights' fees in Herefordshire under the Lacys, two of these being at Llancillo in Ewyas Lacy and at King's Pyon. In 1148-55 Earl Roger of Hereford and his wife Cecily, daughter of Payn fitzJohn, allowed Robert de Esketot and Gilbert his son and Robert's brother Gerard (or Geoffrey) to give a hide of land at Keephill near Bromyard, within his wife's *maritagium*, to St. Guthlac's Priory, Hereford.[64] A further Richard de Esketot held the 3 knights' fees mentioned above and at the same time a Roger de Esketot had 1 'new' fee at Bitterley in 1166. As a 'new' fee the fief at Bitterley had been created since 1135. Richard de Esketot also had 1 knight's fee at Bullinghope and Clehonger held from Richard de Cormeilles of Tarrington, the Clehonger part being held under him by a Gilbert de Esketot.[65] Between 1172 and 1177 Roger de Esketot gave rents from the mill of Bitterley to Haughmond Abbey in a charter confirmed by Hugh II de Lacy; Roger de Esketot son of Hugh confirming this grant about 30 years later.[66] Later members of this branch of the family took the surname Bitterley. In 1242-3 and 1255 Stephen of Bitterley had 1 fee in Bitterley. A Roger of Bitterley had the fee in 1284/5 and he was still alive in 1301.[67]

Corfton, Middlehope and Patton

The Lacys had the Furches family as their military subtenants at these places. In 1085 a Herbert de Furches had witnessed the agreement between Roger de Lacy and the bishop of Hereford mentioned above on Roger's behalf. A year later Herbert is recorded as holding Corfton, Middlehope and Patton in Shropshire of Roger as well as Bodenham Moor and Houghton in Herefordshire, and he was also a benefactor of Shrewsbury Abbey.[68] This Herbert de Furches or a later member of his family gave ¹/₂ hide of land at Patton to Wenlock Priory. In 1166 William II de Furches held 3 knights' fees of the 'old' enfeoffment from Hugh de Lacy, but denied that he owed Hugh the service of one of them.[69] Henry of Hereford, lord of Brecknock and brother and heir to earl Roger of Hereford and to Walter of Hereford, gave 10 *librates* of land at Kingstone, Herefordshire, to this William for the service of ¹/₂ knight's fee.[70] In 1242-3 William V de Furches held 1 knight's fee at Corfton and Middlehope from the heirs of Walter de Lacy and 1 knight's fee at Kingstone from the lord of Brecknock.[71] The fee at Corfton included the feudal service due from Patton. In 1255 Hugh of Patton had ¹/₂ hide of land at Patton which he held from the prior of Wenlock by payment of one mark annually and doing castle-guard at Montgomery Castle in time of war for 10 days, with two serjeants and horses and two hauberks (or the equivalent of the service from one-third knight's fee), through William de Furches, lord of Corfton. The feudal service due from this ¹/₂-hide of land may well have been established before it was given to Wenlock Priory. Also at Patton was another ¹/₂ hide of land that Hugh of Patton held of Walter of Hopton (of Hopton Castle) for ¹/₄ knight's fee and Walter of William de Furches.[72] The heir of this William for most of his lands was his sister Amice who married William de Lucy of Charlecote, Warwickshire, son of the William de Lucy who had been granted the constableship of Ludlow in 1234, but Corfton passed to Robert Burnell of Acton Burnell, bishop of Bath and Wells, who died in 1292 holding 1 knight's fee at Corfton and

Middlehope from the heir of Peter de Geneville for suit of court at Ludlow. In 1284/5 Walter of Cooksey held Corfton from the bishop.[73]

Hopton Cangeford

A knight called Auti had 3 hides in Stanton Lacy in 1086 and these probably lay at Hopton.[74] He may have been the progenitor of the Hopton family. In 1166 William of Hopton had 1 'new' fee here but Eyton is inclined to doubt whether this was a new enfeoffment rather than a regranting on different terms of an 'old' fee.[75] Nicholas of Hopton had 1 fee at Hopton Cangeford in 1242-3, Thomas of Hopton in 1255 and Roger of Hopton in 1284/5.[76] In 1256 Thomas of Hopton was accused of illegally depriving Philip of Greet of three acres of land in Hopton Cangeford and in 1309 John of Hopton *Kandivant* had ¹/₂ fee there.[77]

Pool and Ayntree (in Stanton Lacy)

In 1242-3 and 1255 John Piron had ¹/₄ fee at Pool.[78] As with the Doville fief at Wigley, this fee may represent the lands one of 3 knights had in Stanton Lacy in 1086. At Easter 1234, at Furness in Lancashire, a Ralph Pirun witnessed Walter II de Lacy's charter to the abbey of Furness endowing it with certain lands in Ireland[79] and the family may have been of Irish extraction, since a William Pirun was bishop of Glendalough in Leinster in *c*.1200. If they were, they must have replaced the original Lacy feoffee here in or after 1172. The John Piron of 1242-3 and 1255 was the son of Walter Pirun and in 1256 John was called to vouch to warrant John of Pool and Richelda his wife in possession of half a virgate of arable at Pool.[80] In 1284/5 Walter Pirun had ¹/₄ fee at Pool but in 1327 the fief was centred on Ayntree.[81] In 1289 Walter Pirun *de la Pole* and Margery his wife had sold one virgate of land at Whettleton in Stokesay to Laurence of Ludlow.[82]

Stoke-on-Tern, Stokesay and Wheathill

Theodoric de Say, the earliest known member of the Say family to hold from the Lacys the manors of Stokesay, Stoke-on-Tern (with Moreton Say)

and Wheathill in Shropshire and Childrey, Berkshire, was presumably related to Robert 'Picot' de Say, who was lord of Clun in 1086 and who came from Sai, a few kilometres east of Argentan (Orne),[83] although in what degree is unknown. He was a benefactor of Shrewbury Abbey between 1094 and 1102 and as Tiri de Say witnessed Hugh I de Lacy's grant of the church of St. Peter at Hereford to Gloucester Abbey in 1100 or 1101,[84] although he held no lands from Roger de Lacy in 1086. Between 1086 and 1100, therefore, he became one of the two largest honourial barons within the Lacy barony (the other being Robert de Baskerville of Eardisley), holding no less than 5 knights fees from them. In 1166 it was reported of Elias de Say, his great-grandson, that he 'acknowledges the service of three knight's fees, but denies of old the service of a further two knight's fees'.[85] In 1172-7 Hugh de Say gave the church of Stokesay to Haughmond Abbey for the souls of his father Elias and his mother Egeline and in 1242-3 Hugh's son Walter de Say had 3 fees on the Shropshire manors and 1 fee at Childrey, the latter held from him by John Maltravers.[86] Walter died without issue and Stokesay and Stoke-on-Tern passed to his nephew Hugh, who gave them to John de Verdun, the chief lord of the fee, in exchange for lands in Ireland. John de Verdun had 2 knights' fees in Stokesay *ad castellum de Lodelawe* in 1255, one of which owed service at Montgomery Castle and one, which is probably the knight's fee the lords of Stokesay had at Childrey, at Ludlow, as already noted. John de Verdun also had 1 knight's fee at Stoke-on-Tern (with Moreton Say) *de feodo de Ludelow* by exchange with Hugh de Say for service at Shrawardine Castle. For lands at Eaton-on-Tern in Stoke, Hugh of Eaton provided a horseman at Shrawardine for 40 days at his own cost through John de Verdun (*ex eodem feodo*) and in 1309 this was reckoned to be the equivalent of $\frac{1}{2}$ knight's fee. At the same time Walter Hacket held 1 knight's fee at Wheathill from Hugh de Say for service at Montgomery Castle.[87] In 1274 Reginald de Grey of Wilton, Herefordshire, was Verdun's feoffee at Stokesay

and his son John sold the manor to Laurence of Ludlow, a great wool merchant, in 1281. In 1284/5 Laurence held 1 knight's fee in Stokesay from John de Grey, who held from the lord of Ludlow.[88] Laurence died in 1294 and was succeeded by his son William who died in 1316.

Wootton (in Stokesay)

A knight called Aldred had a 'member' of Aldon in 1086 which was probably at Wootton and he is possibly also the unnamed knight who had 1 hide of land in Onibury at the same date.[89] In 1166-76 Hugh de Lacy gave William of Wootton lands at Wootton and Onibury 'to hold by service of $\frac{1}{2}$ knight's fee in the host and castle-guard; and if the chief or lord paramount levied any aid on his knights, then William and his heirs were to pay in proportion to $\frac{3}{4}$ fee'. William was possibly a descendant of Aldred. Robert of Wootton had $\frac{1}{2}$ fee at Wootton in 1242-3 and died in 1246. His widow Agnes then married Peter de Lacy and their daughter and sole heir Amice married Robert de Lacy. Robert de Lacy had the $\frac{1}{2}$ fee in 1255 and in 1267 he disseised Richard Bacon of right of common in Wootton appurtenant to his tenement of Shelderton. Robert died in 1271 and Amice then married Thomas of Greet.[90] Thomas of Greet held the $\frac{1}{2}$ fee at Wootton 'of the heir of Amice his wife' (that is, Gilbert de Lacy, son of Robert and Amice) in 1284, but by 1295 Philip Burnell, nephew and heir of Bishop Robert Burnell, was holding the manor and fishery of Wootton of the lord of Stanton Lacy by service of finding a horseman at Ludlow in time of war for 40 days at his own cost and suit at Ludlow every three weeks.[91]

Onibury and Walton (in Onibury)

As already noted the knight who had 1 hide at Onibury in 1086 may be Aldred of Wootton. Robert de Lacy had 20s rent in Onibury and Walton in 1255 and in 1284/5 Thomas of Greet had $\frac{1}{4}$ fee at those places as well as $\frac{1}{2}$ fee at Wootton.[92]

Downton (in Stanton Lacy)

Aldred or his descendants seem to have acquired land here, possibly formerly belonging to one of the three knights holding 1 1/2 hides each in Stanton Lacy in 1086, for the service of 1/4 knight's fee, since in 1255 it is found in the hands of the same Robert de Lacy who then had Wootton, Onibury and Walton. His son Gilbert de Lacy had it in 1284-5.[93]

Aldon (in Stokesay)

In 1086 a knight called Richard had 1 hide here.[94] Since the 'fee of *Cauledone* [Aldon]' was held for 1/2 'new' fee in 1166 Eyton surmises Richard's tenancy lapsed (perhaps because he shared Roger de Lacy's exile) and that it was regranted after 1135. He also suggests that the terminology used in 1166 indicates that the fief created after 1135 was already in the hands of coheirs, the state in which it always appears in the 13th century.[95] These coheirs were five in number, perhaps representing families into which five heiresses had married. In 1242-3 Roger le Poer 'and parceners' held 1/2 fee in Aldon and in 1255 the five parceners were said to be John (le Poer), parson of Bishopstone in Herefordshire, Thomas of Lea, Stephen of Smethcott, Thomas Purcel and Richard of Thonglands.[96] An earlier Roger le Poer had in 1166 held one knight's fee at Bishopstone from the bishop of Hereford and in about 1220 John le Poer witnessed a charter of Walter de Lacy's relating to the lands of the priory of Llanthony Secunda (Llanthony-by-Gloucester) in Ireland,[97] In 1284/5 John Purcel had 1/2 fee at Aldon and in 1292 the parceners were John Purcel, John of Lea, Reginald Scot and Isabel his wife, and Gilbert de Lacy.[98]

The following few holdings were on lands that did not belong to the Lacys in 1086 and were acquired by them at a later date:

Henley (in Bitterley)

A knight called Roger held Henley from sheriff Reginald in 1086[99] and does not appear to have left any descendants. The family of Clinton who held Henley in Shropshire and Pixley Clinton in Herefordshire from the 12th century onwards are said to have been decended from William, one of the younger sons of Geoffrey de Clinton, baron of Kenilworth and chamberlain and treasurer to King Henry I.[100] Payn fitzJohn, who was Clinton's fellow *curialis* in the service of King Henry, probably enfoffed William both here and at Pixley. In 1194 Ives de Clinton, William's grandson, was lord of Henley. In 1242-3 Philip de Clinton (called Philip 'of Henley' in 1255) had 1/2 knight's fee at Henley and his cousin Simon one-tenth knight's fee at Pixley Clinton.[101] In 1256 Philip de Clinton was summoned to answer William son of Hugh's plea that Philip should permit him to have his reasonable estover in his wood in Stanton Lacy. Philip's grandson Ives had 1/2 fee in Henley in 1284/5 and he was still living in 1301.[102]

Great Sutton and Witchcot

In 1086 Herbert held Great Sutton (including Witchcot) under his father, Helgot of Castle Holdgate.[103] Payn fitzJohn made this fee appurtenant to Ludlow. In 1166 Herbert de Castello, son of Herbert and grandson of Helgot, held 2 'new' fees from Hugh II de Lacy.[104] One of these fees was at Great Sutton and Witchcot and the other, probably, at Castle Frome in Herefordshire. Herbert de Castello is often found in the company of Hugh II de Lacy in England in contemporary records and in 1174-7 witnessed Hugh's confirmation of the church of Stokesay to Haughmond Abbey.[105] He died without issue and in 1242-3 Thomas Mauduit, the great grandson of his sister, held 1 fee in Sutton and Witchcot; William Mauduit had it in 1255.[106] In 1284/5 Robert Burnell, bishop of Bath and Wells, had 1/2 fee at Sutton and Robert Brown 1/2 fee at Witchcot, but by the time of his death in 1302 the bishop was holding both places for 1 knight's fee and suit of court at Ludlow. In 1305 Philip Burnel held Great Sutton by suit of court at Ludlow every three weeks and Witchcot and Great Poston by service of £1 17s 0d yearly rent.[107]

Cressage

A manor here had belonged to Ranulf Peverel in 1086[108] but it had been forfeited to the crown by 1130. Shortly after 1135 it belonged to William Peverel of Peak, Derbyshire, but it was not among the lands Duke Henry seized from William in 1153-4, probably because it had been annexed to Ludlow by Payn fitzJohn in the interim. By about 1180 a junior line of the Lacy family had become enfeoffed there, the enfeoffer probably being Hugh II de Lacy.[109] In 1284/5 Adam de Lacy held it and in 1316 John de Lacy.[110] When Joan, widow of Peter de Geneville, died in 1323 it was said that John de Lacy, now dead, had formerly held Cressage of the manor of Stanton Lacy by service of $\frac{1}{4}$ knight's fee.[111]

References & Notes

Abbreviations

Anglo-Norman Families   L.C. Loyd, *The Origins of Some Anglo-Norman Families*, Harleian Society, Leeds, 1951.

'Attack'   'The Attack on the Council in the Marches, 1603-1642', *Trans. Cymmrodorion Soc.*, 1961.

CDI   *Calendar of Documents, Ireland, 1171-1251*, PRO, 1875.

CChR   *Calendar Charter Rolls.* PRO.

CCR   *Calendar of Close Rolls.* PRO.

CPR   *Calendar of Patent Rolls.* PRO.

DB   *Domesday Book*, Record Commission, 1783.

Eyton   R.W. Eyton, *The Antiquities of Shropshire*, 12 vols, 1854-60.

FA   *Feudal Aids*, 6 vols., PRO, 1899-1920.

Faraday   M. Faraday, *Ludlow 1085-1660: A Social, Economic and Political History*, Phillimore, 1991.

Fees   *Book of Fees*, 3 vols., P.R.O.,1920-31.

FFW   E.J. Hathaway, P.T. Ricketts, C.A. Robson & A.D. Wilshire (eds.), *Fouke le fitz Waryn*, Anglo-Norman Texts Society, pp.26-8 (1975).

Flenley   R. Flenley, *Calendar of the Register of the Council in the Marches of Wales*, London, 1916.

GEC   G.E. Cockayne, *The Complete Peerage*, ed. V. Gibbs *et al.*, 13 vols., London, 1910-59.

GS   *Gesta Stephani*, ed. & trans. K.R. Potter, London, 1968.

Haughmond Cartulary   U. Rees (ed. & trans.), *The Cartulary of Haughmond Abbey*, Cardiff, 1985.

HDB   V.H. Galbraith & J. Tait (eds.), *The Herefordshire Domesday Book 1160-70*, Pipe Roll Society, 1950.

Hope   W.H. St. John Hope, 'The Castle of Ludlow', *Archaeologia*, LXI, 1908.

Ipm   *Calendar of Inquisitions Post Mortem*, PRO.

JW   *John of Worcester: Chronicle*, vol. 3, ed. & trans. P. Mcgurk, Oxford, 1998.

Lloyd   D. Lloyd, *Ludlow Castle, A History and Guide,* castle guide, nd.

OV   Orderic Vitalis: *Ecclesiastical History*, ed. & trans. M. Chibnall, 6 vols., Oxford, 1969-80.

PatR   *Calendar of Patent Rolls*, PRO.

PR   *Pipe Roll*, as published by the Pipe Roll Society.

PRO   Public Record Office.

RBE   H. Hall (ed.), *The Red Book of the Exchequer*, 3 vols., Rolls Series, 1896.

RH   *Rotuli Hundredorum*, 2 vols., Record Commission, 1812-18.

RRAN   H.W.C. Davis, C. Johnson, H.A. Cronne and R.H.C. Davis (eds.) *Regesta Regum Anglo-Normannorum*, 3 vols, 1913-68.

Shrewsbury Cartulary   U. Rees (ed.), *The Cartulary of Shrewsbury Abbey*, 2 vols., Aberystwyth, 1975.

Shropshire Eyre   A. Harding (ed. & trans.), *The Roll of the Shropshire Eyre of 1256*, Selden Society, (1981).

SRO   Shropshire Record Office.

StGC   'Cartulary of St. Guthlac's Priory, Hereford', Balliol College Oxford MS p.271.

TSAS   *Transactions of the Shropshire Archaeological Society.*

TSAHS   *Transactions of Shropshire Archaeological and Historical Society.*

TWNFC   *Transactions of the Woolhope Naturalists' Field Club.*

VCH   *Victoria County History, Shropshire.*

Wightman   W.E. Wightman, *The Lacy Family in England and Normandy 1066-1194*, Oxford, 1966.

'Wigmore Chronicle'   J.T. Dickinson and P.T. Ricketts (eds. & trans.), *The Anglo-Norman Chronicle of Wigmore Abbey*, *TWNFC* (1969), pp.414-445.

Wright   T. Wright, *The History of Ludlow and its Neighbourhood*, Ludlow, 1852.

Chapter 1 The Geology

1. P. Toghill, *Geology in Shropshire*, Swan Hill Press, 1990.
2. *ibid.*
3. The British Geological Survey Lexicon of Named Rock Units. See website:www.bgs.ac.uk.
4. J.R. Earp and B.A. Hains, *British Regional Geology: The Welsh Borderland*, 3rd edn., HMSO, 1971.
5. T. Rowley, *The Norman Heritage 1966-1200*, 1983, pp.99-103.
6. M. Annd Scard, *The Building Stones of Shropshire*, Swan Hill Press, 1990, pp.49-57.
7. *ibid*, p.54.
8. *ibid*, pp.49-57.
9. N.A. Ruckley, 'Water Supply of Medieval Castles in the United Kingdom', *Fortress* Vol.7 (1990) pp.14-26.
10. S. Toy, *The Castles of Great Britain*, Heinemann, 1963, pp.100-1.

Chapter II Ludlow Town

1. N. Pevsner, *The Buildings of England: Shropshire*, 1958. p.184.
2. L.F. Chitty, 'The Clun-Clee Ridgeway', pp.171-92 in J.L. Foster, & L. Alcock, (eds.), *Culture and Environment,* 1963.
3. S.C. Stanford, *The Archaeology of the Welsh Marches*, 1991, pp.34-7.
4. Stanford, 1991, p.56.
5. P.S. Gelling, 'Excavations at Caynham Camp ... Final report', *TSAS*, 57, 1963, pp.91-100.
6. Stanford, 1991, Fig.19, pp.55-7.
7. I.D. Margery, *Roman Roads in Britain*, 1967, pp.315-32 (Specifically roads numbered 193, 6b, 6c, 613); D.R. Dudley, 'The Herefordshire Area in the Roman period', *TWNFC*, 1951, pp.120-9.
8. I. Soulsby, *The Towns of Medieval Wales*, 1983, pp.93-4.
9. L.T. Smith (ed.), *The Itinerary of John Leland*, 2, 1964, p.78; Jervoise, *Ancient Bridges of Wales and the West of England*, p.148.
10. Stanford, 1991, pp.76, 89.
11. Stanford, 1991, pp.113-5.
12. C. Fox, *Offa's Dyke*, 1955.
13. Smith, 1964, 3, p.103.
14. Smith, 1964, 3, p.103.
15. Since the demolition of the Market Hall, a building that was described by Pevsner, 1958, p.188 as 'Ludlow's bad luck.
16. Renn, D. '"Chastel de Dynan" : The First Phase of Ludlow', pp.55-74, in J.R. Kenyon & R. Avent (eds.), *Castles in Wales and the Marches*, 1987, p.56.
17. T. Rowley, *The Shropshire Landscape*, 1972, p.183.
18. Rowley, 1972, p.182fn.
19. D. Renn, *Norman Castles in Britain*, 1973, p.233.
20. Faraday, p.1.
21. Faraday, p.1; Rowley, 1972, p.182; B.P. Hindle, *Medieval Town Plans*, 1990, esp. pp.56-61.
22. Rowley, 1972, p.45.
23. M.R.G. Conzen, 'The Use of Town Plans in the Study of Urban History', in H.J. Dyos (ed.) *The Study of Urban History*, 1968.
24. E.L. Morley, 'A Thirteenth century Mystery: Walter de Lacy's "moat"', *Shropshire Magazine*, December 1964, p.27; Rowley, 1972, p.185; M.A. Faraday, 'The "Chronica Landavensis", an important find in the British Library during the summer', *Ludlow Heritage News*, December 1985; T.R. Slater, 'English Medieval New Towns with Composite Plans', pp.60-82 in *The Built Form of Western Cities*; M.R.G. Conzen, 'Morphogenesis. Morphological Regions and Secular Human Agency in the Historic Townscape', in D. Denecke & G. Shaw, (eds.), *Urban Historical Geography*, 1988.
25. Quoted in C.J. Train, *The Walls and Gates of Ludlow*, 1999, pp.20-6.
26. Hindle, 1990. p.61.
27. eg W.H.St.J. Hope, 'The Ancient Topography of ... Ludlow', *Archaeologia*, 61, 1909, pp.383-8; Rowley, 1972, p.182 and others.
28. Hindle, 1990, p.57.
29. W.G. Hoskins, *Local History in England*, 1959.
30. Train, 1999, pp.6-14.
31. H.L. Turner, *Town Defences in England and Wales*, 1971, appendix C, pp.238-43.
32. Turner, 1971, p.207.
33. Buildings in similar positions outside the gates of Hereford had to be pulled down during the Civil War to provide good fields of view (R. Shoesmith, *The Civil War in Hereford*, 1995, pp.83-6).

Chapter III Ludlow Castle

1. Daniel Defoe, *A Tour through the Whole Island of Great Britain*, 1974 edition, 2, p.48.
2. *DB.*

3. R.K. Morriss, 'Ludlow Castle—Survey and Analysis of the Solar Block', *Hereford Archaeology Series*, 128, report by the City of Hereford Archaeology Committee, 1991.

4. Hope, pp.257-358.

5. Lloyd.

Chapter IV From Foundation to Anarchy

1. The family came from Lassy and Campeaux (Calvados), which they held under the bishop of Bayeux by service of two knights' fees. They also had lands at La Rocque, just south of Lassy. *Anglo-Norman Families*, p.53; Wightman, pp.215-226.

2. The castle is first called Ludlow in 1138 by Henry of Huntingdon, a contemporary chronicler. The late 13th century source, Fouke le fitz Waryn, was written by a Ludlow man and he seems to be voicing a local tradition which said that it was originally called Dinham. However, the author confuses the name of the locality, Dinham, with forms of the surname of Joce de Dinan, its owner in the mid-12th century, and this results in his calling *chastel de Dynan* after Joce rather than after the local place-name.

3. W.E. Wightman, 'The Palatine Earldom of William fitz Osbern in Gloucestershire and Worcestershire', *English Historical Review*, 77, (1962), pp.6-17.

4. J. Tait, 'Introduction to Shropshire Domesday', *VCH*, I, (1908), pp.288-90.

5. *OV*, ii, pp.260-1 - 'He [the king] gave William fitzOsbern, the Isle of Wight and the county of Hereford, and set him up in the marches with Walter de Lacy and other proved warriors, to fight the bellicose Welsh.' J. Rhys and J.G. Evans (eds.), *The Book of Llan Dâv* (Oxford,1893), p.276 - 'In the time of king William and earl William and Walter de Lacy ...', and p.280 '... and which he [Herewald] held in all episcopal subjection in the time of king William and earl William and Walter de Lacy'.

6. *DB*, ff.179b, 180,181,185-6. Two (Holme Lacy and Llanwarne) were held under the bishop, one under St. Guthlac's Priory, Hereford, one under Osbern fitzRichard of Richard's Castle and one under Urse d'Abitot, sheriff of Worcestershire. Apart from his Shropshire lands, which are dealt with in more detail in the text, Walter had 24 manors in Gloucestershire (*DB*, ff.162,166-8), 12 in Worcestershire (*DB*,ff.172b, 173, 173b, 174, 176b. 5 held under Worcester Cathedral Church, 1 under Westminster Abbey and 1 under Gilbert fitzThorold), 5 in Oxfordshire (*DB*, ff.156b, 161. One was held under St. Mary's Abbey at Abingdon: the other 4 are specified as having been within 'Earl William's holding'), 4 in Berkshire (*DB*, ff.56b, 62b, 73) and 3 in Staffordshire, all held under Roger de Montgomery, earl of Shrewsbury; *DB*,f.248). The Gloucestershire lands were worth £119, Oxfordshire £29, Worcestershire £27, Berkshire £17 and Staffordshire £5, which, with £70 in Shropshire, gives a total annual value of about £423.

7. Of the other 18, he (and his son after him) held 16 under the earl of Shrewsbury, 1 (Onibury) under the bishop of Hereford and 1 under Reginald de Balliol, the sheriff (*DB*,ff.252, 255, 256, 256b).

8. The 4 manors the Lacys had in Berkshire and the 3 they had in Staffordshire were all in demesne in 1086, but these represented only a very small part of the whole honour or barony. In the other four counties (apart from Shropshire) where the Lacys had substantial amounts of land, there were small concentrations around Yarkhill and Weobley in Herefordshire, but being valued at only £13 and £12 respectively do not compare in any way with the Shropshire situation. (In the 1160s Yarkhill 'and appurtenances' was said to be worth £20 yearly in the reign of Henry I and Weobley £10: *HDB*, p.81.) A similar concentration at Painswick in Gloucestershire, valued at £30 and representing 44% of the value of all demesne lands in that county, though large, is still not comparable with the area around Ludlow. Ewyas Lacy, where considerable potential lay, had not been developed politically or economically by 1086.

9. Wightman, pp.134-5.

10. For this and much of what follows see B. Coplestone-Crow 'Payn fitzJohn and Ludlow Castle', *TSAHS*, 70, (1995), pp.171-183.

11. Wightman, p.185 estimates the grants between 1086 and *c*.1150 to have been worth £40.

12. *GS*, pp.24-5.

13. J.H. Round (ed.), *Ancient Charters...Prior to AD1200* (Pipe Roll Society, 1888), no.21.

14. *Rotuli Curiae Regis* (2 vols., Record Commission, 1835), i, p.144.

15. *JW*, pp.228-9; *GS*, pp.24-5; *OV*, vi, pp442-3.

16. He was with the king at Westminster at Easter 1136: *RRAN*, iii, no.944.

17. Round (ed.), *Ancient Charters* ..., no.21.

18. Henry of Huntingdon: *Chronicle*, p. 267; William of Malmesbury: *Historia Novella* (ed. & trans. K.R. Potter, Oxford, 1955), p.23; J.Beeler, *Warfare in England 1066-1189* (Ithaca, New York, 1966), pp.97, 99 assumes Ludlow was in the hands of the opponents of Stephen at this time without identifying who those opponents were.

19. *JW*, pp.242-5, 250-1; *OV*, vi, pp.520-3.

20. *GS*, pp.58-62.

21. R. Pearse Chope, *The Book of Hartland* (1940), pp26-7,37; K.S.B. Keats-Rohan, 'William I and the Breton Contingent in the Non-Norman Conquest 1066-87', *Anglo-Norman Studies*, 13 (1990), pp.157-72.

22. Keats-Rohan, *loc. cit.* Abbot William was at Monmouth in March 1101 or 1102 when the priory church was dedicated: J.H. Round (ed. & trans.), *Calendar of Documents Preserved in France* (P.R.O., 1899), nos. 1136, 1138.

23. Henry of Huntingdon: *Chronicle*, p.270.

24. J. Bradbury, *Stephen and Matilda and the Civil War of 1139-53* (Stroud, 1996), p.59.

25. *JW*, pp.266-7.

26. Beeler, *Warfare in England...*, p.100

27. After he took Shrewsbury Castle in 1138 Stephen retained it for the rest of his reign, thereby ensuring that the county never succumbed to the Angevin cause, despite the Angevin sympathies of many of its chief lords.

28. *JW*, pp.278-9, 282-3.

29. *RRAN*, iii, no.437. 'Newton', where the charter was issued (see the proposed itinerary for Stephen in *ibid*., iii, pp.xli-xlii), is possibly the location of the motte and bailey castle on the north side of the River Teme by Tenbury Wells, which would have lain on Stephen's route between Little Hereford and Worcester. The castle lay in the manor of Burford which belonged to the lord of Richard's Castle, one of the king's few allies in the area. On the castle in general and on the strategic importance of the adjacent crossing of the Teme, see W. Phillips & H.R.H. Southam, 'Castle Tump, near Tenbury', *Transactions of the Shropshire Archaeological and Natural History Society*, 2nd ser, 2 (1902), pp.162-3 and the unpaginated plan and views, and M. Jackson, *Castles of Shropshire* (Shropshire Libraries 1988), p.59.

30. D. Crouch, *The Beaumont Twins: the Roots and Branches of Power in the Twelfth Century* (Cambridge, 1986), pp.48-9.

31. *RRAN*, iii, no.820 dated not later than 7 April 1141.

32. 'Wigmore Chronicle', p.425. The land Gilbert took from the canons is called in the text *Lanton*, which the editors suggested (p.444 note 9), was Letton in Letton, Walford and Newton, Herefordshire, but *Lanton* does not accord well with other early forms of this place-name (see m *Herefordshire Place-Names*, BAR British Series, 214 (1989) p.127). However, it does accord with 12th century forms of the place-name Llanthony found in the Llanthony cartulary (*Llanthon*: D.Crouch (ed.), *Llandaff Episcopal Acta* (Cardiff, 1988), nos.20-22, 36 dated between 1148 and 1191) and elsewhere. The form *Lanton* itself occurs in the cartulary of St. Augustine's Abbey, Bristol, (D.Walker (ed.), *The Cartulary of St. Augustine's Abbey, Bristol*, Bristol and Gloucester Archaeological Society, 1998), Additional Documents, no.15 dated 1187-91), in certain Gloucester Abbey deeds (R.B. Patterson (ed.), *Original Acta of St Peter's Abbey, Gloucester, c1122-1263* (Bristol and Gloucester Archaeological Society, 1998), no.368 dated 1188), in the St. Guthlac cartulary (StGC, f.63v, no.258 dated *c*.1170-91) and in *HDB* (73, dated 1160-70). In the extended form *Lantonia* or *Lantoni(e)* it occurs in both Hereford Cathedral charters (W.W. Capes (ed.) *Charters and Records of Hereford Cathedral* (Hereford, 1908), 7, 10 dated 1132-48) and in the Brecon cartulary (R.W. Banks (ed.), 'Cartularium Prioratus S. Johannis Evang. de Brecon' in *Archaeologia Cambrensis*, 14 (1883),p.153, dated 1155-*c*.60). In giving Llanthony to Merlimond, it may have been Miles' intention that his canons at Shobdon should found a cell in Ewyas to replace the canons of the same order he had settled at Gloucester, and so remove all trace of the Lacy foundation.

33. The quarrel between Hugh de Mortimer and his steward, after which Oliver goes to earl Miles 'his close friend', and his subsequent driving-out of the Shobdon canons is in 'Wigmore Chronicle', pp.424-7. See Dr. Julia Barrow's note to *English Episcopal Acta VII: Hereford 1079-1234* (Oxford,1993), no.36 for the very plausible suggestion that it was these canons whom bishop Robert arranged to take refuge at Llanthony Secunda. As the late 12th century account of the founding of Llanthony Secunda in Sir William Dugdale, *Monasticon Anglicanum* (6 vols. in 8, 1856), vi, p.132, says, land called Moor came into its possession when 'He [bishop Robert] bestowed on the new Llanthony a territory called *Mora* upon condition of its receiving into its bosom twenty brethren who had attempted to establish a monastery in a wooded and barren tract of country, but failed and were driven out by famine. They laid their case before the bishop who in this manner negotiated for their reception into Llanthon' and a virtually identical passage in William of Wycombe's 'Life of Robert de Betune, Bishop of Hereford', where there is the additional information that they had been trying for five years to found their monastery before giving up (H.Wharton (ed.), *Anglia Sacra* (2 vols., London, 1691), ii, p.314). They returned to Shobdon after a conference at Leominster that may have taken place in 1147.

34. *FFW*, pp.ix, xxvii.

35. *Ibid*, p.10. An English translation is in J. Stevenson, 'Gesta Fulconis filii Warini' in *Radulphi de Coggeshall Chronicon Anglicanum*, (Rolls Series, 1875), p.277 onwards.

36. *FFW*, pp.ix, xxxvii-xxxix.

37. 'Wigmore Chronicle', pp.428-31.

38. A. Morey and C.N.L. Brooke, *The Letters and Charters of Gilbert Foliot* (Cambridge, 1967), no.114.

39. Hawise was eventually married to Fulk and her sister Sybil to Hugh de Plugenet, a knight in the service of the empress Matilda: M. Chibnall, *The Empress Matilda* (Oxford, 1991), pp.123-4; J. Meisel, *Barons of the Welsh Frontier: the Corbet, Pantulf and Fitz Warin families, 1066-1272* (Lincoln, Nebraska, 1980), pp.35-6, 94-6.

40. *FFW*, p.4 (Stevenson translation, pp.279-80).

41. *FFW*, pp.10-12 (Stevenson, pp.294-300).

42. *FFW*, p.13 (Stevenson, p.302).

43. Eyton, v, p.247.

44. *FFW*, p.14 (Stevenson, p.303).

45. *FFW*, pp.14-8 (Stevenson, pp.303-13).

46. *FFW*, pp.18-21 (Stevenson, pp.313-21); *Great Roll of the Pipe for the Second,Third and Fourth Years of the Reign of King Henry the Second* (Record Commission,1844), p.34.

47. 'Wigmore Chronicle', p.421.

48. Joce witnesses a deed of earl Miles in 1142-3: D.Walker (ed.), 'Charters of the Earldom of Hereford 1095-1201', *Camden Miscellany*, 22, (1964), no.68.

49. Wightman, p.240.

50. Some time after 1148 bishop Gilbert Foliot consecrated cemeteries *ad refugium paupereum* or *cogente guerra* at several places to the north-east of Hereford (Morey & Brooke (eds.), *op. cit.*,nos. 290, 335)   and they may date from this period.

51. B.A. Lees (ed.), *Records of the Templars in England in the Twelfth Century*, British Academy Records of the Social and Economic History of England and Wales, 9 (1935), p.47. His grants of lands and other facilities in Ewyas Lacy to the priory at Ewyas Harold (D. Walker (ed.),'A Register of the Churches of the Monastery of St. Peter, Gloucester', in *An Ecclesiastical Miscellany*, Bristol and Gloucs. Archaeological Society, Records Section, 11 (1976), nos.139,140) and to Dore Abbey, which had been founded in 1147, (Dugdale, *Monasticon Anglicanum*, v, p.555 Charter X) probably also date from this time. He also gave his assent to an exchange of lands in Castle Frome between the prior of St. Guthlac's and Walter fitzHingan (StGC, f.51, no.190).

52. *Great Roll of the Pipe for the Second, Third and Fourth Years of the Reign of King Henry the Second*, pp.144, 170; V.L. de Lisle & É. Berger (eds.), *Receuil des Actes de Henri II, Roi d'Angleterre et Duc de Normandie*, (Chartes et Diplômes Relatifs à l'Histoire de France, 4 vols., Paris, 1909-27), no.141.

53. D. Walker, 'A Letter from the Holy Land', *English Historical Review*, 72 (1957), p.665, where a letter to the king from Walter of Hereford, then at Jerusalem, is witnessed by *fratribus Templi* Gilbert de Lacy and Warin de Mountchesney.

54. The author of *Gesta Stephani* says of him in 1138 that he was already 'a man of judgement and shrewd and painstaking in every operation of war': pp.58-9.

Chapter V The End of the Anarchy to the de Genevilles

1. see Walker (ed.), 'Register of the Churches of the Monastery of St. Peter's, Gloucester', no.142, where a writ of King Henry's addressed to the sheriff of Herefsordshire and to Hugh de Lacy must date from before chancellor Thomas Becket, one of its witnesses, ceased to be chancellor in 1162.

2. Wightman, p.191.

3. Richard was the son of Gilbert fitzGilbert of Clare, earl of Pembroke. Earl Gilbert's sister, Rose, married Baderon of Monmouth and was the mother of Rose who was Hugh's current wife.

4. Middleton, Ingardine, Monkhall, Upper Ledwyche, Plaish and Higford. The first four of these had belonged to the Pantulf's of Wem in 1086, but Ivo Pantulf exchanged them with Payn fitzJohn for the chief tenancy of Waters Upton: see my 'Payn fitzJohn and Ludlow Castle', p.175.

5. *PR 23 Henry II*, p.52 (where he received £4 2s 6d *de quarta parte anni ad custodiam castelli de Ludelawa*, showing that the castle was taken by the king about the end of June 1177, or about a month after Hugh returned to Ireland), through to *PR 2 Richard I*, p.45.

6. Gerald of Wales: *Expugnatio Hibernica* (ed. & trans. A.B. Scott & F.X. Martin (1978), pp.193-5,199.

7. *PR 33 Henry II*, p.66.

8. *PR 2 Richard I*, pp.7, 124.

9. *PR 2 Richard I*, p.49; *RBE*, p.74; *PR 6 Richard I*, pp.138,140.

10. L. Landon, *The Itinerary of King Richard I* (Pipe Roll Society, 1935), p.86. In 1196 Walter paid £51 on 51 fees of the scutage of Normandy: *PR 8 Richard I*, p.91; *RBE*, p.114.

11. A.J. Otway-Ruthven, *A History of Medieval Ireland* (1968), p.73, and see the writ of 4 September 1199 to Meilyr fitzHenry, justiciar of Ireland, in respect of a certain Henry Tyrell and asking him to enquire 'whether he sided with John de Courcy and Walter de Lacy and aided them in destroying the king's land of Ireland': *CDI*, no.90. The Tyrells were Walter's military subtenants at Little Marcle in Herefs and at Castleknock in Meath.

12. *PR 9 Richard I*, p.196; Eyton, v, pp.257-8.

13. *PR 10 Richard I*, pp.213-4. To give some idea of the huge financial burden this represented to Walter, Wightman (p.244) estimates the 3,100 marks (£2,066 13s 4d) to be equal to about three times the annual revenue he could expect from all his lands in England, Wales, Ireland and Normandy at this time.

14. Roger of Howden: *Chronica Magistri* (ed. W. Stubbs, 4 vols., Roll Series, 1868-71), iv, pp.21, 35; J.E. Lloyd, *A History of Wales* (London,1911), p.584 note 48; Landon, *Itinerary of King Richard I*, p.125; J.T. Appleby, *England Without Richard 1189-99* (London, 1965), p.213. Howden (iv, p.21) makes Hubert Walter's campaign in Wales follow more or less straight on from Rhys ap Gruffydd's death in April 1197 ... *ad quam exstinguendam* [the discord between his heirs] *Hubertus Cantuariensis archiepiscopus, regis justiciarus, fines Gwalliae adiit et pacem into illos fecit.* However, it seems more logical to suppose that his visit to Hereford at the end of that year, when he *recepit in manu sua castellum de Hereford et castellum de Briges et castellum de Ludelawe, expulsis inde custodibus qui ea diu custodierant: et tradidit ea aliis custodibus, custodienda ad opus regis* (Howden, iv, p.35), was for the purpose of entering Wales to bring peace among the heirs of Rhys, his placing of his own men in the three castles being intended to provide him with a secure base from which to conduct the campaign. Landon certainly dates the Welsh campaign to January 1198 rather than 1197.

15. *Rotuli Curiae Regis* (2 vols., Record Commission, 1835), i, p.144; R.A. Brown (ed.), *The Memoranda Roll for the Tenth Year of King John, 1207-9* (Pipe Roll Society, 1957), p.110.

16. *Rotuli de Oblatis et de Finibus* (Record Commission, 1835), p.38.

17. Landon, *Itinerary of King Richard I*, p.125; *PR 1 John*, p.218; *RBE*, p.123; *Rotuli Chartarum* (Record Commission, 1837), i, 23b-24.

18. *Rotuli Normanniae* (Record Commission, 1835), pp.59, 74.

19. *PR 5 John*, pp.63, 70.

20. Eyton, v, p.259.

21. *Rotuli Litterarum Clausarum* (Record Commission, 1833), 71b.

22. *Rotuli Litterarum Patentium* (Record Commission, 1835), p.69b. Braose seems to have used his period as custodian of Ludlow to obtain from Bromfield Priory three small manors at Bromfield ('Bromfield Simon'), Oakly and West (or Lady) Halton that are later found in the hands of the Bohun and Mortimer families (*RH*, ii, p.70; *FA*, iv, p.223), members of these families having married two of the coheiresses of his grandson William.

23. *Rotuli Litterarum Clausarum*, i, p.79, 80.

24. *Rotuli Litterarum Patentium*, p.74

25. *CDI*, nos.324, 325.

26. *Rotuli Litterarum Patentium*, 80b.

27. *CDI*, no.402. In 1210 sheriff Engelard de Cigogné accounted for £102 10s 0d on 51¼ knights' fees of Walter de Lacy, amerced because they did not do service in Ireland: *PR 12 John*, p.147.

28. *PR 16 John*, pp.121,136. 20 marks of tallage was still owing in 1219, when the *villata* paid off half of it: *PR 3 Henry III*, pp.6, 7.

29. *Rotuli Litterarum Clausarum*, i, pp.173b,175.

30. *Rotuli Litterarum Patentium*, p.132b

31. List of Sheriffs, 59.

32. *PatR 1216-25*, p.376; T. Jones (ed. & trans.), *Brut y Tywysogion: Peniarth MS 20 Version* (Cardiff, 1952), p.100 - 'And both of them, that is, the prince and the earl, came before the king and the archbishop and the council at Ludlow, but they failed to be reconciled'; see also D.A. Carpenter, *The Minority of Henry III* (London, 1990), p.308.

33. *PatR 1216-25*, p.483; *CDI*, no.1180.

34. *PatR 1216-25*, p.435.

35. *CDI*, no.1289; G.H. Orpen, *Ireland Under the Normans 1169-1216* (4 vols., Oxford, 1911), ii, pp.45-6. It was about this time that Walter founded the Grandmontine priory of Craswall within his lordship of Ewyas Lacy and gave to it the ninth sheaf of every kind of corn, except oats, of wheat and of rye at Stanton Lacy, Ludlow and Rock: A.T. Bannister, 'A Lost Cartulary of Hereford Cathedral', *TWNFC* (1917), p.272.

36. *CCR 1227-31*, p.464. In 1230 Gilbert had been quit of scutage on all 51¼ fees in the barony: *PR 14 Henry III*, p.222.

37. W. Dugdale, *The Antiquities of Warwickshire* (ed. W. Thomas, 2 vols, London, 1730), i, p.502; Eyton, v, pp.270-1. When in 1225 Walter had fined 3,000 marks for his Irish lands William de Lucy had gone surety for him in the sum of 20 marks: *CDI*, no.1289).

38. J. Hillaby, 'Hereford Gold: Irish, Welsh and English Land, Part 2: The clients of the Jewish Community at Hereford 1179-1253: Four Case Studies', *TWNFC* (1985), pp.215, 231; Orpen, iii, p.47; *Excerpta e Rotulis Finium* (2 vols., Record Commission, 1835-6), i, pp.445-6.

39. Hillaby, *op. cit.*, p.238-9; Faraday, p.66; *CCR 1237-42*, pp.122,123.

40. *Excerpta e Rotulis Finium*, i, p.337.

41. Matthew of Paris: *Chronica Majora* (ed. H. Luard, 7 vols., Rolls Series, 1872-83), iv, pp.94, 174.

42. *CCR 1237-42*, pp.279, 376-7.

43. *Excerpta e Rotulis Finium*, i, p.413. Henry had previously offered her marriage to Guy de Russillon, another Savoyard: *PatR 1232-47*, p.261.

44. *Ibid.*, p.421.

45. *CCR 1242-7*, p.186.

46. *Ibid.*,p.198.

47. *Excerpta e Rotulis Finium*, i, pp.445-6.

48. Matthew of Paris: *Chronica Majora*, (ed. Luard), v, pp.90-1; *Excerpta e Rotuli Finium*, ii,p.61.

49. *CCR 1251-3*, p.142.

50. F.M. Powicke, *King Henry III and the Lord Edward* (Oxford, 1947), p.699

51. *RH*, ii, pp.72b, 99. Stanton Lacy and the town of Ludlow were represented by their own jurors at the Shropshire eyre of 1256 and not the jurors of Munslow, the hundred in which they had formerly lain: *Shropshire Eyre*, nos.638-642 & 650-5; G.C. Baugh, 'The Franchises', *VCH*, vol. 3 (1979), pp.38-9.

52. *Ibid.*, p.49.

53. See *ibid.*, pp.35-6 for the role of sheriffs in the formation of some Shropshire Marcher liberties.

54. *RH*, ii,100b; W. Rees, *Map of South Wales and the Border in the Fourteenth Century* (Ordnance Survey, 1933).

55. On reductions in the full *servicium debitum* demanded from baronies by the crown from the early 13th century onwards, see I.J. Sanders, *Feudal Military Service in England* (Oxford, 1956), pp.50-90.

56. GEC, v, p.630 & note b. For the division of the borough, see Faraday, pp.13-15.

57. *CCR 1261-4*, pp.275, 279.

58. Powicke, *King Henry III and the Lord Edward*, p.477.
59. *Flores Historiarum* (3 vols., ed. H. Luard, Rolls Series, 1890), iii, p,264; Powicke, *King Henry III and the Lord Edward*, p.498.
60. *Ipm*, i, no.767; Eyton, v, pp.275-6; *Excerpta e Rotuli Finium*, ii, pp.548-9.
61. Eyton, v, p.277 quoting BM Add MS 6041, f.xxxvii.
62. 'Acornbury Priory Cartulary' calendared in Appendix II to *8th Report of the Deputy Keeper of Public Records* (1847), p.135; Eyton, v, p.277.
63. *RH*, i, p.99.
64. *Placita Abbreviatio* (Record Commission, 1811), p.276; Eyton, v, p.278 note 84; GEC, v, p.632. Eyton, v, p.278; GEC, v, p.632 note d, both say the 'Mansell' of the original is Mansell Lacy, whereas it was Mansell Gamage that was involved. Mansell Lacy belonged to the barony of Radnor, and was held under it by Catherine de Lacy in 1243. Mansell Gamage was held from the Lacy barony of Weobley by the Gamages family.
65. *Ipm*, iii, no.43; GEC, v, p.650 & viii, 441.
66. GEC, v, 629.
67. *Ipm*, v, no.187 & vi, no.54; *FA*, iv, p.228.
68. *Ipm*, vi, no.344.
69. *Ibid.*, x, no.307.

Chapter VI The Mortimer Lordship
1. J.J. Crump, 'The Mortimer Family and the Making of the March', *Thirteenth Century England VI, Proceedings of the Durham Conference 1995*, ed. M. Prestwich, R.H. Britnell and R. Frame (Woodbridge, 1997), pp.117-126.
2. B. Penry Evans, The Family of Mortimer, (Unpublished Thesis, University of Wales, 1934), p.511, citing The Wigmore Chronicle, l066-1306, (John Rylands Library Latin MS215).
3. *CIPM*, Vol. IV (Edward I), No.235.
4. *CCR, 1302-07*, pp.175-76, 545.
5. R. Frame, *English Lordship in Ireland, 1318-1361*, (Oxford, 1982), p.183, n.108; *Chartularies of St. Mary's Abbey, Dublin, I II, Annals of Ireland*, ed. J.T. Gilbert, (Rolls Series, 1884), pp.345, 348, Appendix II, 1, pp.407-9.
6. *Vita Edwardi Secundi*, edited N. Denholm-Young, (London, 1957), p.68.
7. *CPR, 1313-17*, p.563; *Annals of Ireland*, pp.355, 358; *CPR, 1317-21*, pp.317, 558.
8. *Chronicon de Lanercost*, ed. J. Stevenson, (Edinburgh, 1839), p.229; *Vita Edwardi Secundi*, pp.118-9; *Annales Paulini, Chronicles of the Reigns of Edward I and Edward II*, I, (Rolls Series, 1882), p.301.
9. *CCR, 1318-23*, p.415; *CPR, 1321-24*, p.77; *CCR, 1323-27*, p.87.
10. *CCR, 1323-27*, pp.140-1; *Vita Edwardi Secundi*, p.134; Thomas Walsingham, *Historia Anglicana*, I, (Rolls Series, 1863), p.176; *CCR, 1323-27*, pp.578-9; *Chronicon Galfridi le Baker de Swynbroke*, ed. E. Maunde Thompson, (Oxford, 1889), p20.
11. *CCR, 1323-27*, p.590; *Annales Paulini*, p.314.
12. *Annales Paulini*, pp.319-20; *Adae Murimuth Continuatio Chronicarum*, (Rolls series, 1889), pp.50-1.
13. *Lanercost*, p.258; *Murimuth*, p.56; *PRO*, E.101/332/21; E.101/333/3.
14. *CPR, 1327-30*, pp.141-43.
15. *CChR., 1327-41*, p.55; *CPR, 1327-30*, pp.192, 546; *CFR, 1327-37*, pp.147-48.
16. *CFR, 1327-37*, p.19; *Chronicon Henrici Knighton* I (Rolls Series, 1889), p.449.
17. *The Brut or Chronicles of England*, I, ed. F.W.D. Brie, (Oxford, 1906), pp.261-2.
18. *CChR. 1327-41*, p.94; R.H. Clive, *Documents connected with the History of Ludlow and the Lords Marchers*, (London, 1841), p,17.
19. W. Dugdale, *The Baronage of England* I, (London, 1675), p.145; *Annales Paulini*, p.305; *CPR, 1327-30*, p.343.
20. *CPR, 1354-58*, p.87.
21. *CPR. 1327-30*, p.14; T.F. Dukes, *Antiquities of Shropshire*, (Shrewsbury, 1844), p.63.
22. Dukes, *op. cit.*, p.56n. 'Rex Edwardus III at Marchiam transit, et in castris Domini Rogeri Comitis Marchiae a se creati de Loddelowe et de Wigmore, forestique et hastiluelys, magnificisque donariis regaliter per nonnullos dies tractatur quem nec non debite remunerabit'.
23. *PRO*, E.101/384/9; E.403/246; E.101/384/1.
24. *CCR, 1330-33*, pp.65-6; *CPR, 1330-33*, p.13.
25. *CCR, 1330-33*, pp.99, 111.
26. *CCR, op. cit.*, p.346.
27. For the date of Mortimer's death: W. Dugdale, *Monasticon Anglicanum*, VI, pt.l, (London, 1849), p.352; the description is found in a grant relating to Stratford Mortimer, Berkshire, dated 22 January 1354, *CPR, 1350-54*, p.540.
28. *CIPM*, Vol. IX, (Edward III), No.247.
29. *CFR, 1327-37*, pp.293, 344.
30. *CPR, 1334-38*, pp.266, 311.
31. G. Wrottesley, 'Crécy and Calais from the Public Records', *Collections for a History of Staffordshire edited by William Salt, Archaeological Society*, XVIII, (London, 1897), p.114; *Murimuth*, p.199.

32. *Register of the Black Prince*, I, England 1346-48, pp.55-6.
33. *le Baker*, pp.103-11; *Chronicon Anglie, 1328-1388*, (Rolls Series, 1874), p.41; H. Knighton *Chronicon* II, (Rolls Series, 1889), pp.107-8.
34. *CCR, 1346-49*, p.101.
35. Dugdale, *Monasticon*, p.352.
36. *CPR, 1354-58*, pp.159-60, 267, 319; *CCR, 1354-60*, pp.18, 50-1.
37. *CIPM*, Vol. X (Edward III), No.291, Elizabeth, wife of William de Bohun, mother of Roger Mortimer, Earl of March her heir; No.307, Joan, wife of Roger Mortimer, Earl of March. This shows that Joan held the manor of Stanton Lacy by Ludlow and a moiety of the town of Ludlow with the castle, in fee tail of the king in chief by gift of Geoffrey de Geneville, father of Joan whose heir she was; Dolforyn Castle and the land of Cydewain; and Ceri. In Herefordshire she held Mansell Lacy manor, Wolferlowe manor, held of the king in chief; Walterston manor and a moiety of the town of Ewyas Lacy as well as the manors of Pembridge, Kingsland, Orleton, Marden and Winforton. In addition she held in the county 23 knights' fees of the king in chief by service of $1/2$ knight's fee, which included holdings at Staunton, Byford, Eardisley and Mansell Gamage. This holding at Mansell Gamage has been referred to in the previous chapter as a manor. The manor should be Mansell Lacy.
38. *CFR, 1356-68*, pp.25-6.
39. *CPR, 1354-58*, p.522.
40. *CIPM*, Vol. IX (Edward III), No.379; *CPR, 1358-61*, p.44
41. The origins and development of uses is examined at length, J.M.W. Bean, *The Decline of English Feudalism 1215-1540*, (Manchester, 1968), pp.104-179.
42. *CPR, 1358-61*, pp.266-7.
43. Dugdale, *Monasticon*, p.353.
44. *CPR, 1370-74*, p.337.
45. *CIPM*, Vol. XIII (Edward III), No.293.
46. *CCR, 1360-64*, pp.113-4; *CPR, 1358-61*, p.374.
47. *CCR, 1360-64*, pp.46-7.
48. *CPR, 1358-61*, p.454.
49. *op. cit.*, p.500.
50. *op. cit.*, pp.577-8.
51. *CPR, 1364-67*, pp.37-8.
52. *CFR, 1356-68*, p.357.
53. Dugdale, *Monasticon*, p.354.
54. *CCR, 1369-74*, pp.55-6, 418.
55. J. Sherborne, ed. A. Tuck, *War, Politics and Culture in Fourteenth Century England*, The Battle of La Rochelle, (London, 1994), p.48; *Historia Anglicana*, 1, pp.318-9.
56. G. Holmes, *The Good Parliament*, (Oxford, 1975) pp.93-5.
57. 'Et in rebus agendis summa prudencia fultus'; *The Westminster Chronicle 1381-1394*, edited L.C. Hector and B.F. Harvey, (Oxford, 1982), p.22.
58. *Chronicon Anglie 1328-1388*, pp.107-8.
59. *CPR, 1377-81*, p.383.
60. *The Chronicle of Adam Usk 1377-1421*, edited C. Given-Wilson, (Oxford, 1997), p.46.
51. Dugdale, *Baronage*, p.150; Dugdale, *Monasticon*, p.353.
62. *CPR, 1374-77*, pp.33-4. Peter de la Mare was the earl of March's steward. In 1376 he became the first Speaker of the House of Commons. Bishopston, 'clerc et familier del dit Conte de la Marche', appeared for the earl in Parliament. Walter de Colmpton was keeper of the earl's wardrobe. Hugh de Boraston was his attorney.
63. G.A. Holmes, *The Estates of the Higher Nobility in Fourteenth Century England*, (Cambridge, 1957), p.51.
64. *CCR, 1377-81*, p.365.
65. J. Nichols, *A Collection of all the Wills of the Kings and Queens of England* (London, 1780). 'In a list of Austin Friaries almost the only feature of interest is the importance given to the house at Ludlow which was the head of a group of western houses including Cleobury Mortimer, Droitwich, Newport and Shrewsbury', D. Knowles, *The Religious Orders in England*, I, (Cambridge,1950), p.201.
66. Dugdale, *Monasticon*, p.354.
67. *CFR, 1377-83*, p.302.
68. *CIPM*, Vol. XV (1-7 Richard II), No.556, p.223.
69. *CPR, 1381-85*, p.184.
70. *op. cit.*, p.65; *CFR, 1377-83*, p.357. Philip Holygot was one of the executors of the Countess Philippa. David Hanmer, a serjeant-at-law, was appointed Justice of South Wales in September 1381. He was a Justice of the King's Bench in February 1383. *CPR, 1381-85*, pp.42, 242, 264. His career is outlined, R.A. Griffiths, *The Principality of Wales in the Later Middle Ages*: I, South Wales 1277-1536 (Cardiff, 1972), pp.114-5.
71. *CFR, 1383-91*, pp.22-3. 'From their governance, Roger coming to full age had restored to him castles, manors and other

houses well-repaired, well supplied with household furniture; manors and agricultural land well ploughed; and a treasury of 40,000 marks'. Dugdale, *Monasticon*, p.354.

72. G.A. Holmes, *The Estates of the Higher Nobility in Fourteenth Century England,* (Cambridge, 1957), pp.60, 76-7.

73. I am grateful to Professor R.R. Davies for allowing me to see a copy of his forthcoming article for the *Yearbook of the Langland Studies*, about Walter Brugge, which makes clear the extent of Brugge's involvement with the Mortimers.

74. BL. Egerton Roll, 8744. The year is not given, but of three possible years 1387 seems the most probable, though 1392 cannot be ruled out.

75. BL. Egerton Roll, 8732.

76. R.R. Davies, *Lordship and Society in the March of Wales, 1282-1400,* (Oxford, 1978), p.195.

77. BL. Egerton Roll, 8741.

78. B. Penry Evans, The Family of Mortimer, p.453.

79. *CIPM*, Vol. XV (1-7 Richard II), No.448.

80. *PRO*, SC6/965/10.

81. *PRO*, SC6/861/2.

82. *CPR, 1391-96*, p.375.

83. BL. Egerton Roll, 8740.

84. CPR, 1391-96, p.715.

85. 'If, as God forbids the King were to die childless it would be upon one of these brothers [Earl Roger and his younger brother Edmund] that the crown of England would devolve by hereditary right'. *The Westminster Chronicle 1381-1394*, p.194.

86. *CCR, 1396-99*, p.222.

87. *The Chronicle of Adam Usk 1377-1421*, p.146.

88. *CPR, 1396-99*, p.336; *CCR, 1396-9*, p.325.

89. Dugdale, *Monasticon*, p.355.

90. *CPR, 1396-99*, pp.403, 431.

91. *CCR. 1396-99*, pp.451-3.

92. *The Chronicle of Adam Usk 1377-1421*, p.146.

93. *CIPM*, Vol. XIX (7-14 Henry IV 1405-12), Nos.47-49, pp.11-2; *CPR, 1405-08*, p.l0l.

94. *CCR, 1405-09*, p.65.

95. 'The town of Ludlow was prefixed to the castle of Wigmore'. R.H. Clive, *Documents connected with the History of Ludlow and the Lords Marchers* (London, 1841), p.61; 'Roger Mortimer preferred Ludlow Castle to his patrimonial seat at Wigmore and henceforth the chief transactions of the House of Mortimer have relation to Ludlow Castle', 'George Sandford, Ludlow Castle and its connection with the Marches of Wales', *TSAS*, Vol.I (1878), p.229; but: 'Under Mortimer rule Ludlow gave place to Wigmore their chief seat and the centre of their oldest estates and main power', G.T.C., Ludlow Castle, *TSAS*, Vol.VI (1883), p.296.

96. 'By mid 14th Century, Ludlow had replaced Wigmore as the capital of the Mortimer empire'. R.R. Davies, *Lordship and Society in the March of Wales*, p.54; 'Wigmore was eclipsed in value and importance by Ludlow'. B. Penry Evans, The Family of Mortimer, p.432.

99. B. Penry Evans, The Family of Mortimer, p.432, n.5; R.R. Davies, *Lordship and Society*, p.54.

98. *CPR, 1399-1401*, p.359.

99. *CFR. 1399-1405*, p.22.

100. *op. cit.*, p.142.

101. Dugdale, *Monasticon*, p.354; *Eulogium Historiarum* III, (Rolls Series 1863) p.398.

102. *The Chronicle of Adam Usk 1377-1421*, p.160.

103. *CPR, 1401-5*, p.140.

104. *op.cit.*, p.137

105. *op.cit.*, p.140.

106. *Issues of the Exchequer, Henry III-Henry IV*, ed. F. Devon (Record Commission, 1847), p.295.

107. *Eulogium* p.396; *The Chronicle of Adam Usk 1377-1421*, p.160.

108. *CPR, 1401-5*, p.237.

109. *op.cit.*, p.229.

110. *op.cit.*, p.407.

111. *op.cit.*, p.485.

112. *CPR, 1405-8*, p.67.

113. *op.cit.*, pp.352, 394.

114. *CPR, 1405-08*, p,483; K.M. McFarlane, *John Wycliffe and the Beginnings of English Nonconformity* (London, 1952), pp.169-72.

115. Dugdale, *Monasticon*, p.355.

116. 300 marks a year was allocated from the Mortimer lordship of Clare in Suffolk for their maintenance. *CPR, 1399-1401*, p.380.

117. *CPR, 1401-5*, p.108.
118. Dugdale, *Monasticon*, p.355.
119. *CPR, 1408-13*, p.149.
120. *CPR, 1413-6*, p.45.
121. T.B. Pugh, *Henry V and the Southampton Plot* (Alan Sutton, 1988), p.79.
122. Dugdale, *Monasticon*, p.355.
123. *CCR, 1413-9*, p.98.
124. *op.cit.*, p.240.
125. T.B. Pugh, *Henry V and the Southampton Plot,* pp.80-1, 87, n.46.
126. The Southampton Plot is examined in detail, T.B. Pugh, *op.cit.*
127. *Report of the Deputy Keeper of the Public Records,* 41 (1880), p.690. March was present at Windsor in November 1422 when Henry V's Great Seal was delivered to the Bishop of Durham, *CCR, 1422-9*, p.49.
128. *CPR, 1422-9*, p.96.
129. *Collections of A Citizen of London in the 15th Century, Wm. Gregory's Chronicle*, (Camden Society, 1876), p.158.
130. *CPR, 1422-9*, pp.272-3.
131. *CFR, 1422-30*, p.202.
132. *op.cit.* pp.249, 260-62.
133. P.A. Johnson, *Duke Richard of York 1411-1460* (Oxford, 1988), pp.10-11.

Chapter VII Ludlow During the Wars of the Roses

1. *The Parish Church of St. Laurence, Ludlow* (10th edn, Ludlow, [1970]); D. Lloyd, *The Concise History of Ludlow* (Ludlow, 1999), pp.43-6.
2. Wright, pp.456-63, 478-9; *Historic Ludlow* (Birmingham, n.d.), p.5.
3. Faraday, pp.157-8; D. Lloyd, *Broad St., its Houses and Residents through Eight Centuries* (Ludlow Research Paper no. 3, Birmingham, 1979), p.22.
4. *Ibid.*, p.17; Faraday, p.185; Lloyd, *Concise History*, p.43; E M. Carus Wilson, 'The Overseas Trade of Bristol', in E. Power and M.M. Postan (eds.), *Studies in English Trade in the Fifteenth Century* (London, 1933), pp.187-8, 228; E.B. Fryde, *Peasants and Landlords in later Medieval England, c.13 80-c.1535* (Stroud, 1996), pp.106-7, noting Venetian merchants buying expensive Ludlow cloths in the early 1440s.
5. N. Pevsner, *The Buildings of England: Shropshire* (1st edn, London, 1958; repr. 1979), pp.177-90 (with the quotation on p.187); Lloyd, *Broad St.*, passim.
6. *Historic Ludlow*, pp.4, 7.
7. W. Rees (ed.), *Calendar of Ancient Petitions relating to Wales* (Cardiff, 1975), pp.330-2; Faraday, pp.27, 185-90 (with useful lists of bailiffs); J.C. Wedgwood, *History of Parliament, 1439-1509: Register* (London, 1938), p.673.
8. Faraday, ch. 4. William Parys, draper, the warden between 1422 and 1440, had previously been bailiff of Ludlow in 1416-19; his son, John Parys, hosier, who is portrayed in the Annunciation window, commissioned for the parish church by his wife Katherine, who also figures, was warden in 1443-9 after having served as bailiff in 1439-40 (and becoming so again in 1446-7). Faraday, pp.185-6; Lloyd, *Concise History*, pp.34, 54.
9. C. Liddy, 'The Palmers' Guild Window, St. Laurence's Church, Ludlow: A Study of the Construction of Guild Identity in Medieval Stained Glass', *TSAHS.*, LXXII (1997), pp.26-37. For subscriptions sought in Salisbury, Marlborough and Devizes in Wiltshire in the early 16th century, see A.D. Brown, *Popular Piety in Late-Medieval England: The Diocese of Salisbury, 1250-1550* (Oxford, 1995), p.133, quoting E.G.H. Kempson, 'A Shropshire Guild at Work in Wiltshire', *Wiltshire Archaeological and Natural History Magazine*, LVII (1958-60), pp.50-5. For earlier examples, see SRO LB/5/3/1 (1460-1, including Henry VI's step-father, Owain Tudor, and other members of the royal household), and LB/5/1/2 (1488-9).
10. R. Horrox, 'Urban Patronage and Patrons in the Fifteenth Century' in R.A. Griffiths (ed.), *Patronage, the Crown and the Provinces in Later Medieval England* (Gloucester, 1981), p.156; *VCH*, II, pp.134-40; Faraday, pp.86-7.
11. C. Platt, *The Architecture of Medieval Britain: A Social History* (London and New Haven, 1990), pp.108-9.
12. R.H. Clive, *Documents connected with the History of Ludlow and the Lords Marchers* (London, 1841), p.9; *Calendar of Fine Rolls, 1422-30*, p.202.
13. *Ibid.*, pp.9-10; *CPR, 1429-36*, pp.514-15. See P.A. Johnson, *Duke Richard of York, 1411-1460* (Oxford, 1988), esp. pp.1-16, for Richard's early financial difficulties.
14. Faraday, pp.86-7; J.T. Rosenthal, 'The Estates and Finances of Richard, Duke of York (1411-1460)', in W.M. Bowsky (ed.), *Studies in Medieval and Renaissance History*, vol. II (Lincoln, Nebraska, 1965), pp.169-77 (noting Ludlow as the 'traditional nerve center of Mortimer power' [p.170]).
15. For the charter, see Faraday, pp.12, 27-8; Wright, p.27; SRO 356/2/1 f.33.
16. R.A. Griffiths, 'Duke Richard of York's Intentions in 1450 and the Origins of the Wars of the Roses', *Journal of Medieval History*, I (1975), pp.187-209; and M.A. Hicks, 'From Megaphone to Microscope: The Correspondence of Richard, Duke of York with Henry VI in 1450 Revisited', *ibid.*, XXV (1999), pp.243-56.
17. R.A. Griffiths, *The Reign of King Henry VI* (London, 1981; 2nd edn, Stroud, 1998), p.305, quoting G.L. and M.A. Harriss (eds.), 'John Benet's Chronicle for the years 1400 to 1462', in *Camden Miscellany*, XXIV (Camden Soc., 1972), p.202.

18. B.P. Wolffe, *Henry VI* (London, 1981), pp.250-1.

19. Griffiths, *Reign of Henry VI*, pp.693-4, with the statement in J. Gairdner (ed.), *The Paston Letters* (6 vols, London, 1904), I, p.96.

20. PRO, E403/786 m.9; R. Flenley (ed.), *Six Town Chronicles* (Oxford, 1911), p.139. Thomas Kent set out from Westminster on 1 February: R.L. Storey, *The End of the House of Lancaster* (London, 1966), p.98n, citing PRO, E404/68/79.

21. For the second statement, see H. Ellis (ed.), *Original Letters illustrative of English History*, 1st series (3 vols, London, 1825), I, pp.11-13. See Griffiths, *Reign of Henry VI*, pp.694, 709 n.132 (for later copies of the lost original).

22. Faraday, p.18. For Mulso's service to York, see Griffiths, *Reign of Henry VI*, p.671; and for Milewater, Johnson, *Duke Richard of York*, p.235. On 10 February 1452, at Ludlow, a payment was made to Mulso on York's behalf. PRO, SC6/1113/11 m.3.

23. Griffiths, *Reign of Henry VI*, pp.696-7. For a letter sealed by the duke at Ludlow Castle in the later 1440s or early 1450s, see M.L. Kekewich et al. (eds.), *The Politics of Fifteenth-Century England: John Vale's Book* (Stroud, 1995), p.264.

24. Faraday, p.19; Johnson, *Duke Richard of York*, pp.115-16; C.L. Kingsford, *English Historical Literature in the Fifteenth Century* (Oxford, 1913), p.368.

25. Wolffe, *Henry VI*, p.370; *CPR, 1446-52*, pp.580-1; Faraday, pp.19, 64; Flenley, *Six Town Chronicles*, p.107.

26. For these two letters, see C.D. Ross, *Edward IV* (London, 1971; 2nd edn, London and New Haven, 1997), plate opposite p.48, and printed in Ellis, *Original Letters*, 1st series, I, pp.9-10; and (the second letter) S. Bentley (ed.), *Excerpta Historica* (London, 1831), pp.8-9.

27. J. Gairdner (ed.), *Three Fifteenth-Century Chronicles* (Camden Soc., 1880), p.151.

28. Gairdner, *Paston Letters*, III, p.132.

29. Faraday, p.56.

30. For the campaign of Ludford Bridge, see Griffiths, *Reign of Henry VI*, pp.817-22; G. Hodges, *Ludford Bridge and Mortimer's Cross* (Almeley, 1989), pp.18-28. The most recent account is M.A. Hicks, *Warwick the Kingmaker* (London, 1998), pp.164-7.

31. J.S. Davies (ed.), *An English Chronicle* (Camden Soc., 1856), pp.81-3; *Reports from the Lords' Committee ... on the Dignity of a Peer* (5 vols., London, 1820-9), IV, pp.940-4, for the king at Leominster.

32. Griffiths, *Reign of Henry VI*, p.848 n. 299.

33. *Ibid.*, p.848 n. 300. For lists of the nobles on each side at Ludford Bridge, see C.F. Richmond, 'The Nobility and the Wars of the Roses, 1459-61', *Nottingham Medieval Studies*, XXI (1977), pp.74-7.

34. William Hastings, another of York's retainers, may have been reluctant to fight against the king; he was pardoned and not attainted afterwards: E. Acheson, *A Gentry Community: Leicestershire in the Fifteenth Century* (Cambridge, 1992), p.26; *CPR, 1452-61*, pp.552, 577. Reynold Grey, esquire, deserted York: T.B. Pugh, 'Magnates, Knights and Gentry', in S.B. Chrimes, C.D. Ross and R.A. Griffiths (eds.), *Fifteenth-Century England, 1399-1509: Studies in Politics and Society* (Manchester, 1972; 2nd edn, Stroud, 1995), p.126 n. 122; *CPR, 1452-61*, p.573. Richard Croft and Roger Kynaston were also pardoned and fined, the former being the young man in Ludlow Castle in 1454: H.T. Evans, *Wales and the Wars of the Roses* (Cambridge, 1915; 2nd edn, Stroud, 1995), p.65.

35. Griffiths, *Reign of Henry VI*, p.775. The royalist view of the campaign is recorded in *Rotuli Parliamentorum*, V (London, 1783), pp.348-50; J. Gairdner (ed.), *The Historical Collections of a Citizen of London in the Fifteenth Century* (Camden Soc., 1876), pp.206-7.

36. *Historic Ludlow*. The Carmelite prior's plea to Edward IV for help six years later did not refer to building damage, but to the plundering of furniture and fittings: *Calendar of Papal Registers, 1458-71*, p.425 (4 May 1465).

37. Gairdner, *Historical Collections*, p.207; Davies, *English Chronicle*, p.83.

38. *CPR, 1452-61*, pp.555, 561 (14 October).

39. *Ibid.*, pp.586-7, 594.

40. Wright, p.301. At Hereford he met his duchess, who had been put in the charge of her sister, the duchess of Buckingham, after Ludford Bridge.

41. R.A. Griffiths and R.S. Thomas, *The Making of the Tudor Dynasty* (Gloucester, 1985), p.52.

42. *Historic Ludlow*, p.4; Faraday, pp.12, 28-30; *CChR, 1427-1516*, pp.155-61; W. Fenton (ed.), *Copies of the Charters and Grants to the Town of Ludlow* (London, 1821). For the Devereux as alternating patrons of St. Laurence's rectory, see Clive, *Documents*, p.36. For Edward IV's sojourn in Ludlow in September 1461, see Evans, *Wales and the Wars of the Roses*, p.83.

43. *CPR, 1461-7*, p.79; Faraday, p.30. He died in 1488. For Fryse, see C.H. Talbot and E.A. Hammond, *The Medical Practitioners in Medieval England* (London, 1965), pp.96-8. It is unclear whether Edward had been acquainted with Fryse, a Cambridge graduate, before 1461 from his Ludlow days.

44. Faraday, pp.28-9, 31; Wright, pp.317-18; *CPR, 1477-85*, p.144. For a later copy of Richard III's charter, see SRO, LB/1/2.

45. For this analysis, see Faraday, pp.31, 37, 43, 185-90 (and for lists of bailiffs and wardens); and, for MPs, Wedgwood, *History of Parliament; Register*, p.673. For Hubbold's wealth at the time of his death before August 1501, see Lloyd, *Concise History*, p.95.

46. Faraday, p.43. For Beaupie, see Wedgwood, *History of Parliament: Biographies* (London, 1936), pp.58-9.

47. Faraday, pp.54, 62; *Calendar of Papal Registers, 1458-71*, p.425.

48. D. Lloyd and P. Klein, *Ludlow: An Historic Town in Words and Pictures* (Chichester, 1984), introduction; Faraday, pp.86-7; *VCH*, II, pp.134-40.

49. *Historic Ludlow*, p.4. For the almshouses, see N. Orme, *The English Hospital, 1070-1570* (London and New Haven, 1995), p.116; *VCH, Shropshire*, II, p.108. Richard III licensed its establishment on 8 February 1485, and Hosyer's executors, Richard Sherman and John Dale, made the arrangements: SRO, LB/7/1160-1.

50. Faraday, p.112.

51. Lloyd, *Broad St.*, pp.17-19, 45.

52. Wedgwood, *History of Parliament: Biographies*, s.n.; Ross, *Edward IV*, p.197.

53. Faraday, p.31; *CChR, 1427-1516*, p.155.

54. Faraday, p.56; R.A. Griffiths, 'Wales and the March', in Chrimes, Ross and Griffiths, *Fifteenth-Century England*, p.165.

55. Wright, pp.320-1; Ross, *Edward IV*, pp.222, 424; L. Attreed (ed.), *York House Books, 1461-90* (2 vols., Gloucester, 1991), II, p.697 (a letter under Prince Edward's signet from Ludlow, probably 26 June 1482); Griffiths, in Chrimes, Ross and Griffiths, *Fifteenth-Century England*, p.161. The prince and his entourage seem to have been in no hurry to set out for London after hearing the news on 14 April of his father's death: C.A.J. Armstrong, 'Some Examples of the Distribution and Speed of News in England at the Time of the Wars of the Roses', in R.W. Hunt et al. (eds.), *Studies in Medieval History presented to F.M. Powicke* (Oxford, 1948), p.118.

56. Hope, pp.304-16; R.A. Brown et al., *The History of the King's Works: The Middle Ages* (2 vols, London, 1963), II, p.732.

56. On 16 May 1483, when Richard, duke of Gloucester was protector, those who had been left in charge of Ludlow Castle when Prince Edward left were ordered to hand it over to Henry Stafford, duke of Buckingham, though whether this was implemented before Buckingham's rebellion in October 1483 may be doubted. R. Horrox and P.W. Hammond (eds.), *British Library, Harleian Manuscript 433* (4 vols., Gloucester, 1979-83), III, p.2.

57. Faraday, p.30; *CPR, 1485-94*, pp.453, 332 (£10 per annum to Haseley, 16 November 1490); Wright, p.324.

58. Faraday, p.30; *CPR, 1485-94*, p.333 (25 November 1490). For annuities granted by Henry VIII to some of his household servants, see Faraday, p.30.

59. *Ibid.*, p.87; Brown, *Popular Piety*, p.133; SRO, LB/5/1/2 m.5.

60. *Parish Church of St. Laurence*, p.11; G. Kipling (ed.), *The Receyt of the Ladie Kateryne* (Early English Text Soc., 1990), pp.82-7, for the funeral. The body was moved from his chamber in the castle to lie in state in the choir of the parish church on St. George's day.

61. Faraday, p.87.

62. Lloyd, *Broad St.*, p.6; Wright, p.467; for Leland's comment, se J. Chandler (ed.), *John Leland's Itinerary: Travels in Tudor England* (Stroud, 1993), pp.356-7.

Chapter VIII The Council in the Marches of Wales

1. Much of this and the following paragraphs is based on the first and later chapters of Penry Williams *The Council in the Marches of Wales under Elizabeth I*, Cardiff (1958), a work, which with the same scholar's articles 'Activity of the Council in the Marches under the Early Stuarts' in*Welsh Hist. Rev.*, I (1961), pp.133-64 and 'Attack' pt I, pp.1-22, form the most comprehensive and authoritative corpus of work on the Council that there is at the time of writing.

2. *CPR 1485-94*, p.453.

3. T.B. Pugh (ed.) *The Marcher Lordships of South Wales 1415-1536*; Select Documents, (Univ. Wales Press, 1963), pp.30, 257-8.

4. *DNB*.

5. Letters & Papers of Henry VIII, vol. 5, p.991.

6. 26 Henry VIII, *c*.6; 34 & 35 Henry VII, *c*.26.

7. *Statutes of the Realm*, iii, pp.500-3, 926.

8. G.R. Elton, *The Tudor Constitution*, (Cambridge, 1968), pp.198-9.

9. British.Library; Harleian MS 4220; Herefordshire County Record Office: Diocesan Records, Acts of Office, vols 136-8.

10. A. Harding, *The Law Courts of Medieval England*, (London, 1973), p.107; G.E. Aylmer, *The King's Servants*, (2nd. ed., London, 1974) p.50.

11. M. Blatcher, *The Court of King's Bench, 1450-1550*, (London, 1978), pp.29, 164.

12. Flenley, p.31n.

13. *Ibid.*, pp.31-4.

14. *Ibid.*, p.31.

15. PRO, Star Chamber Proceedings, Stac.2/17/73

16. PRO, Star Chamber Proceedings, Stac.5/B.50/32; B.55/31; B.57/18; B.68/19.

17. PRO, Chancery Proceedings, C.3/250/60.

18. PRO, Chancery Proceedings, C.2/Eliz.I./P9/35.

19. PRO, Court of Requests, Req.2/191/74.

20. PRO, Star Chamber Proceedings, Stac.8/82/19; 269/28; M.A. Faraday, 'The Enticement of Susan Blashfield' in*Shropshire Magazine*, vol. 31, no. 10 (1979)).

21. PRO, Chancery Pproceedings, C.2/James I/W12/20.

22. PRO, Chancery Proceedings, C.2/James I/E.6/1.
23. Faraday, pp.96-102.
24. *Letters & Papers of Henry VIII*, 1515-8, p.1489.
25. British Library; Lansdowne 38, ff.97, 99; PRO: Exchequer, Accounts Various, E.101/533/22; E.101/675/41; E.101/616/15, E.101/123/20.; Penry Williams, *The Council in the Marches*, pp.326-9.
26. PRO, Exchequer, Accounts Various, E.101/533/26; E.101/675/41.
27. *Letters & Papers of Henry VIII*, vol. 5, pp.310. 318, 320.
28. *Letters & Papers of Henry VIII*, vol. vi, 2155.
29. BL, Lansdowne MSS: Burghley papers, Lansd. MS 111, fo.23.
30. PRO, Exchequer, Accounts Various, E.101/533/26; E.101/124/3; E.101/675/41; E.101/613/13; CPR, 1580.
31. PRO, Exchequer, Accounts Various, E.101/613/13; State Papers Domestic SP46/164, ff.50-84.
32. PRO, State Papers Domestic, SP46/164, ff.50-84.
33. PRO, Special Collections, SC6/1236/9, SC6/1305/15; SC6/966/15-17.
34. *Letters & Papers of Henry VIII*, vol vi,1393.
35. *Letters & Papers of Henry VIII*, vol. vi; P.R.O.; Special Collections, SC6/Hen.viii/7437.
36. PRO, Exchequer, Accounts Various, E.101/613/13; Special Collections, SP46/164. fos.50-84.
37. BL, Lansdowne MSS, Burghley Papers, Lansd. MS 111 f.20.
38. M.A. Faraday & E.J.L. Cole, *Hereford Probates, Administrations & Wills 1407-1581*, (London, 1989).
39. Williams: 'Attack'.
40. GEC, *Complete Peerage*, ix, pp.677-8.
41. Aylmer, p.377
42. Williams 'Attack'.
43. British Library; Collection of Pamphlets, 1642, pp.6-8.
44. 16 Charles I, c. 10. s.2; *Statutes of the. Realm*, iv, p.110.
45. Faraday, pp.174-8.
46. J.R.S. Phillips, *The Justices of the Peace in Wales and Monmouthshire 1541-1689* (Cardiff, 1975), *passim*; *Complete Peerage*, II, pp.311-2; IX, pp.769-72; *DNB*.
47. *Calendar of State Papers Domestic, 1660-1*, pp.212, 279, 465, 495, 496, 525.
48. *Calendar of State Papers Domestic, 1661-2*, pp.11, 36, 99.
49. *Calendar of State Papers Domestic, 1661-2*, pp.91, 99.
50. *Calendar of State Papers Domestic, 1661-2*, pp.112, 158, 164.
51. *Calendar of State Papers Domestic, 1661-2*, pp.370, 408, 436, 586.
52. *Calendar of State Papers Domestic, 1667*, p.139.
53. Aylmer, pp.131-2.
54. *Calendar of State Papers Domestic, 1670*, pp. 297, 339; *Complete Peerage*, vol. IX, pp.769-77; Penry Williams, *Council in the Marches*, pp.158, 159.
55. *Calendar of State Papers Domestic, 1673*, p. 195; *Complete.Peerage*, vol. I, pp.216-7.
56. *Calendar of State Papers Domestic, 1661-2*, pp.163, 306.
57. *Calendar of State Papers Domestic, 1663-4*, p.399; *1664-5*, pp.169, 273, 347, 363, 373, 494; *1665-6*, p.565.
58. *Calendar of State Papers Domestic, 1668-9*, p.645; *1670*, p.355; *1671*, p.63.
59. *Calendar of State Papers Domestic, 1683-4*, p.89; *1687-9*, p.1090.
60. *Calendar of State Papers Domestic, 1673-5*, p.204; BL, Harleian MS f.220
61. *Calendar of State Papers Domestic, 1689-90*, p.60, p.114.
62. 1 William and Mary c.27 (*Statutes of the Realm*, vi, p.93).

Chapter IX The Civil War
1. Clarendon, *History of the Rebellion*, VI, p.270.
2. R. Hutton, *The Royalist War Effort 1642-1646* (1982), pp.11-13.
3. D. Underwood, *Revel, Riot and Rebellion: Popular Politics and Culture in England 1602-1660*, (Oxford, 1985).
4. T.T. Lewis (ed.), *Letters of the Lady Brilliana Harley*, (Camden Soc. 1st series 58, 1854), p.167.
5. Nehemiah Warton. 'Letters from a Subaltern Officer of the Earl of Essex's Army written in the summer and autumn of 1642' H. Ellis (ed.), *Archaeologia* 35 (1853), p.332.
6. Penry Williams, 'Government and politics at Ludlow 1590-1642', *Shropshire Archaeol. and Nat. Hist. Soc. Trans.* 56 (1957-60), p.290.
7. *Letters of Lady Brilliana Harley*, p.172.
8. J. Mitchell 'Nathan Rogers and the Wentwood case', *Welsh History Review* 14, no.1 (1988), pp.23- 53. For a similar situation on Exmoor see M. Style, *Loyalty and Locality : Popular Allegiance in Devon During the Civil War*, (Exeter, 1994), pp.170-182.
9. Thomas Auden's claim that Essex captured Ludlow in October 1642 after a stiff fight (*Memorials of Old Shropshire* [London 1906], p.165) is based on *True Intelligence and Joyfull Newes from Ludlow; Declaring a battell fought by the*

Earl of Essex against Prince Robert... (sic) Thomason Tracts E 121 (12) p.176. This, a work of mendacious fiction, is presumably a product of the period when London anxiously awaited the outcome of the Edgehill campaign.

10. Auden, *Memorials of Old Shropshire* p.169, citing the minutes of a Council of War held by Capel in the library of Shrewsbury School on 3 April 1643. On Woodhouse see P.R. Newman *Royalist Officers in England and Wales 1642-1660* (Garland Press, 1981), p.421. According to Symonds *Diary of the Marches of the Royalist Army* (Camden Soc., 1859), p.248 he was a former page of the Marquess of Hamilton.

11. *Letters Lady Brilliana Harley* p.202, J.R. Phillips *Memoirs of the Civil War in Wales and the Marches 1642-1649,* (London, 1874), Vol 2, pp.196-7.

12. S. Reid, *Officers and Regiments of the Royalist Army* (Partizan Press, N.D.) Vol IV, p.192. Richard Herbert was given a commission to raise a regiment of foot by the King at Nottingham on 3 September 1642, He was made governor of the town and castle of Ludlow on 28 September 1643 and governor of Aberystwyth on 18 April 1644. (*Historical Manuscripts Commission Tenth Report*, Powis Castle MSS, p.399.)

13. *Calendar of the Proceedings of the Committee for Compounding 1643-1660*, ed. M.A.E. Green, (1889-1892, 5 vols), p.1484.

14. *Ibid.,* p.1485 (William Bowdler), p.2788 (Thomas Crump senior and junior). John Young (*ibid.;* p.1185) was in the Ludlow garrison as Steward of the Household to the Council in the Marches of Wales. His son and namesake served in the Royalist army.

15. J.A. Bradney (ed.), *The Diary of Walter Powell of Llantilio Crossenny 1603-1654,* (Bristol, 1907); Petition of William Jones of the Hardwick - J.A. Bradney, *A History of Monmouthshire Vol 1 Part 2 a Abergavenny Hundred,* (London, 1906), pp.183-5.

16. *Calendar for Compounding* p.1060 (Walcot), p.1373 (Vernon). Walter Powell (n.12 above) was imprisoned at Raglan for failing to collect his neighbour's taxes. For conditions in prison at Ludlow Castle see *Letters of Lady Brilliana Harvey* p.202.

17. Hutton, *Royalist War Effort*, pp.129-142.

18. P. Bigglestone, 'The Civil War' in *The Gale of Life, Two Thousand Years in South-West Shropshire*, (Almely, 2000), p.163.

19. First hand accounts of sieges of Hopton Castle and Brampton Bryan in *Historical Manuscripts Commission : Marquess of Bath Papers* Vol 1 by Captain Priamus Davies (pp.22-33) and Captain Samuel More (pp.36-40). Woodhouse's reports on the siege of Brampton Bryan to Prince Rupert are in E. Warburon *Memoirs of Prince Rupert and the Cavaliers* (London, 1849), vol 1, pp.525-6. The parish register of Hopton records 'Occisi fuere 29 in castro Hoptoniensi inter quos Henricus Gregorye, senex'.

20. SRO Box 298 - Papers of the Bailifffs of Ludlow, quoted in Hutton, *Royalist War Effort*, pp.97-8.

21. Newman, *Royalist Officers in England and Wales 1642-1660*, p.421.

22. For Myddleton's account see *Historical Manuscripts Commission* 6th report (1877), 28a. *Herbert Correspondence* ed. W.J. Smith (University of Wales Press, 1964), no.172.

23. Bodleian Library, *Firth Mss* ff.162, 167. See *Archaeologia Cambrensis* 141 (1992), p.119.

24. National Library of Wales, *Herbert Mss* series 2, no 9. ff .3-4, printed in *Montgomeryshire Collections* 22, (1888), pp.179-83.

25. Sources for Battle of Montgomery - *Montgomeryshire Collections* 22, (1888), p.98 and J.R. Phillips, pp.201-9.

26. *Archaeologia Cambrensis* 142 (1993), pp.210-225.

27. J. Gardner and J. Brewer (ed.), *Letters and Papers, Foreign and Domestic, of the Reign of Henry VIII,* Vol XII, part 2, no.896.

28. E. Warburton, *Memoirs of Prince Rupert and the Cavaliers*, (London, 1849), Vol 1, p.526.

29. Warburton, *op. cit* 1, p.530.

30. Letters, Brereton to Committee of Both Kingdoms, 3 and 10 February 1645. *Calendar of State Papers Domestic 1644-5*, pp.283, 298.

31. *Intelligence from Shropshire, of Three Great Victories Obtained by the Forces of Shrewsburie (commanded by the committee there); viz The taking of Stokesay and Cause-castles, places of great strength...* (Thomas Underhill, London, 28 June 1645). *National Library of Wales : Catalogue of Tracts of the Civil War* (Aberystwyth, 1911), no.64, p.16.

32. Destruction of suburbs - S. Porter *Destruction in the English Civil Wars*, (1994), p.78. For an inventory of the castle in 1650 see Wright, pp.422-34.

33. *op.cit.*, p.78.

34. K. Parker, *The Civil War in Radnorshire*, (Almeley, forthcoming).

35. Revd. John Webb and T.W. Webb (ed.), *Roe, Military Memoir of Colonel John Birch* (Camden Soc., 1873), p.30.

36. *Roe*, p.235.

37. The chronology is not wholly clear. The Webbs (in *Roe* p.129, n and p.235) date the beginning of the siege to 24 April, with surrender on 20 May, though this does not agree exactly with Roe's statement (p.30) that Brereton and Birch took the castle and town 'within 33 days'. I have assumed that 20 May saw Woodhouse suing for terms, and that the surrender took place on about 26 May. The need for Birch to return from Goodrich may have delayed the surrender.

38. Those claiming Ludlow articles included Viscount Molineux ; the young brother of Lord Brereton (*Calendar of the Proceedings of the Committee for Compounding* pp.1343, 1836); and two local M.P.s, Charles Baldwin and Ralph

Godwin (do. 1227, 1474). Colonel Randolph Egerton claimed to have been the 'effective instrument in the surrender of Ludlow', and claimed Ludlow articles, but in 1659 was involved in Sir George Booth's royalist rising in Cheshire (do. 1521).

39. *Calendar of State Papers Domestic 1645-7* p.534

40. Parliamentary governors included Colonel Samuel More, Captain William Botherell, Captain John Groom and Wroth Rogers, *Calendar of Committee for Compounding* pp.750, 1007, 1026. *Calendar of State Papers Domestic 1652-3* pp.113, 412.

41. *Historical Manuscripts Commission 13th Report Appendix 1, Portland Mss 1*, p.693.

42. *Calendar of State Papers Domestic 1663-4*, p.399. Do. *1664-5* pp.273, 347, 363.

Chapter X Decline

1. Wright, pp.422-35.

2. *Ibid.* pp.436-9.

3. *Ibid.* pp.453/4.

4. *Ibid.* pp.453/4.

5. Daniel Defoe, *A Tour through the Whole Island of Great Britain*, (1962) Vol.2 p.48.

6. Wright , pp.453/4.

7. SRO 552/26/2 uncalendared material dated 1829. In the material in the PRO CRES 2/1147/2, the governor is called Alexander Stewart.

8. SRO 552/26/2 uncalendared material dated 1826. Opinion as to liability of the castle to poor rate. It should be noted that the Ludlow material in the Powis collection still awaits cataloguing.

9. PRO CRES 2/1147/2.

10. SRO 552/26/2 uncalendared material dated 1829.

11. PRO CRES 2/1147/2.

12. Quoted from *Archaeologia Cambrensis*, Vol.XIV (1868), pp.142-6, in J. Ionides, *Thomas Farnolls Pritchard of Shrewsbury*, (Ludlow, 1999), p.195. Ref. from J. Ionides.

13. PRO MR1/54. A number of copies of this survey are extant, but the map seems to be only available at the PRO.

14. Ionides, *Pritchard*, p.195.

15. PRO CRES 2/1147.

16. SRO 552/26/2 Accounts dated 1784 - 1810; also at PRO CRES 2/1147.

17. PRO CRES 2/1147.

18. Additional correspondence regarding this episode can be found in SRO 552/26/2.

19. SRO 552/26/2.

20. SRO 552/26/4 uncalendered maps.

21. SRO 552/26/3 & 4.

22. SRO 552/26/1.

23. PRO CRES 2/1147.

24. SRO 552/26/2.

Chapter XI Symbolism & Assimilation

1. C. Coulson, 'Structural Symbolism in Medieval Castle Architecture' in *Jnl. of the British Arch. Assoc.* CXXXII (1979), pp.73-90; C. Coulson, 'Specimens of Freedom to Crenellate by Licence' in *Fortress*, 18 (1993), pp.3-15; *Castle Studies Group Newsletter* 12 (1998-9), pp.43-50.

2. The early Welsh word *din* is taken to mean 'fort' and many important medieval Welsh castles occupy sites which had previously been prehistoric or Dark Age settlements, often associated with princely power. Some examples are Dinas Powys in Glamorgan, Denbigh in Clwyd and, closer to Ludlow, Dinas in Brecknock and Cefnllys in Radnorshire (originally known as *Dinyetha*). See D.J. Cathcart-King, *Castellarium Anglicanum* (1983), *passim*. In the adjoining county of Worcestershire, the presence of castles within the ramparts of the British Camp on the Malverns and Elmley Camp on Bredon Hill has also been noticed and explained in symbolic terms. The existence of a castle on the site of a *din* does not imply physical continuity but the ancient associations of the site were probably just as clear in the Middle Ages as they are today. The ridge upon which the castle of Dinham was founded was certainly occupied before *c*.1090. Wright, pp.13-4 refers to the ancient burials beneath the parish church, which traditionally were thought to have been those of Irish monks. He also records the importance of the name Dinham as, more recently, does D. Renn '"Chastel de Dinham" the first phase of Ludlow' in J. Kenyon and R. Avent (eds.), *Castles in Wales and the Marches,* (1987), pp.55-65. Camden in *Britannia* is the first to notice that Ludlow was first called Dinham and '*Lys-twysoc,* that is, the prince's palace'.

3. The great tower at Thornbury (*c*.1515) uses as its model William Herbert's hexagonal gate tower at Raglan. For Leland there was no doubt that Thornbury was built 'after the manner of a castle'. J. Chandler (ed.), *Itinerary*, (1993), p.186; J. Scarisbrick, *Henry VIII* (1971), p.164.

4. N.J.G. Pounds, *The Medieval Castle in England and Wales* (1990), pp.270-1; M.W. Thompson, *The Decline of the Castle* (1987), pp.75-6; A. Curry and M. Hughes (eds.), *Arms, Armies and Fortifications in the Hundred Years War* (1994), p.98.

5. Wright, p.224; H.T. Weyman, *Royal Visits to Ludlow* (1911), p.24.

6. G.M. Woolgar, *The Great Household in Late Medieval England* (1999), 179.

7. Charles Ross, *Edward IV* (1974), p.197.

8. For a general discussion of the role of castles in the Wars of the Roses see A. Goodman, *The Wars of the Roses* (1981), pp.181-93.

9. G. Hodges, *Ludford Bridge and Mortimer's Cross* (1989), pp.18-28; Wright, p.291; Ross, *Edward IV* pp.274-7.

10. *Proceedings and Ordinances of the Privy Council* VI, pp.304-8.

11. Goodman, *Wars of the Roses*, pp.183-5, 190-2; H.M. Colvin, *History of the King's Works* II (1963), pp.656, 732, 764, 783; Thompson, *Decline of the Castle* pp.78, 93-5.

12. Ross, *Edward IV* p.197.

13. Hope, pp.213-4; Coulson, 'Structural Symbolism', p.80.

14. P. Williams, *The Council in the Marches of Wales* (1958), p.10; J. Harvey (ed.), *William of Worcestre Itineraries* (1969), p.201; W. Camden, *Britannia* (Gibson, 1695), p.541; Arthur's marriage to Catherine of Aragon had been celebrated by a pageant in which a model castle was assaulted by knights - M. Girouard, *Robert Smythson and the Elizabethan Country House* (1983), p.218.

15. Williams, *Council in the Marches* p.12; *Letters and Papers of Henry VIII*, Vol. IV, Pt. 1, p.1698; Girouard, *Robert Smythson*, pp.216-8.

16. *Letters and Papers of Henry VIII*, Vol. VIII, pp.947, 1264, 1409; IX, pp.780, 793; X, p.211; XIV, p.155; XV, pp.398, 557, 562.

17. Williams, *Council in the Marches*, pp.249-75; Camden, *Britannia,* p.541; Girouard, *Smythson,* pp.210-1.

18. *DNB* (Compact Edition), p.1923-4.

19. Flenley, pp.50-1; For Philip Sidney's chivalric dreams - A. Young, *Tudor and Jacobean Tournaments* (1987), pp.154-62. The Landsdowne Mss. reciting Sidney's repairs to the castle is most accessible in R.H. Clive (ed.), *Documents Connected with the History of Ludlow* (1841), pp38-40. See also Faraday, p.100. Thomas Churchyard's poem is recited in several antiquarian sources including Felton (pub.), *A Description of the Town of Ludlow* (n.d.), pp.66-8.

20. Clive, *Documents*, pp.195-280.

21. Flenley, p.193; J. Newman, *The Buildings of England: West Kent and the Weald* (1969), pp.436-40; I. Donaldson (ed.), *Ben Jonson, Poems* (1975), pp.87-91; Girouard, *Robert Smythson,* p.108. Pembroke's pompous inscription on his new stable block constructed in the outer court shows him to been a man of haughty conceits - R.W. Banks (ed.), *The Progress of his Grace Duke of Beaufort through Wales in 1684* (1888), cxxiv.

22. Clive, *Documents*, p.39; Hope, p.321; A.A. Ringler (ed.), *The Poems of Sir Philip Sidney* (1962), pp.11-130; Felton, *Description*, p.66; E. Woodhouse, 'Kenilworth, the earl of Leicester's pleasure grounds following Robert Laneham's letter' in *Garden History*, 27 (1999), pp.136-41.

23. Clive, *Documents*, pp.58-80.

24. D. Lloyd and P. Klein, *Ludlow* (1984), pp.46-7; C.C. Brown, *John Milton's Aristocratic Entertainments* (1985), pp.28-36; F.R. Leavis, *Revaluation: Tradition and Development in English Poetry* (1936), pp.42-64; P.W. Thomas, 'Two Cultures? Court and Country under Charles I' in *The Origins of the English Civil War*, Conrad Russell (ed.) (1973), pp.168-193; C. Hussey, *The Picturesque* (1927), pp.22, 44, 194; S. Robinson, 'The Forests and Woodland Areas of Herefordshire' in *TWNFC* (1923), pp.208-14; Woodhouse, *Kenilworth*, pp.129-31.

25. Banks, *Progress*, cxxiv-v.

26. W. Stukeley, *Itinerarium Curiosum* (1724), pp.70-1; D. Defoe, *A Tour through the whole Island of Great Britain* (Penguin, 1971), p.371.

27. Rose Macauley, *Pleasure of Ruins* (1953), pp.441-54; T. Wright, *The History and Antiquities of Ludlow* (1826), p.143; J. Price, *The Ludlow Guide* (1797), p.34; Felton, *Description*, p.76; G. Lipscomb, *Journey into South Wales* (1802), pp.258-60; A.Janowitz, *England's Ruins* (1990), pp.67-71.

28. W. Hodges, *An Historical Account of Ludlow Castle* (1794), pp.44-5; Lloyd and Klein, *Ludlow* pp.68-70; Wright, p.435.

29. F. Grose, *Antiquities of England and Wales* (1765), p.14; Wright, pp.436, 454; C. Brooks, *The Gothic Revival* (1999), pp.190-3. The poem is reprinted in Wright, *History and Antiquities* (1826), p.143; In Herefordshire Eastnor Castle (1812) and Goodrich Court (1838) both had great halls providing settings for that 'central symbolic act of good lordship'. The local gentry were very keen to buy up redundant royal castles in the Marches - Colvin, *King's Works* III (1975), p.176.

30. C.H. Collins Baker & M.1. Baker, *The Life and Circumstances of James Brydges, first Duke of Chandos* (1949), p.213; Herefordshire Record Office A81/IV/386.

31. Lloyd & Klein, *Ludlow*, p70. See also Pat Hughes this volume.

32. C. Bruyn Andrews, *The Torrington Diaries* I (1934), p.132; *The Tourist's Guide to Ludlow* (1879), To the Reader (unpaginated).

33. SRO 552/6/2. Many thanks to Pat Hughes for help in cracking this collection.

34. S.J. Wright, 'Sojourners and lodgers in a provincial town' in *Urban History Yearbook* 17 (1990), pp.14-38; P. Borsay, *The English Urban Renaissance* (1989), passim; Bruyn Andrews, *Torrington Diaries* I, pp.130, 132, 185, 227.

35. R. Porter, 'Enlightenment and Pleasure' in R. Porter & M. Mulvey Roberts (eds.), *Pleasure in the Eighteenth Century*, (1996), pp.1-18.

36. M. Batey, 'The Picturesque: An Overview' in *Garden History*, 22 (1994), pp.121-32; D. Jacques, *Georgian Gardens* (1983), pp.75-6; M. Andrews, *The Search for the Picturesque* (1989), pp.42-4.

37. A. Bury, *Francis Towne* (1962), pp.71, 95, Pl. XYXVI.

38. D. Morris, *Thomas Hearne and his Landscape* (1989), p.103, Pl. 81.

39. Nottingham Castle Museum Catalogue, *Ruins* (1988), Pl. 30.

40. E. Shanes, *Turner's Picturesque Views in England and Wales 1825-1838* (1979), p.34, Pl. 37.

41. see colour section, this volume.

42. see Fig. 8.

43. Richard Payne Knight, *The Landscape* (1794), pp.50, 53, 57; Janowitz, *England's Ruins*, pp.63-5; Andrews, *Picturesque* pp.49-50.

44. F. Calvert, *Ludlow Castle*, early 19th century.

45. P. Stamper, *Historic Parks and Gardens of Shropshire* (1996), Pl. 36.

46. *The Tourist's Guide to Ludlow* (1879), p.25.

47. Price, *Ludlow Guide*, p.34; P. Larkin, 'Church Going' in *Collected Poems* (1988), pp.97-8
'.......   I wonder who
Will be the last, the very last to seek
This place for what it was; one of the crew
That tap and jot and know what rood lofts were?'

48. Lipscomb, *Journey*, p.265-7; A. Ballantyne, *Architecture, Landscape and Liberty: Richard Payne Knight and the Picturesque* (1997), pp.251-9; J. Macve, 'James Plumtre at Downton' in *The Picturesque*, 29 (1999), pp.29-31.

49. Pritchard's Survey SRO 552/8/1000-1009; Ionides, *Pritchard*, pp.195-6; Lloyd & Klein, *Ludlow*, p.73.

50. SRO 552/6/2.

51. *Ibid.*; Price, *Ludlow Guide*, pp.41-3.

52. Uvedale Price, *Essays on the Picturesque* II (1810), pp.259-60.

53. SRO 552/6/1 - cutting from the *Dumfries Standard* August 1873 - describing a visit to the castle; T. Wright, 'An Historical and Descriptive Sketch of Ludlow Castle' in *Wooley's Ludlow Guide* (1909), p.12; Hodges, *Historical Account*, pp.44-5; Bruyn Andrews, *Torrington Diaries* I, p.132, 241.

54. SRO 552/6/1-2; Hope, p.257.

55. SRO 552/6/3.

56. *Ibid.* For the debate about sensibility and convenience see D. Whitehead, 'Belmont Herefordshire: the Development of a Picturesque Estate 1788-1827' in *The Picturesque*, 12 (1995), pp.1-11.

57. SRO 552/6/2-3.

58. The role of the picturesque ruin in 'homogenizing' the past and helping to bridge the cultural gap between the élite and the industrial classes is discussed by Janowitz, *England's Ruins*, pp.64-5, 89-91.

59. SRO 552/6/1-3.

Chapter XIII The Norman Military Works

1. This chapter is a revised and expanded version of my paper '"Chastel de Dynan" : the first phases of Ludlow', in J.R. Kenyon and R. Avent (eds.),*Castles in Wales and the Marches; essays in honour of D.J. Cathcart King*, (Cardiff, University of Wales Press, 1987), pp. 55-73. I am indebted to Bruce Coplestone-Crow for much constructive criticism and fresh ideas.

2. Wightman, Chapter IV, especially pp.121-4, 134-5. He suggests the alternative possibility of the castle's foundation by Hugh de Lacy I, 1094 x 1115. For fitzOsbern's castles, see Derek Renn,'The First Castles in England 1051-1071' in *Château Gaillard 1: colloque des Andelys 1962* (Centre des Recherches Archéologiques Médiévales, Université de Caen,1964) pp.127-32.

3. D. Austin, 'Barnard Castle, County Durham' in *Château Gaillard IX-X; colloques de ... Durham 1980*, (Centre des Recherches Archéologiques Médiévales, Université de Caen, 1992), pp.293-300, summarizes and updates his two interim reports 'Barnard Castle, Co. Durham ... Excavations in the Town Ward 1974-6' *Journal of the British Archaeological Association* CXXXII (1979), pp.50-72 and *ibid.*, ... 1976-8',... CXXXIII (1980), pp.74-96. R. Shoesmith, *Goodrich Castle*; G. Coppack, *Wigmore Castle*, forthcoming English Heritage monographs. A.J. Taylor, (Official guidebook to) *Monmouth Castle and Great Castle House*, (London, HMSO, 1951).

4. Hope, pp.257-328, at p.323.

5. Austin (note 3), 1979 p.52, 1980 p.74.

6. Many of the upper parts of the castle are inaccessible without scaffolding or ladders, so I have had to rely here on the observations of St. John Hope and Mr. Richard Morriss.

7. British Library Royal Ms. 12C XII; printed as *Anglo-Norman Texts* 26-28, ed. E.J. Hathaway, P.T. Ricketts, C.A. Robson and A.D. Wilshire, (Oxford, Blackwell for the Anglo-Norman Text Society, 1975), at 3.31, 12.35; Hope (note 4), p.298 note c.

8. See this volume.

9. Martin Biddle, (Official guidebook to) *Wolvesey, the Old Bishop's Palace, Winchester, Hampshire*, (London,   English

Heritage, 1986). Pamela Marshall, 'The Twelfth Century Castle at Newark' in *Southwell and Nottinghamshire: medieval art, architecture and industry*, ed. J.S. Alexander, British Archaeological Association Conference Transactions XXI for 1995 (1998), pp.110-25.

10. G.T. Clark, 'Ludlow Castle', *Archaeologia Cambrensis*, fourth series, 8 (1877), pp.165-92.

11. The only records of the excavation seem to be the account in Hope (note 4), pp.306-7, with two photographs (plate XXXIX and Fig.23), together with two sentences in his notebooks and Harold Brakspear's large-scale architectural plans, called here 'the excavation plan' to distinguish it from the coloured and published versions (Society of Antiquaries of London, Ms.785 and Roll Room respectively).

12. Two pivot-stones for a drawbridge were re-used (inner bailey, west wall). The wooden door itself may be medieval.

13. Richard Gem has argued that the cushion capital first arrived in England soon after 1070 at Canterbury (both at St. Augustine's abbey and at the cathedral) from the Marquise quarries near Boulogne, the border between French and German influences: 'Canterbury and the Cushion Capital: a commentary on passages from Goscelin's "De Miraculis Sancti Augustini"' N. Stratford (ed.) *Romanesque and Gothic: essays for George Zarnecki*, (Woodbridge, Boydell, 1987), pp.95-6. He denies H.M. Taylor's thesis of a native Anglo-Saxon development: *Anglo-Saxon Architecture III* (Cambridge University Press, 1978), pp.1049-50. Double cushions above multiple half-shafts occur in the presbytery of Durham Cathedral 1093 x 1096: J. Bilson, 'Le chapiteau a godrons en Angleterre' *Congres Archaeologique* 75 (Caen), 1908, ii ,pp, 634-46.

14. On an unfinished drawing kept with the excavation plans at the Society of Antiquaries of London, the main passage arch orders are only pencilled in, although carefully squared up. A spiral stair in the north-west angle and a wallspace running south are very roughly sketched in pencil but crossed out. Although both St. John Hope and the plans make both walls of the main passage equally thick, the relative size of the pickaxe and shovels on the published photograph (plate XXXIX) suggests that the west wall may have been thinner than the claimed 8.5 feet. If it really was that thick, perhaps there was a wallstair starting at a higher level than that to the east and running either east or south.

15. Hope, plates XXXIX, XL and XLI.

16. (Bridgend) Royal Commission on Historical Monuments and Ancient Constructions in Wales, *Glamorgan III.i: The early castles* (Cardiff, HMSO, 1991), pp.325-36; M.W. Thompson, (Official guidebook to) *Kenilworth Castle, Warwickshire* (London, HMSO, 1977); D.A. Casey, 'Lydney Castle', *The Antiquaries Journal* XI (1931), pp.240-61; K.J. Barton and E.W. Holden, 'Excavations at Bramber Castle, 1966-67', *The Archaeological Journal* 134 (1977) esp. pp.36-8,74-5; S.R. Blaylock, *Exeter castle gatehouse: architectural survey 1985, preliminary report* (Exeter Museums Archaeological Field Unit. 1985). P.R. White, 'Castle gateways during the reign of Henry II', *The Antiquaries Journal*, 76, (1996), pp.241-7.

17. C.R. Peers does not mention the casing in his description of the castle in *Victoria County History of Yorkshire, North Riding* 1 (London, Constable, 1914) fig.12 but it is shown in his (official guidebook to) *Richmond Castle, Yorkshire* (London, HMSO, 1926). It may have been exposed during the repairs to the castle, some of which are described in his Annual Report of the Inspector of Ancient Monuments for 1912-13 (London, HMSO), pp.23-28.

18. D.F. Renn, 'The "Turris de Penuesel": a reappraisal and a theory' *Sussex Archaeological Collections* 109 (1971), pp.55-64; D.F. Renn with J. Munby, 'Description of the buildings' in B.W. Cunliffe and J. Munby, *Excavations at Portchester Castle IV: the inner bailey* (Society of Antiquaries of London Research Report,1985), pp.72-119; J.G. Coad and A.D.F. Streeten, 'Excavations at Castle Acre, Norfolk 1972-77: country house and castle of the Norman earls of Surrey', *The Archaeological Journal* 139 (1982) pp.138-301.

19. Henry, Archdeacon of Huntingdon, *Historia Anglorum*, ed. and trans. D. Greenaway, (Oxford Medieval Texts 1996), pp.718-9; *JW*, III, pp.266-7 for the siegeworks and their date. *Fouke le Fitz Waryn* (note 7) 4.14, 13.28, 17.29,18.36; Pipe Rolls of Henry II and Richard I *passim*. After 1200, control of Ludlow changed frequently (see chapters V and VI).

20. Wightman, pp.204-5; *Fouke le Fitz Waryn*, ed.ix.

21. H.M. Colvin et al., *The History of the King's Works: Medieval*, (London, HMSO, 1963) II, s.a..

22. Maylis Baylé, *L'architecture normande au moyen âge 2: les étapes de la création*, (Presses Universitaires de Caen, editions Charles Corlet, 1997), pp.14-15, 32-36; K.J. Conant, *Carolingian and Romanesque Architecture*, Pelican History of Art Z13 (Harmondsworth, 1959) fig.22; F. Kreusch, 'Kirche, Atrium und Portikus de Aachener Pfalz' and L. Hugol, 'Die Pfalz Karl der Grosser in Aachen', in W. Braunfels and H. Schnitzler (eds.) *Karl der Grosser: Lebenswerk und Nachleben*, (Düsseldorf, L. Schwann Verlag 1967), 3, pp.483-88, 534-72.

23. D.F. Renn, 'Burhgeat and gonfanon: two sidelights from the Bayeux Tapestry', *Anglo-Norman Studies XVI: proceedings of the 1993 Battle conference* (Woodbridge, Boydell, 1994), esp. pp.178-86.

24. S.R. Blaylock, *Exeter castle gatehouse*; J. Munby et al: *Oxford Castle: a heritage study*, forthcoming.

25. C.J. Bond, 'Church and Parish in Norman Worcestershire', in W.J. Blair (ed.) *Minsters and Parish Churches: The Local Church in Transition 950-1200*, (Oxford University Committee for Archaeology, monograph 17, 1988) esp. Figs. 36 & 40.

26. (note 7), 18.36.

27. The tower windows have no glass grooves, but there is evidence for bars and shutters. The transoms and mullions of the upper south windows were still in place in 1903: St. John Hope (note 10), Fig 5.

28. Hope, pp.310, 316; H.M. Colvin (note 21), p.732.

29. (note 10) facing page 165.

30. Hope, Figure 1.

31. SRO, Walcot Estate Office papers, box 682; H.T. Weyman, 'Ludlow Castle and Church', *TWNFC,* 1914-17, p.130; Society of Antiquaries of London, Roll Room.
32. T. Hearne (ed.) *Leland, Collecteana* , (London, Richardson, 1770), III, p.407; note of (incomplete) permission for the men of Ludlow to enclose the town, *CPR Henry III 1232-47* (London, HMSO, 1906), p.35. Murage grants for the town are almost continuous from 1260 to 1460: H.L. Turner, *Town Defences in England and Wales* (London, 1971), Appendix C.

Chapter XIV Changes to the Castle Keep
1. G.T. Clark, *Medieval Military Architecture in England*, ii, (1884) p.273ff.
2. Hope, pp.257-328.
3. *op.cit.,* p.276.
4. R. Allen Brown, *The Architecture of Castles*, (London, 1984), p.28.
5. F.J.E. Raby and P.K. Baillie Reynolds, *Framlingham Castle* (HMSO, 1977).
6. RCHME, *An Inventory of the Historical Monuments in Dorset, 1 - West*, (HMSO, 1952), pp.64-6.
7. C.R. Peers, *Richmond Castle* (HMSO, 1926).
8. P. Marshall, 'The Twelfth Century Castle at Newark' in J.S. Alexander (ed.), *Southwell and Nottinghamshire: medieval art, architecture and industry*, BAA Conference Trans. xxi, (1998), pp.110-25.
9. RCHME, *Ancient and Historical Monuments in the City of Salisbury*, (HMSO, 1980), pp.1-15.
10. D.J.C. King and J.C. Perks, 'Manorbier Castle', in *Archeaol. Cambren.*, cxix, pp.83-118.
11. S.R. Blaylock, *Exeter Archaeology 1984-5*, pp.18-23.
12. R.A. Brown, H.M. Colvin and A.J. Taylor, *History of the King's Works*, (HMSO, 1963), ii, pp.844-5. There is no reliable plan of Tickhill.
13. K.J. Barton and E.W. Holden, 'Excavations at Bramber Castle, Sussex, 1966-7', in *Archaeological Journal*, cxxxiv, pp.11-79.
14. D.J.C. King and J.C. Perks, 'Carew Castle', in *Archaeological Journal*, cxix, (1966), pp.270-307.
15. P.R. White, 'Castle Gateways during the reign of Henry II', in *Antiquaries Journal*, lxxvi, (1996), pp.241-7, discusses and gives locations of surviving examples.
16. Clark, *op.cit.*, i, pp.186-95; S. Toy, *Castles, A Short History of Fortifications from 1600 BC to AD 1600*, (1939), pp.64, 73; C.L. Salch, *Dictionnaire des Châteaux, et des fortifications du moyen âge in France*, (1979), pp.62-3; J. Mesqui, *Châteaux et enceintes de la France médiévale*, (1991), p.260.
17. Clark, *op.cit.*; D.F. Renn, *Kenilworth Castle*, (HMSO, 1973), pp.9-11; M.W. Thompson, *Kenilworth Castle*, (HMSO, 1977), pp.9-11 also has a clearer plan.
18. RCHAMW, *The Early Castles, from the Norman Conquest to 1217*, Inventory of the Ancient Monuments in Glamorgan, (HMSO, 1991), iii, Pt 1a.
19. B.H.St.J. O'Neill with P.R. White, *Peveril Castle*, (HMSO, 1983).
20. J.F.A. Mason, *The Borough of Bridgenorth 1157-1957*, (Bridgnorth, 1957).
21. C.J. Spurgeon, 'St. Donat's Castle—A recent revised interpretation by the RCHAMW', *Arch. J.* cl pp.169-75.
22. C.A.R. Radford, *Goodrich Castle*, (HMSO, 1958).
23. A.J. Taylor, 'White Castle in the thirteenth century: a reconsideration', *Medieval Archaeology*, v, pp.169-75.
24. F. Stackhouse Acton, *The Castles and Old Mansions of Shropshire*, (Shrewsbury, 1868), pp.36-7.
25. J.K. Knight, 'Usk Castle and its Affinities' in *Ancient Monuments and their Interpretation: Essays presented to A.J. Taylor* (Phillimore, 1977), pp.139-154.
26. R. Shoesmith, *A Short History of Castle Green and Hereford Castle*, (City of Hereford Arch. Comm., 1980).
27. P.R. White and A.M. Cook, *Sherborne Old Castle,* (EH Official Guide).
28. A.M. Cook and P.R. White, *Sherborne Old Castle, Dorset*, (EH Monograph, forthcoming).
29. J.K. Knight, *Chepstow Castle*, (CADW Official Guide, 1991).
30. M. Wood, *The English Medieval House*, (London, 1981), p.38.
31. M. Biddle, *Wolvesey, the Old Bishop's Palace, Winchester, Hampshire* (EH, London, 1986).
32. R.D.H. Gem, 'Lincoln Minster: ecclesia pulchra, ecclesia fortis' in T.A. Heslop and V.A. Sekules (ed.). *Medieval art and architecture at Lincoln Cathedral*, BAA Conference Trans. viii, (1986), pp.9-28.
33. RCHAMW, *The Later Castles after 1217*, An Inventory of the Ancient Monuments in Glamorgan, iii, pt ib forthcoming.
34. Brown et al, *History of the King's Works*, i, pp.293-408, ii, pp.1027-40.
35. D.J.C. King, *Castellarium Anglicanum*, (1983), i, p.235.

Chapter XV The Round Chapel of St. Mary Magdalene
1. See T. Wright, *The History of Fulk Fitz Warine* (London, Wharton Club, 1855), and Rolls Series 66.
2. Hope, pp.257-328.
3. C. Oman, *Castles* (London, 1926), p.141.
4. C.R. Peers, *Pevensey Castle* (London, 1985), p.27.
5. For the chapel at Hereford, see F.G. Heys, 'Excavations at Castle Green, 1960: a lost Hereford church', *TWNFC* 36 (1960), 343-57; and a re-evaluation by R. Shoesmith, 'Excavations at Castle Green', *Hereford City Excavations* I (Council for British Archaeology, London 1980), particularly pp.45-59.

6. B. Morley and D. Gurney, 'Castle Rising Castle, Norfolk', *East Anglian Archaeology* 81 (1997), pp.24-38.

7. W. Rodwell and K. Rodwell, 'St Peter's Church, Barton on Humber: Excavations and Structural Study, 1978- 81', *Antiquaries Journal* 62 (1982), pp.183-315 and particularly Fig. 3.

8. For the early development of this church see W.F. Grimes *The Excavation of Roman and Medieval London,* (London, Routledge and Kegan Paul 1968), pp.184-87 and Pl. 81; and D. Morgan, *St Brides's Church, Fleet Street in the City of London,* (London, 1969).

9. For Garway see Royal Commission on Historical Monuments, *An Inventory of the Historical Monuments in Herefordshire: Vol 1 South West* (Oxford, 1931), p.xxx and N. Pevsner, *The Buildings of England: Herefordshire,* (London, 1963), pp.135-136. For Hereford, see RCHM *op. cit.* p.xxx. There is some confusion concerning the origins of the chapel of St. Giles in Hereford, for there are no documentary sources to support a Templar presence in Hereford, *vide* D. Knowles and R.N. Hadcock, *Medieval Religious Houses; England and Wales* (London, 1953), pp.234-39. Its attribution to the Templars by more recent scholars appears to stem from a misreading of Alfred Watkins' note on its discovery in 1926; 'St. Giles Chapel, Hereford', *TWNFC* 1927-29, pp.102-5.

10. N. Pevsner, *The Buildings of England: Cambridgeshir*e (London, 1970), pp.230-1.

11. N. Pevsner and B. Cherry, *The Buildings of England: Northamptonshire* (London, 1973), pp.322-4.

12. Lloyd, pp.3 and 13.

13. Hope *op cit* in note 2, p.275, quoting BL Ms Lansdowne 111, no 9.

14. Bodleian Ms Blakeway 11, f 221. This miscellany comprises papers from the collection of W. Mytton, the source of which was admitted in the ms to be Mr. Perkes. If this is the case, this is likely to be a local source of exceptional value, not simply for the chapel but for other parts of the castle too.

15. Hope, pp.275-76.

16. For an appreciation of Hope's and Brakspear's archaeological techniques see G. Coppack, *Abbeys and Priories* (London, 1990), pp.22-5.

17. For the context of this drawing see R.W. Banks (ed), *The Progress of His Grace Henry Duke of Beaufort through Wales in 1684* (London, 1888), cxxv.

18. See for instance the early 20th century photographs published by Oman *op cit* in note 3, facing pp.131 and 136. The vertical terminations of several areas of plaster were first commented on by Hope who could not offer an explanation. They do not result from abutting buildings that have been demolished, and the most likely explanation is that they demonstrate that the exterior wall was plastered in sections and not all at one time, the plaster being laid up to battens fixed to the wall in alternating panels. The battens were then removed and the remaining areas plastered.

Chapter XVI The Solar Block

1. J. Bony, *The English Decortaed Style,*1979, p.11.

2. R.K. Morris, 'Development of Later Gothic Mouldings' in *Architectural History*, 21, 1978, p.31.

3. J.H. Maddison, 'The Choir of Chester Cathedral' in *Journal of the Chester Archaelogical Soc.*, 66, 1983, p.41; A.J. Taylor, *Caernarfon Castle and Town Walls*, 1953, p.7.

Chapter XVII The Great Hall & Great Chamber Block

1. H.T. Weyman, 'Ludlow Castle and Church', *TWNFC*, 1814-17, pp.126-36.

Chapter XVIII The Tudor Lodgings & use of the North-East Range

1. Pantin, W.A., 'Chantry Priests' Houses and other medieval lodgings', in *Medieval Archaeology*, 3, (1959), pp.216-58.

2. Hope, p.298.

3. Lloyd; see also chapter XVI.

4. Wright, pp.422-35.

5. R.W. Banks (ed.), *The Progress of his Grace Duke of Beaufort through Wales in 1684* (1888).

6. From Perkes Papers (town clerk 1719-1751), in Blakeway MS. 11.

7. R.W. Banks (ed.) (1888).

Chapter XX The Outer Bailey

1. Hope p.259.

2. *Ibid.*

3. G.T. Clark, 'Ludlow Castle', *Archaeologia Cambrensis*, fourth series, 8 (1877), facing p.165.

4. Hope fig. 1.

5. SRO552/1 Walcot Estate Papers box 682; H.T. Weyman, 'Ludlow Castle and church', *TWNFC*, 1914-17, p.130; Society of Antiquaries of London, Roll Room.

6. R.K. Morriss & R. Shoesmith, 'Ludlow Castle: Watching brief and recording of the collapsed south-eastern section of the curtain wall', *Herefordshire Archaelogical Series* 79 (Hereford Archaeological Unit, 1990)

Chapter XXI Mortimer's Tower

1. T. Churchyard, *The Worthines of Wales, a poem*, (London, 1776), p.82.
2. G.T. Clark, *Mediaeval Military Architecture in England*, 2, (Wyman, 1884), p.275; Hope, particularly pp.264-66.
3. P.E. Curnow, 'Ludlow Castle', *Archaeological Journal* 138 (1981), 12; D. Renn, '"Chastel de Dynan": the first phases of Ludlow', in J.R. Kenyon and R. Avent (eds), *Castles in Wales and the Marches* (University of Wales Press, 1987), p.58. See also Derek Renn's contribution to this volume.
4. R.H. Clive, *Documents Connected with the History of Ludlow, and the Lords Marchers* (Van Voorst, 1841), pp.51-2. The secretary's chamber in 1650 contained a bed, table, hangings, curtains and a carpet, whilst in the study there was a velvet chair, cushions, a table, a blue rug, a stool, as well as a close-stool. The scullery had a 'furnace', shelving and a bed in the chamber that formed part of the scullery, possibly the area opposite the fireplace on the ground floor.
5. Renn, *op cit* in note 3, 59.
6. Renn, *op cit* in note 3.
7. J. Mesqui, *Châteaux et Enceintes de la France Médiévale.1. Les Organes de la Défense* (Picard, 1991), ch. 5.
8. P.E. Curnow, 'Some developments in military architecture c.1200: le Coudray-Salbart', in R.A. Brown (ed.), *Proceedings of the Battle Conference on Anglo-Norman Studies II, 1979* (Boydell Press, 1980), pp.42-62, 172-73. This paper also examines similar features at Bressuire.
9. C.J. Spurgeon, 'Aberystwyth Castle and borough to 1649', in I.G. Jones (ed.), *Aberystwyth 1277-1977* (Gomer Press, 1977), pp.28-45.
10. D.J.C. King, 'Pembroke Castle', *Archaeologia Cambrensis* 127 (1978), pp.75-121.
11. The writers are indebted to Derek Renn for his views on the Constable's Gate at Dover Castle.
12. T.E. McNeill, 'Trim Castle, Co. Meath: the first three generations', *Archaeological Journal* 147 (1990), pp.308-36. See Fig. 11 (p.329) for comparisons of the plans of the gates at Le Coudray-Salbart, Bressuire and the south-east gate at Trim. See also D. Sweetman, *Medieval Castles of Ireland* (The Collins Press, 1999), pp.44-47.
13. Philippe Auguste's castle of the Louvre in Paris, completed by 1202, had a fine twin-towered gatehouse on its east side (M. Fleury and V. Kruta, *The Medieval Castle of the Louvre* (Editions Atlas, 1989)). The excavated remains now stand in the basement of the Louvre, together with curtain wall and round keep. The outer gatehouse at Chepstow may now date to the closing years of the 12th century, following the dendrochronological analysis of its timber door (R. Turner, 'The oldest castle doors in Europe?', *Heritage in Wales* 13 (1999), pp.6-9. Also, the gatehouse into the inner ward at Pevensey is now argued as being of a similar date to the Chepstow example (J. Goodall, *Pevensey Castle, East Sussex*, English Heritage, 1999), although not convincingly. We should not forget the twin-towered gatehouses of the 1180s to Henry II's inner ward at Dover, although the towers here are not rounded but square.
14. The authors are indebted to Tony Daly for redrawing the floor plans of the tower from a set in the possession of PEC, with some editorial amendments, and also to David Sweetman for the photograph of Trim Castle.

Chapter XXII St. Peter's Chapel & the Court House

1. From Perkes Papers (town clerk 1719-1751), in Blakeway MS. 11 ff. 221, 222. as quoted in Hope p 327.
2. P.M. Remfry, *Brampton Bryan Castle, 1066 to 1309 and the Civil War, 1642 to 1646*, (Malvern, 1997).

Chapter XXIII The Porter's Lodge, Prison and Stable Block

1. eg C.P.S. Platt, *The Castle in Medieval England and Wales*, Secker & Warburg, 1982, eg J. R. Mathieu 'New Methods on Old Castles: Generating New Ways of Seeing', in *Med. Arch.* vol.43, 1999, pp.115-42.
2. T. Wright, *History and Descriptive Sketch of Ludlow Castle and of the Church of St Laurence, Ludlow* 1856, p.4.
3. Hope, plate 40, pp.255-325.
4. R. Stone, R., 'Ludlow Castle, Shropshire: An Interim Report on Excavations to the west of the Gateway to the Outer Bailey', City of Hereford Archaeology Unit internal report, *Hereford Archaeology Series* 187, 1994.
5. eg Anon, *The History and Antiquities of Ludlow*, (Ludlow, 1882), p.117.; Anon, *A brief historical sketch of Ludlow Castle* (Ludlow, 1835), p.15.
6. Lloyd, p.5.
7. W. Hodges, (ed.), *An historical account of Ludlow Castle*, (Ludlow, 1794), pp.92-95.
8. Lloyd, p.4.
9. *ibid*.
10. Anon, *The history of Ludlow Castle, with many original and valuable Records, Anecdotes, occasional notes etc. compiled from original manuscripts by several gentlemen*, (Ludlow, 1794), pp.29-32.
11. Anon, *The Ludlow Guide*, (Ludlow, 1801), pp.35-6.
12. P. Hughes, this volume.
13. P. Hughes, this volume.
14. J.B. Blakeway, 'Description of the castle' [of Ludlow], in J. Britton, *The architectural antiquities of Great Britain*, vol. 4, 1814, pp.31-135; G.T. Clark, 'Ludlow Castle', *Transactions of the Shropshire Archaeological and Natural History Society*, First Series, vol. 6, 1883, pp.271-298.
15. Hope, p.262.

Appendix I

1. A prior is recorded in 1132 but not again until 1155, the year in which it was refounded by Bishop Gilbert Foliot as a cell of Gloucester Abbey: M. Chibnall, 'The Priory of Bromfield', *VCH*, II (1973), 27.

Appendix II

1. StGC, f.51v, no.192.
2. *Ibid.*, f.52, no.198.

Appendix III

1. Wightman, pp.197-8; J.H. Round, *Feudal England* (London, 1909), p.253.
2. *HDB*, p.81. Cecily was divorced from earl Roger of Hereford before his death in 1155. She subsequently married William de Poitou and, after his death, Walter de Mayenne.
3. *RBE*, pp.281-3.
4. *PR 33 Henry II*, p.134.
5. Eyton, viii, pp.62-3.
6. *Ibid.*, p.202.
7. *RH*, ii, pp.71b,80b; *Fees*, pp.846,859.
8. *RH*, ii, pp.70b, 85.
9. *Ibid.*, pp.55b-56, 82b.
10. *Ibid.*, p.56b.
11. *Ibid.*, pp.69b, 80b. Pool is now Pools Farm in Stanton Lacy.
12. *Ipm*, vii, no.710 (p.495).
13. Faraday, p.14 'The hundred rolls provide evidence of tenements outside the borough but within the liberty, where tenure was based on service to the castle.'
14. *RH*, ii, pp.69b, 80b; Eyton, v, pp.273-4.
15. On the vast range of such non-feudal serjeanty services, see E.G. Kimball, *Serjeanty Tenure in Medieval England* (Yale University Press, 1936), pp.16-68.
16. *Fees*, p.964.
17. *RBE*, pp.156, 509; *Ipm*, x, no.307.
18. Eyton, v, pp.15-16.
19. *Shropshire Eyre*, no.130.
20. C.W. Hollister, *The Military Organization of Norman England* (Oxford, 1965), pp.94-6.
21. *Ipm*, iii, no.194.
22. S. Painter, 'Castle-Guard', *American Historical Review*, 40 no.3 (1935), p.451 'For fractions of fees adjustments were made either in the duration or the quality of the service. Thus half a fee might owe twenty days service instead of forty or a sergeant instead of a knight for the full period.'
23. *RH*, ii, p.76.
24. Morey & Brooke (eds.), *Letters and Charters of Gilbert Foliot*, no.310.
25. *Ipm*, ii, no.640 & iii, no.291.
26. *Ibid.*, viii, no.185; R.W. Banks, 'Notes on the early history of the manor of Huntington, Herefordshire', *Archaeologia Cambrensis* (1869), p.229.
27. *Ipm*, i, no.812; *RH*, ii, p.76b.
28. *Fees*, p.963; *Ipm*, xi, nos.270, 400.
29. *RRAN*, i, no.1945; *Placita de Quo Warranto* (Record Commission, 1818), p.269; A.J. Horwood (ed.), *Year Books 20 & 21 Edward I* (Rolls Series,1866), pp.98-100. In 1212 the service of these two mounted serjeants was counted as equivalent to one knight's fee: *Fees*, p.100.
30. *Ipm*, i, no.812; S. Painter, *Studies in the History of the English Feudal Barony* (Baltimore, 1943), p.134.
31. Hollister, *Military Organization of Norman England*, p.208.
32. *Ipm*, i, no.186.
33. *Fees*, p.811; *Ipm*, i, no.197.
34. *Fees*, p.147; *Ipm*, v, no.5.
35. *Ipm*, i, no.812.
36. *RH*, ii, p.107b; *ClR 1279-86*, p.426.
37. Faraday, p.8.
38. StGC, f.53v, no.209 & f.94v, no.418.
39. *DB*, ff.254, 254b, 256b; Eyton, iv, p.89; *Anglo-Norman Families*, p.14.
40. *Shrewsbury Cartulary*, no.279 (p.258) & notes pp.15, 45, 262.
41. *RBE*, pp.272, 283. For *muntatores*, see F.C. Suppe, *Military Institutions on the Welsh Marches: Shropshire, A.D.1066-1300* (Woodbridge, 1994), pp.63-87.
42. Eyton, iv, pp.94-6.

43. *Fees*, p.964; *RH*, ii, p.69b.
44. *Shropshire Eyre*, no.130.
45. Eyton, iv, p.97; *Ipm*, v, no.611.
46. *Ibid.*,vii, no.710.
47. *DB*, f.184.
48. *RBE*, p.282.
49. *Fees*, pp.811,964; *FA*, ii, p.381.
50. Eyton, v, p.24; *FA*, iv, p.224.
51. *Ipm*, vii, no.710.
52. *DB*, ff.184, 184b, 185.
53. *RBE*, p.282.
54. *Fees*, p.964.
55. *FA*, iv, p.224.
56. *Ipm*, viii, no.111.
57. *RH*, ii, p.80b; *DB*, f.260b.
58. *Shropshire Eyre*, nos.918, 947.
59. *RH*, ii, pp.89,101; *Ipm*, vii, no.710.
60. *Anglo-Norman Families*, p.39.
61. V.H. Galbraith, 'An Episcopal Land-Grant of 1085', *English Historical Review*, 44 (1929), p.372.
62. *DB*, f.167b; W.H. Hart (ed.), *Historia et Cartularium Monasterii Sancti Petri Gloucestriae* (3 vols., Rolls Series, 1863-7),
    i, p.73.
63. *DB*, 186b.
64. StGC, f.48v, no.173 & f.78, no.333.
65. *RBE*, pp.282, 285; Eyton, iv, p.368; *HDB*, p.62; W. Capes (ed.), *Charters and Records of Hereford Cathedral*, p.21.
66. *Haughmond Cartulary*, nos.204-6.
67. *Fees*, p.964; *RH*, ii, p.69b; *FA*, iv, p.216; *Shrewsbury Cartulary*, no.279.
68. *DB*, ff.184, 256b; *Shrewsbury Cartulary*, no.36 & notes pp.xv, xix, 44, 261.
69. Eyton, v, p.43; *RBE*, p.282.
70. See my 'Grant of the Manor of Kingstone in Return for Knight-Service', *TWNFC*, (1995), pp.295-303; Eyton, v, p.48 note
    26.
71. *Fees*, pp.812, 813, 964.
72. *RH*, ii, pp.70b, 85; *FA*,iv, p.223.
73. *FA*, iv, p.223.
74. *DB*, ff.256b, 260b.
75. *RBE*, p.283; Eyton, v, pp.12-13 '...the fees of the new in [Hugh de] Lacy's barony ... seem to have been classified as of
    new enfeoffment under some exceptional circumstances; and I do not think that such classification necessarily implies
    that none of the tenants of 1166 were hereditary representatives of the Domesday tenants or, in other words, of tenants
    by old enfeoffment.'
76. *Fees*, p.964; *RH*, ii, 69b; *FA*, iv, p.224.
77. *Shropshire Eyre*, no.57; *Ipm*, vi, no.54.
78. *Fees*, p.964; *RH*, ii, p.69b.
79. J.C. Atkinson, *The Coucher Book of Furness Abbey*, vol.1, Chetham Society, new series, 9 (1886), p.20.
80. *Shropshire Eyre*, no.305.
81. *FA*, iv, p.225; *Ipm*, x, no.307.
82. Eyton, v, pp.40, 289.
83. *Anglo-Norman Families*, p.96.
84. *Shrewsbury Catulary*, no.35 & note p4; Hart (ed.), *Historia et Cartularium ... Gloucestriae*, i, pp.84-5 & iii, no.995.
85. *RBE*, p.282.
86. *Haughmond Cartulary*, no.1141; *Fees*, pp.846, 964.
87. *RH*, ii, pp.55b-56, 57, 69b, 80b, 82b; *Ipm*, vi, no.54.
88. Eyton, v, pp.36-7; *FA*, iv, p.223.
89. *DB*, ff.252, 260b.
90. *Fees*, p.964; *RH*, ii, p.69b; Eyton, v, pp.17-18.
91. *FA*, iv, p.224; *Ipm*, iii, no.194; Eyton, v, p.18.
92. *RH*, ii, p.69b; *FA*, iv, p.224; Eyton, v, p.56.
93. *RH*, ii, p.69b; *FA*, iv, p.224.
94. *DB*, f.260b.
95. Eyton, v, p.27; *RBE*, p.283.
96. *Fees*, p.964; *RH*, ii, p.70.
97. *HDB*, p.28; *RBE*, p.278; E. St. John Brooks (ed.), *The Irish Cartularies of Llanthony Prima & Secunda* (Irish MSS
    Commission, Dublin,1953), Llanthony Secunda, no.7.

98. *FA*, iv, p. 223; Eyton, v, pp.27-8.

99. *DB*, f.255.

100. J.H. Round, 'A Great Marriage Settlement', *Ancestor*, 11 (1904), pp.153-7.

101. Eyton, iv, pp.375-6; *Fees*, pp.808, 964; *RH*, ii, p.69b.

102. *Shropshire Eyre*, no.345; *FA*, iv, p.225; *Shrewsbury Cartulary*, no.279.

103. *DB*, f.258b.

104. *RBE*, p.282.

105. *Haughmond Cartulary*, no.1142.

106. *Fees*, p.964; RH, ii, 69b.

107. *FA*, iv, p.225; *Ipm*, iii, nos.65,194. Great Poston had been held in demesne by Helgot in 1086. It remained part of the barony of Castle Holdgate, its link with Witchcot in 1305 being personal and not feudal.

108. *DB*, f.256b.

109. Eyton, iv, pp.310-1.

110. *FA*, iv, pp.215, 229.

111. *Ipm*, vi, no.344.

INDEX